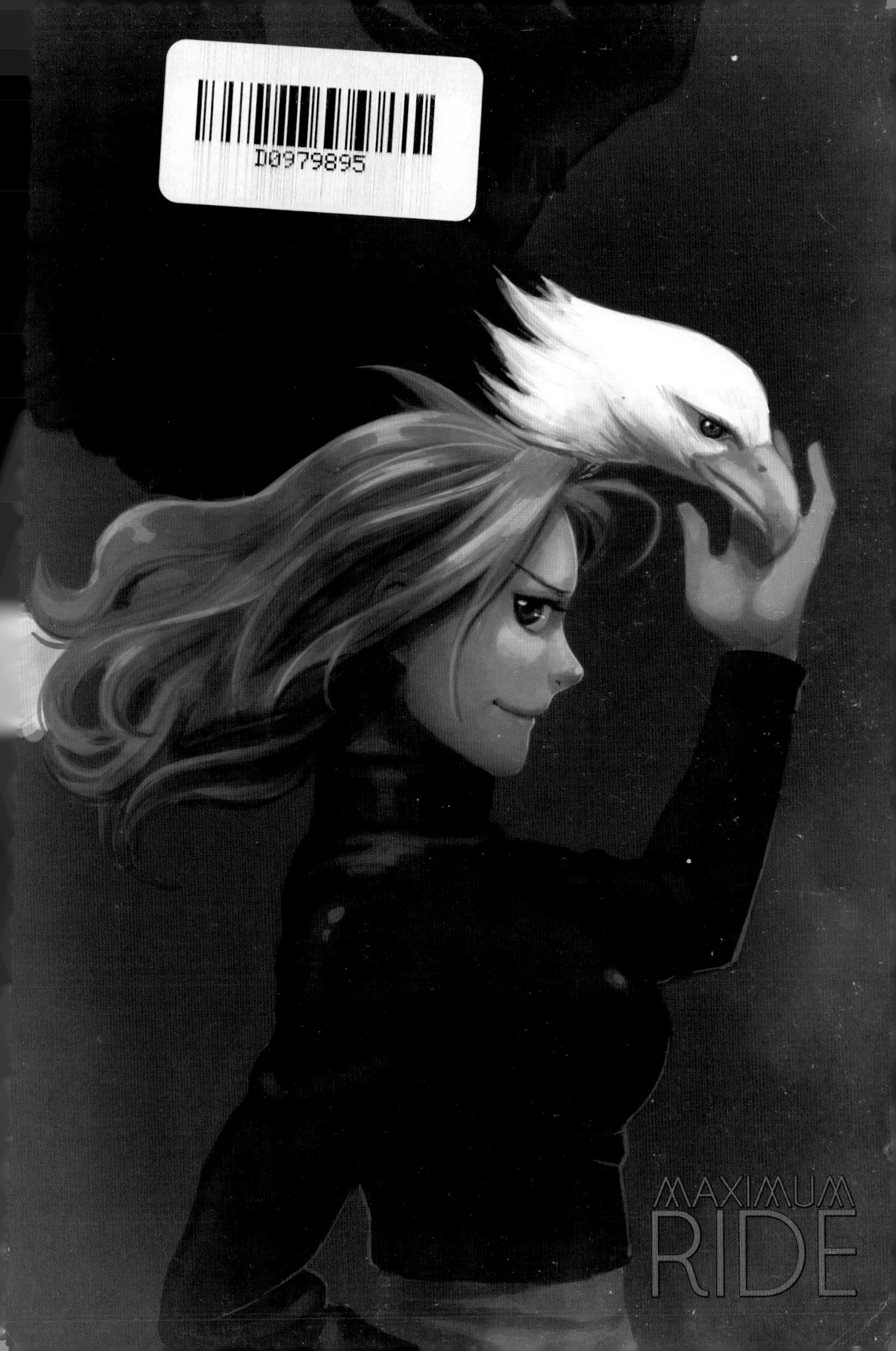
MAXIMUM
RIDE

WHAT CAME BEFORE

Max and her flock are genetic experiments. Created by a mysterious lab known only as the "School," their genetic codes have been spliced with avian DNA, giving them wings and the power to soar. What they lack are homes, families, and memories of a real life.

After escaping from the School, the flock is hunted by Erasers, agents of the School who can transform into terrifying wolf creatures, and Jeb Batchelder, the man they once thought of as a father. Despite the targets on their backs, the flock is desperate to learn about their individual pasts, and their inquiries lead them to Washington, D.C., where they meet Special Agent Anne Walker of the FBI, who takes them in and gives the flock a taste of a normal life — only to betray them in the end.

On their own again, the flock heads to Florida, following a lead on a multi-national corporation called ITEX that seems to have been pulling the flock's strings all along. Once there, Max is kidnapped by ITEX and replaced by a clone of herself — Max 2.0! With a bit of unexpected help from Jeb, Max escapes ITEX and rescues the flock from her doppelgänger.

Heading west, the kids find that ITEX has gone troublingly quiet and decide that a very public appearance is in order to try to draw them out. Unfortunately for the flock, their plan is a bit too successful, as they have their first encounter with the company's new and improved mechanical Erasers. Where it all goes truly wrong, however, is when one of their own switches sides... Who would have expected Angel to turn on the others in an effort to secure her survival in the world that remains after ITEX reduces the world's population by half?

As Max and the flock await extermination, will Angel turn out to be their executioner...or their salvation?

CHARACTER INTRODUCTION

MAXIMUM RIDE
Max is the eldest member of the flock, and the responsibility of caring for her comrades has fallen to her. Tough and uncompromising, she's willing to put everything on the line to protect her "family."

FANG
Only slightly younger than Max, Fang is one of the elder members of the flock. Cool and reliable, Fang is Max's rock. He may be the strongest of them all, but most of the time it is hard to figure out what is on his mind.

IGGY
Being blind doesn't mean that Iggy is helpless. He has not only an incredible sense of hearing, but also a particular knack (and fondness) for explosives.

NUDGE
Motormouth Nudge would probably spend most days at the mall if not for her pesky mutant-bird-girl-being-hunted-by-wolf-men problem.

MAXIMUM RIDE

GASMAN

The name pretty much says it all. The Gasman (or Gazzy) has the art of flatulence down to a science. He's also Angel's biological big brother.

ANGEL

The youngest member of the flock and Gazzy's little sister, Angel seems to have some peculiar abilities — mind reading, for example.

ARI

Just seven years old, Ari is Jeb's son but was transformed into an Eraser. He appears to have a particular axe to grind with Max.

JEB BATCHELDER

The flock's former benefactor, Jeb was a scientist at the School before helping the flock to make their original escape.

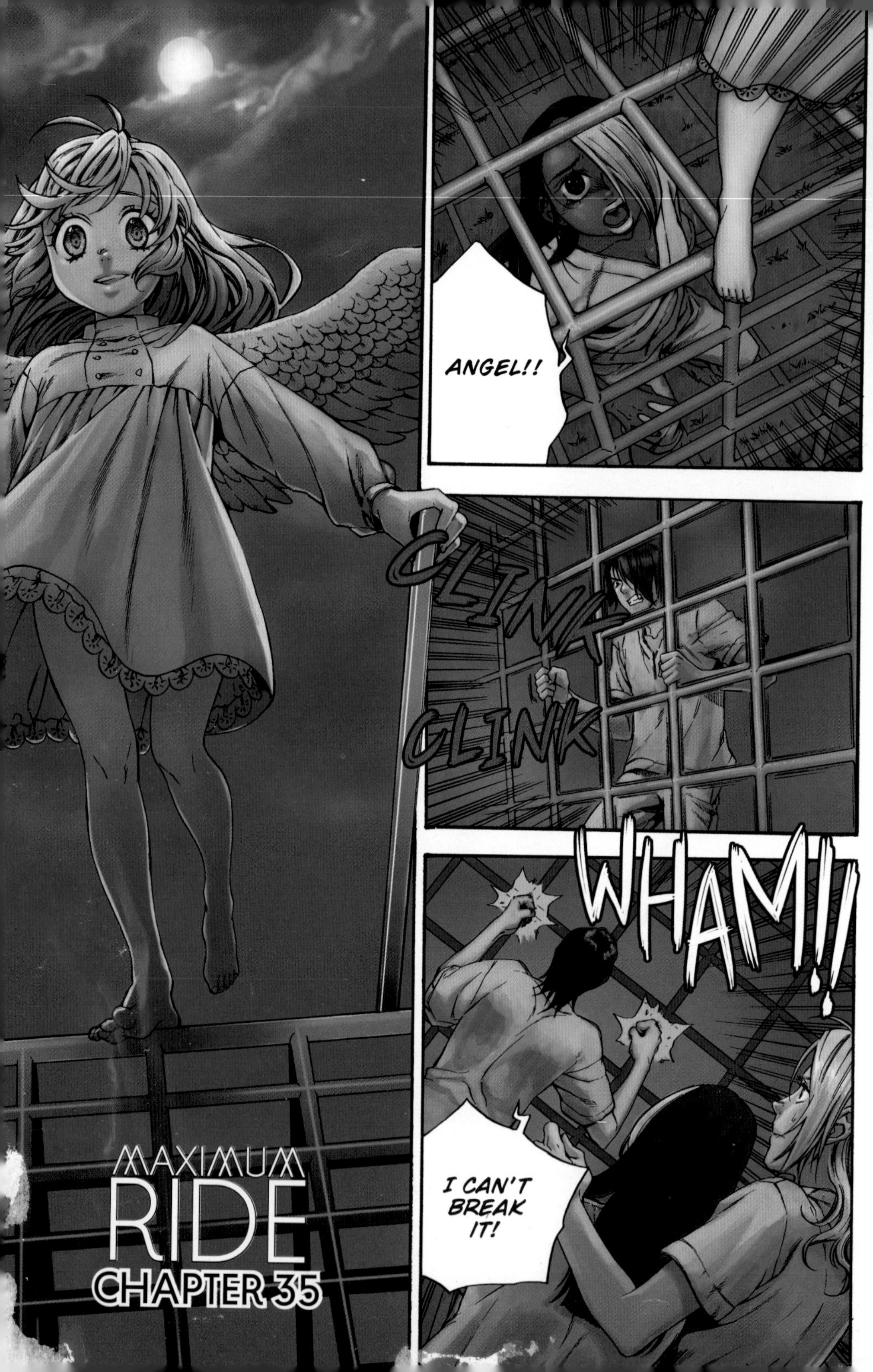
MAXIMUM RIDE
CHAPTER 35
ANGEL!!
CLINK
CLINK
WHAM!!
I CAN'T BREAK IT!

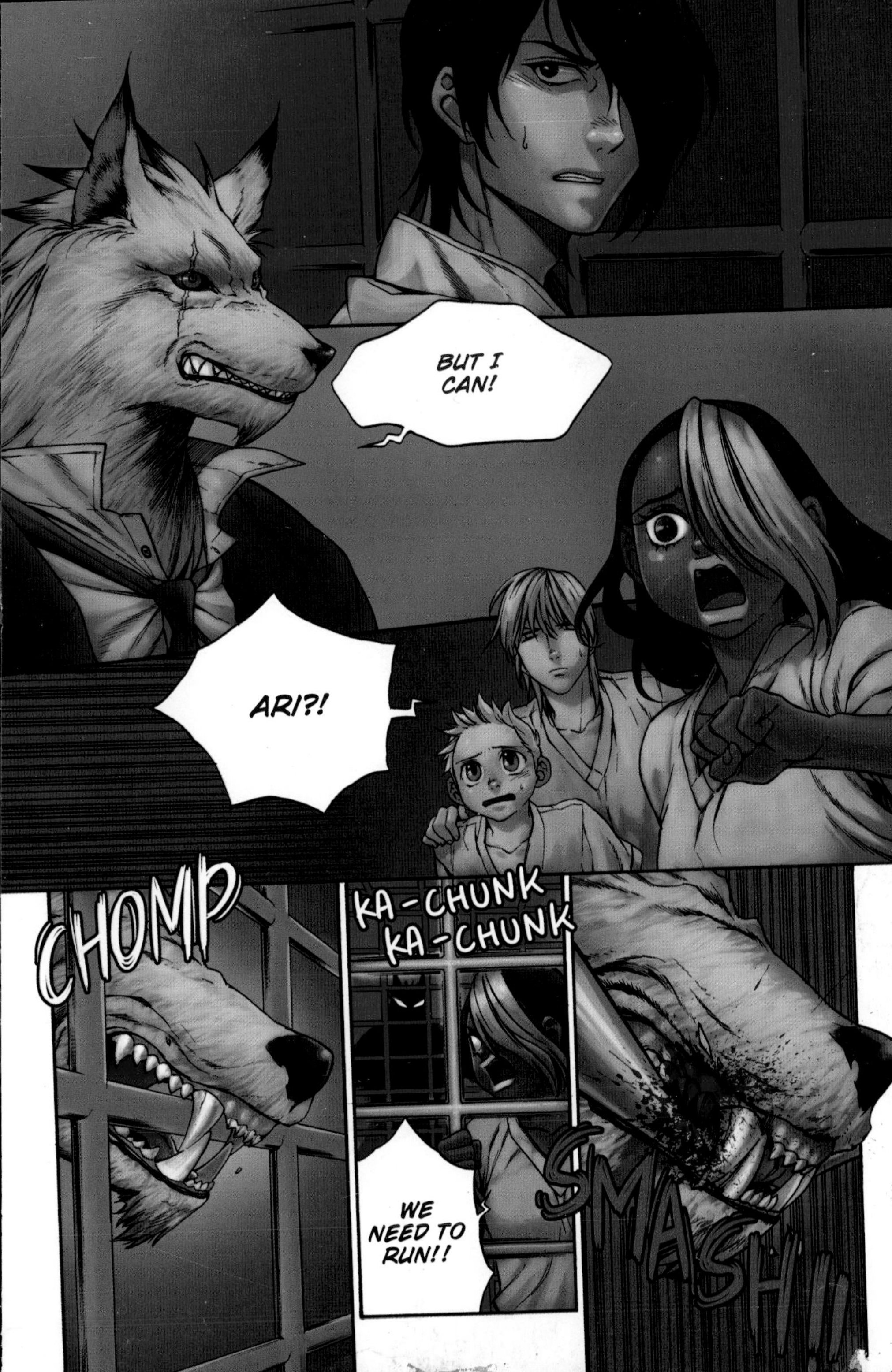
BUT I CAN!
ARI?!
CHOMP
KA-CHUNK
KA-CHUNK
WE NEED TO RUN!!
SMASH!!!

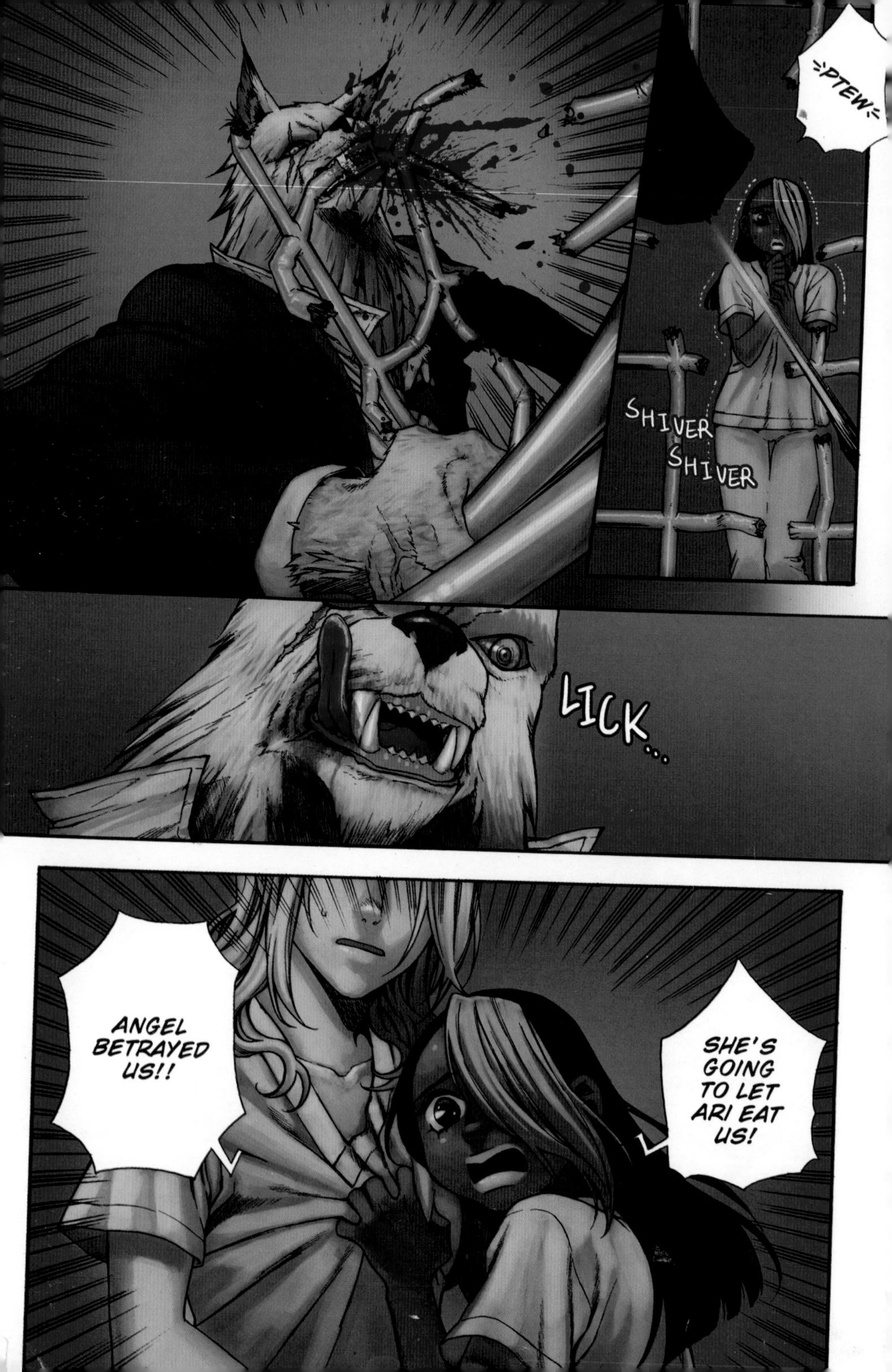
PTEW
SHIVER SHIVER
LICK...
ANGEL BETRAYED US!!
SHE'S GOING TO LET ARI EAT US!

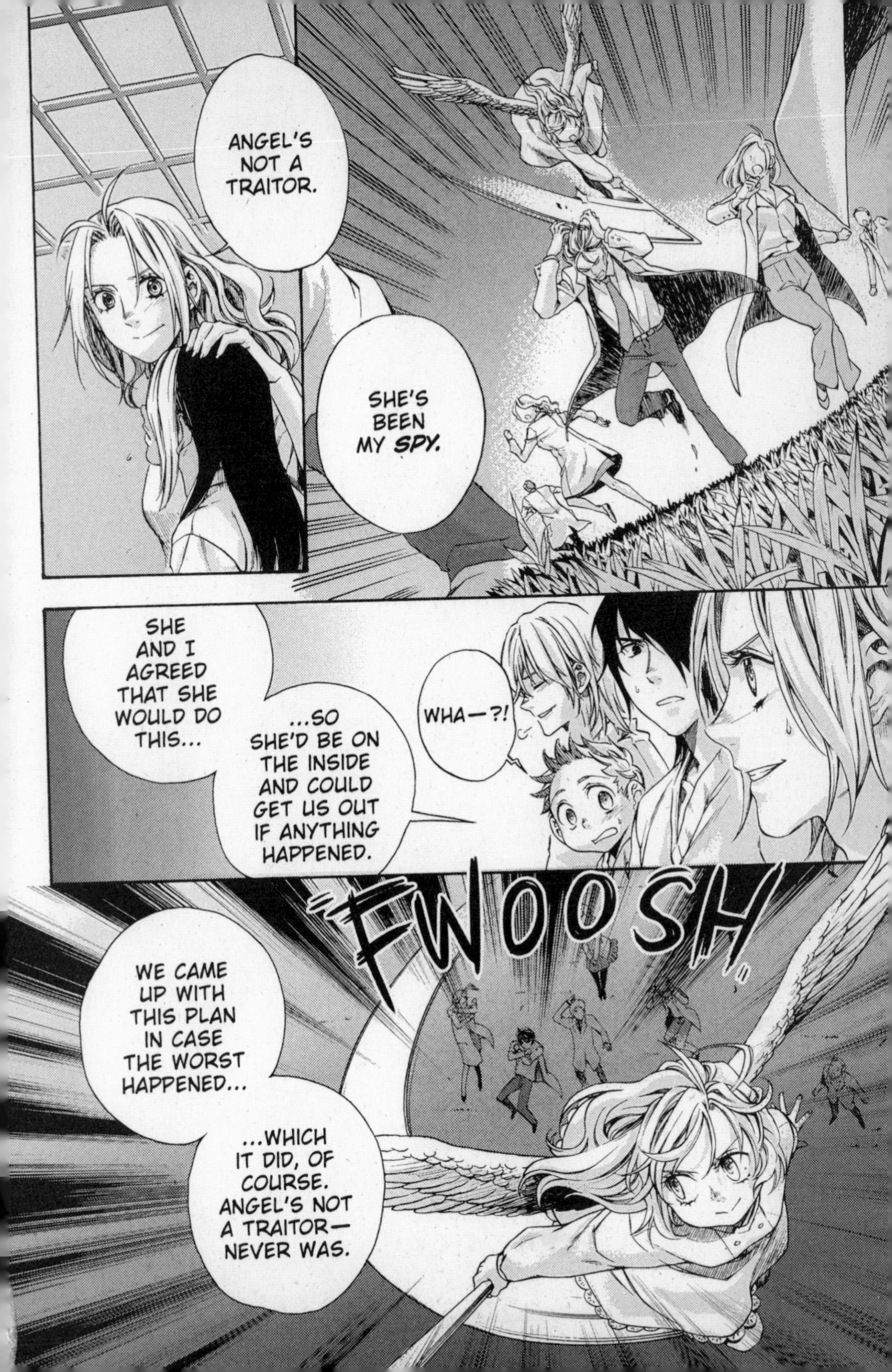
ANGEL'S NOT A TRAITOR.
SHE'S BEEN MY SPY.
SHE AND I AGREED THAT SHE WOULD DO THIS...
...SO SHE'D BE ON THE INSIDE AND COULD GET US OUT IF ANYTHING HAPPENED.
WHA—?!
FWOOSH
WE CAME UP WITH THIS PLAN IN CASE THE WORST HAPPENED...
...WHICH IT DID, OF COURSE. ANGEL'S NOT A TRAITOR— NEVER WAS.

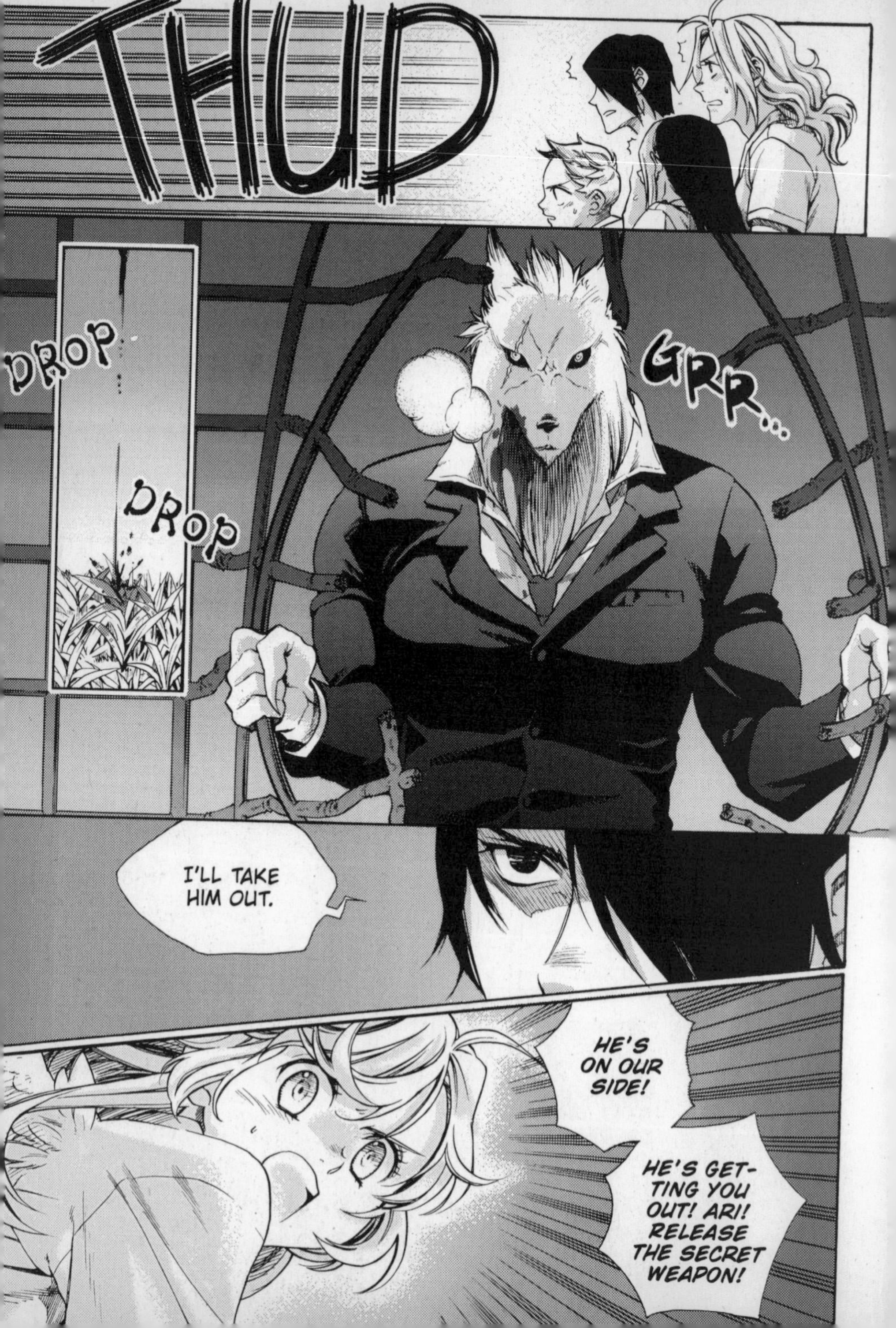
THUD
DROP
DROP
GRR...
I'LL TAKE HIM OUT.
HE'S ON OUR SIDE!
HE'S GET-TING YOU OUT! ARI! RELEASE THE SECRET WEAPON!

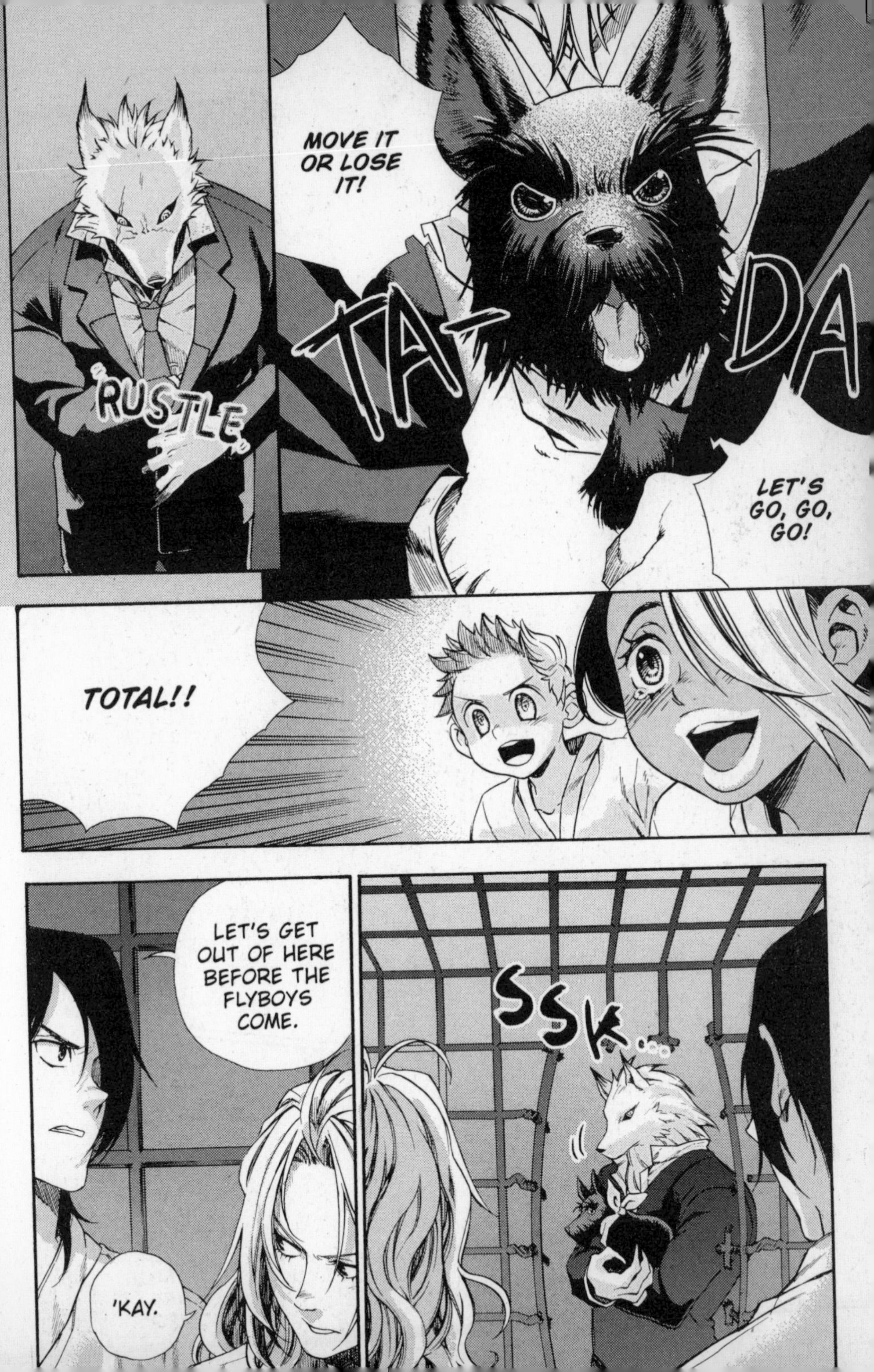
MOVE IT OR LOSE IT!
RUSTLE
TA-DA
LET'S GO, GO, GO!
TOTAL!!
LET'S GET OUT OF HERE BEFORE THE FLYBOYS COME.
SSK...
'KAY.

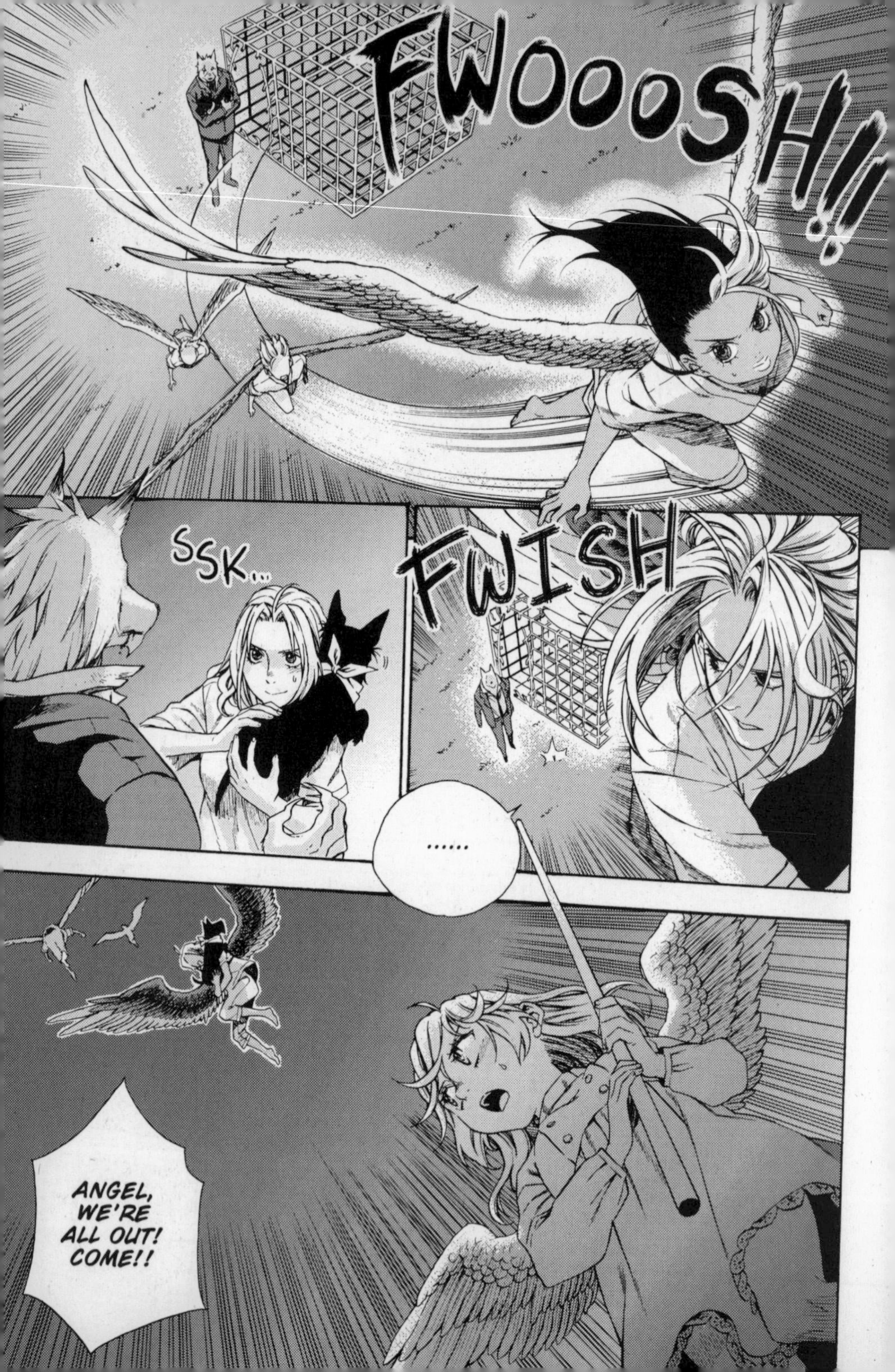
FWOOOSH!!
SSK...
FWISH
......
ANGEL, WE'RE ALL OUT! COME!!

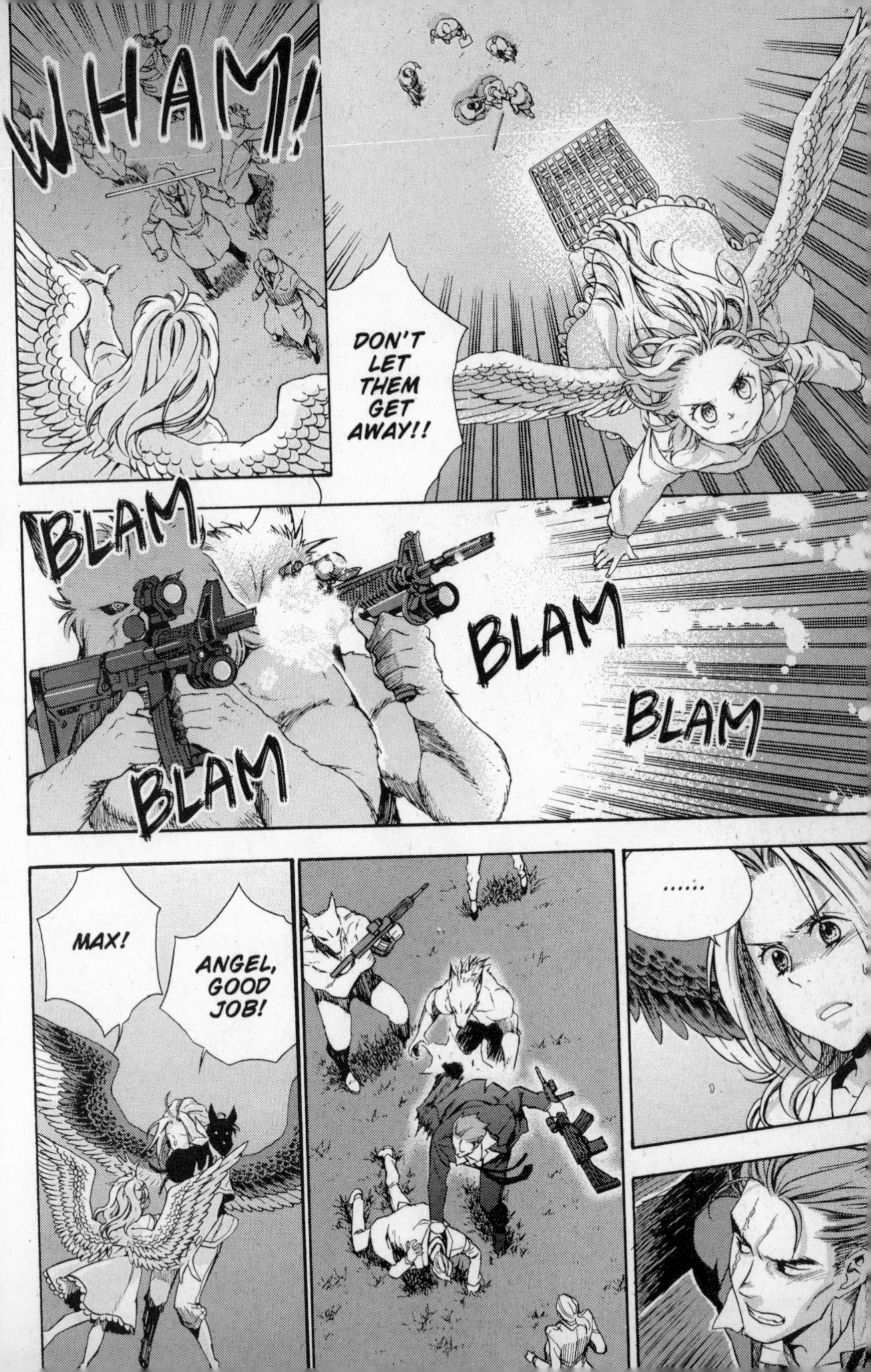
WHAM!
DON'T LET THEM GET AWAY!!
BLAM
BLAM
BLAM
BLAM
......
MAX!
ANGEL, GOOD JOB!

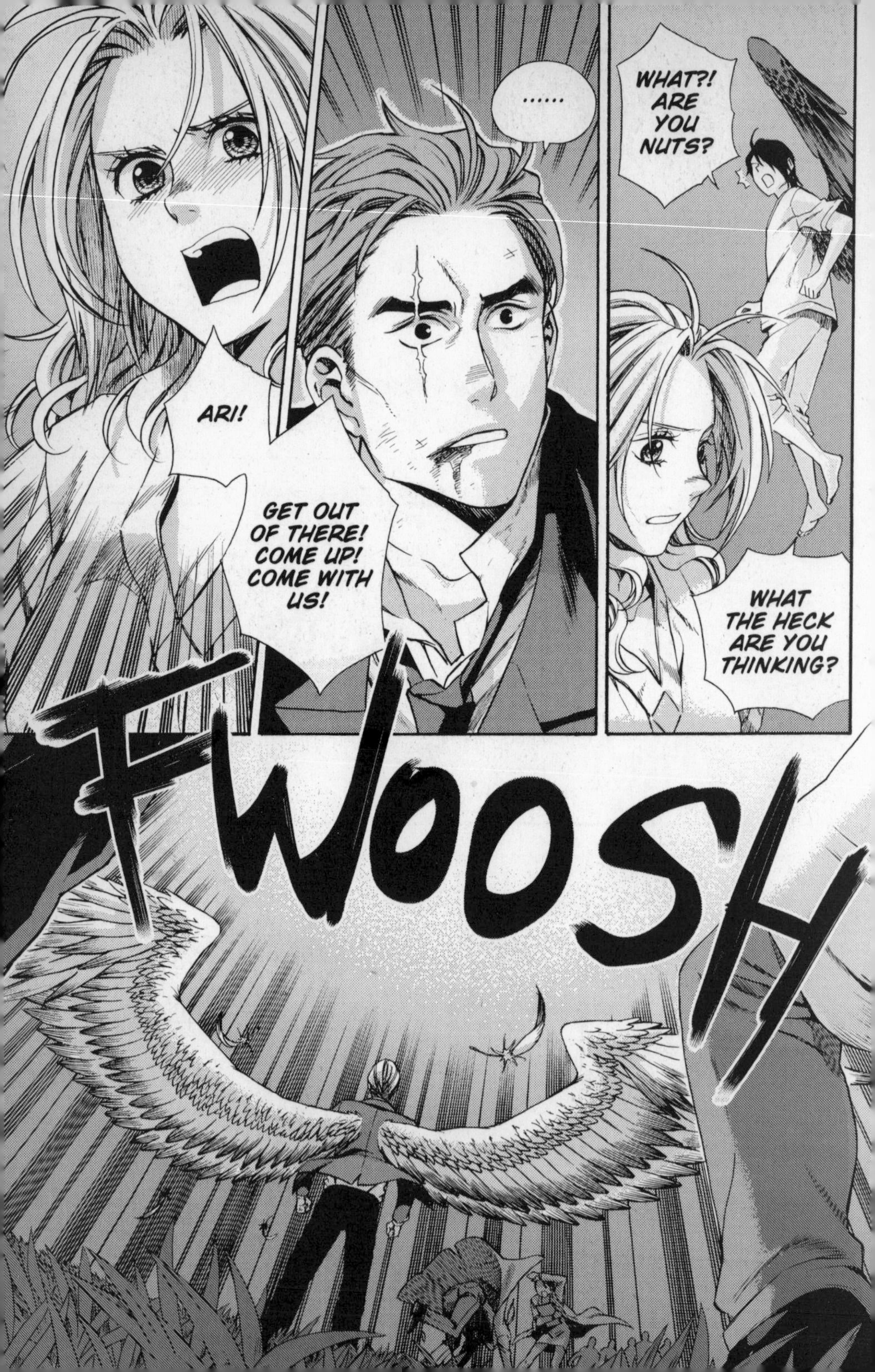
WHAT?! ARE YOU NUTS?
WHAT THE HECK ARE YOU THINKING?
......
ARI!
GET OUT OF THERE! COME UP! COME WITH US!
FWOOSH

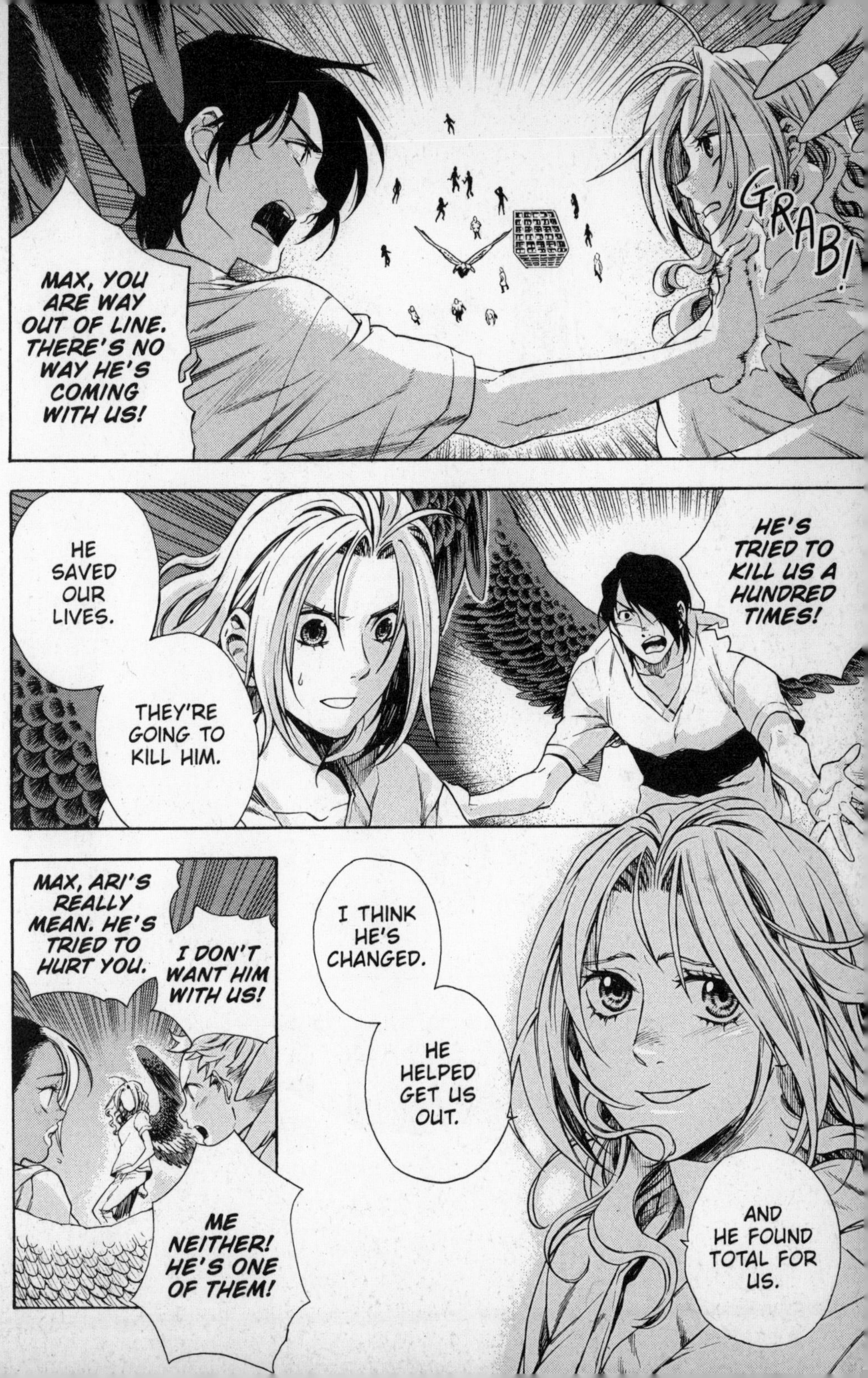
GRAB!
MAX, YOU ARE WAY OUT OF LINE. THERE'S NO WAY HE'S COMING WITH US!
HE SAVED OUR LIVES.
HE'S TRIED TO KILL US A HUNDRED TIMES!
THEY'RE GOING TO KILL HIM.
MAX, ARI'S REALLY MEAN. HE'S TRIED TO HURT YOU.
I DON'T WANT HIM WITH US!
ME NEITHER! HE'S ONE OF THEM!
I THINK HE'S CHANGED.
HE HELPED GET US OUT.
AND HE FOUND TOTAL FOR US.

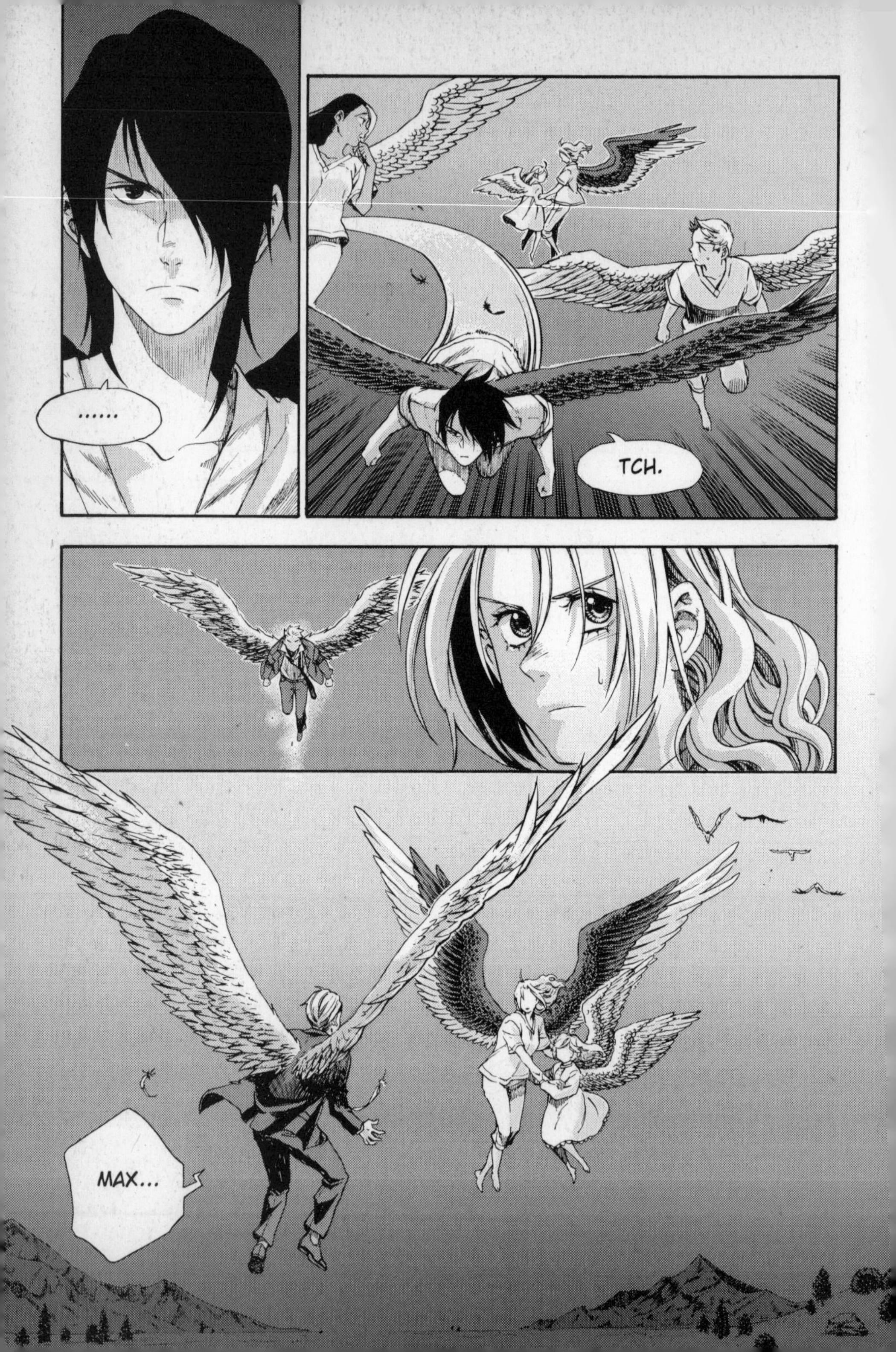
......
TCH.
MAX...

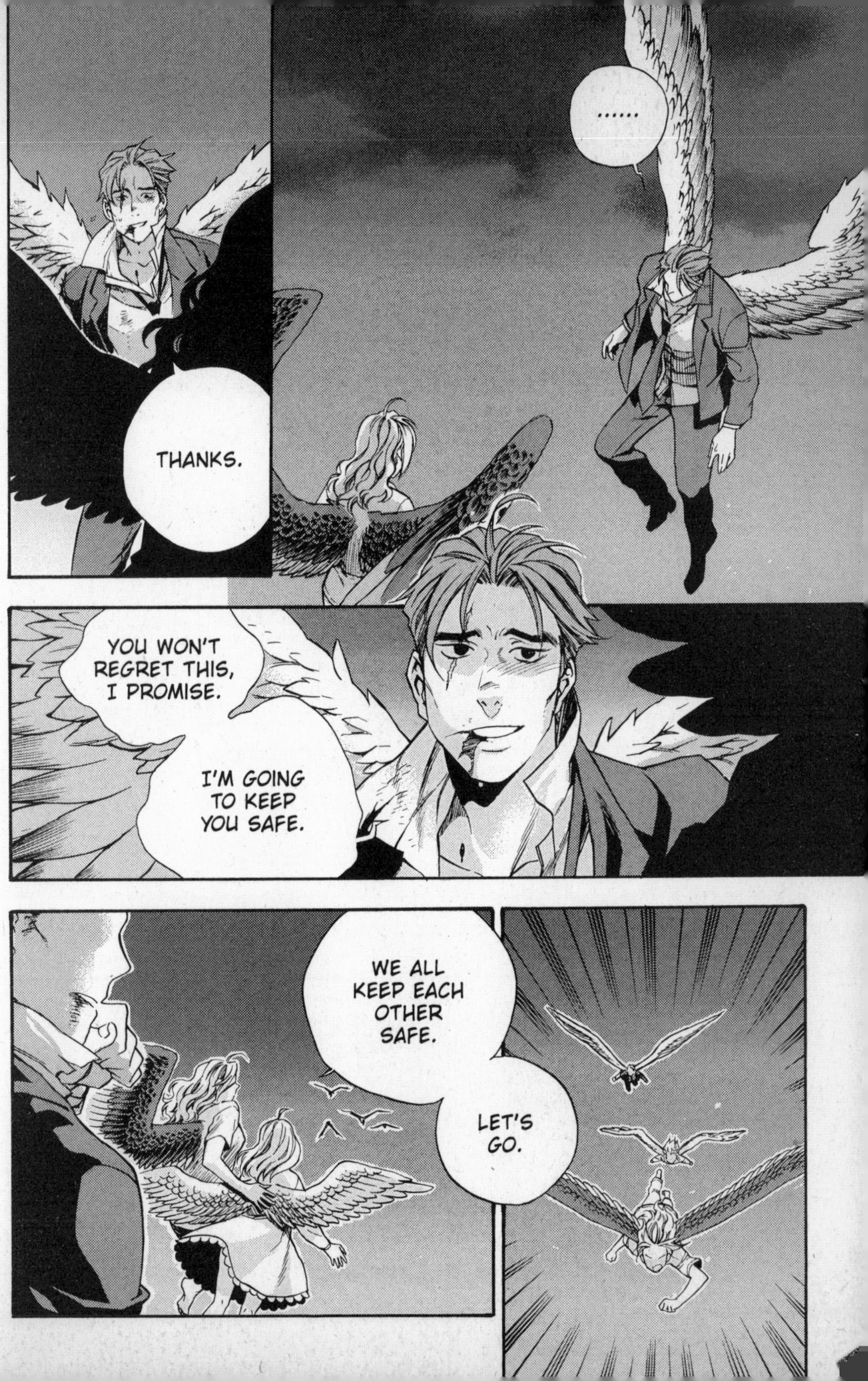
......
THANKS.
YOU WON'T REGRET THIS, I PROMISE.
I'M GOING TO KEEP YOU SAFE.
WE ALL KEEP EACH OTHER SAFE.
LET'S GO.

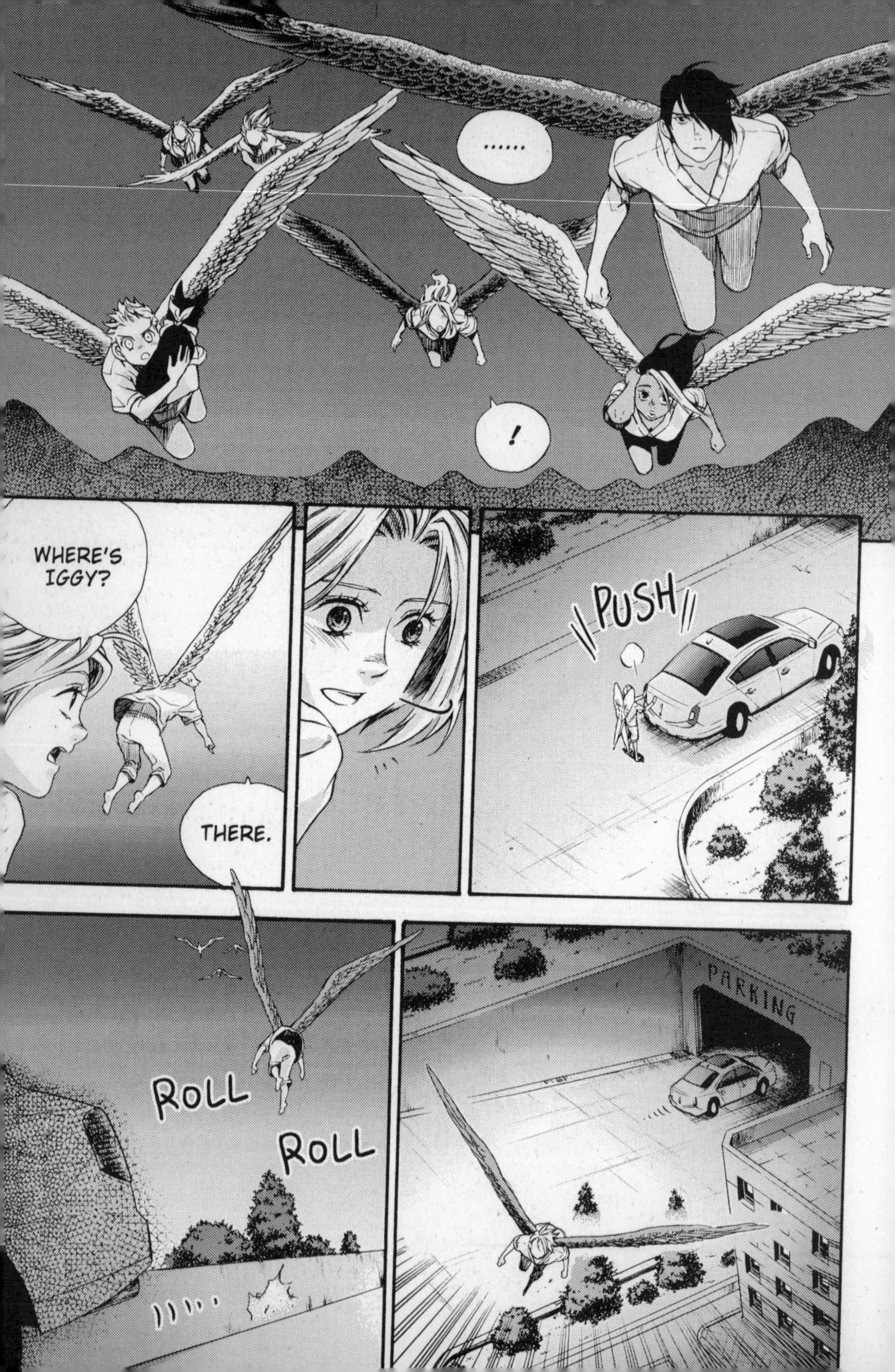
......
!
WHERE'S IGGY?
THERE.
PUSH
ROLL
ROLL

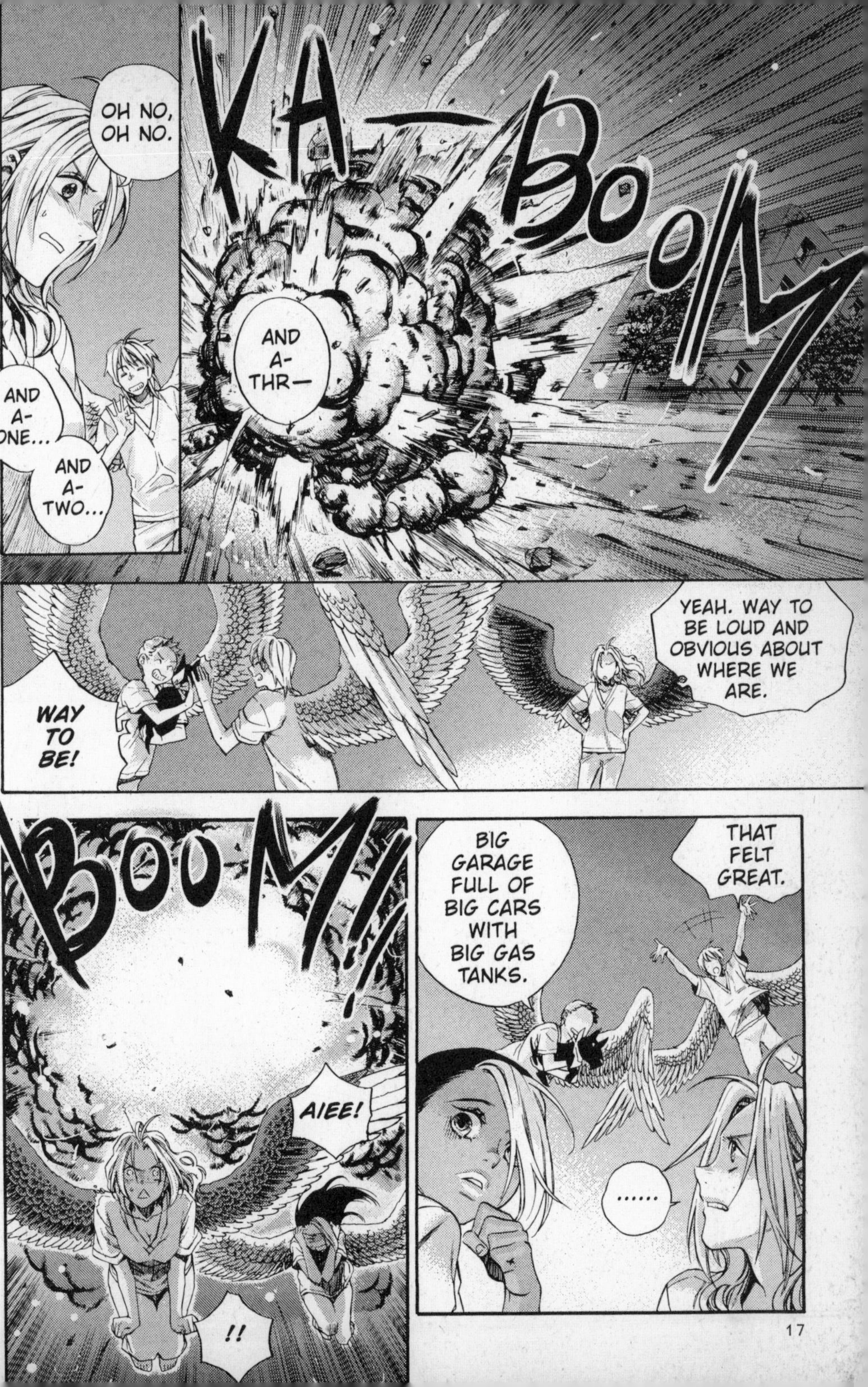
KA—BOOM
OH NO, OH NO.
AND A-ONE...
AND A-TWO...
AND A-THR—
YEAH. WAY TO BE LOUD AND OBVIOUS ABOUT WHERE WE ARE.
WAY TO BE!
THAT FELT GREAT.
BIG GARAGE FULL OF BIG CARS WITH BIG GAS TANKS.
BOOM!!
AIEE!
!!
......

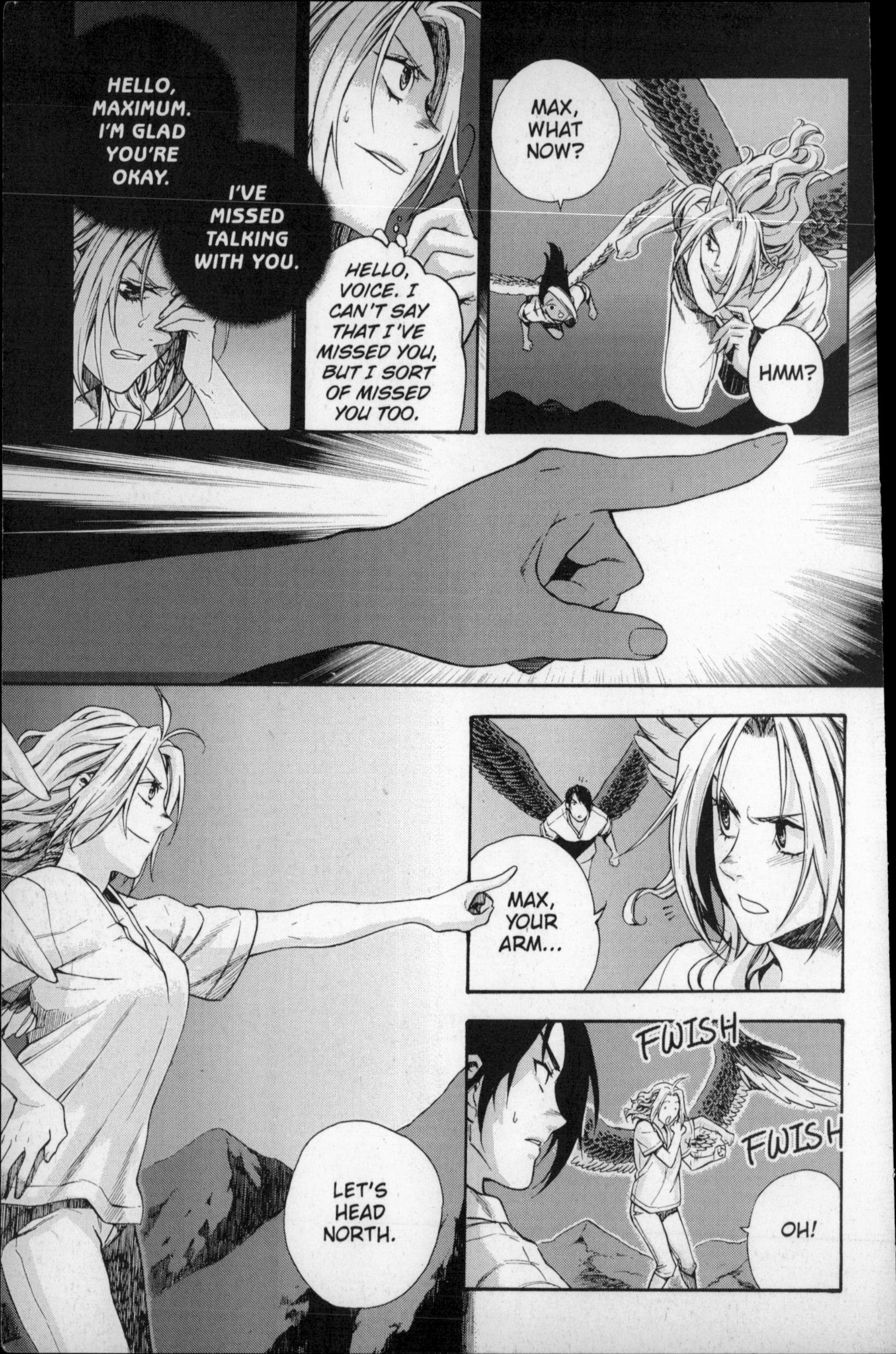
HELLO, MAXIMUM. I'M GLAD YOU'RE OKAY.
I'VE MISSED TALKING WITH YOU.
HELLO, VOICE. I CAN'T SAY THAT I'VE MISSED YOU, BUT I SORT OF MISSED YOU TOO.
MAX, WHAT NOW?
HMM?
MAX, YOUR ARM...
LET'S HEAD NORTH.
FWISH
FWISH
OH!

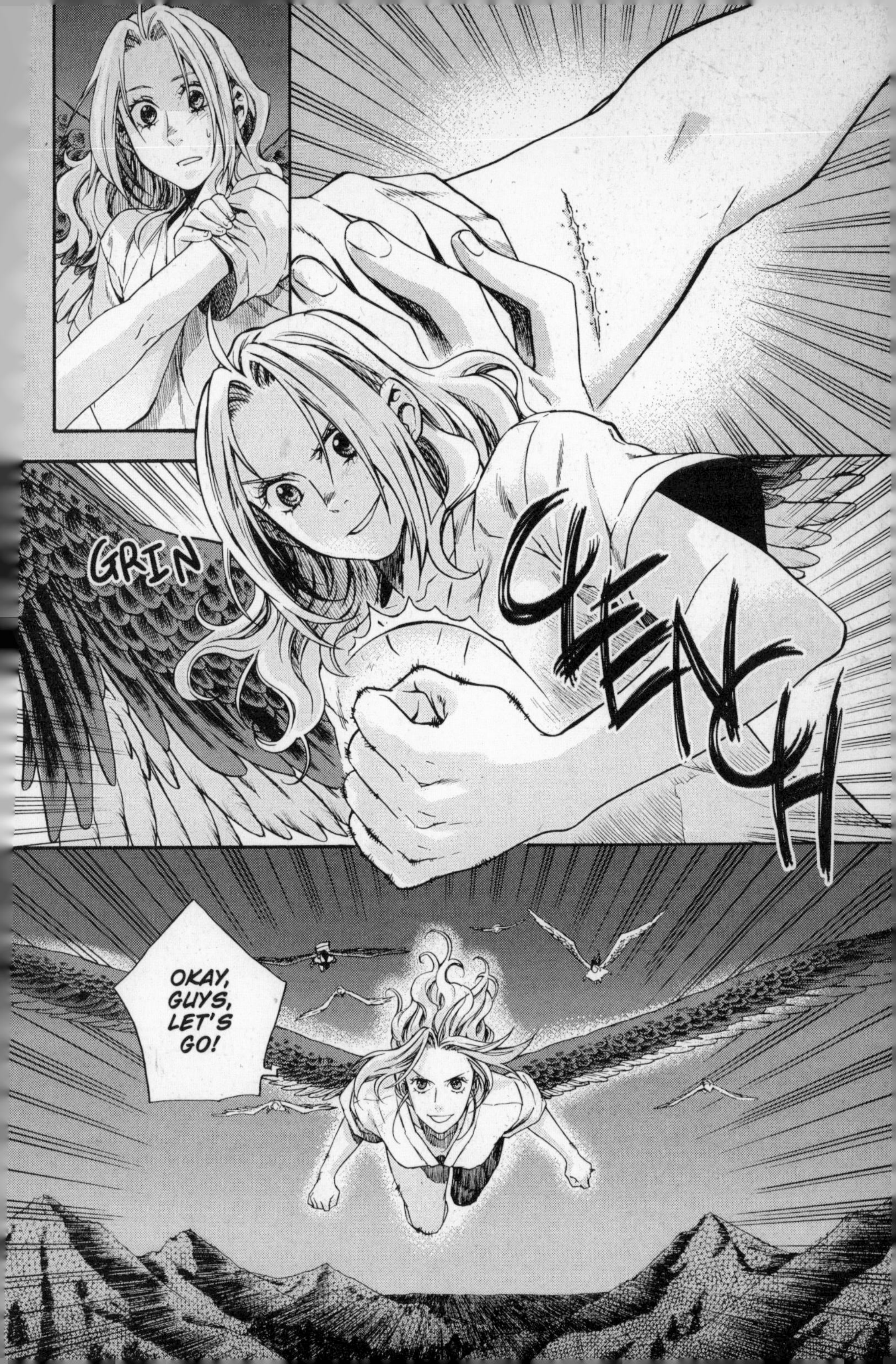
GRIN
CLENCH
OKAY, GUYS, LET'S GO!

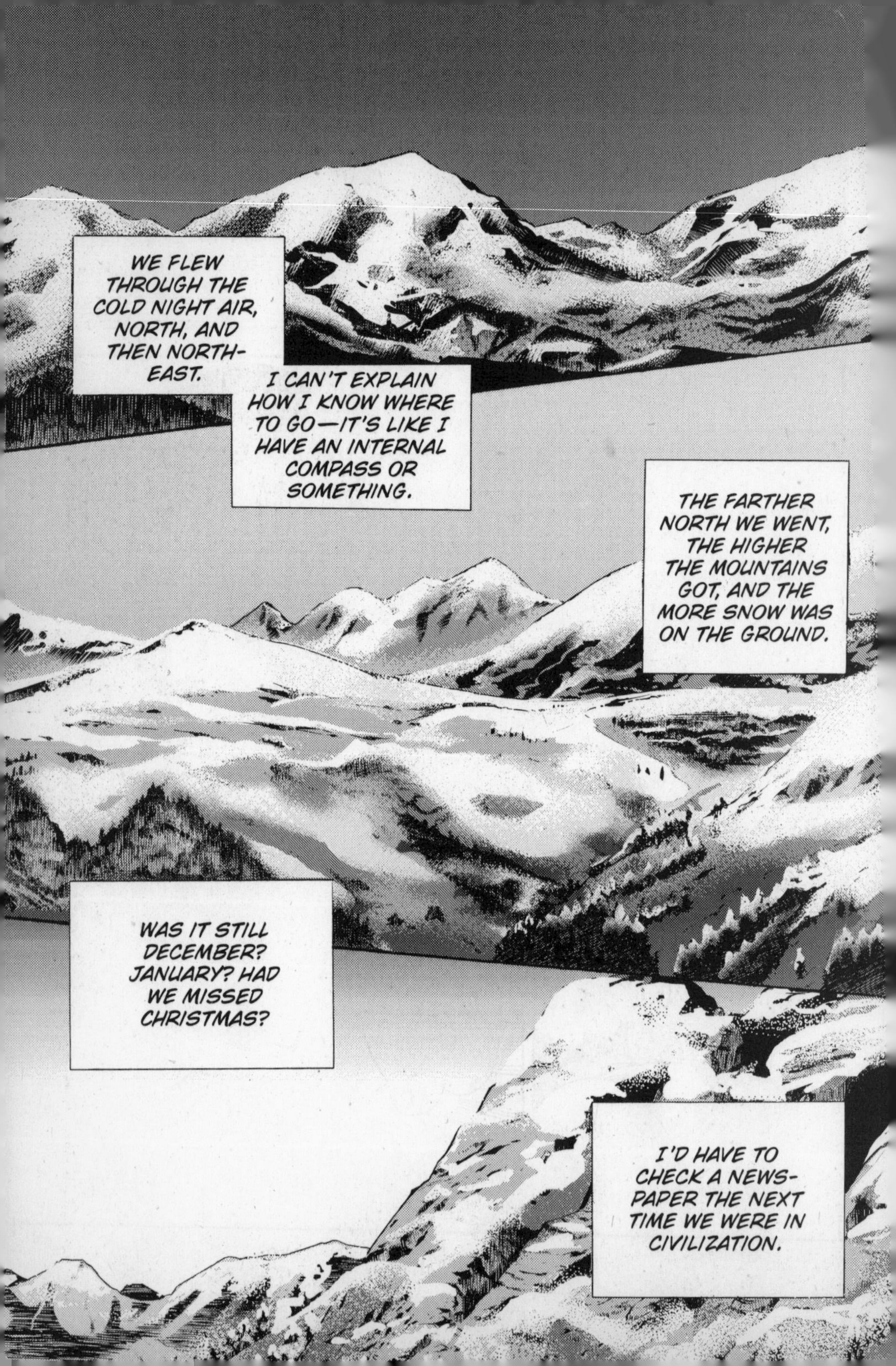
WE FLEW THROUGH THE COLD NIGHT AIR, NORTH, AND THEN NORTH-EAST.
I CAN'T EXPLAIN HOW I KNOW WHERE TO GO—IT'S LIKE I HAVE AN INTERNAL COMPASS OR SOMETHING.
THE FARTHER NORTH WE WENT, THE HIGHER THE MOUNTAINS GOT, AND THE MORE SNOW WAS ON THE GROUND.
WAS IT STILL DECEMBER? JANUARY? HAD WE MISSED CHRISTMAS?
I'D HAVE TO CHECK A NEWS-PAPER THE NEXT TIME WE WERE IN CIVILIZATION.

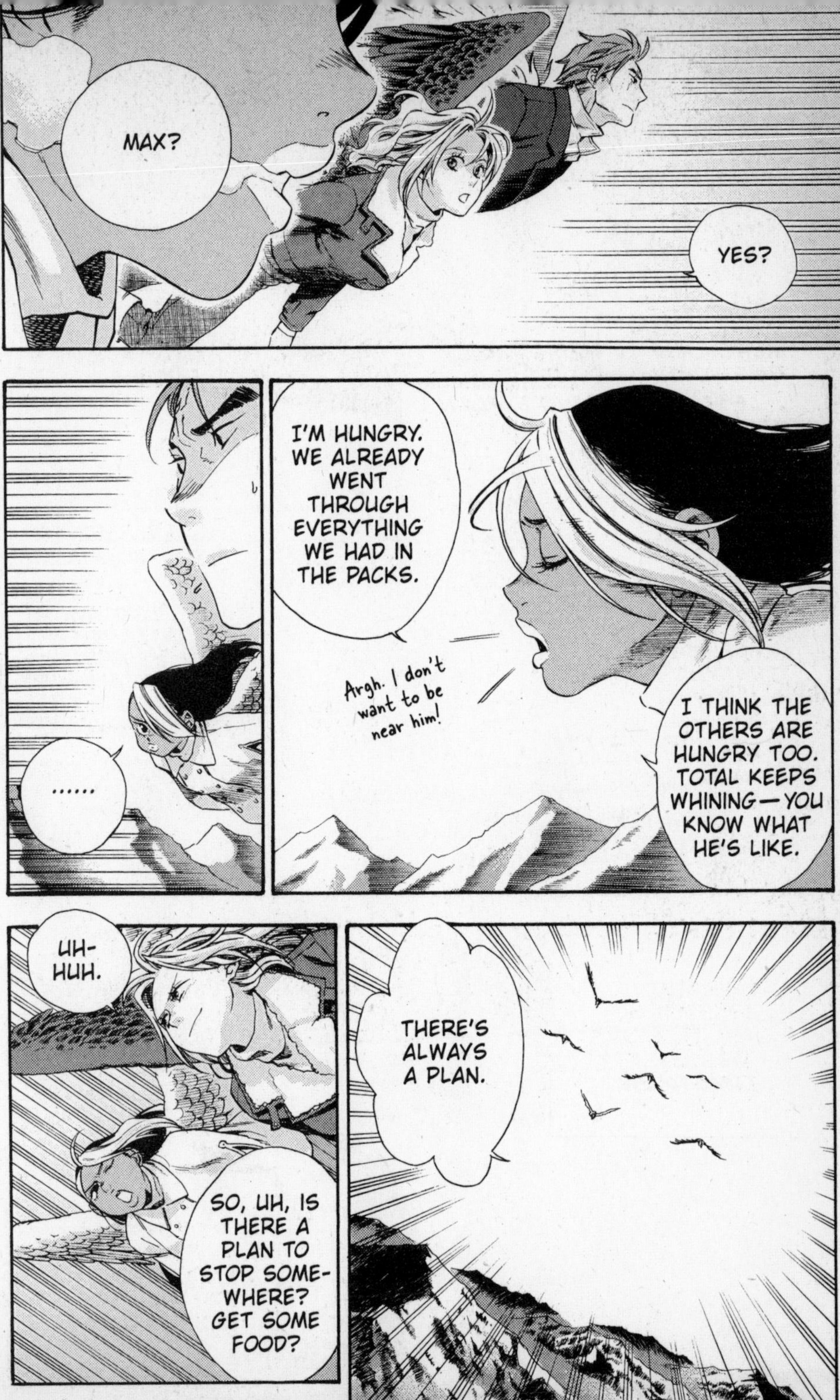
MAX?
YES?
I'M HUNGRY. WE ALREADY WENT THROUGH EVERYTHING WE HAD IN THE PACKS.
Argh. I don't want to be near him!
I THINK THE OTHERS ARE HUNGRY TOO. TOTAL KEEPS WHINING—YOU KNOW WHAT HE'S LIKE.
......
UH-HUH.
SO, UH, IS THERE A PLAN TO STOP SOME-WHERE? GET SOME FOOD?
THERE'S ALWAYS A PLAN.

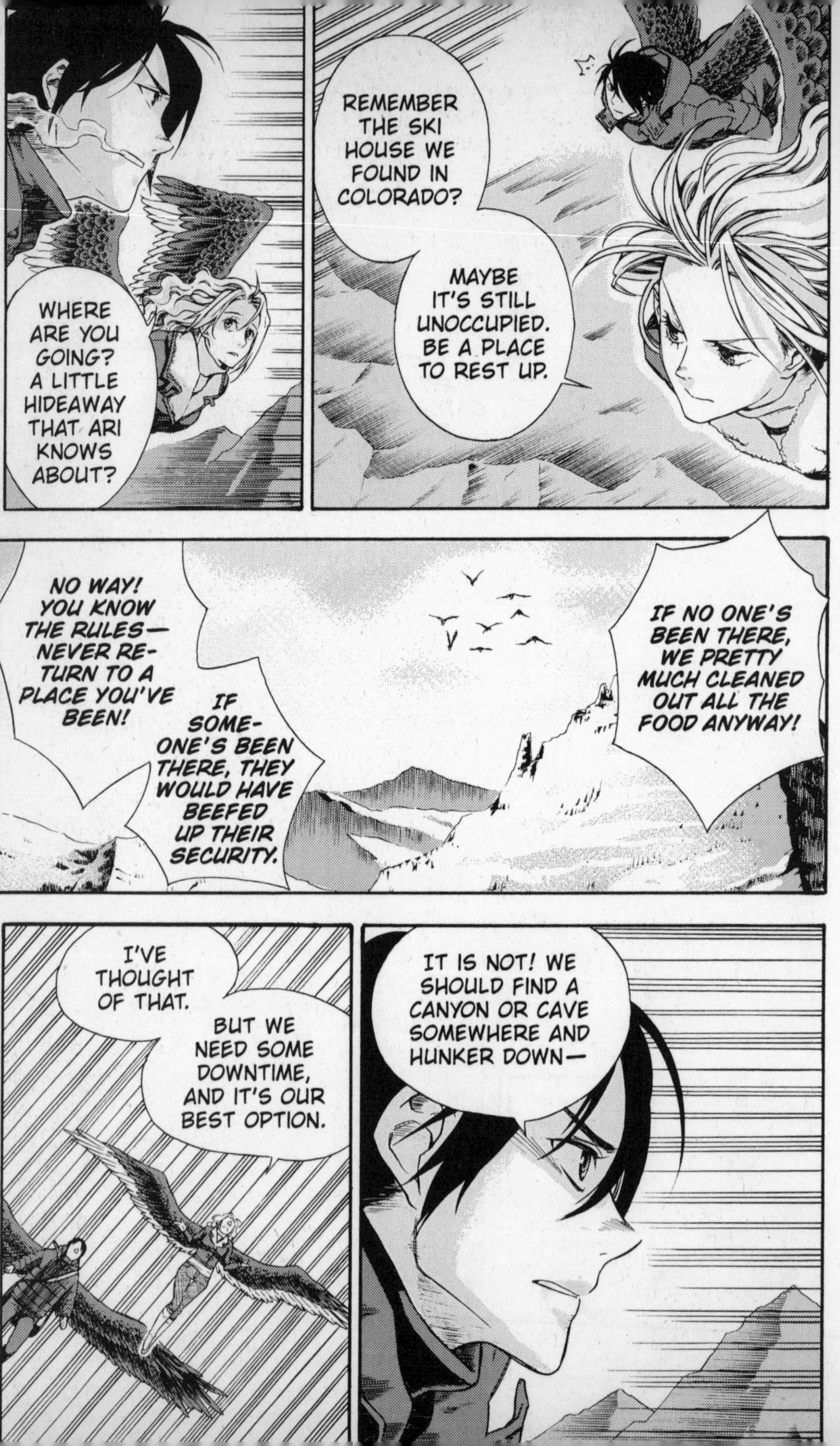
WHERE ARE YOU GOING? A LITTLE HIDEAWAY THAT ARI KNOWS ABOUT?
REMEMBER THE SKI HOUSE WE FOUND IN COLORADO?
MAYBE IT'S STILL UNOCCUPIED. BE A PLACE TO REST UP.
NO WAY! YOU KNOW THE RULES— NEVER RE-TURN TO A PLACE YOU'VE BEEN!
IF SOME-ONE'S BEEN THERE, THEY WOULD HAVE BEEFED UP THEIR SECURITY.
IF NO ONE'S BEEN THERE, WE PRETTY MUCH CLEANED OUT ALL THE FOOD ANYWAY!
I'VE THOUGHT OF THAT.
BUT WE NEED SOME DOWNTIME, AND IT'S OUR BEST OPTION.
IT IS NOT! WE SHOULD FIND A CANYON OR CAVE SOMEWHERE AND HUNKER DOWN—

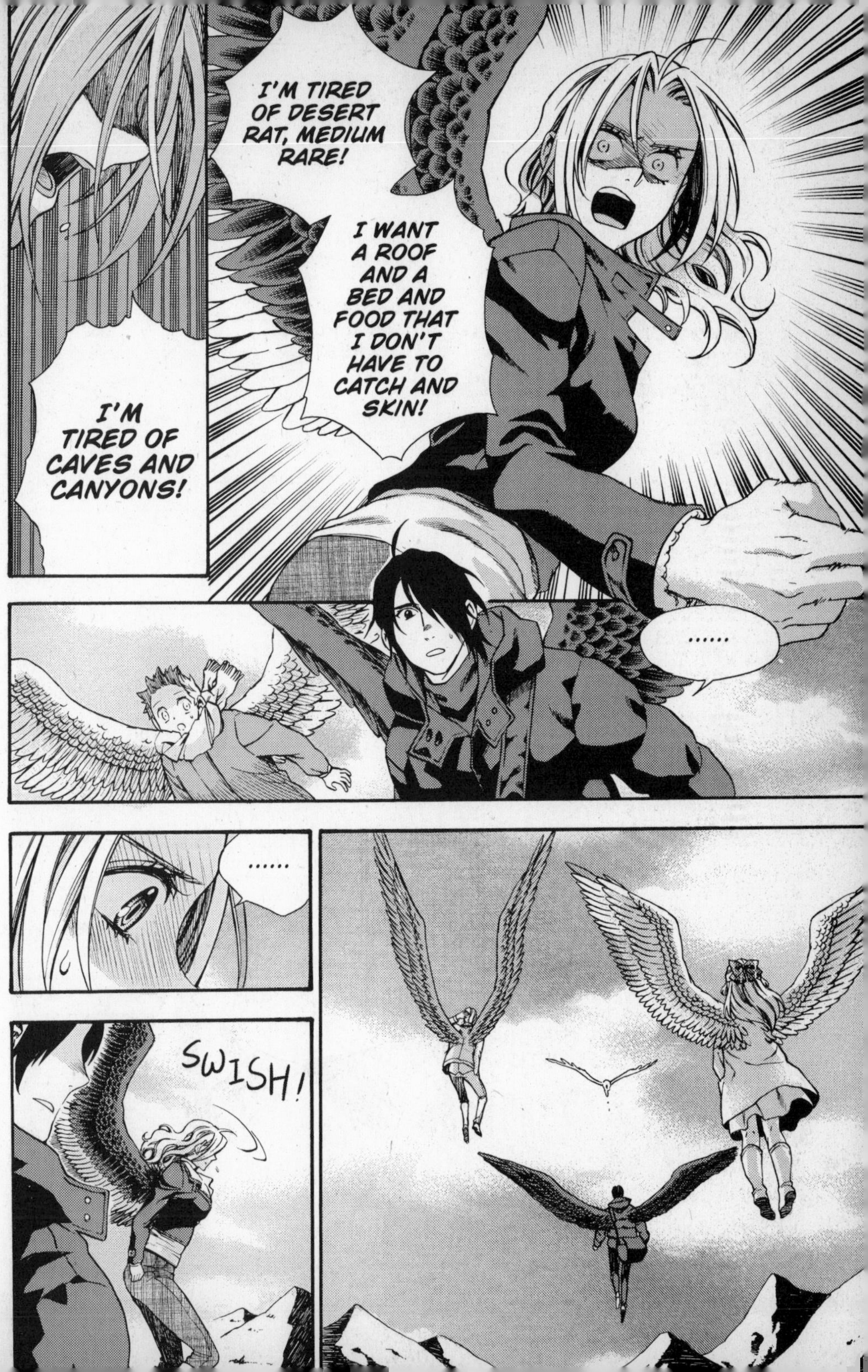
I'M TIRED OF DESERT RAT, MEDIUM RARE!
I WANT A ROOF AND A BED AND FOOD THAT I DON'T HAVE TO CATCH AND SKIN!
I'M TIRED OF CAVES AND CANYONS!
......
......
SWISH!

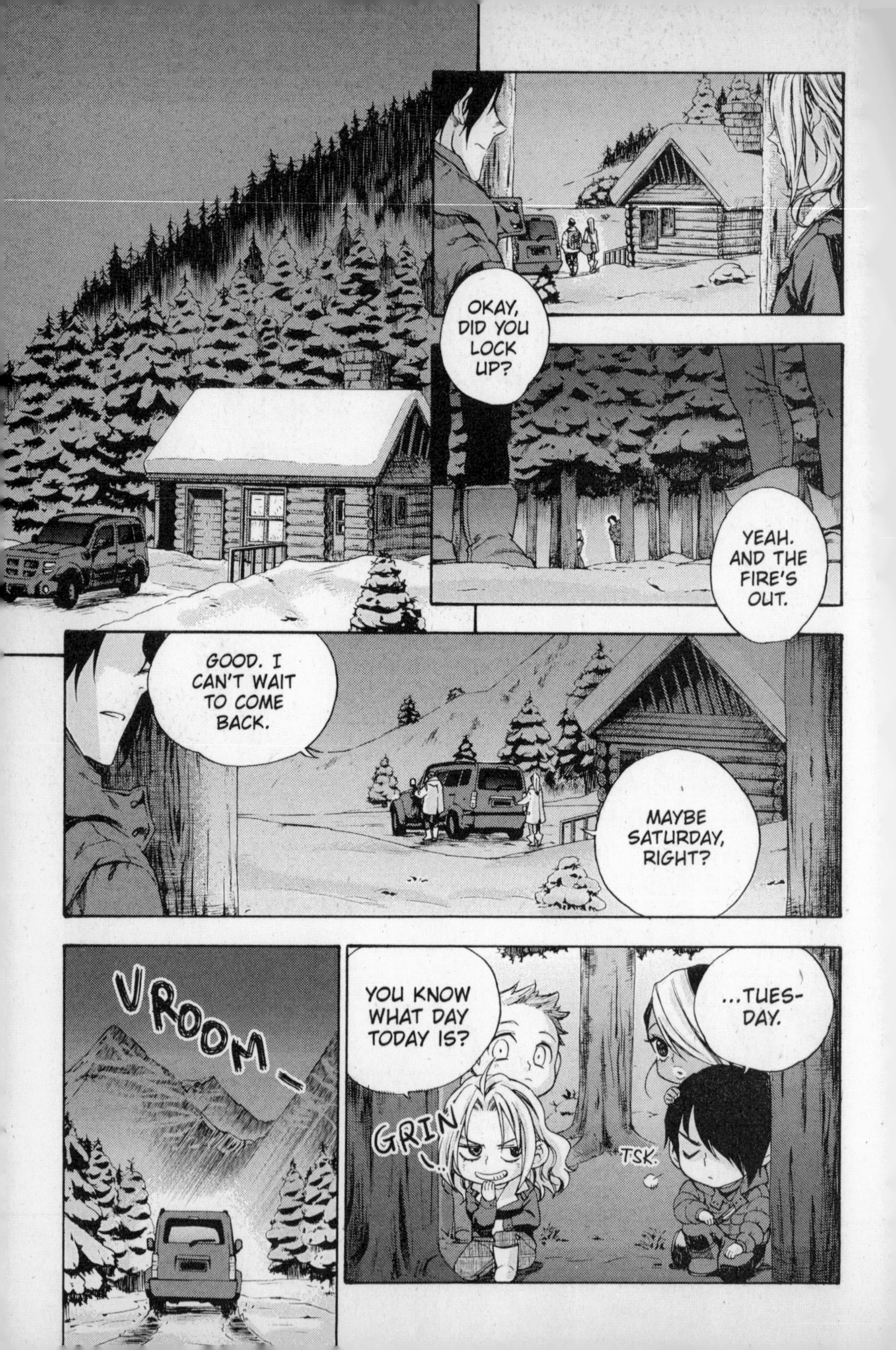
OKAY, DID YOU LOCK UP?
YEAH. AND THE FIRE'S OUT.
GOOD. I CAN'T WAIT TO COME BACK.
MAYBE SATURDAY, RIGHT?
VROOM-
YOU KNOW WHAT DAY TODAY IS?
...TUES-DAY.
GRIN...
TSK.

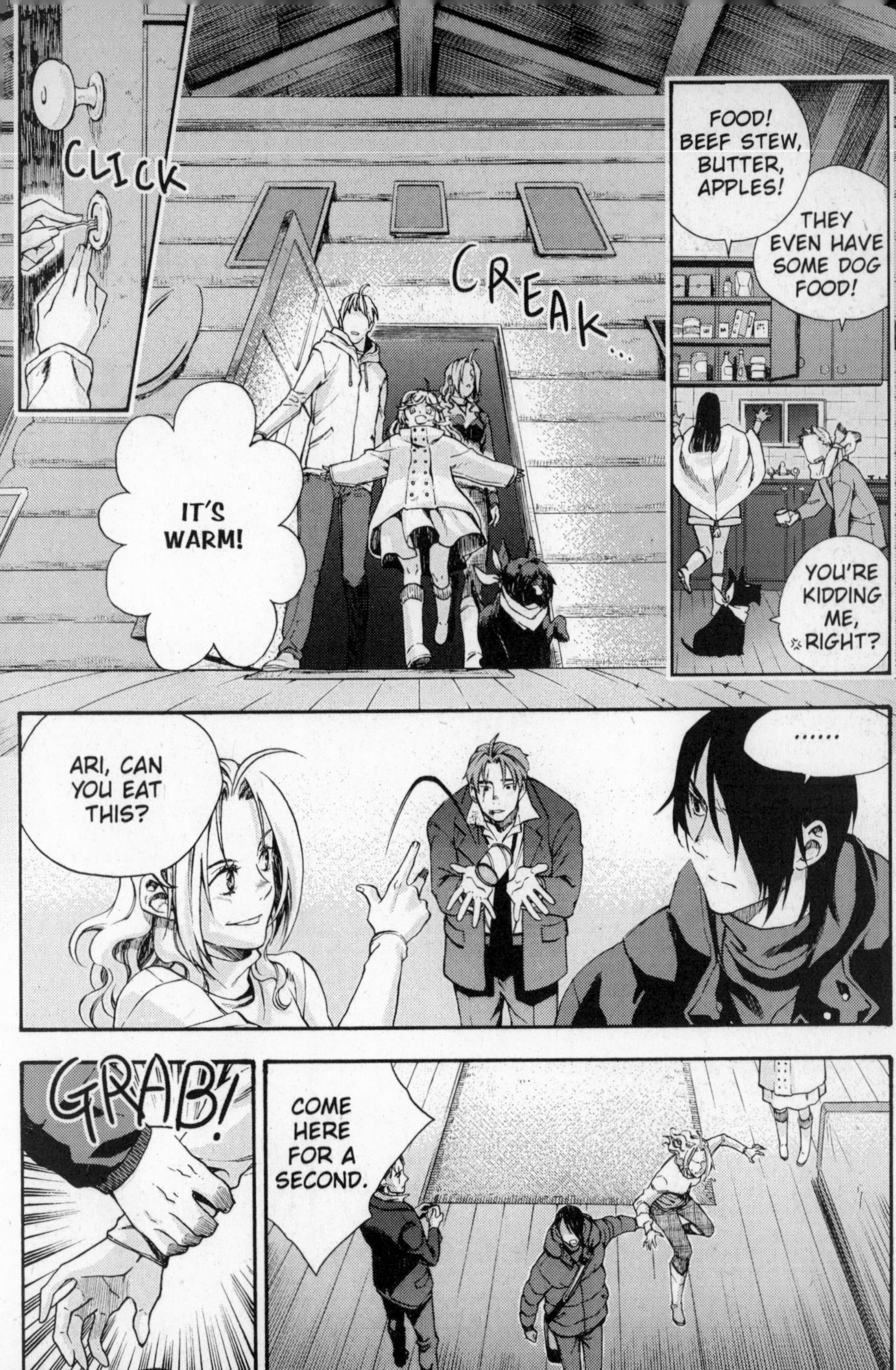
CLICK
CREAK...
IT'S WARM!
FOOD! BEEF STEW, BUTTER, APPLES!
THEY EVEN HAVE SOME DOG FOOD!
YOU'RE KIDDING ME, RIGHT?
ARI, CAN YOU EAT THIS?
......
GRAB!
COME HERE FOR A SECOND.

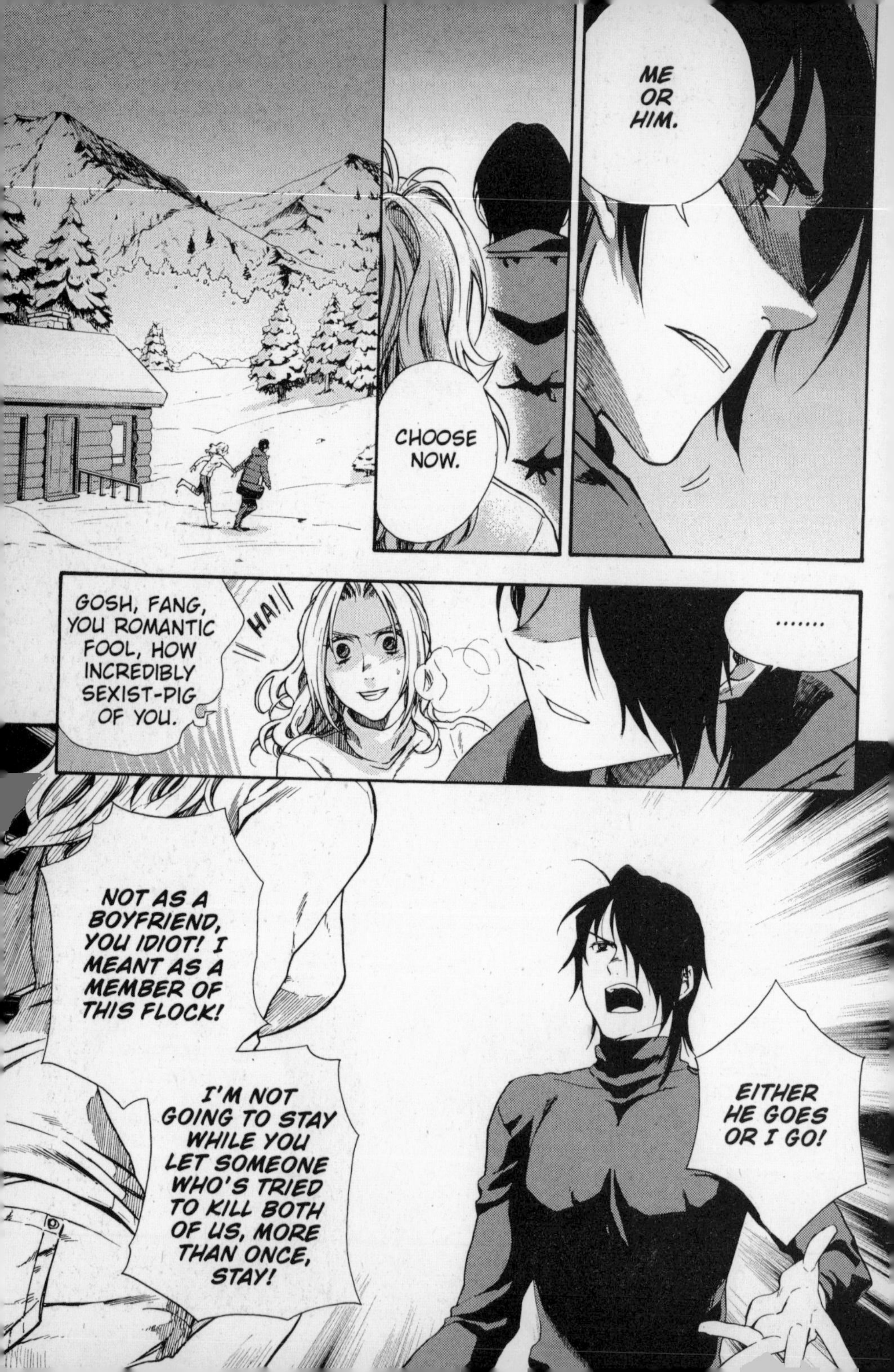
ME OR HIM.
CHOOSE NOW.
GOSH, FANG, YOU ROMANTIC FOOL, HOW INCREDIBLY SEXIST-PIG OF YOU.
HA!
....
NOT AS A BOYFRIEND, YOU IDIOT! I MEANT AS A MEMBER OF THIS FLOCK!
I'M NOT GOING TO STAY WHILE YOU LET SOMEONE WHO'S TRIED TO KILL BOTH OF US, MORE THAN ONCE, STAY!
EITHER HE GOES OR I GO!

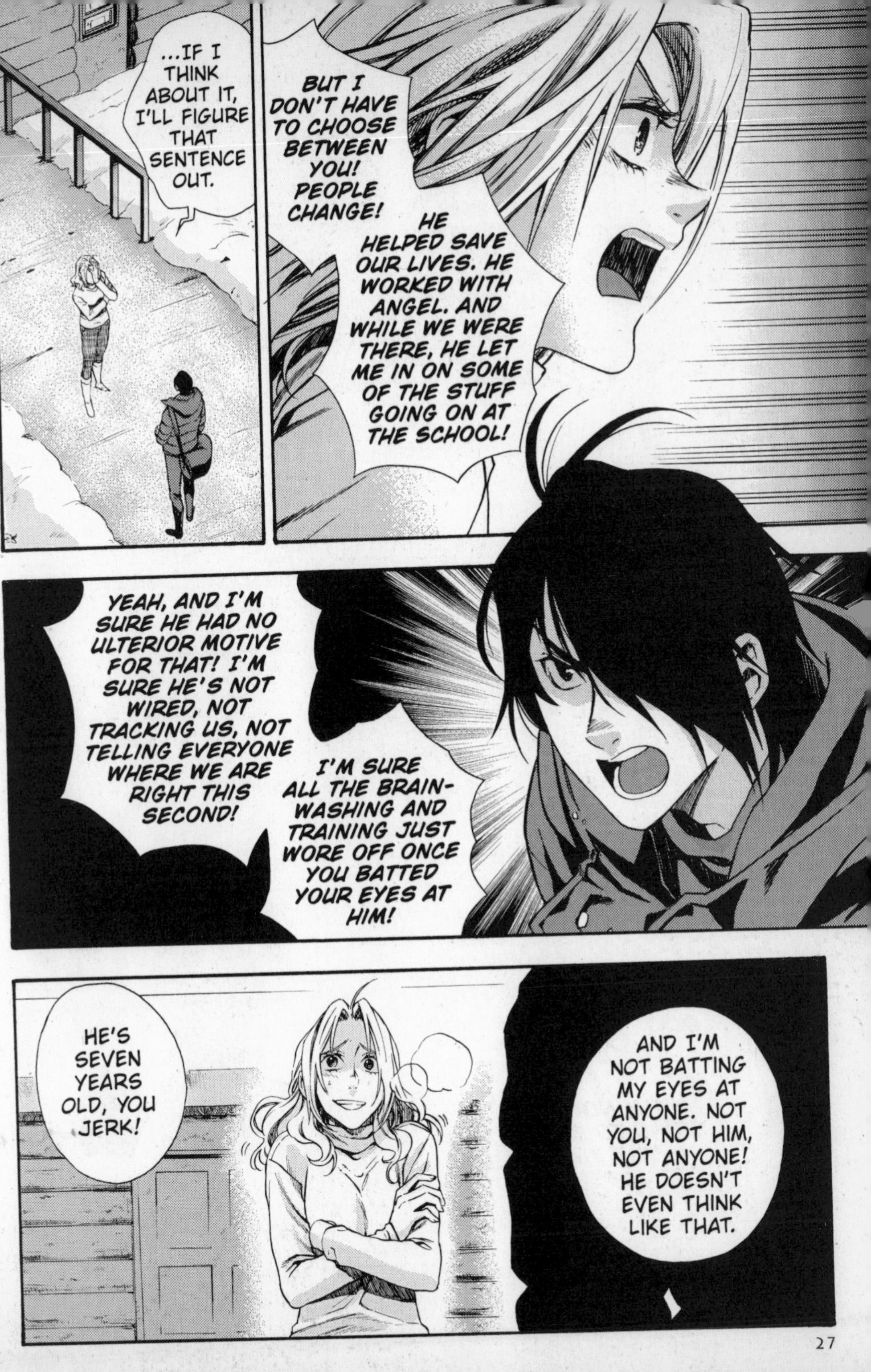

...IF I THINK ABOUT IT, I'LL FIGURE THAT SENTENCE OUT.
BUT I DON'T HAVE TO CHOOSE BETWEEN YOU! PEOPLE CHANGE!
HE HELPED SAVE OUR LIVES. HE WORKED WITH ANGEL. AND WHILE WE WERE THERE, HE LET ME IN ON SOME OF THE STUFF GOING ON AT THE SCHOOL!
YEAH, AND I'M SURE HE HAD NO ULTERIOR MOTIVE FOR THAT! I'M SURE HE'S NOT WIRED, NOT TRACKING US, NOT TELLING EVERYONE WHERE WE ARE RIGHT THIS SECOND!
I'M SURE ALL THE BRAIN-WASHING AND TRAINING JUST WORE OFF ONCE YOU BATTED YOUR EYES AT HIM!
HE'S SEVEN YEARS OLD, YOU JERK!
AND I'M NOT BATTING MY EYES AT ANYONE. NOT YOU, NOT HIM, NOT ANYONE! HE DOESN'T EVEN THINK LIKE THAT.

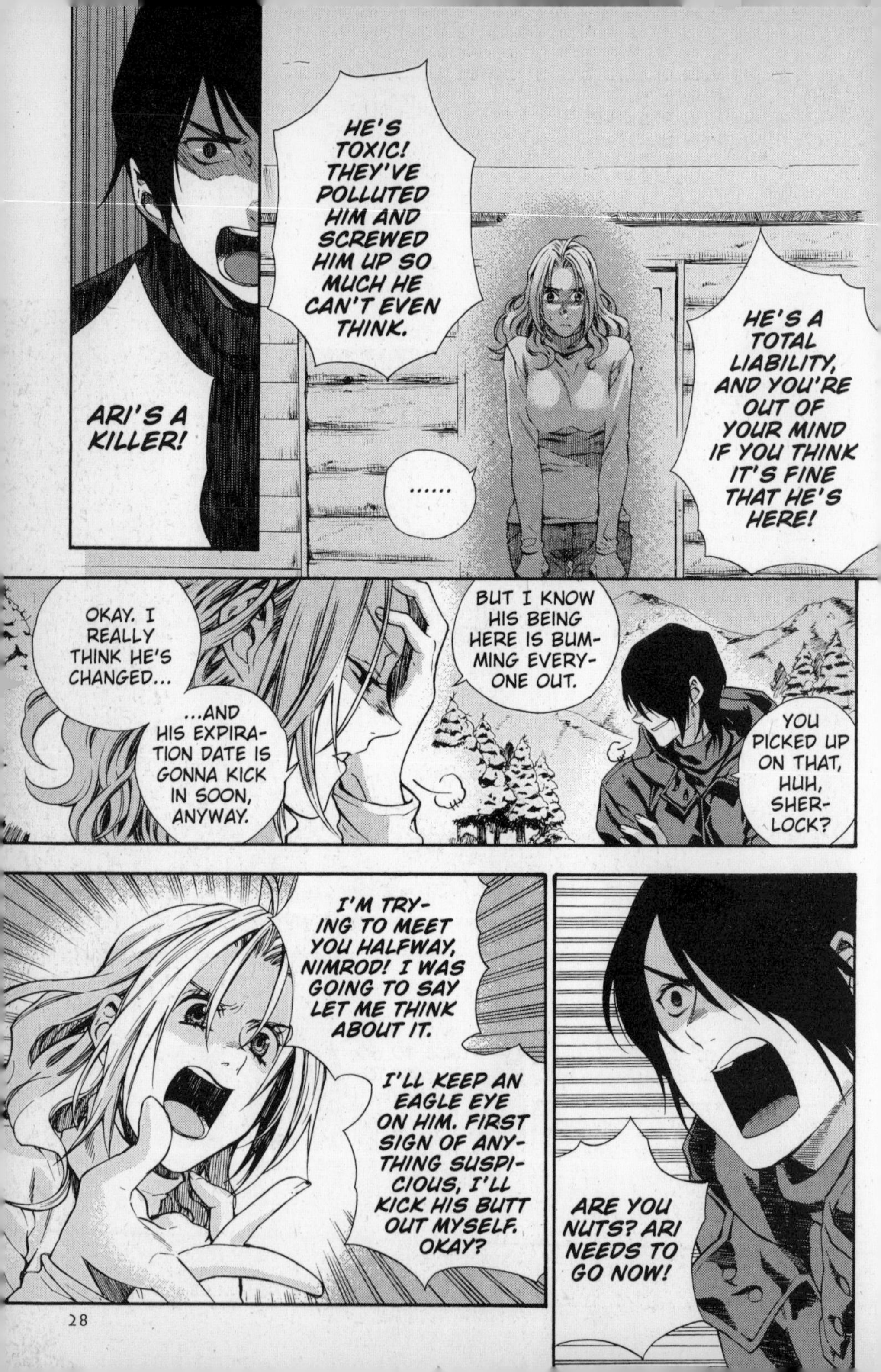
HE'S TOXIC! THEY'VE POLLUTED HIM AND SCREWED HIM UP SO MUCH HE CAN'T EVEN THINK.
ARI'S A KILLER!
HE'S A TOTAL LIABILITY, AND YOU'RE OUT OF YOUR MIND IF YOU THINK IT'S FINE THAT HE'S HERE!
......
OKAY. I REALLY THINK HE'S CHANGED...
...AND HIS EXPIRATION DATE IS GONNA KICK IN SOON, ANYWAY.
BUT I KNOW HIS BEING HERE IS BUMMING EVERYONE OUT.
YOU PICKED UP ON THAT, HUH, SHERLOCK?
I'M TRYING TO MEET YOU HALFWAY, NIMROD! I WAS GOING TO SAY LET ME THINK ABOUT IT.
I'LL KEEP AN EAGLE EYE ON HIM. FIRST SIGN OF ANYTHING SUSPICIOUS, I'LL KICK HIS BUTT OUT MYSELF. OKAY?
ARE YOU NUTS? ARI NEEDS TO GO NOW!

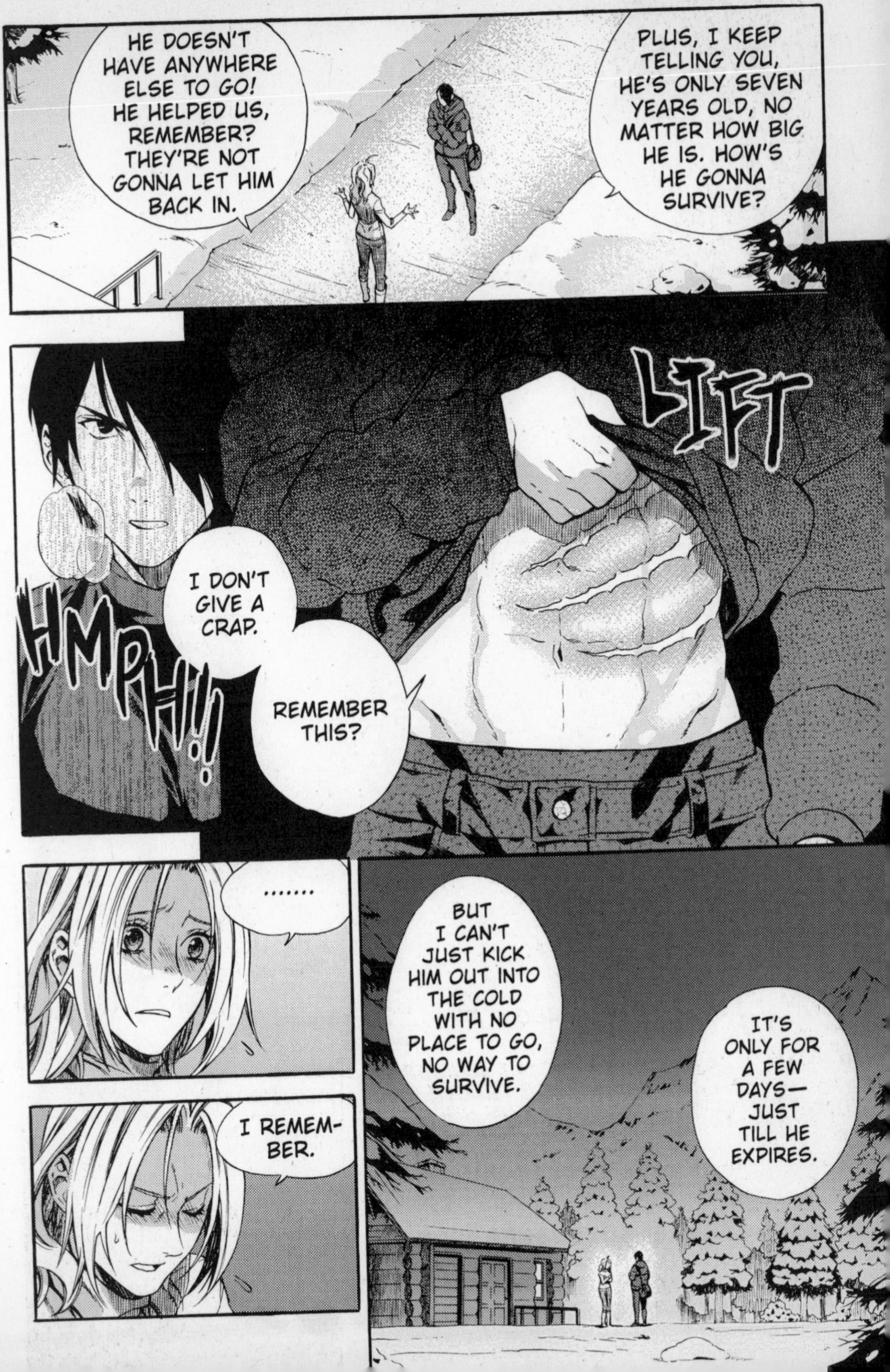
HE DOESN'T HAVE ANYWHERE ELSE TO GO! HE HELPED US, REMEMBER? THEY'RE NOT GONNA LET HIM BACK IN.
PLUS, I KEEP TELLING YOU, HE'S ONLY SEVEN YEARS OLD, NO MATTER HOW BIG HE IS. HOW'S HE GONNA SURVIVE?
LIFT
HMPH!!
I DON'T GIVE A CRAP.
REMEMBER THIS?
....
I REMEMBER.
BUT I CAN'T JUST KICK HIM OUT INTO THE COLD WITH NO PLACE TO GO, NO WAY TO SURVIVE.
IT'S ONLY FOR A FEW DAYS—JUST TILL HE EXPIRES.

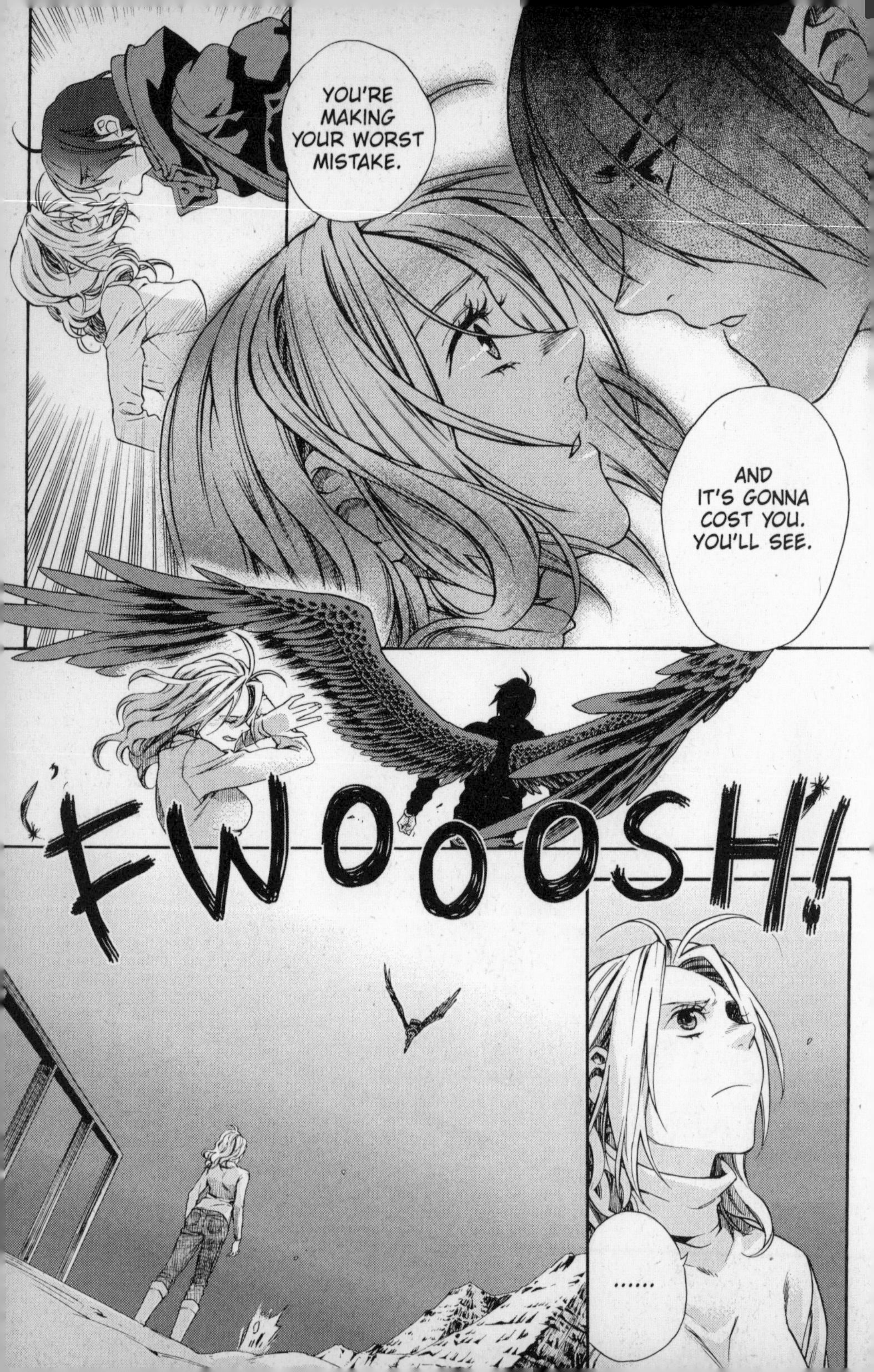
YOU'RE MAKING YOUR WORST MISTAKE.
AND IT'S GONNA COST YOU. YOU'LL SEE.
FWOOOSH!
......

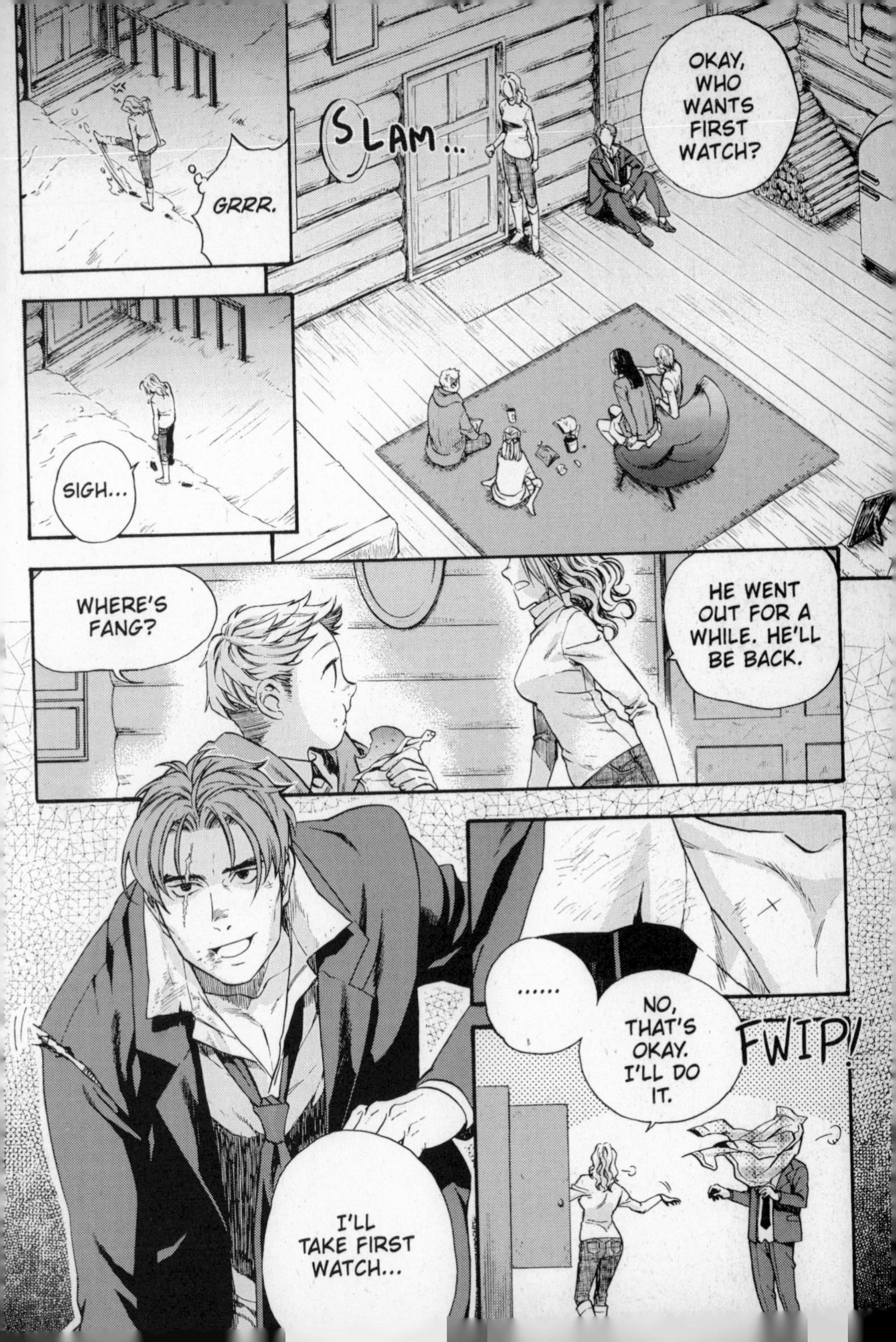
GRRR.
SLAM...
OKAY, WHO WANTS FIRST WATCH?
SIGH...
WHERE'S FANG?
HE WENT OUT FOR A WHILE. HE'LL BE BACK.
I'LL TAKE FIRST WATCH...
......
NO, THAT'S OKAY. I'LL DO IT.
FWIP!

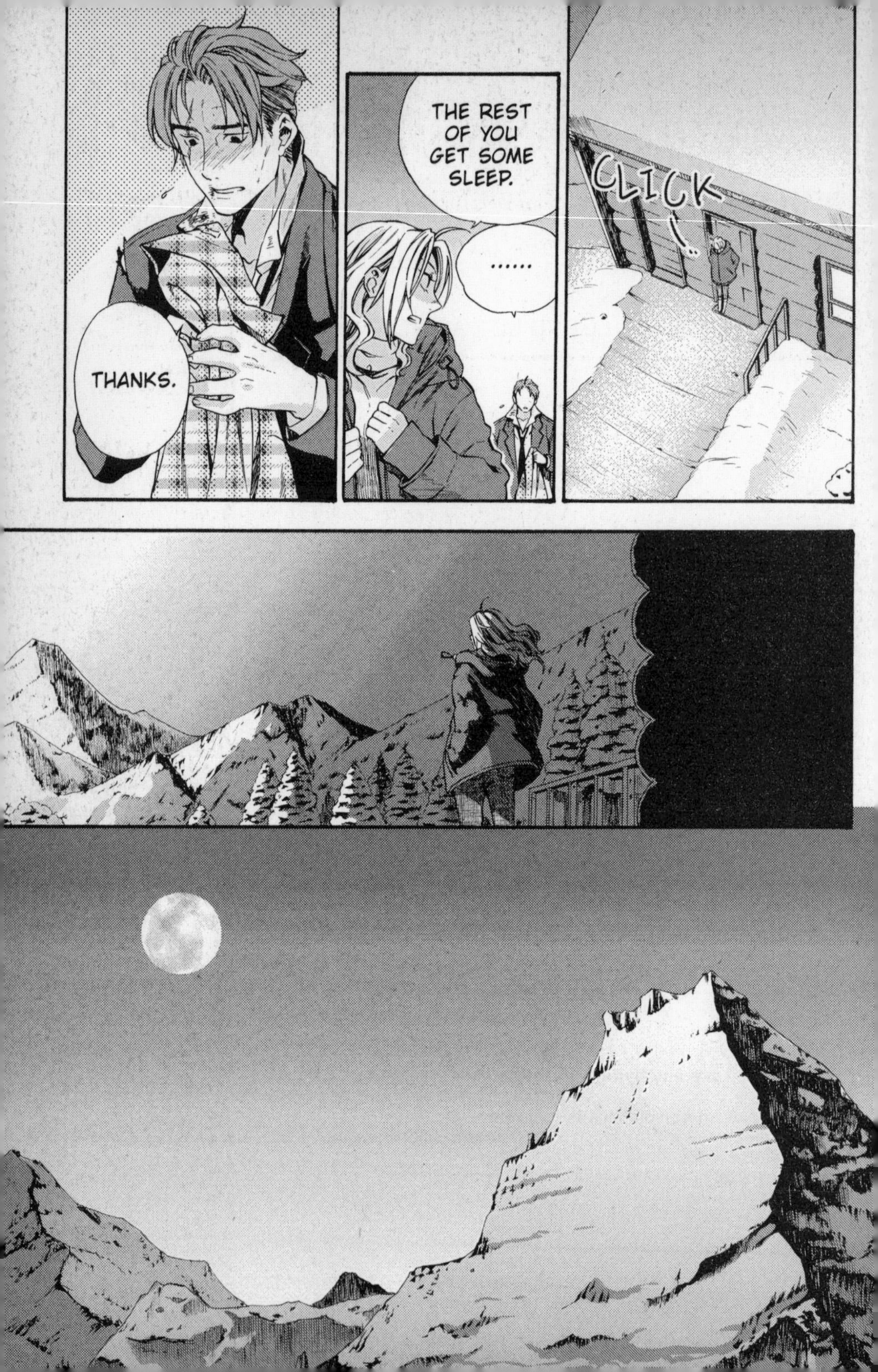
CLICK
THE REST OF YOU GET SOME SLEEP.
......
THANKS.

HOME Blog Posts Discussions Groups Photos Chat BBS

TO EVERYONE, EVERYWHERE
WARNING
HEADS-UP
EVIL SCIENTISTS WILL END LIFE AS WE KNOW IT

And even as we don't know it.
I know what it's called now, folks. It's called the Re-Evolution Plan. And the By-Half Plan. We got out of the School (anyone who wants to bomb them, feel free). Now we're in hiding, ha-ha. While we were there, we found out that the plan is to basically KILL anyone with any kind of disease or weakness. The only people left will be perfectly healthy and have useful skills. So everyone bone up on something useful! Or go into hiding. And if you have the sniffles, crawl under a rock and don't come out.

What would be useful, you ask? I've made a chart.

USEFUL	NOT USEFUL
Plumber	Politician
Carpenter	Publicist
Boat builder	Art history buff
Farmer	Celebrity chef
Sanitation crew	Interior designer
Cattle rancher	Pet psychic
Scientist	Celebrity rock/pop/hip-hop star
Military	Teen idol
Medical personnel	Life coach

So this would be a good time to examine your career goals.
Last time I checked, more than 28 million people had hit this blog. Way to go, people. Save yourselves. Save your brothers and sisters. Don't let the whitecoats get you.

And if you see any flying kids, keep your mouth shut.

— Fang, from somewhere in America

Comment Wall (1,805 comments) ▼

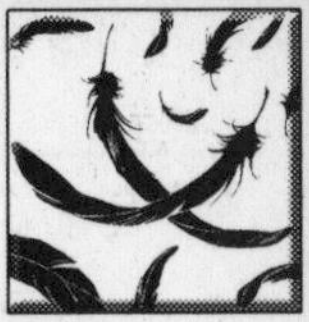

Fang
Today's date: Already Too Late!

Visitor number
28,772,461

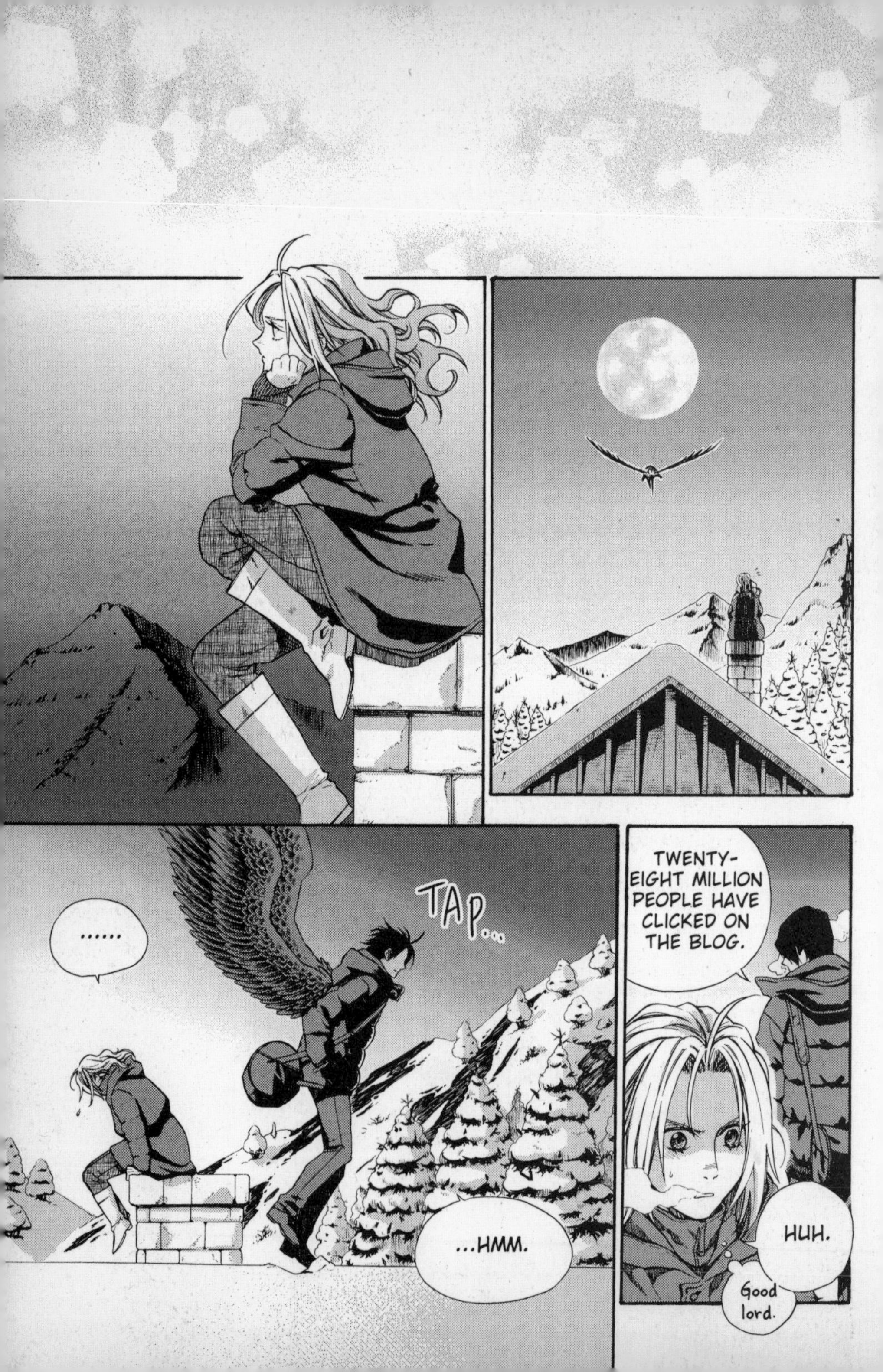

......
TAP...
...HMM.
TWENTY-EIGHT MILLION PEOPLE HAVE CLICKED ON THE BLOG.
HUH.
Good lord.

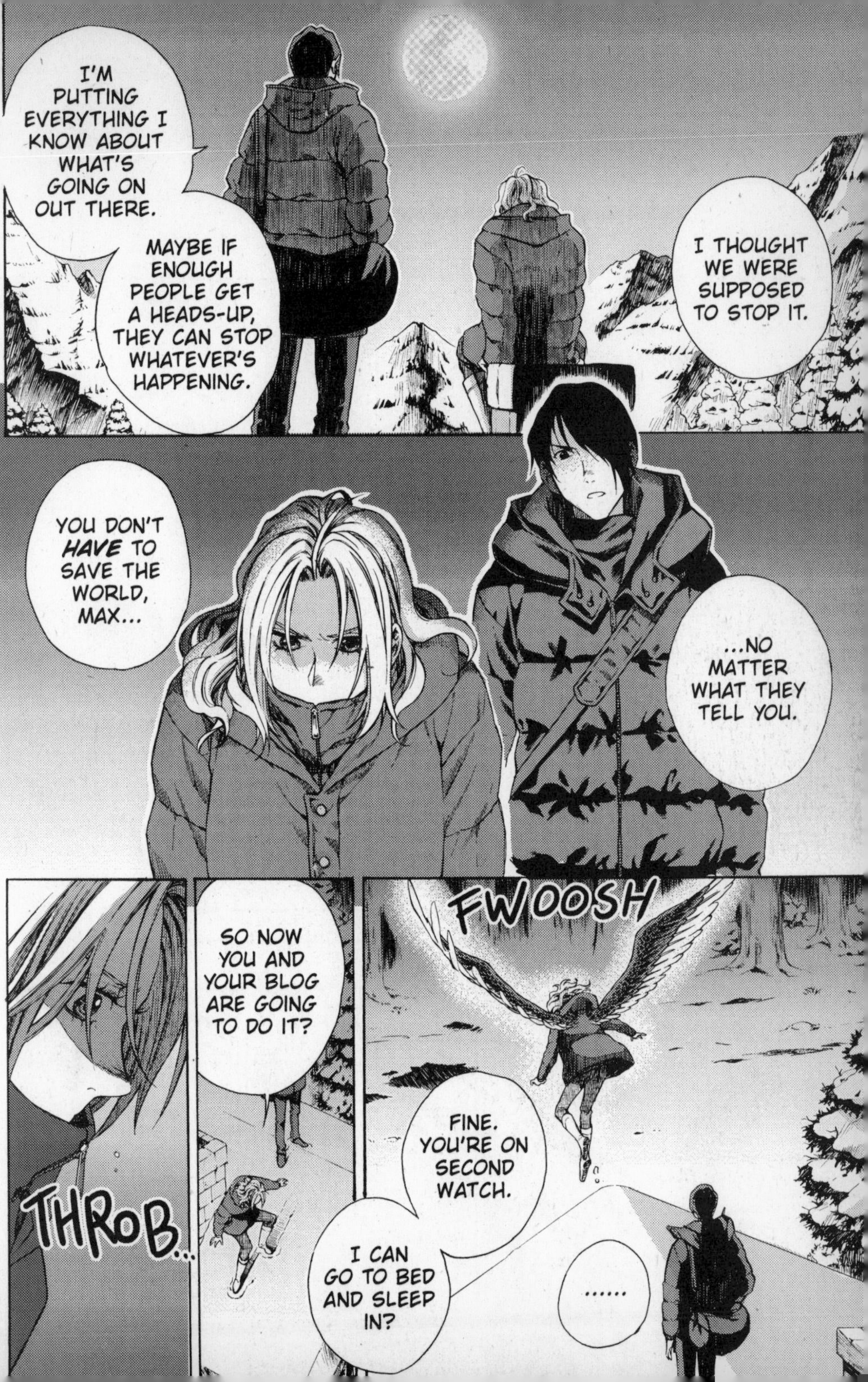
I'M PUTTING EVERYTHING I KNOW ABOUT WHAT'S GOING ON OUT THERE.
MAYBE IF ENOUGH PEOPLE GET A HEADS-UP, THEY CAN STOP WHATEVER'S HAPPENING.
I THOUGHT WE WERE SUPPOSED TO STOP IT.
YOU DON'T *HAVE* TO SAVE THE WORLD, MAX...
...NO MATTER WHAT THEY TELL YOU.
THROB...
SO NOW YOU AND YOUR BLOG ARE GOING TO DO IT?
FWOOSH
FINE. YOU'RE ON SECOND WATCH.
I CAN GO TO BED AND SLEEP IN?
......

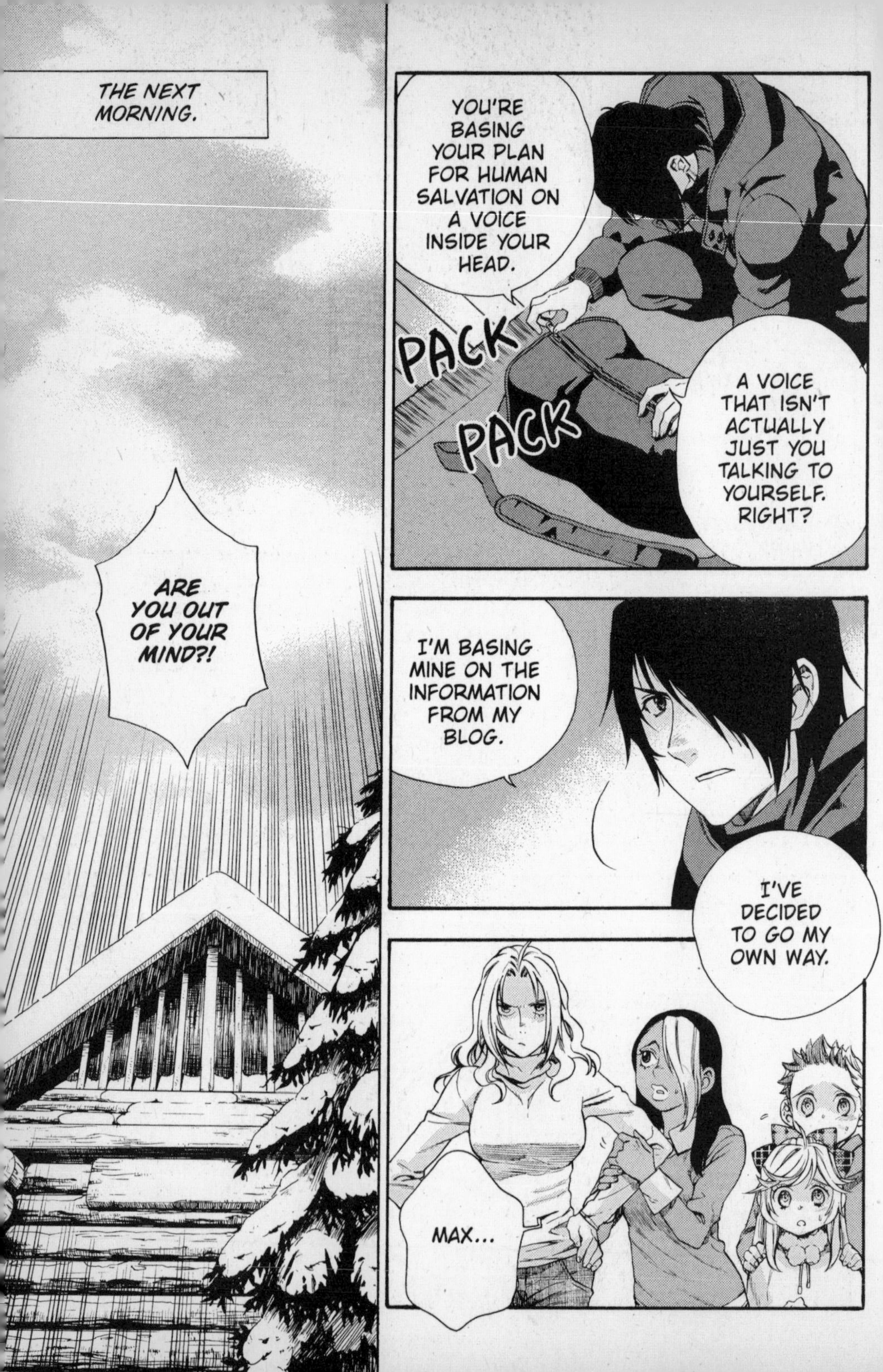
THE NEXT MORNING.
ARE YOU OUT OF YOUR MIND?!
YOU'RE BASING YOUR PLAN FOR HUMAN SALVATION ON A VOICE INSIDE YOUR HEAD.
PACK
PACK
A VOICE THAT ISN'T ACTUALLY JUST YOU TALKING TO YOURSELF. RIGHT?
I'M BASING MINE ON THE INFORMATION FROM MY BLOG.
I'VE DECIDED TO GO MY OWN WAY.
MAX...

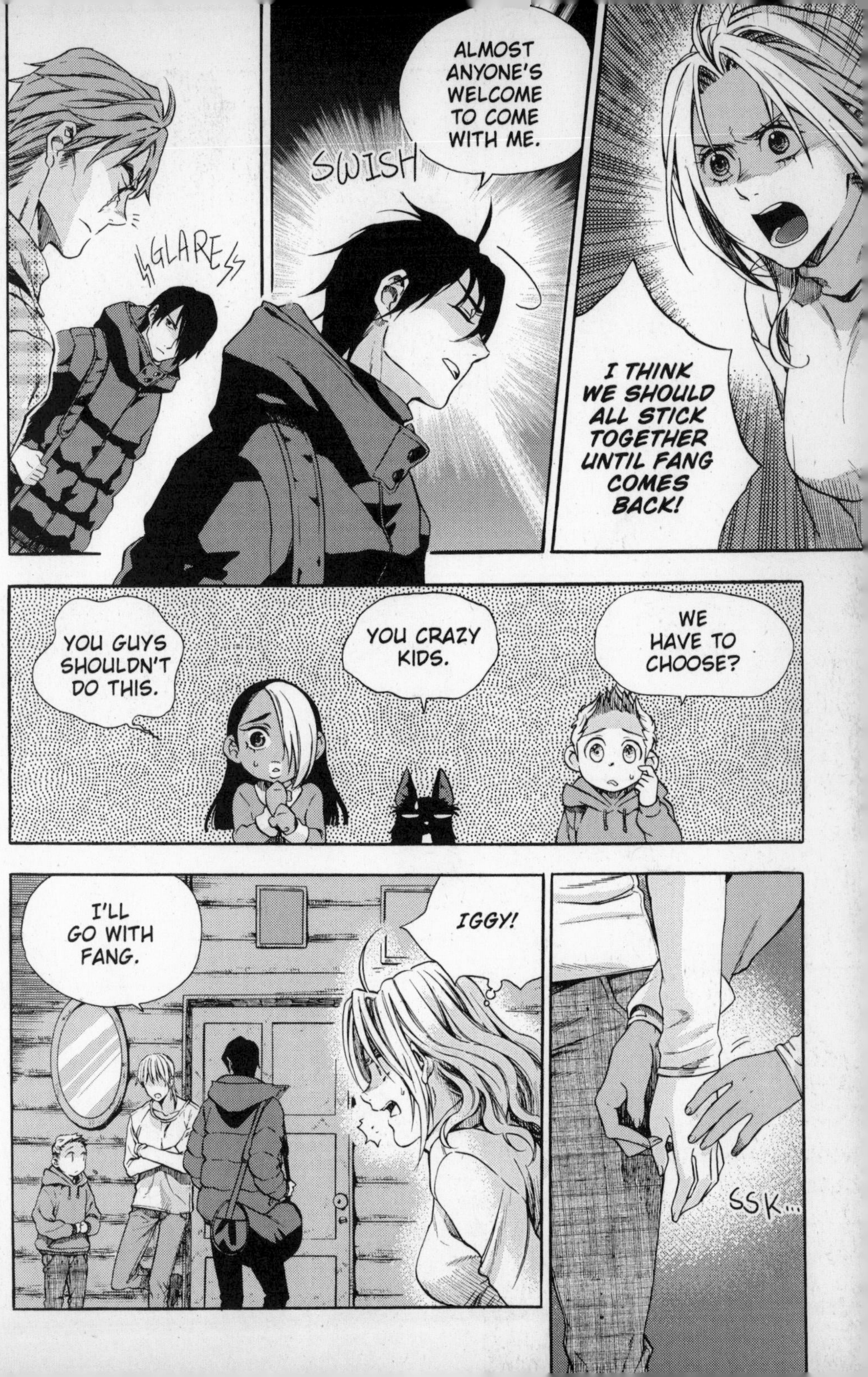
GLARE
SWISH
ALMOST ANYONE'S WELCOME TO COME WITH ME.
I THINK WE SHOULD ALL STICK TOGETHER UNTIL FANG COMES BACK!
YOU GUYS SHOULDN'T DO THIS.
YOU CRAZY KIDS.
WE HAVE TO CHOOSE?
I'LL GO WITH FANG.
IGGY!
SSK...

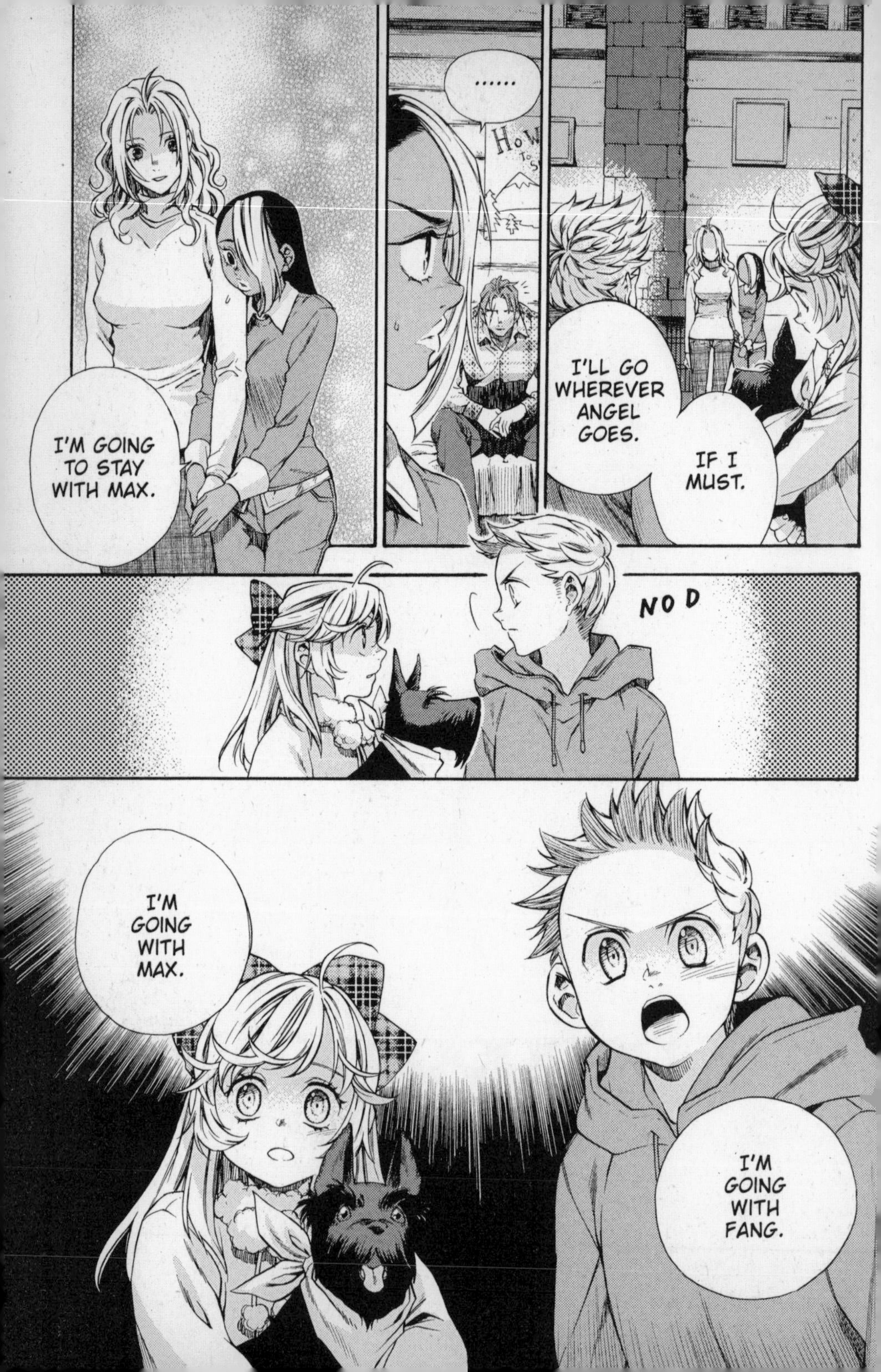

I'M GOING TO STAY WITH MAX.
......
I'LL GO WHEREVER ANGEL GOES.
IF I MUST.
NOD
I'M GOING WITH MAX.
I'M GOING WITH FANG.

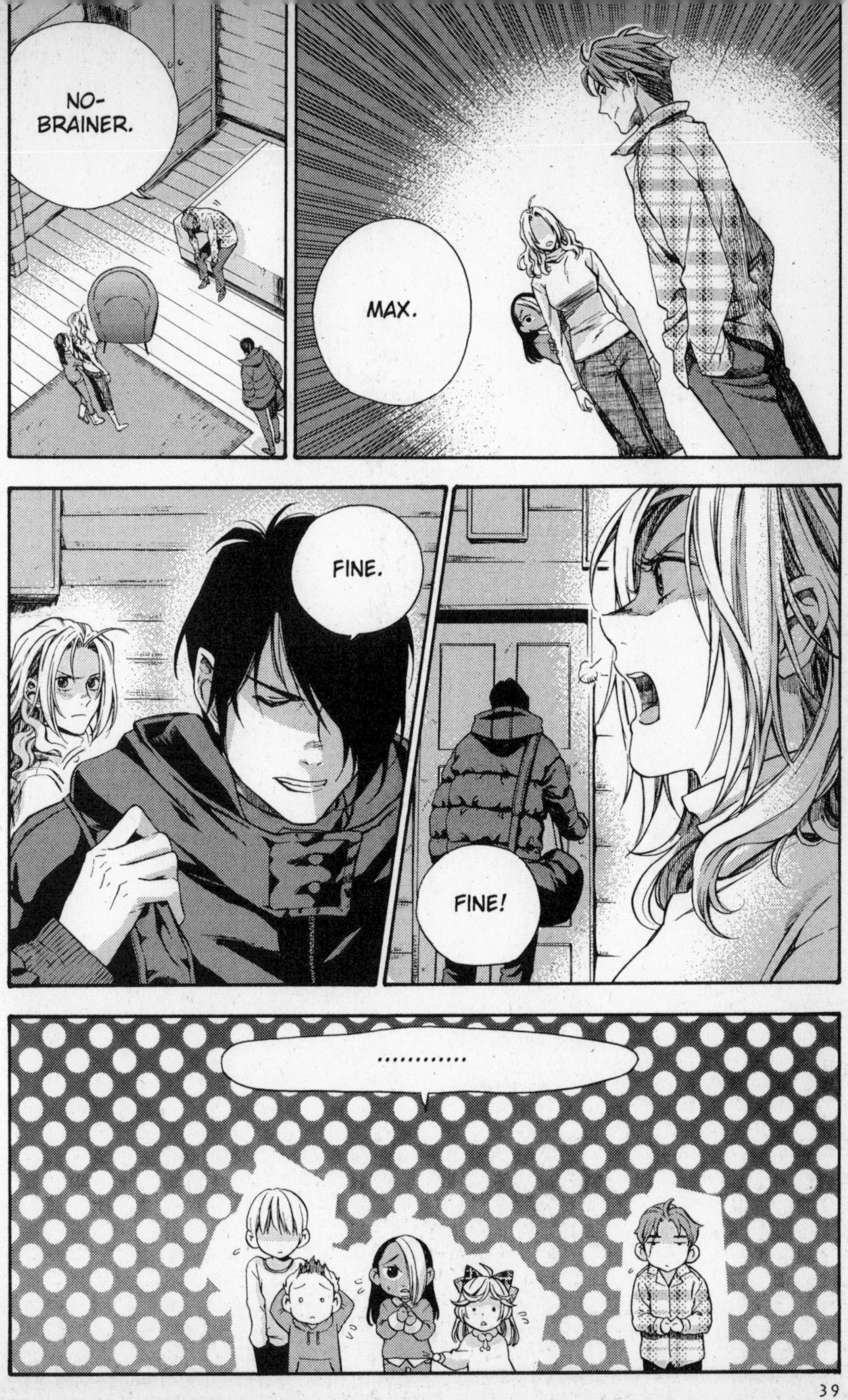
NO-BRAINER.
MAX.
FINE.
FINE!
....

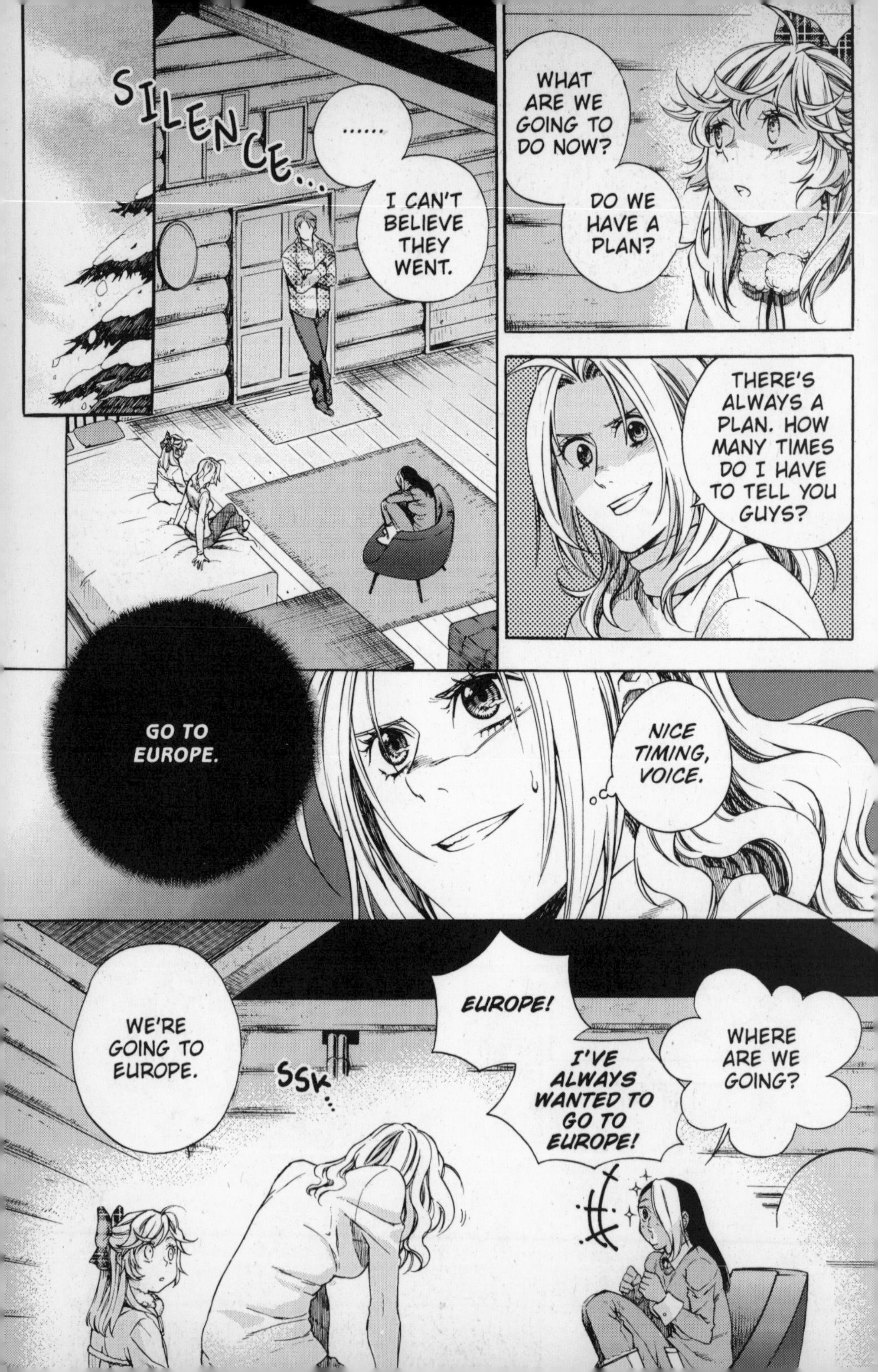
SILENCE...
......
I CAN'T BELIEVE THEY WENT.
WHAT ARE WE GOING TO DO NOW?
DO WE HAVE A PLAN?
THERE'S ALWAYS A PLAN. HOW MANY TIMES DO I HAVE TO TELL YOU GUYS?
GO TO EUROPE.
NICE TIMING, VOICE.
WE'RE GOING TO EUROPE.
SSK...
EUROPE!
I'VE ALWAYS WANTED TO GO TO EUROPE!
WHERE ARE WE GOING?

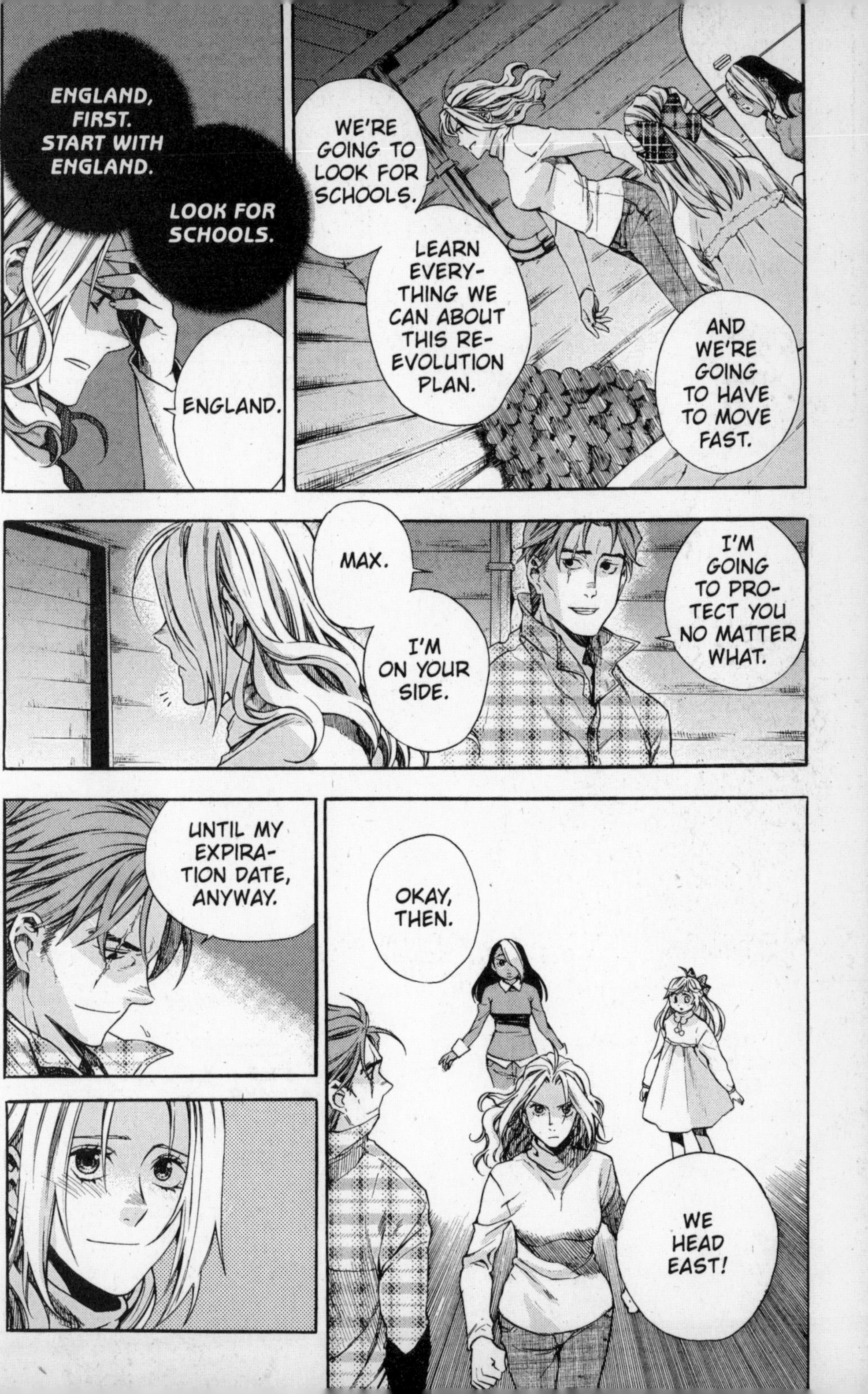
ENGLAND, FIRST. START WITH ENGLAND.
LOOK FOR SCHOOLS.
ENGLAND.
WE'RE GOING TO LOOK FOR SCHOOLS.
LEARN EVERY-THING WE CAN ABOUT THIS RE-EVOLUTION PLAN.
AND WE'RE GOING TO HAVE TO MOVE FAST.
MAX.
I'M ON YOUR SIDE.
I'M GOING TO PRO-TECT YOU NO MATTER WHAT.
UNTIL MY EXPIRA-TION DATE, ANYWAY.
OKAY, THEN.
WE HEAD EAST!

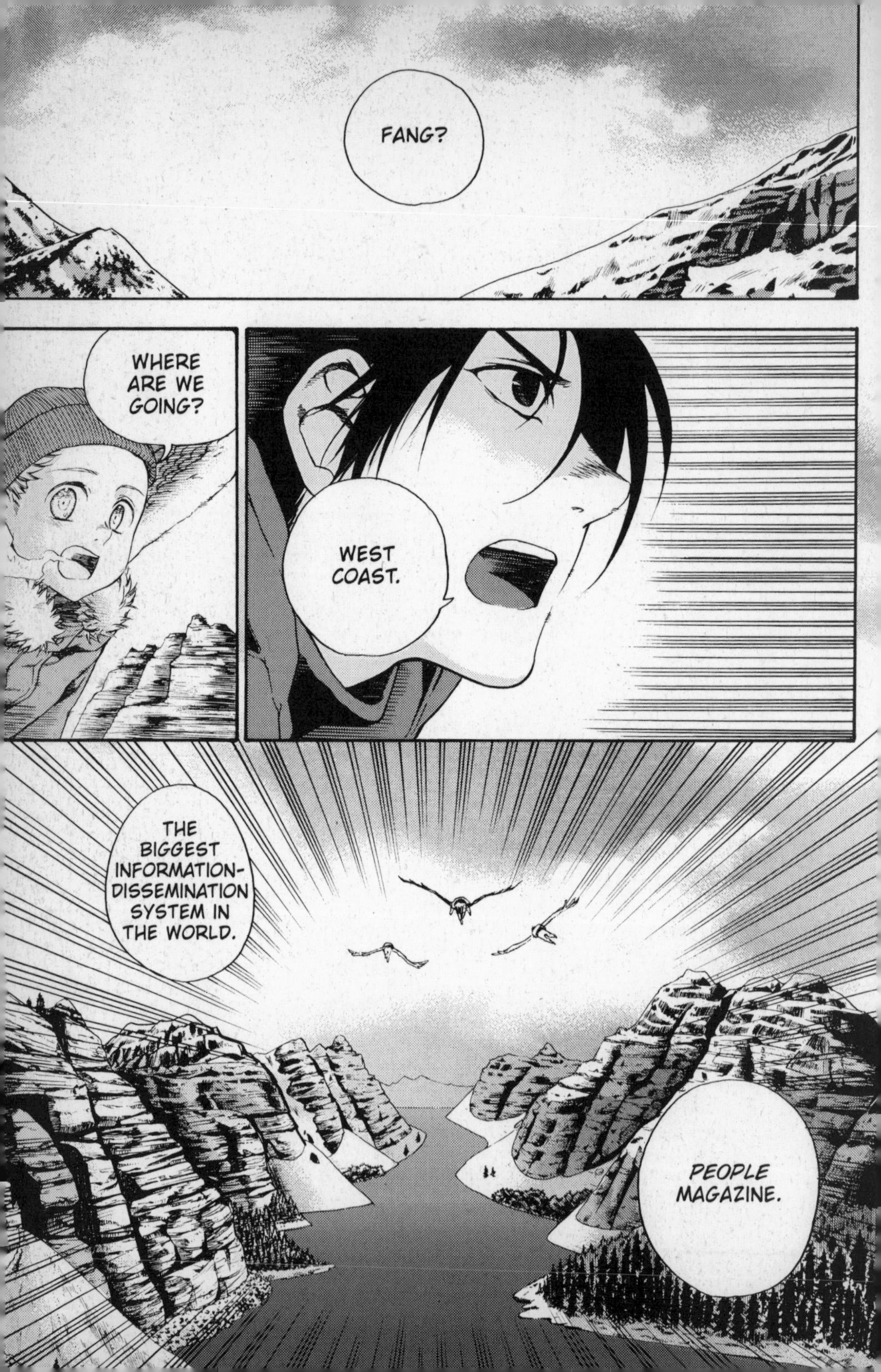
FANG?
WHERE ARE WE GOING?
WEST COAST.
THE BIGGEST INFORMATION-DISSEMINATION SYSTEM IN THE WORLD.
PEOPLE MAGAZINE.

MAXIMUM
RIDE

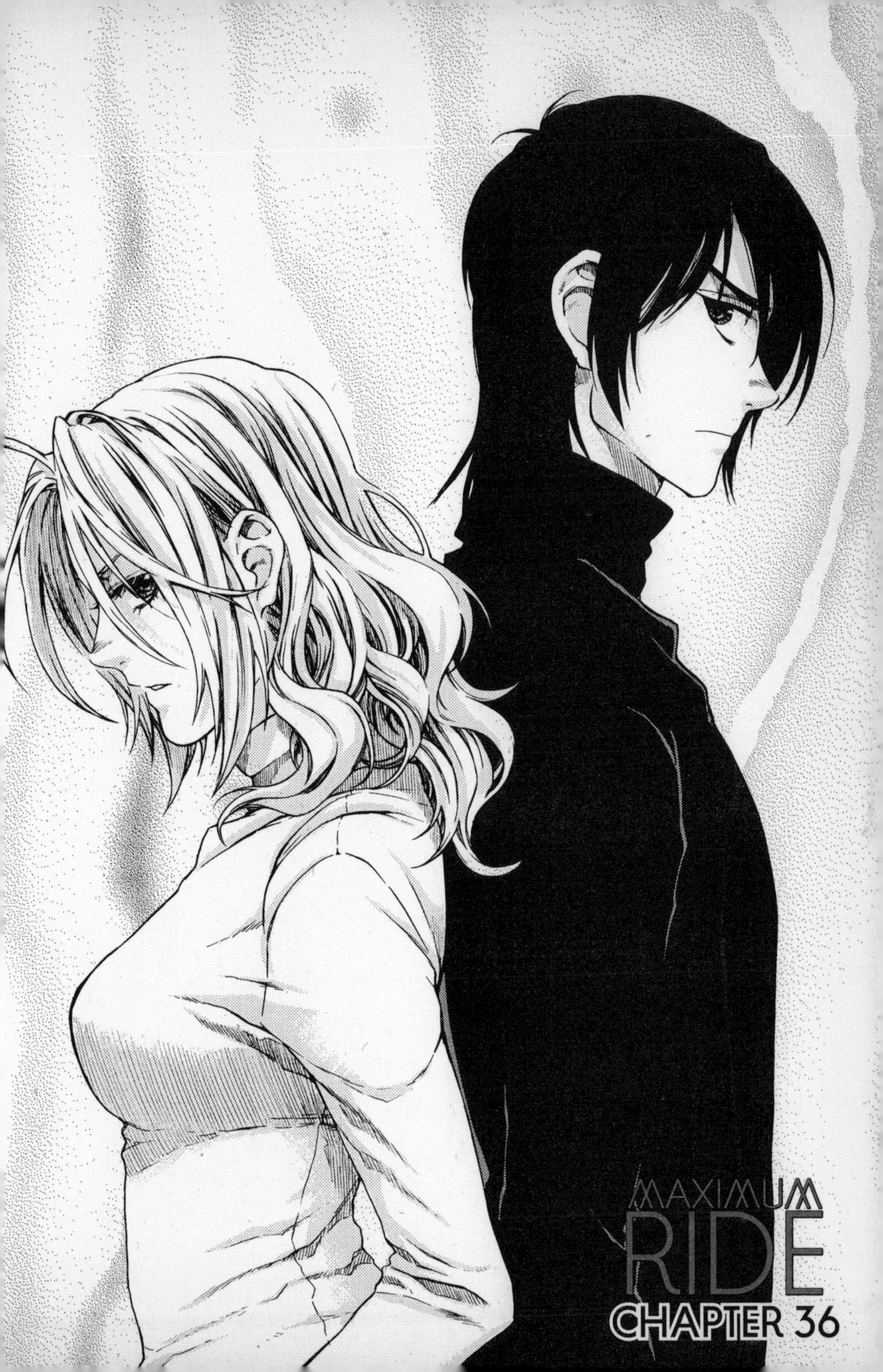
MAXIMUM
RIDE
CHAPTER 36

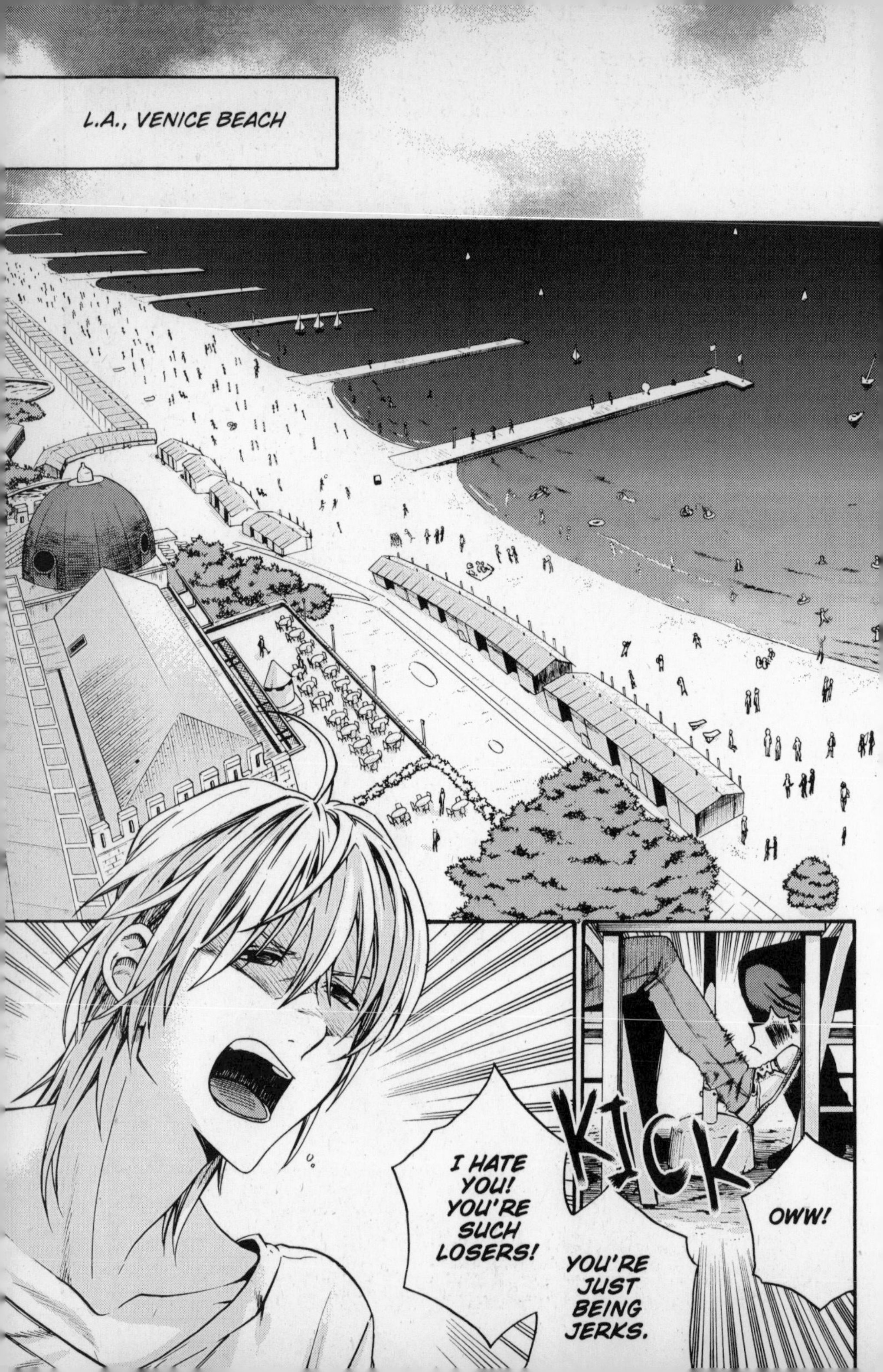
L.A., VENICE BEACH
KICK
OWW!
YOU'RE JUST BEING JERKS.
I HATE YOU! YOU'RE SUCH LOSERS!

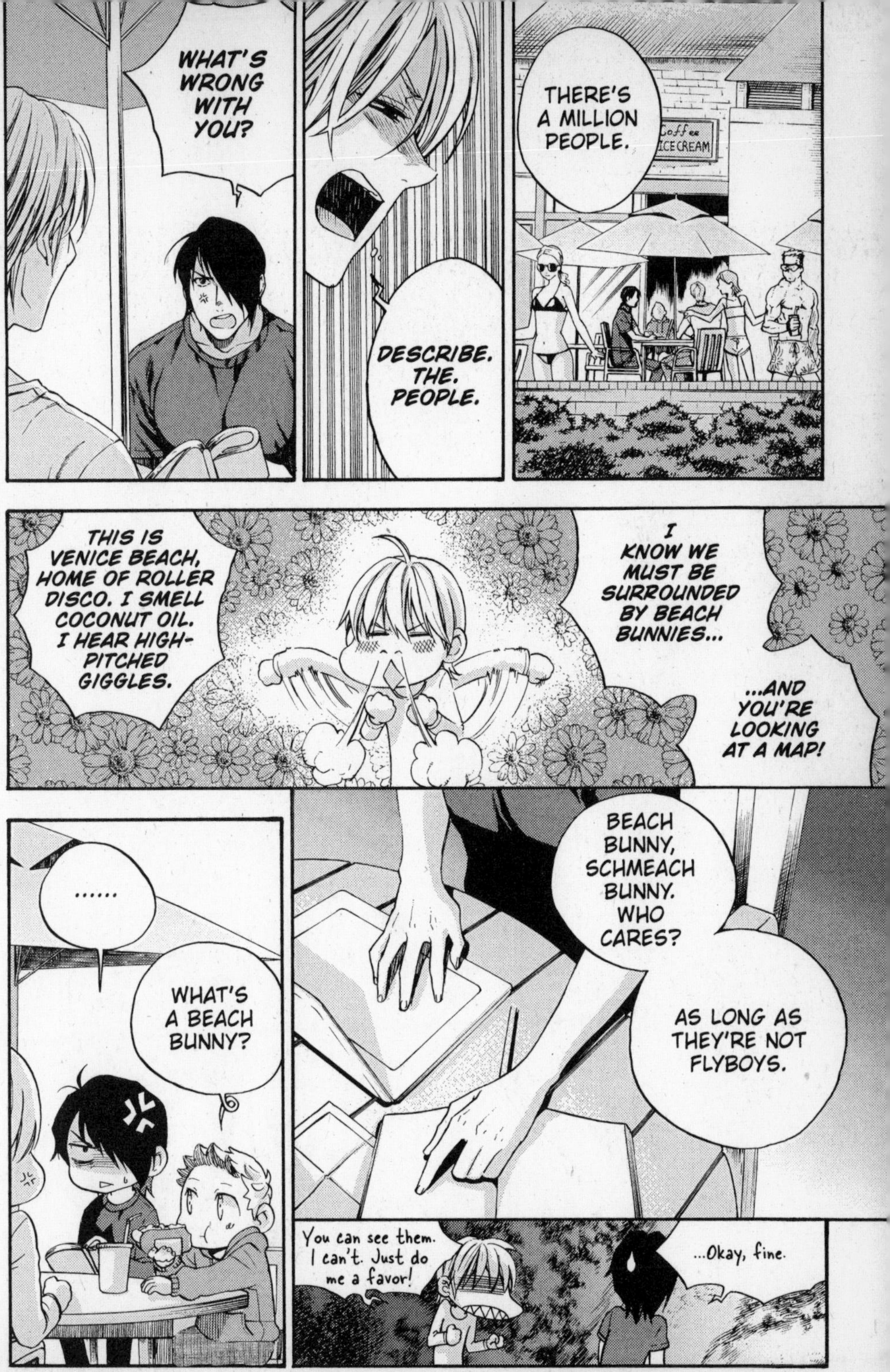
WHAT'S WRONG WITH YOU?
DESCRIBE. THE. PEOPLE.
THERE'S A MILLION PEOPLE.
Coffee
ICE CREAM
THIS IS VENICE BEACH, HOME OF ROLLER DISCO. I SMELL COCONUT OIL. I HEAR HIGH-PITCHED GIGGLES.
I KNOW WE MUST BE SURROUNDED BY BEACH BUNNIES...
...AND YOU'RE LOOKING AT A MAP!
......
WHAT'S A BEACH BUNNY?
BEACH BUNNY, SCHMEACH BUNNY. WHO CARES?
AS LONG AS THEY'RE NOT FLYBOYS.
You can see them. I can't. Just do me a favor!
...Okay, fine.

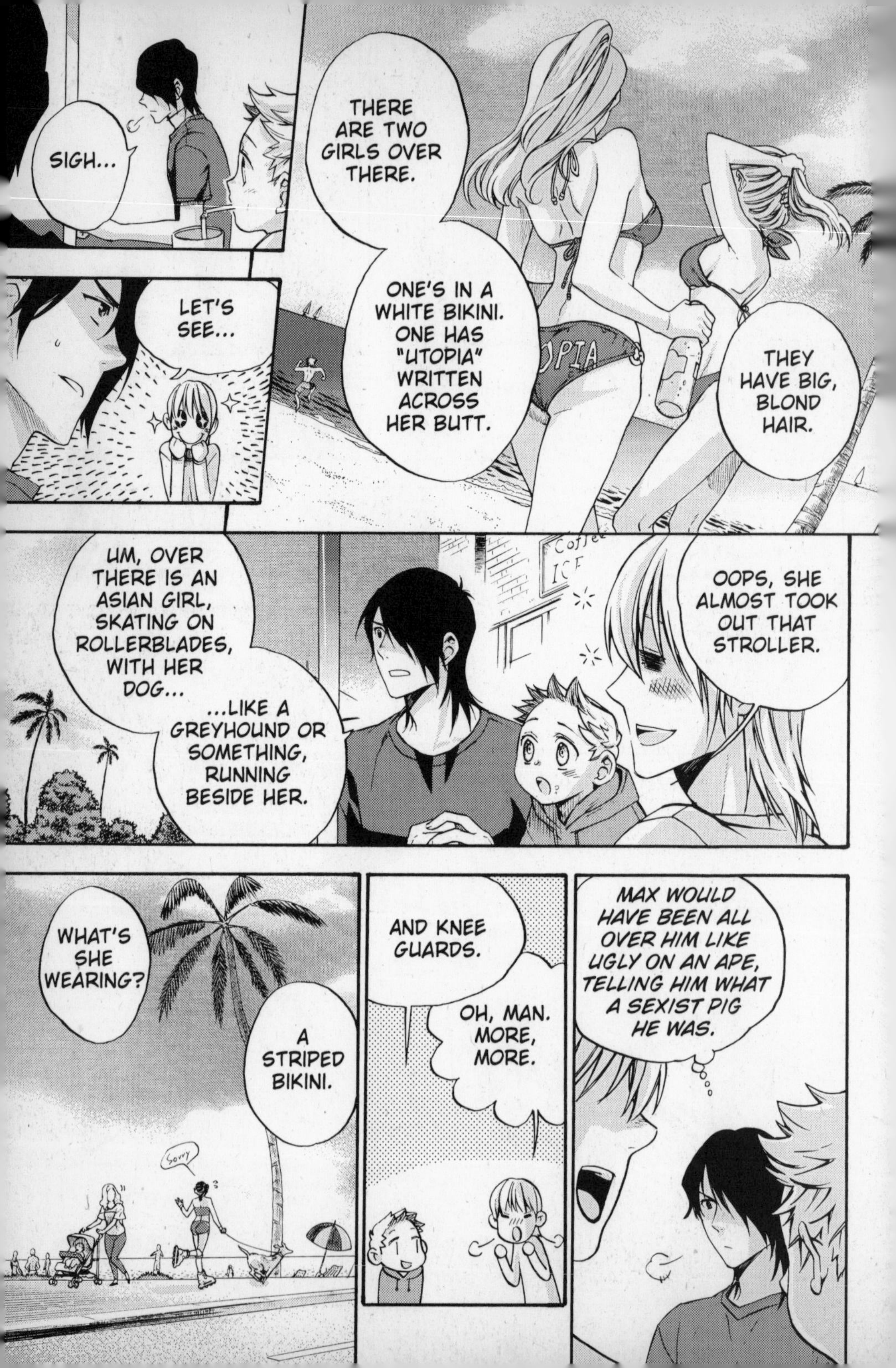

SIGH...
THERE ARE TWO GIRLS OVER THERE.
LET'S SEE...
ONE'S IN A WHITE BIKINI. ONE HAS "UTOPIA" WRITTEN ACROSS HER BUTT.
THEY HAVE BIG, BLOND HAIR.
UM, OVER THERE IS AN ASIAN GIRL, SKATING ON ROLLERBLADES, WITH HER DOG...
...LIKE A GREYHOUND OR SOMETHING, RUNNING BESIDE HER.
OOPS, SHE ALMOST TOOK OUT THAT STROLLER.
WHAT'S SHE WEARING?
A STRIPED BIKINI.
Sorry
AND KNEE GUARDS.
OH, MAN. MORE, MORE.
MAX WOULD HAVE BEEN ALL OVER HIM LIKE UGLY ON AN APE, TELLING HIM WHAT A SEXIST PIG HE WAS.

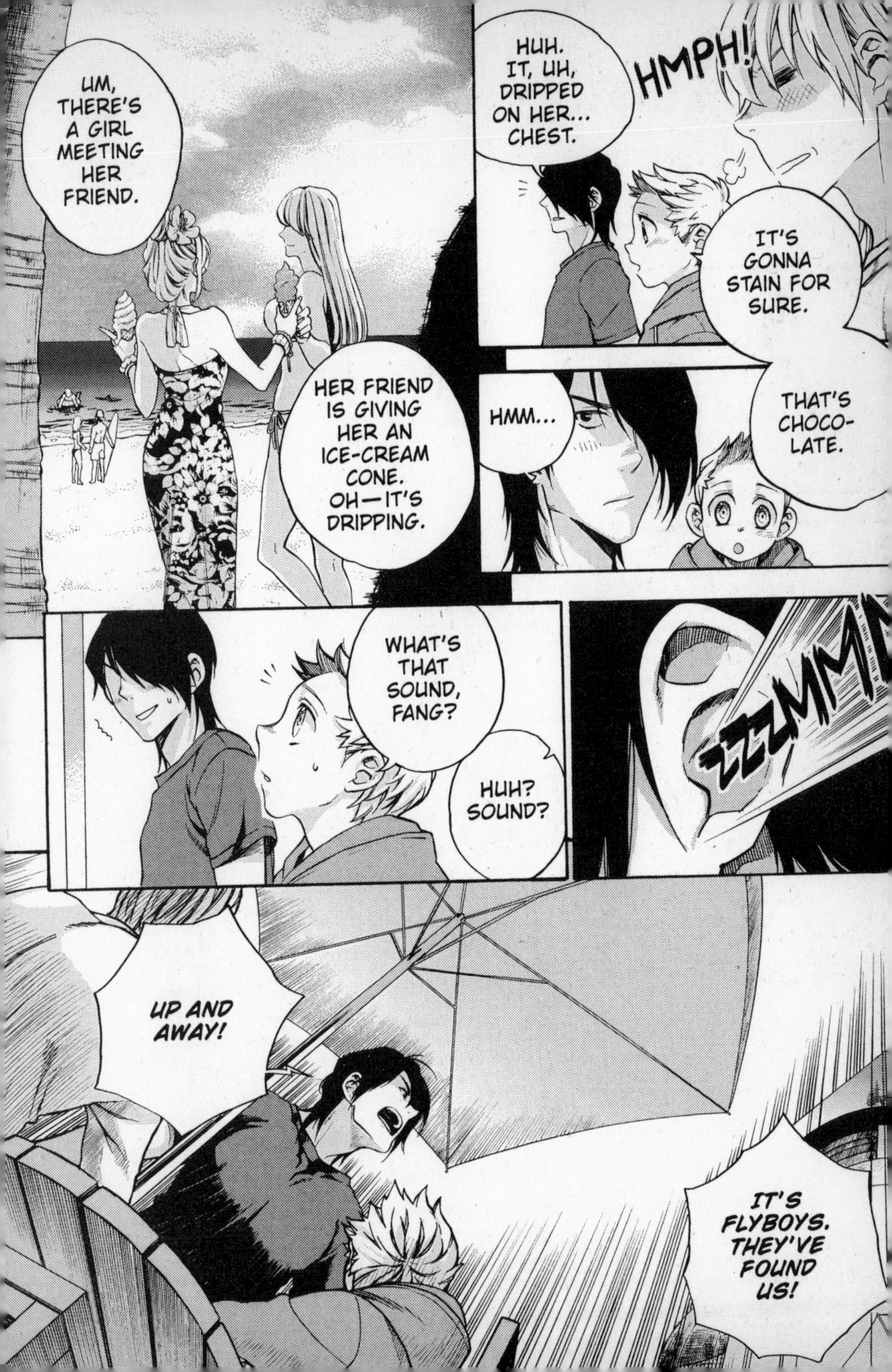
UM, THERE'S A GIRL MEETING HER FRIEND.
HER FRIEND IS GIVING HER AN ICE-CREAM CONE. OH—IT'S DRIPPING.
HUH. IT, UH, DRIPPED ON HER... CHEST.
HMPH!
IT'S GONNA STAIN FOR SURE.
HMM...
THAT'S CHOCO-LATE.
WHAT'S THAT SOUND, FANG?
HUH? SOUND?
ZZZMMM
UP AND AWAY!
IT'S FLYBOYS. THEY'VE FOUND US!

Sign Up Sign In

Fang's Blog

HOME Blog Posts Discussions Groups Photos Chat BBS

Busted-up Hollywood

So, for those of you in the LA area, I need to fess up about the major wreckage over at the big Hollywood sign. A million hopefuls have fixated on that sign as a symbol of future movie careers, and I sure do apologize about it being destroyed. But it wasn't my fault.

The Gasman, Iggy, and I were minding our own business somewhere in the greater LA area (which extends from Tijuana up to Pismo Beach), and suddenly, out of nowhere, a couple hundred Flyboys dropped down on us. How did they know where we were? I always assumed they tracked us either by Max's chip or by Angel's dog.

Which, as you've probably heard, are with us no longer.

So how'd they know where to find us?

Unless one of us three is telling them?

Which is impossible, of course. Anyway, like I told you before, Max saw thousands of Flyboys back at the School, hanging in rows, charging up. So today they let a bunch of 'em go for a test-drive.

I have to tell you people, those things are fast. They're strong. They can go for a long time without stopping. But smart? Not so much.

Gaz, Iggy, and I shot up, fast, from where we'd been innocently hanging out. We're always better off in the air. Of course jaws dropped, eyes popped, small children screamed, etc., when we suddenly whipped out wings and took flight. I guess we're unusual even for LA.

The three of us against a couple hundred Flyboys?

I don't think so. Sure, maybe sixty, or even eighty, no problem. But not two hundred. Not even if Max were there. Well, okay, maybe if Max were there. Maybe the two hundred. But she wasn't there.

Anyway, Gaz, Iggy, and I instinctively implemented a tried-and-true plan of action, Plan Delta, which we've used any number of times and have down to an art. Basically it means "run like hell." Or rather, "fly like hell."

We flew. We zipped out of there like lightning. The Flyboys don't seem to have altitude problems — they followed us easily up into 747 cruising altitude, where even I was getting a little short of breath. Like the Erasers, they're not too nimble, but they're wicked fast and scarily strong.

One of Iggy's newest explosives took out about fifty of them, and sorry to all those folks showered by bits of Flyboy metal and flesh matrix down at that MTV party on the beach. The rest of them tore after us, and we couldn't outrun them.

Then I saw the Hollywood Hills. We flew right for the sign and, at the very, very last second, screamed into a direct vertical climb. I mean, my belt buckle scraped one of the letters. But the three of us made it, shooting straight up like rockets.

The Flyboys were not so fortunate.

One after another, they plowed right into the sign, setting off electrical charges that shorted them out and made quite a few of them explode like metallic, furry popcorn. And if you think that's a gross description, be glad you weren't there, being pelted by the little pieces. I think only about six or seven of them managed to avoid the carnage, and I have no idea what happened to them.

After we'd busted our sides laughing, we blew out of there, and now we're hiding. Again.

Us: roughly 200. Hard to tell with all the parts flying.

Them: 0

Take that, you whitecoat schmucks. Now you owe California a new Hollywood sign.

— Fang, somewhere in the West

Comment Wall(108 comments) ▼

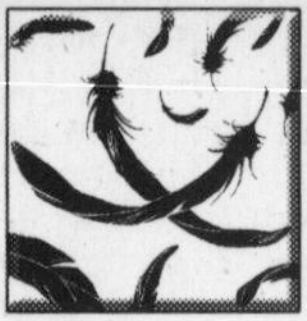

Fang

Today's date: Already Too Late!

Visitor number

972,361,007

Sign Up Sign In

Fang's Blog

HOME Blog Posts Discussions Groups Photos Chat BBS

108 comments ▼

Kewl dude 326 said . . .
O man Fang thats so awesome, i mean when u guys popped all the flyboys. i would a been bustin my gut 2. Keep flyin, man.
San Diego 11:51 AM

Sugargrrl said . . .
Dear Fang, I'm so glad your alright. I hate those flyboys and hope they all crash and burn. If u need a place to stay in Roanoke, Virginia, just e-mail me.
12:14 PM

Heather said . . .
We should all make posses and search everywhere for labs and Schools and stuff! There are millions and millions of kids in the world, and we can fix what the grown-ups have polluted and destroyed! Landfills and oil slicks and endangered species and wiping out forests and driving gas hogs and not caring about the environment and not caring about animals! Their time of destroying everything is over! It's time for Green Kids to unite!
Heather Schmidt
President, GreenKidsforaGreenerPlanet.org
12:57 PM

Streetfightr said . . .
Us kidz got 2 take over! De groneups hav recked everything! Dere destroyin r whole planet! De kidz shuld run everything! Dey want us 2 b quiet! We won't b quiet no more!
Brooklyn 1:20 PM

Chen Wei said . . .
Fang, I was wondering: do u have a girlfriend? Hong Kong
P.S. I am 15 years old but look younger.
2:40 PM

Carlos said . . .
I say we burn all the science labs! Make all the grown-ups into slaves!
Texas 3:07 PM

Anonymous said . . .
Carlos, no, that's stupid. We need science. Science isn't bad by itself. It's just bad when bad people use it to do bad things. We can do good things with science. Like feed the world. I don't want to make all grown-ups slaves. My parents are grown-ups, but they're all right.
Concerned Future Scientist
Louisiana 4:21 PM

Adide said . . .
I am afraid the grown-ups are going to destroy our planet. I want them to stop. I wish they would use science to make better crops and make more rain. Instead of bombs, they should make more schoolbooks for children.
Uganda 4:26 PM

Dita said . . .
I can't believe you and Max split up! You guys should stick together! Now I'm even more worried about all of you! Be extra careful!
Mumbai 6:08 PM

Sean said . . .
Fang, I want to be a bird kid. I don't care what it takes. I would go through anything to be able to fly and be with the flock. Tell me where to meet you. I want to join you today.
Manchester, England 6:35 PM

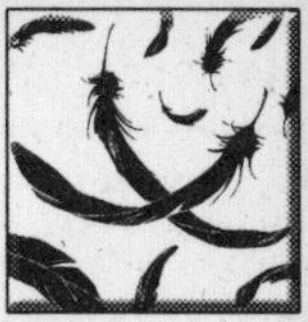

Fang
Today's date: Already Too Late!

Visitor number
972,361,007

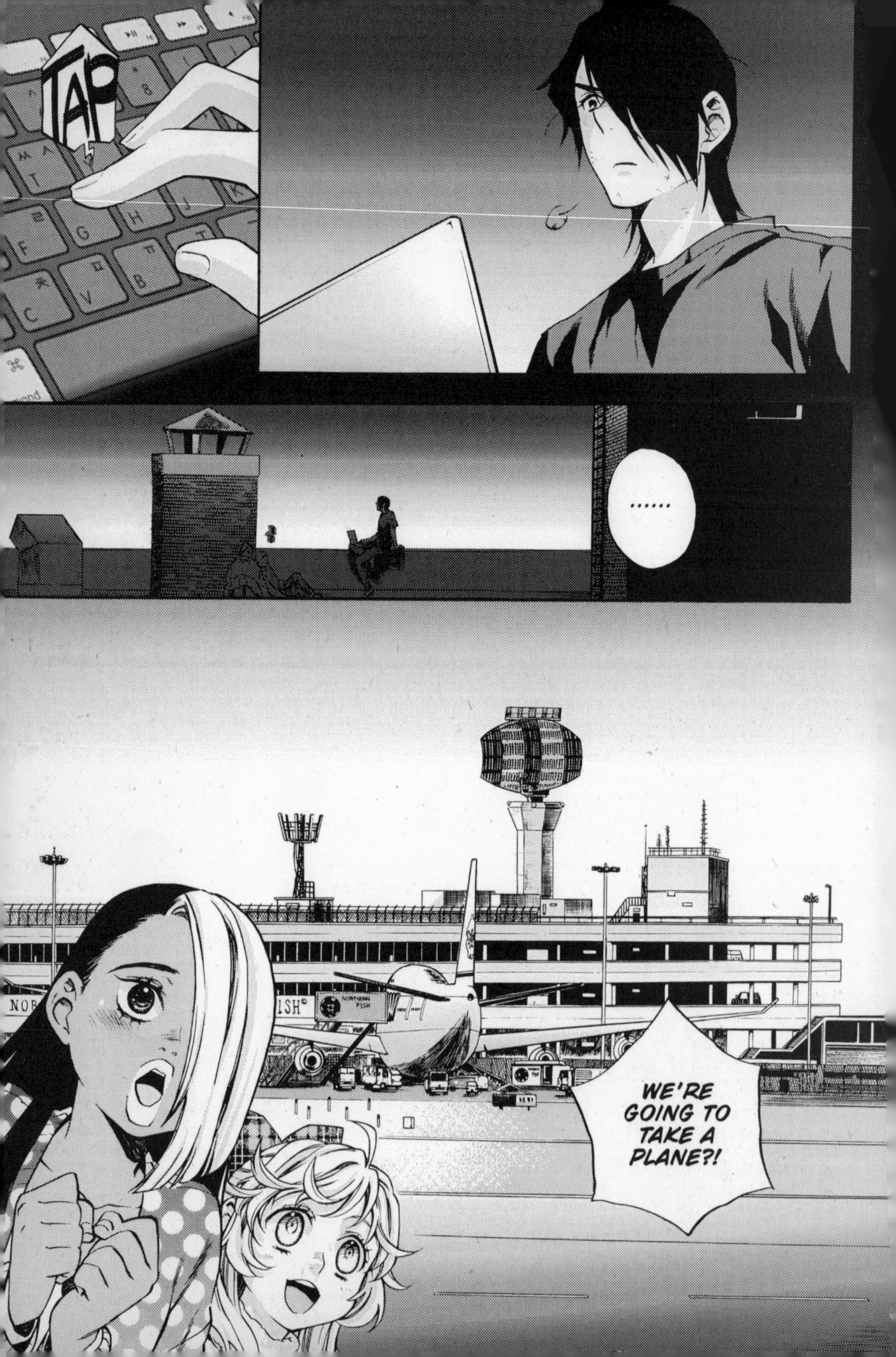
TAP
......
WE'RE GOING TO TAKE A PLANE?!

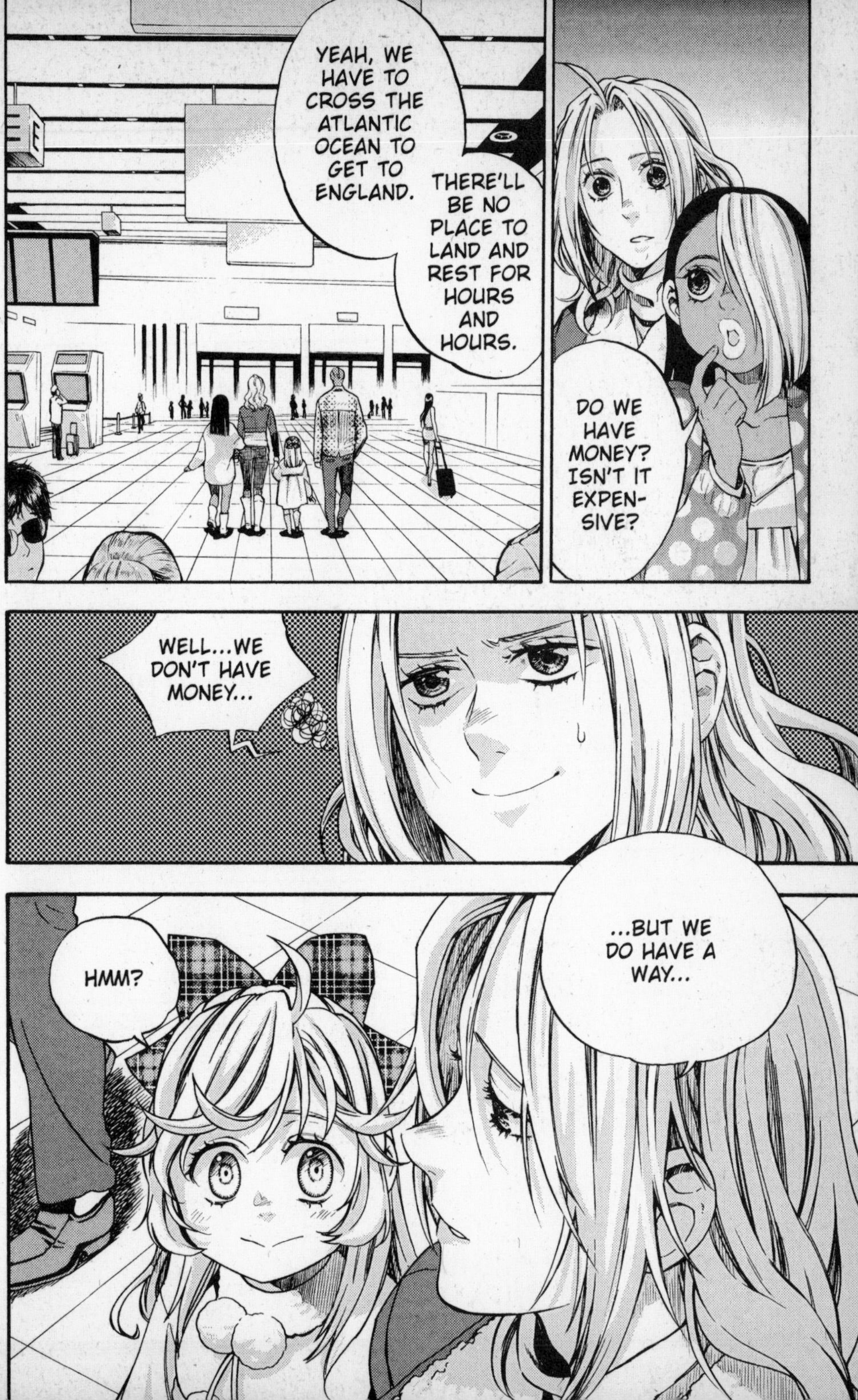
DO WE HAVE MONEY? ISN'T IT EXPENSIVE?
YEAH, WE HAVE TO CROSS THE ATLANTIC OCEAN TO GET TO ENGLAND.
THERE'LL BE NO PLACE TO LAND AND REST FOR HOURS AND HOURS.
WELL...WE DON'T HAVE MONEY...
...BUT WE DO HAVE A WAY...
HMM?

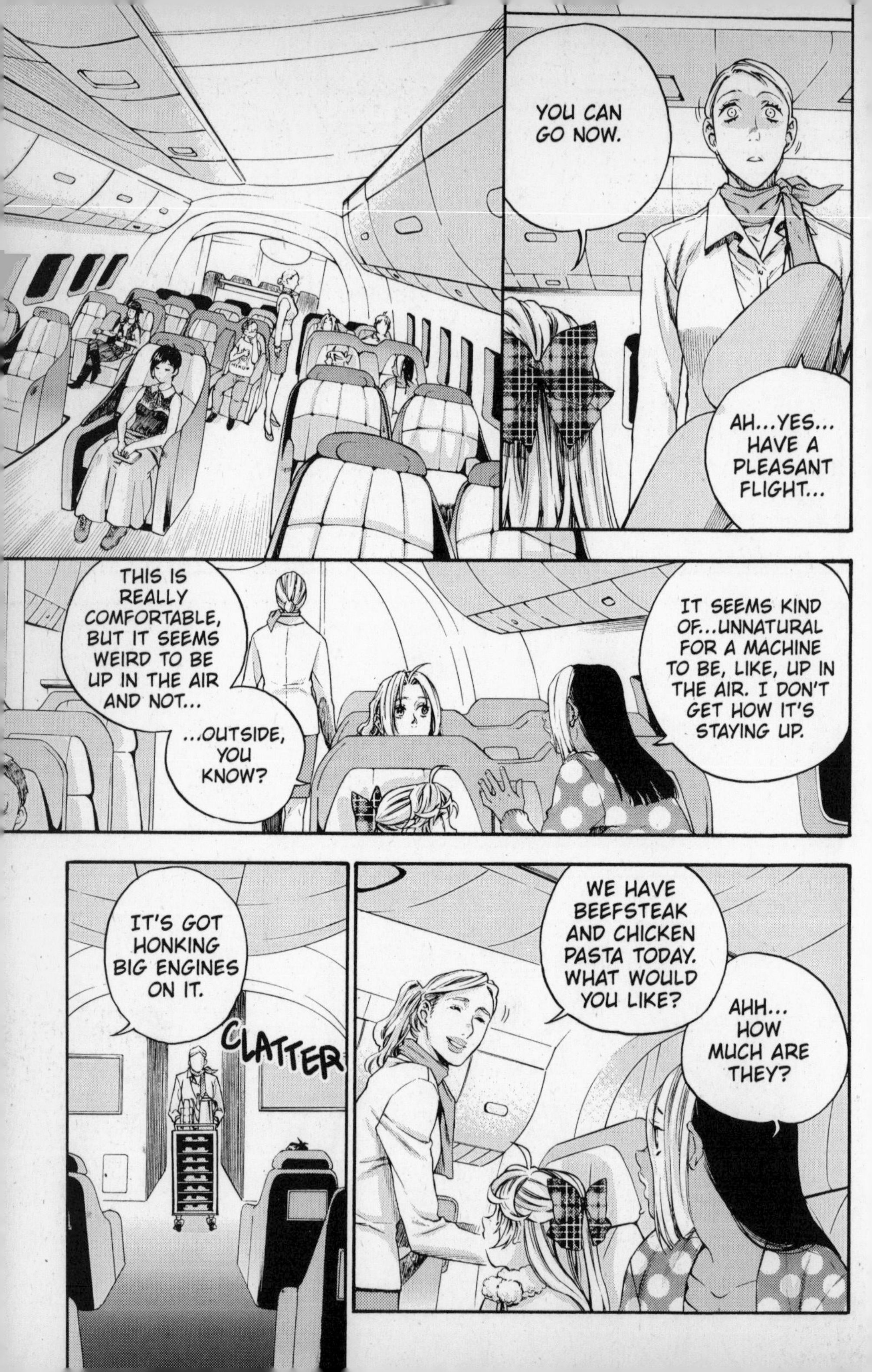
YOU CAN GO NOW.
AH...YES... HAVE A PLEASANT FLIGHT...
IT SEEMS KIND OF...UNNATURAL FOR A MACHINE TO BE, LIKE, UP IN THE AIR. I DON'T GET HOW IT'S STAYING UP.
THIS IS REALLY COMFORTABLE, BUT IT SEEMS WEIRD TO BE UP IN THE AIR AND NOT...
...OUTSIDE, YOU KNOW?
WE HAVE BEEFSTEAK AND CHICKEN PASTA TODAY. WHAT WOULD YOU LIKE?
AHH... HOW MUCH ARE THEY?
IT'S GOT HONKING BIG ENGINES ON IT.
CLATTER

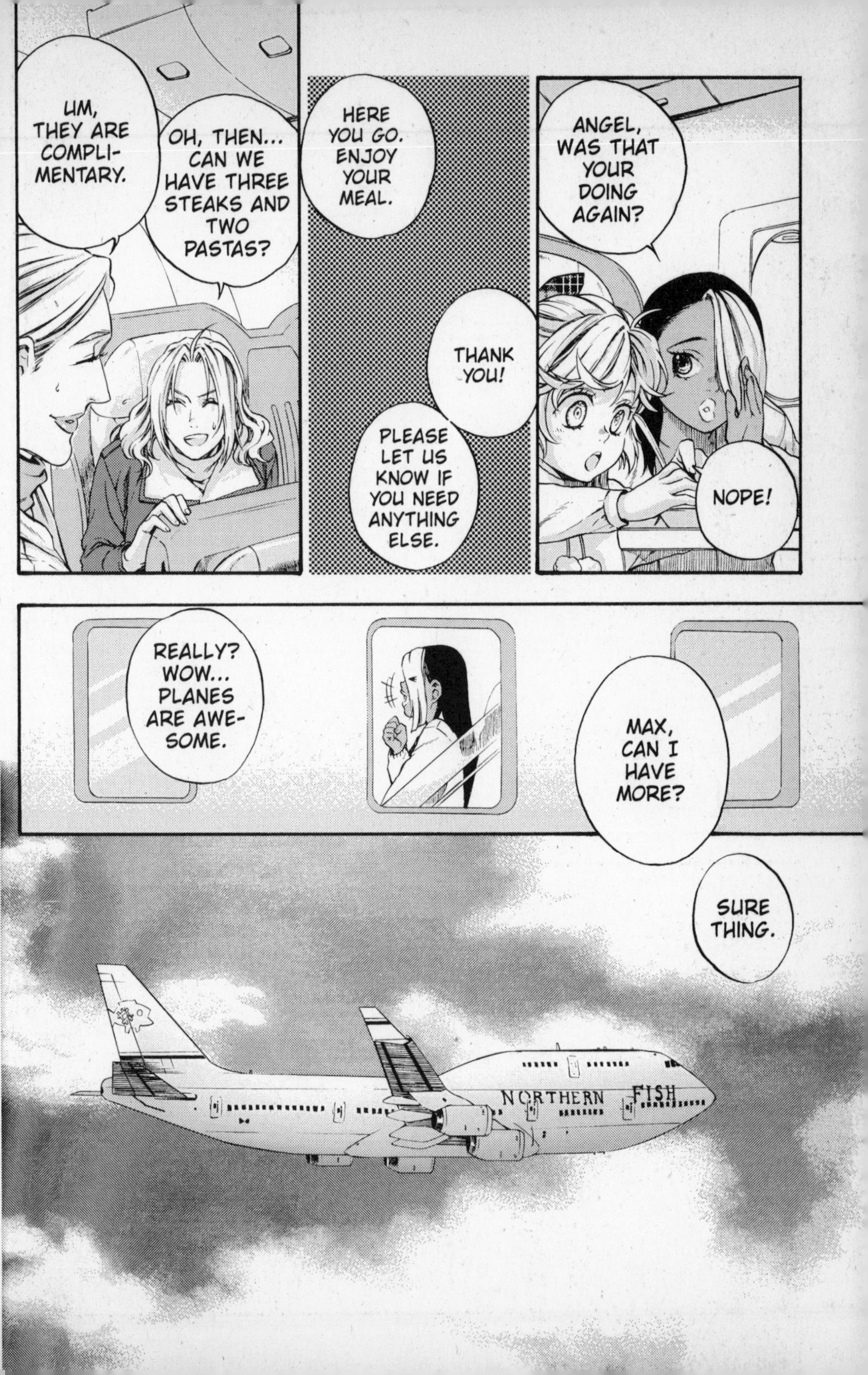
UM, THEY ARE COMPLI-MENTARY.
OH, THEN... CAN WE HAVE THREE STEAKS AND TWO PASTAS?
HERE YOU GO. ENJOY YOUR MEAL.
THANK YOU!
PLEASE LET US KNOW IF YOU NEED ANYTHING ELSE.
ANGEL, WAS THAT YOUR DOING AGAIN?
NOPE!
REALLY? WOW... PLANES ARE AWE-SOME.
MAX, CAN I HAVE MORE?
SURE THING.
NORTHERN FISH

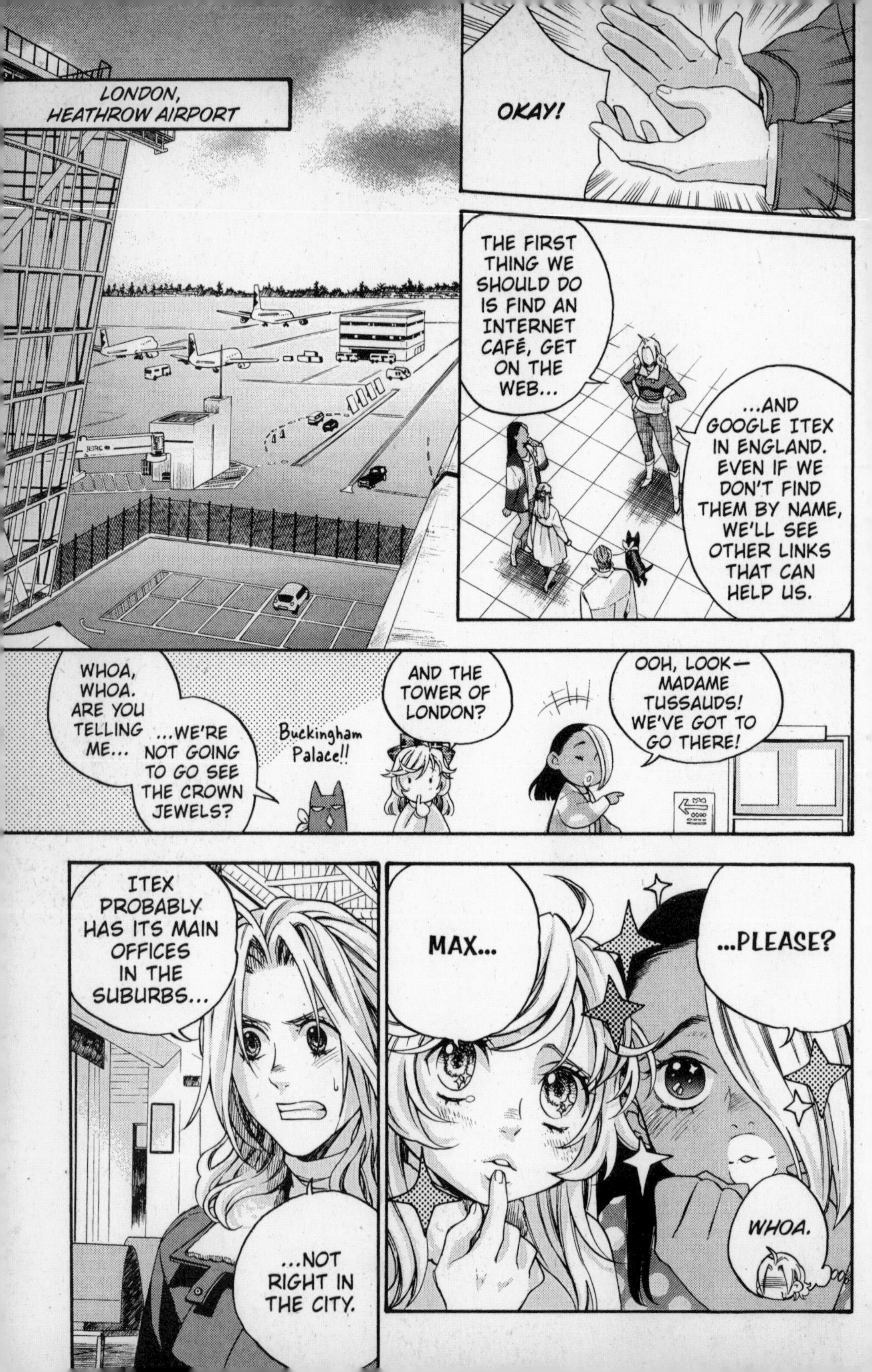

LONDON, HEATHROW AIRPORT
OKAY!
THE FIRST THING WE SHOULD DO IS FIND AN INTERNET CAFÉ, GET ON THE WEB...
...AND GOOGLE ITEX IN ENGLAND. EVEN IF WE DON'T FIND THEM BY NAME, WE'LL SEE OTHER LINKS THAT CAN HELP US.
WHOA, WHOA. ARE YOU TELLING ME...
...WE'RE NOT GOING TO GO SEE THE CROWN JEWELS?
Buckingham Palace!!
AND THE TOWER OF LONDON?
OOH, LOOK—MADAME TUSSAUDS! WE'VE GOT TO GO THERE!
ITEX PROBABLY HAS ITS MAIN OFFICES IN THE SUBURBS...
...NOT RIGHT IN THE CITY.
MAX...
...PLEASE?
WHOA.

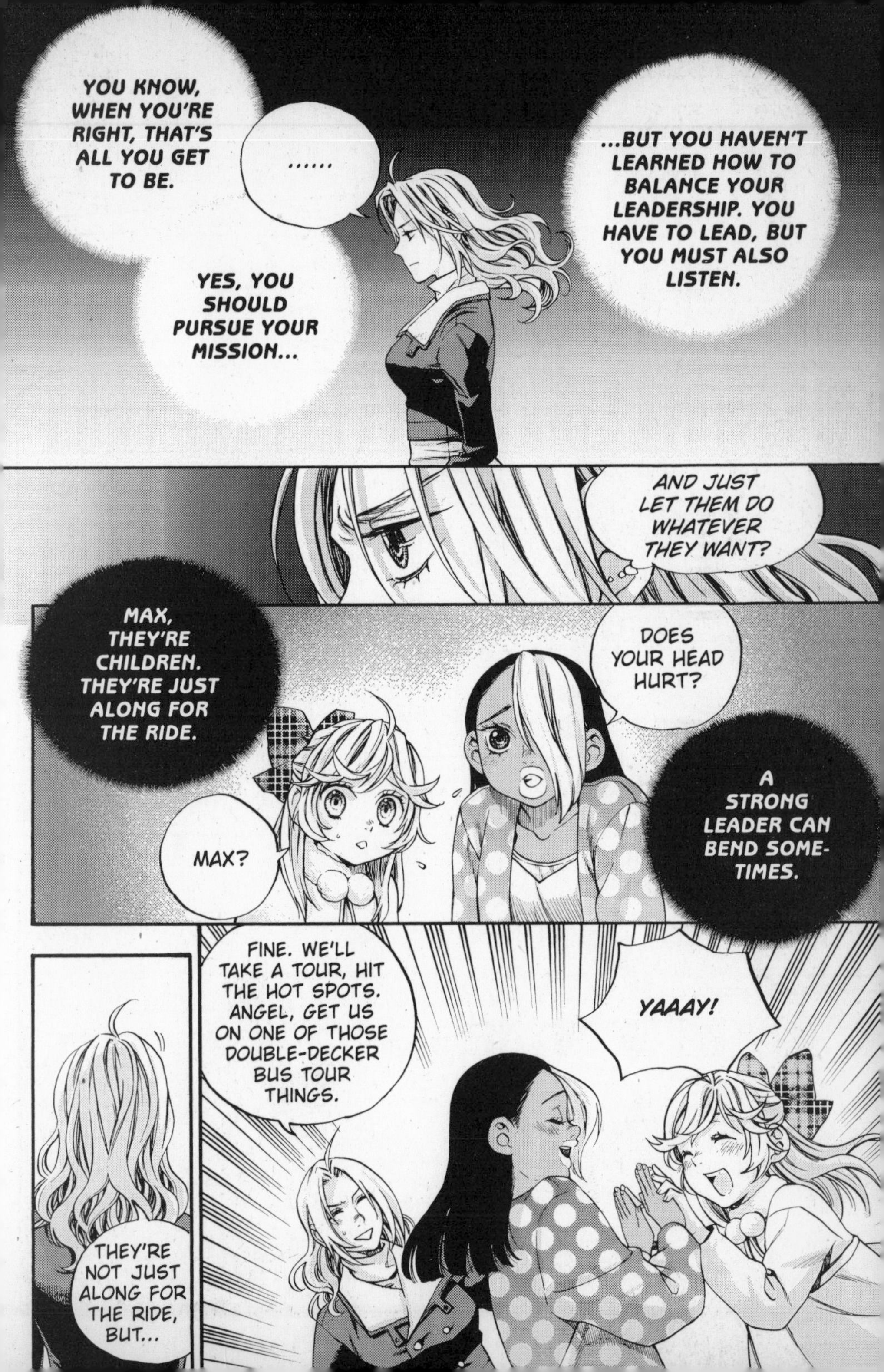
YOU KNOW, WHEN YOU'RE RIGHT, THAT'S ALL YOU GET TO BE.
......
YES, YOU SHOULD PURSUE YOUR MISSION...
...BUT YOU HAVEN'T LEARNED HOW TO BALANCE YOUR LEADERSHIP. YOU HAVE TO LEAD, BUT YOU MUST ALSO LISTEN.
AND JUST LET THEM DO WHATEVER THEY WANT?
MAX, THEY'RE CHILDREN. THEY'RE JUST ALONG FOR THE RIDE.
DOES YOUR HEAD HURT?
MAX?
A STRONG LEADER CAN BEND SOME-TIMES.
FINE. WE'LL TAKE A TOUR, HIT THE HOT SPOTS. ANGEL, GET US ON ONE OF THOSE DOUBLE-DECKER BUS TOUR THINGS.
YAAAY!
THEY'RE NOT JUST ALONG FOR THE RIDE, BUT...

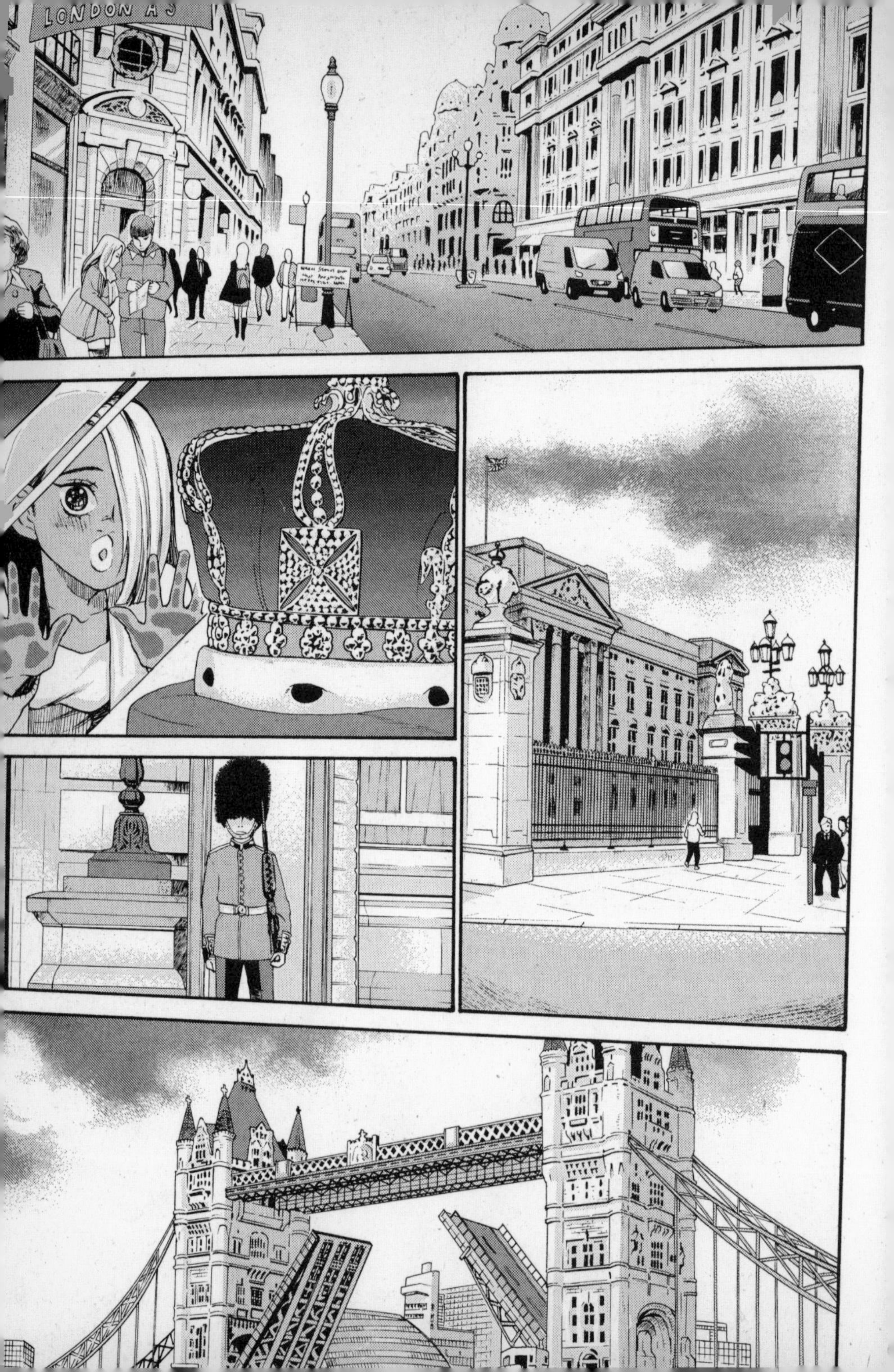
LONDON A S

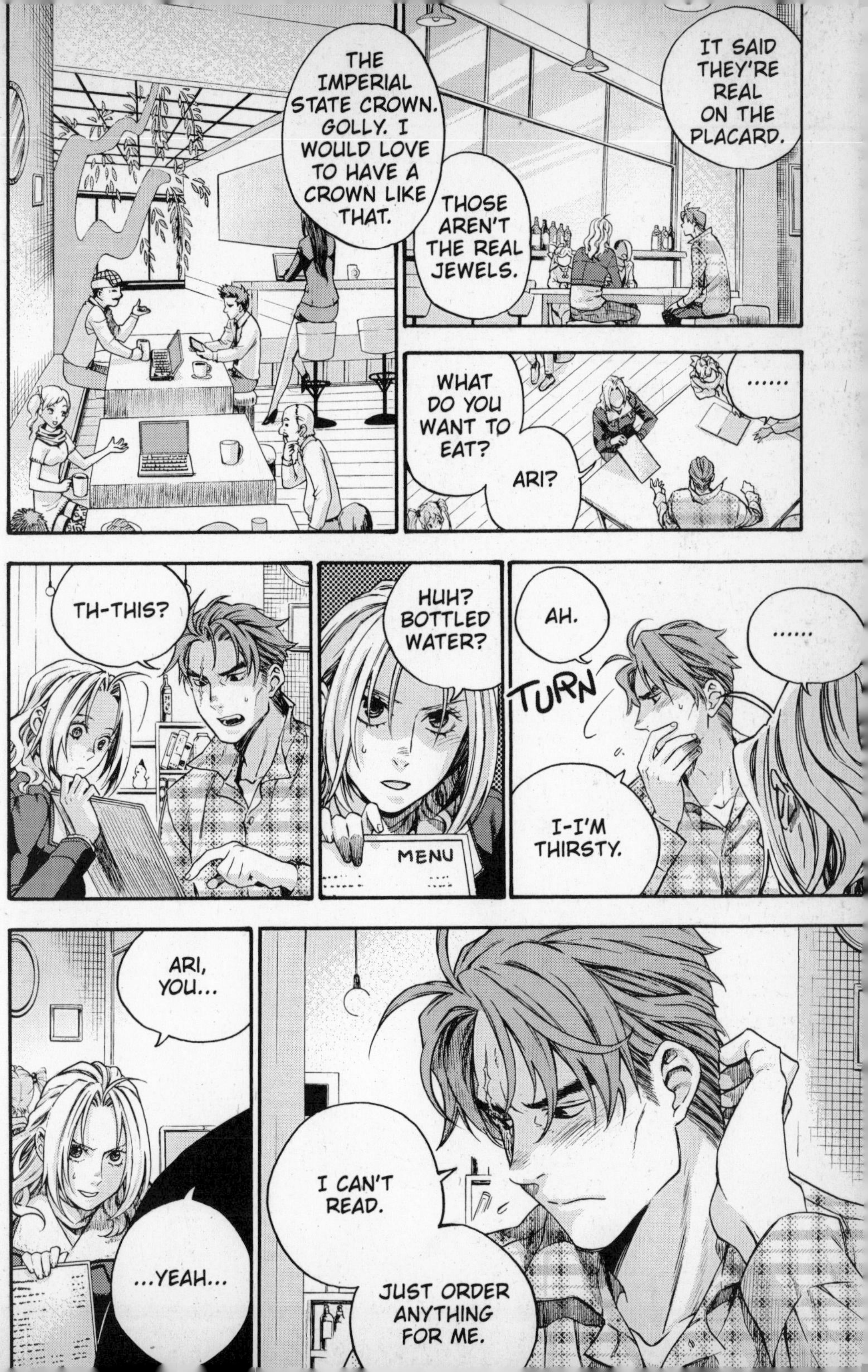
THE IMPERIAL STATE CROWN. GOLLY. I WOULD LOVE TO HAVE A CROWN LIKE THAT.
THOSE AREN'T THE REAL JEWELS.
IT SAID THEY'RE REAL ON THE PLACARD.
WHAT DO YOU WANT TO EAT?
ARI?
......
TH-THIS?
HUH? BOTTLED WATER?
MENU
AH.
TURN
I-I'M THIRSTY.
......
ARI, YOU...
...YEAH...
I CAN'T READ.
JUST ORDER ANYTHING FOR ME.

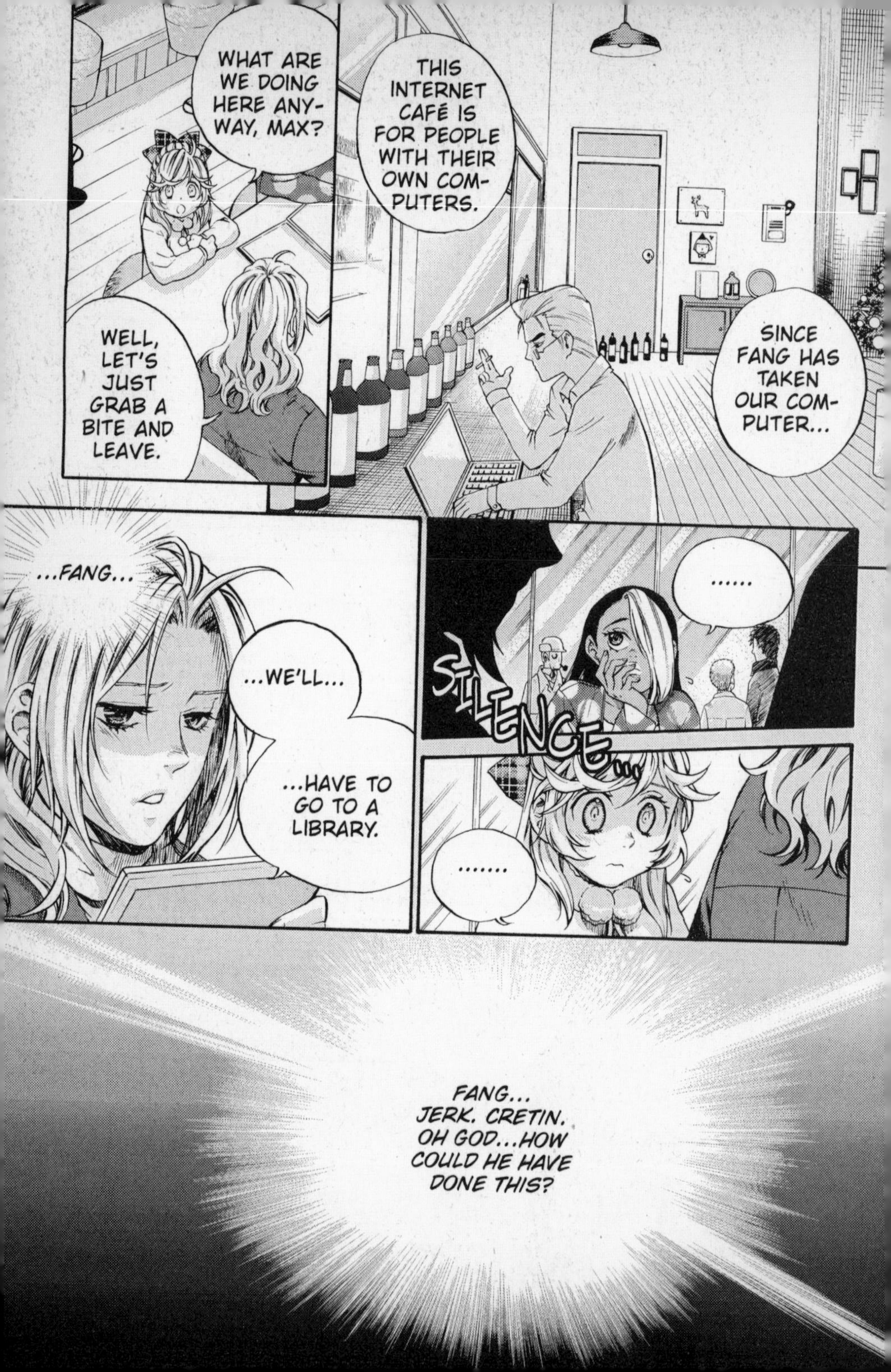
WHAT ARE WE DOING HERE ANYWAY, MAX?
THIS INTERNET CAFÉ IS FOR PEOPLE WITH THEIR OWN COMPUTERS.
WELL, LET'S JUST GRAB A BITE AND LEAVE.
SINCE FANG HAS TAKEN OUR COMPUTER...
...FANG...
...WE'LL...
...HAVE TO GO TO A LIBRARY.
......
SILENCE...
....
FANG... JERK. CRETIN. OH GOD...HOW COULD HE HAVE DONE THIS?

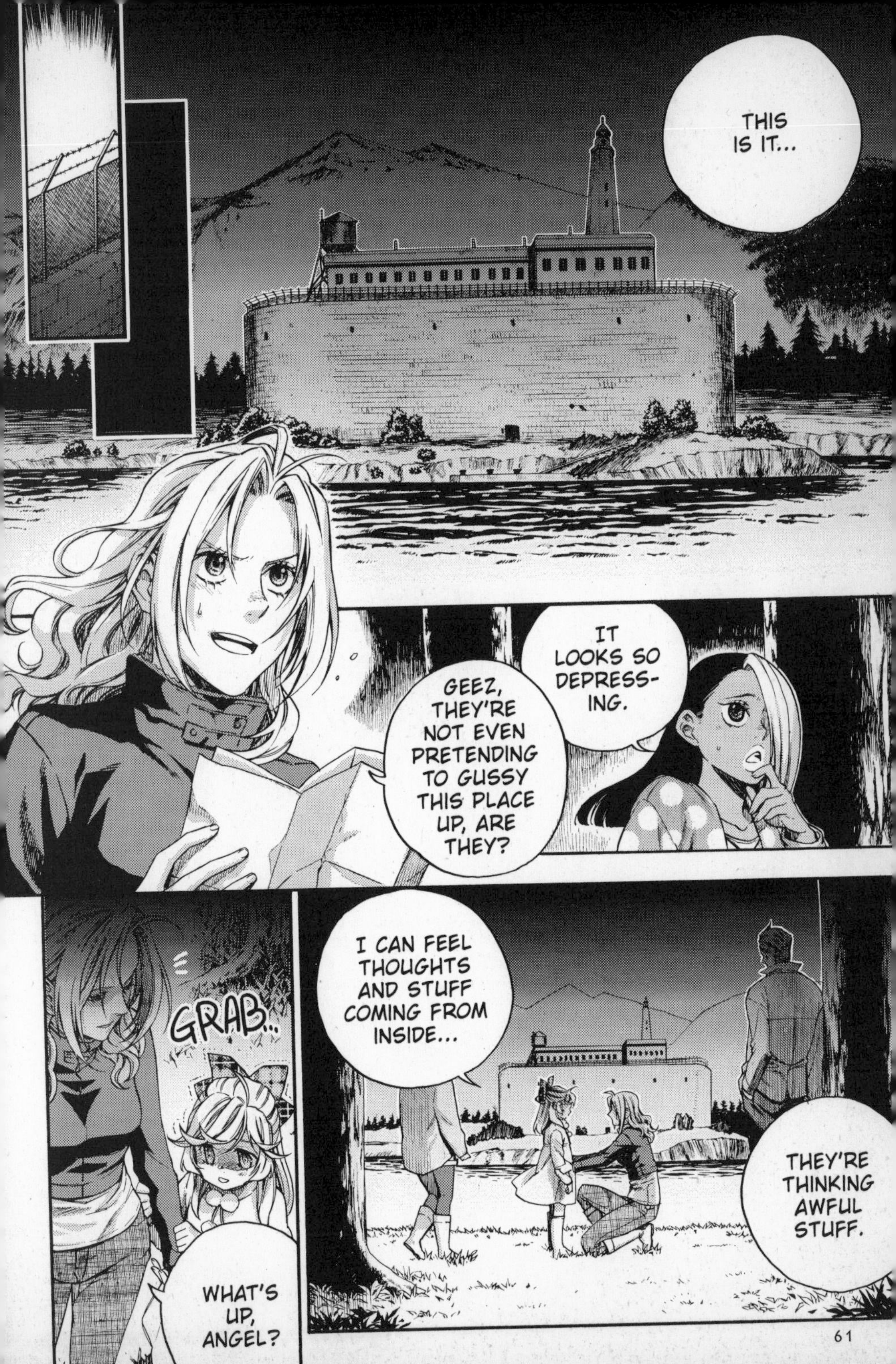
THIS IS IT...
IT LOOKS SO DEPRESS-ING.
GEEZ, THEY'RE NOT EVEN PRETENDING TO GUSSY THIS PLACE UP, ARE THEY?
I CAN FEEL THOUGHTS AND STUFF COMING FROM INSIDE...
THEY'RE THINKING AWFUL STUFF.
GRAB..
WHAT'S UP, ANGEL?

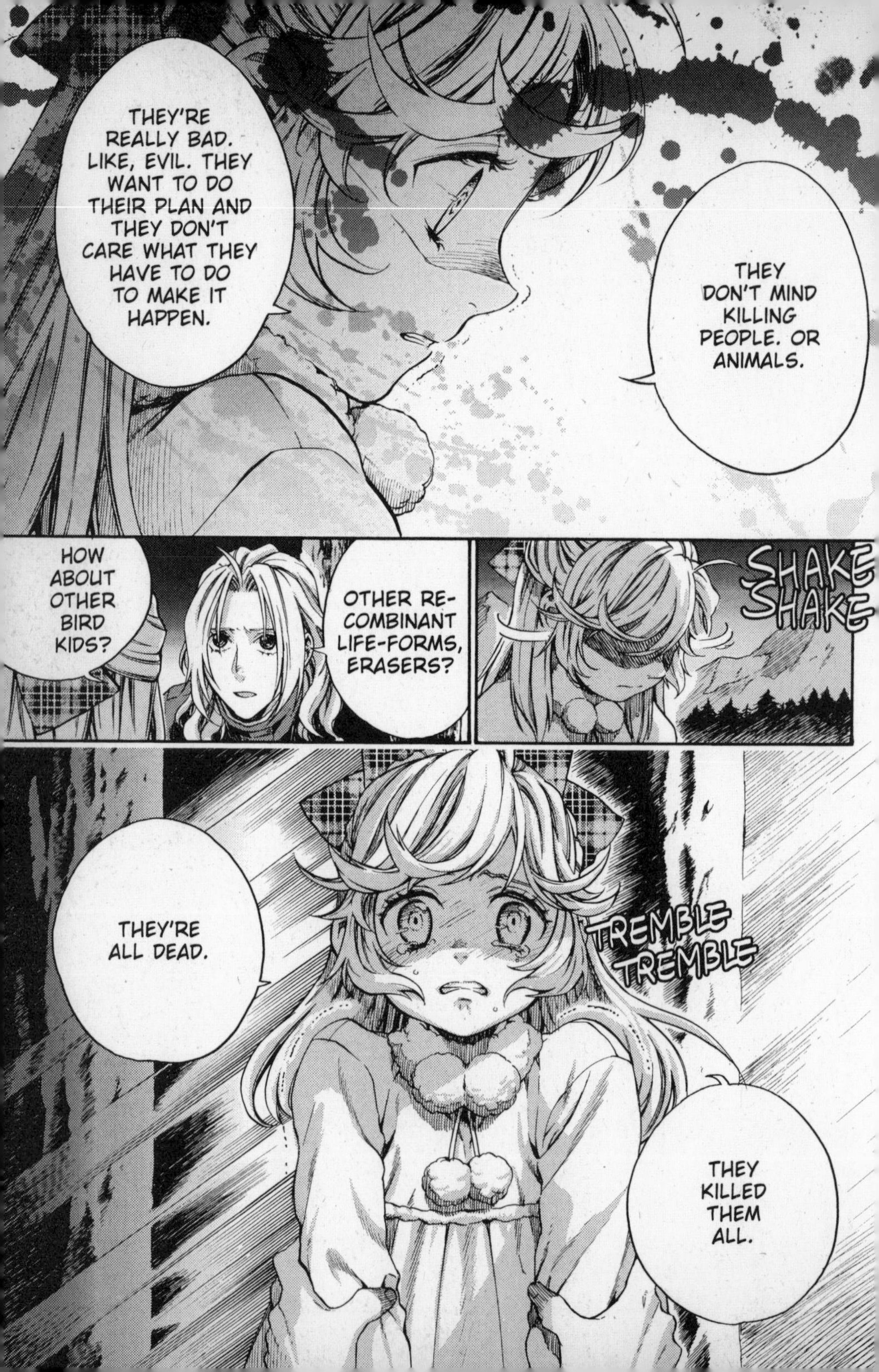
THEY'RE REALLY BAD. LIKE, EVIL. THEY WANT TO DO THEIR PLAN AND THEY DON'T CARE WHAT THEY HAVE TO DO TO MAKE IT HAPPEN.
THEY DON'T MIND KILLING PEOPLE. OR ANIMALS.
HOW ABOUT OTHER BIRD KIDS?
OTHER RE-COMBINANT LIFE-FORMS, ERASERS?
SHAKE SHAKE
THEY'RE ALL DEAD.
TREMBLE TREMBLE
THEY KILLED THEM ALL.

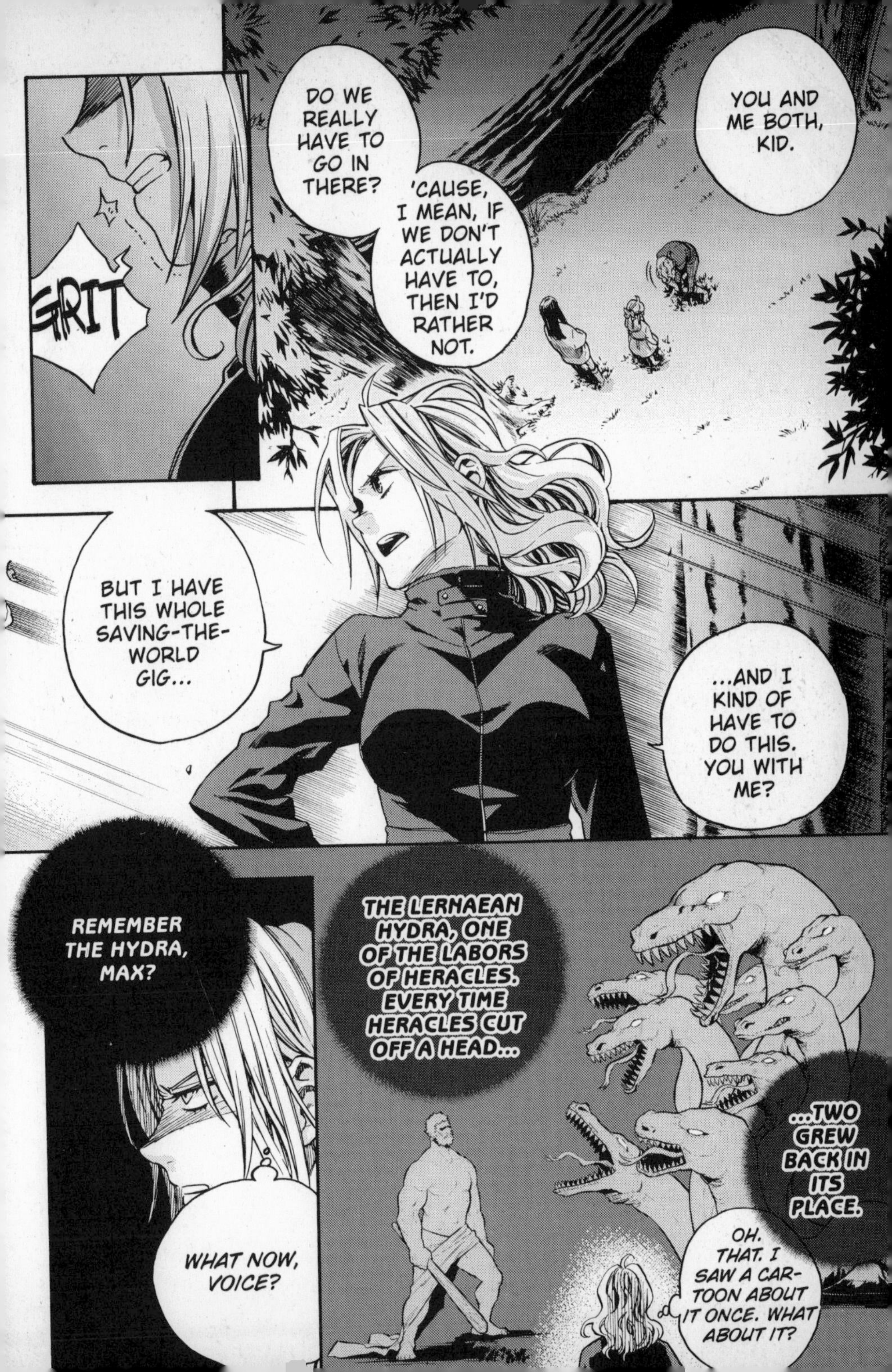
DO WE REALLY HAVE TO GO IN THERE?
'CAUSE, I MEAN, IF WE DON'T ACTUALLY HAVE TO, THEN I'D RATHER NOT.
YOU AND ME BOTH, KID.
GRIT
BUT I HAVE THIS WHOLE SAVING-THE-WORLD GIG...
...AND I KIND OF HAVE TO DO THIS. YOU WITH ME?
REMEMBER THE HYDRA, MAX?
WHAT NOW, VOICE?
THE LERNAEAN HYDRA, ONE OF THE LABORS OF HERACLES. EVERY TIME HERACLES CUT OFF A HEAD...
...TWO GREW BACK IN ITS PLACE.
OH. THAT. I SAW A CARTOON ABOUT IT ONCE. WHAT ABOUT IT?

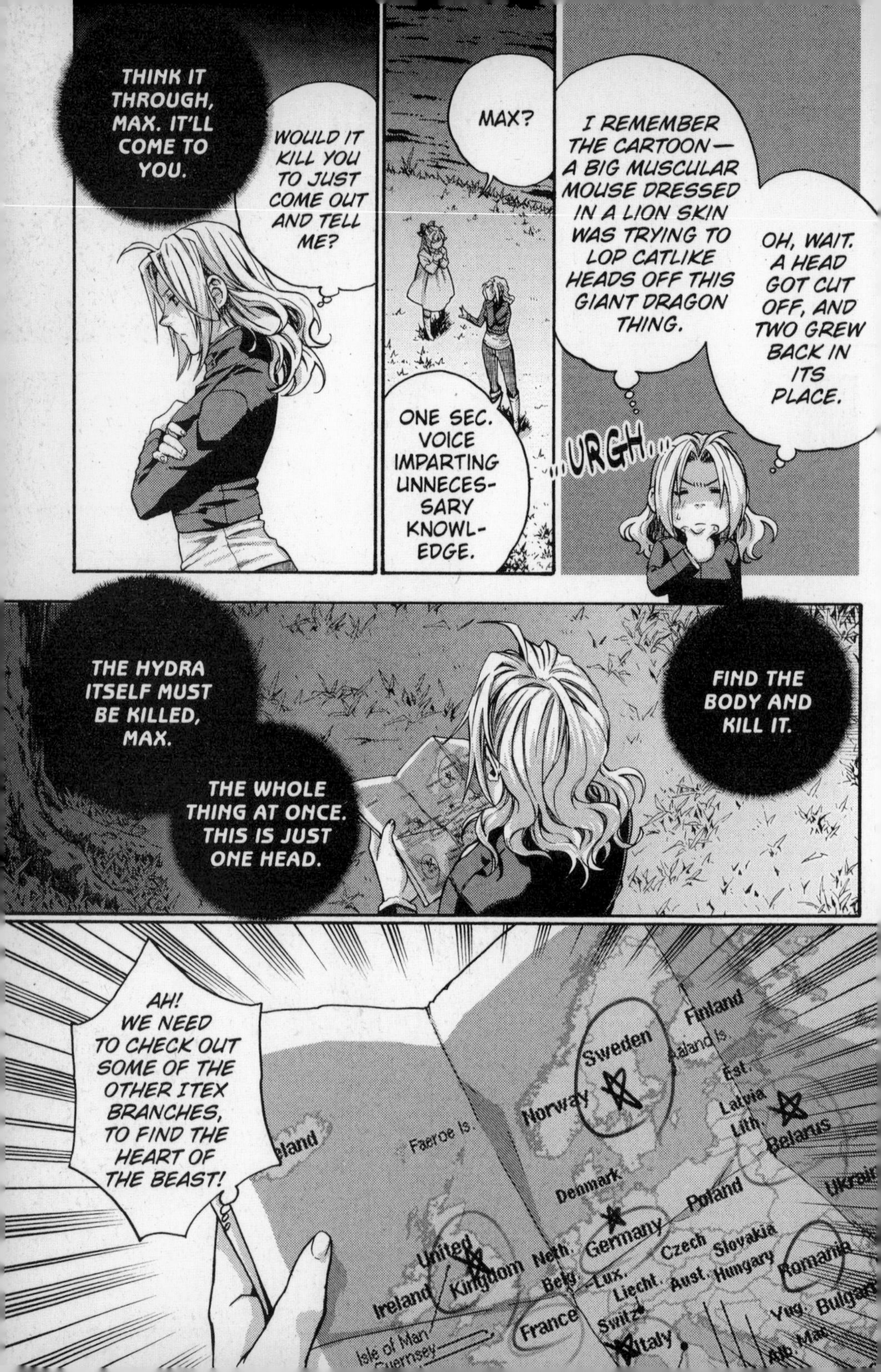
THINK IT THROUGH, MAX. IT'LL COME TO YOU.
WOULD IT KILL YOU TO JUST COME OUT AND TELL ME?
MAX?
ONE SEC. VOICE IMPARTING UNNECES-SARY KNOWL-EDGE.
I REMEMBER THE CARTOON— A BIG MUSCULAR MOUSE DRESSED IN A LION SKIN WAS TRYING TO LOP CATLIKE HEADS OFF THIS GIANT DRAGON THING.
OH, WAIT. A HEAD GOT CUT OFF, AND TWO GREW BACK IN ITS PLACE.
...URGH...
THE HYDRA ITSELF MUST BE KILLED, MAX.
THE WHOLE THING AT ONCE. THIS IS JUST ONE HEAD.
FIND THE BODY AND KILL IT.
AH! WE NEED TO CHECK OUT SOME OF THE OTHER ITEX BRANCHES, TO FIND THE HEART OF THE BEAST!
Finland
Sweden
Aland Is.
Est.
Norway
Latvia
Lith.
Belarus
Faeroe Is.
Denmark
Poland
Germany
United Kingdom
Neth.
Czech
Slovakia
Belg.
Lux.
Liecht.
Aust.
Hungary
Romania
Ireland
France
Switz.
Yug.
Italy
Isle of Man

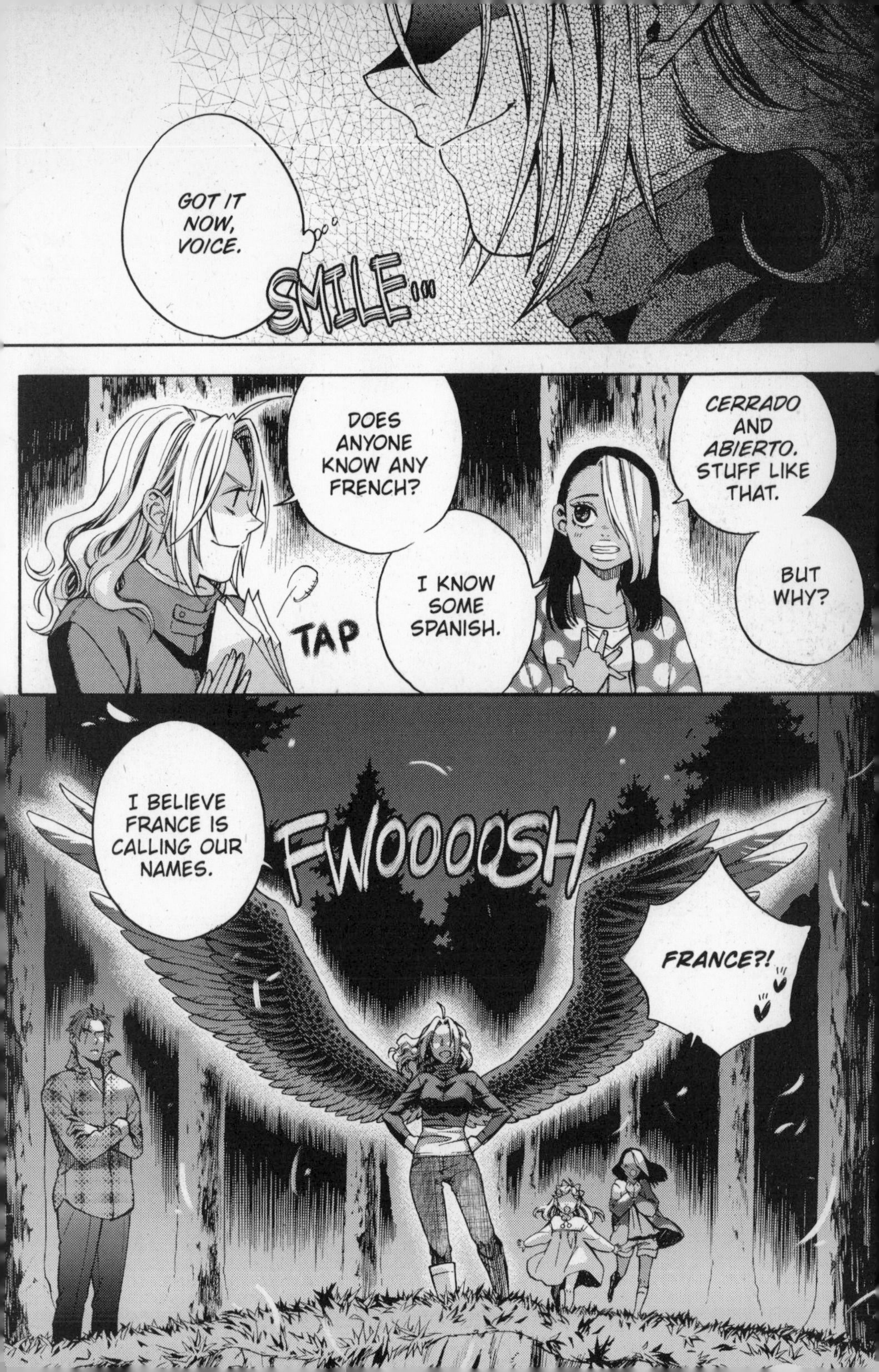
GOT IT NOW, VOICE.
SMILE...
DOES ANYONE KNOW ANY FRENCH?
TAP
I KNOW SOME SPANISH.
CERRADO AND ABIERTO. STUFF LIKE THAT.
BUT WHY?
I BELIEVE FRANCE IS CALLING OUR NAMES.
FWOOOOSH
FRANCE?!

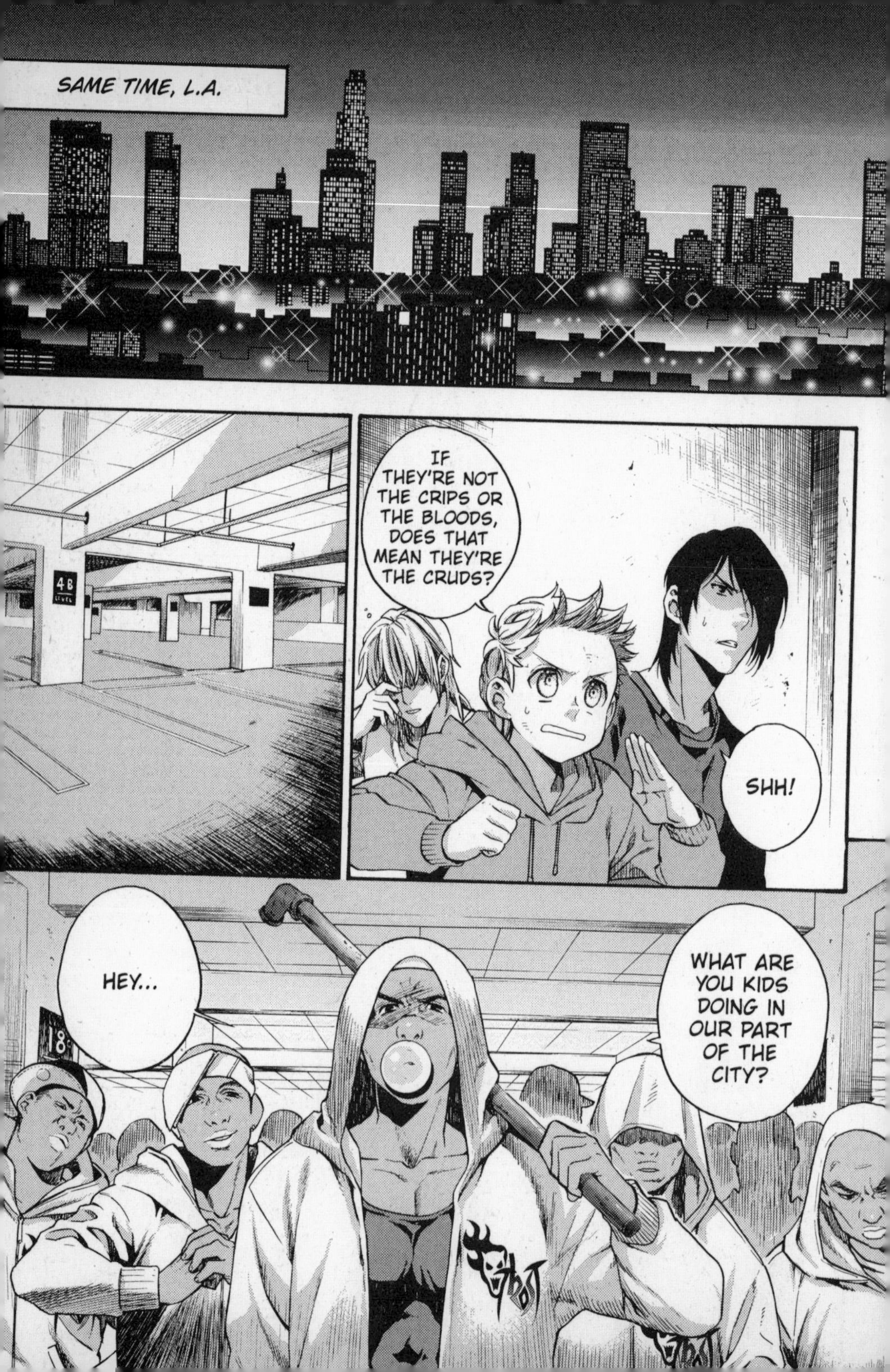
SAME TIME, L.A.
IF THEY'RE NOT THE CRIPS OR THE BLOODS, DOES THAT MEAN THEY'RE THE CRUDS?
SHH!
HEY...
WHAT ARE YOU KIDS DOING IN OUR PART OF THE CITY?

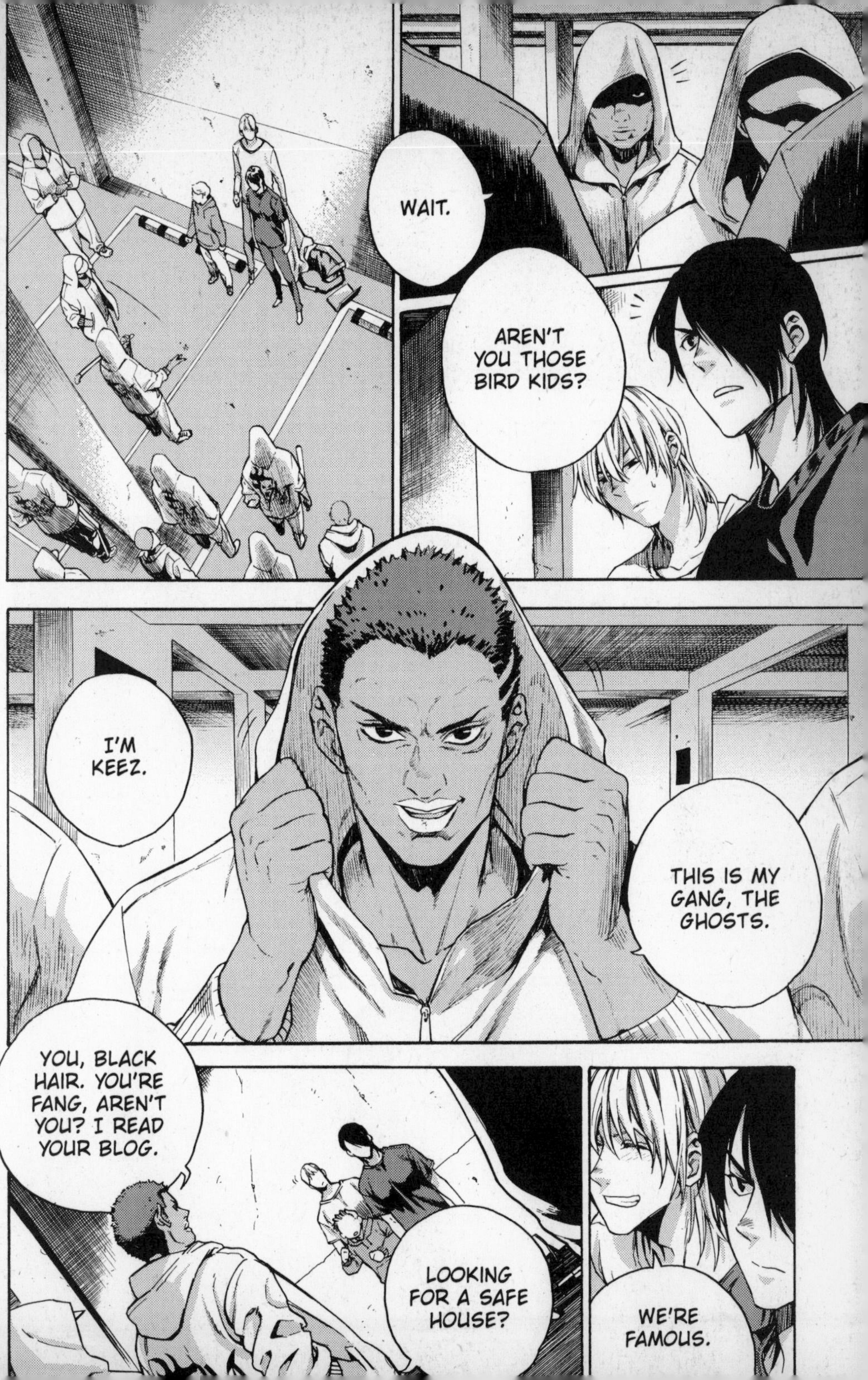
WAIT.
AREN'T YOU THOSE BIRD KIDS?
I'M KEEZ.
THIS IS MY GANG, THE GHOSTS.
YOU, BLACK HAIR. YOU'RE FANG, AREN'T YOU? I READ YOUR BLOG.
LOOKING FOR A SAFE HOUSE?
WE'RE FAMOUS.

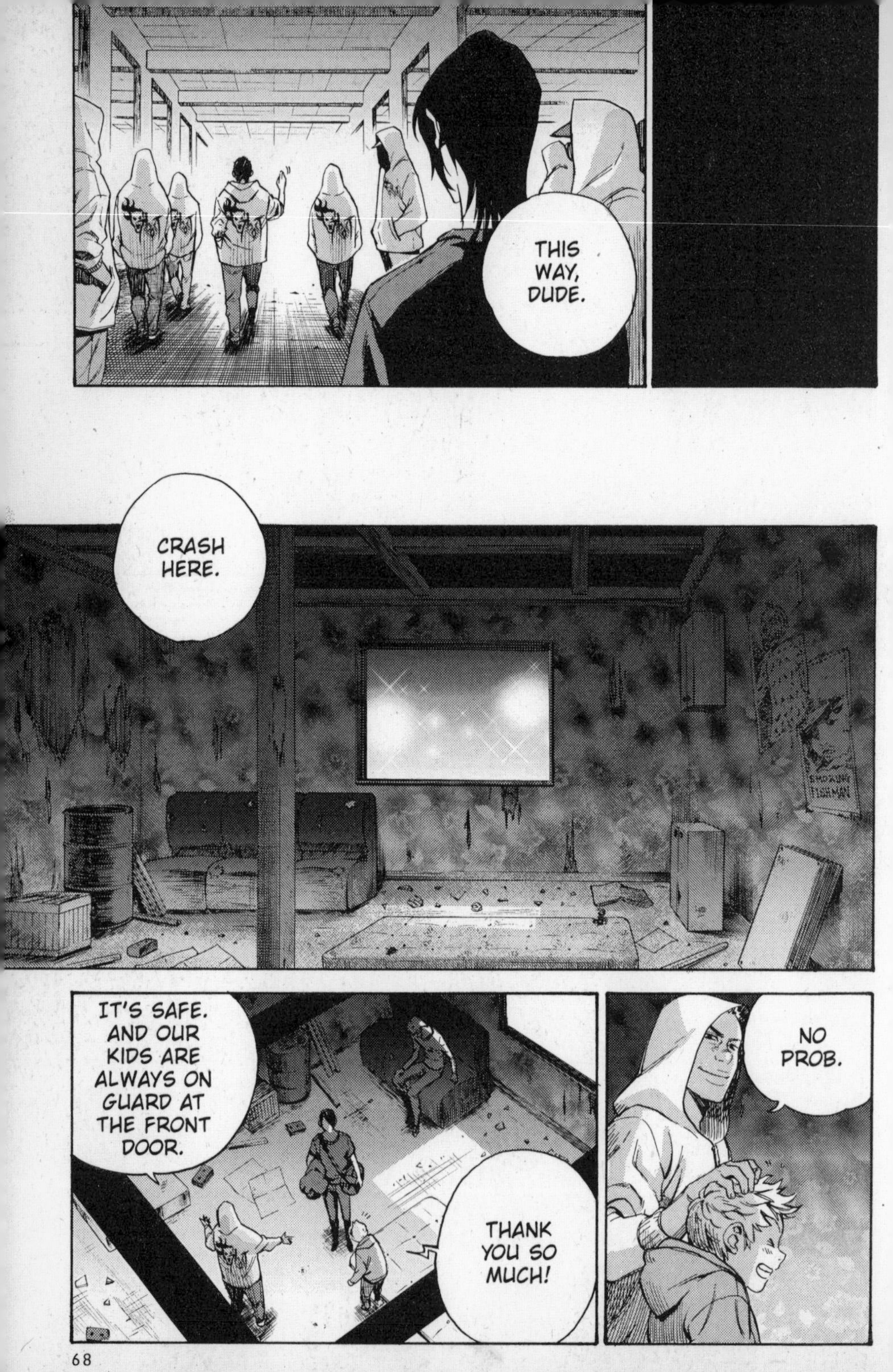
THIS WAY, DUDE.
CRASH HERE.
IT'S SAFE. AND OUR KIDS ARE ALWAYS ON GUARD AT THE FRONT DOOR.
THANK YOU SO MUCH!
NO PROB.

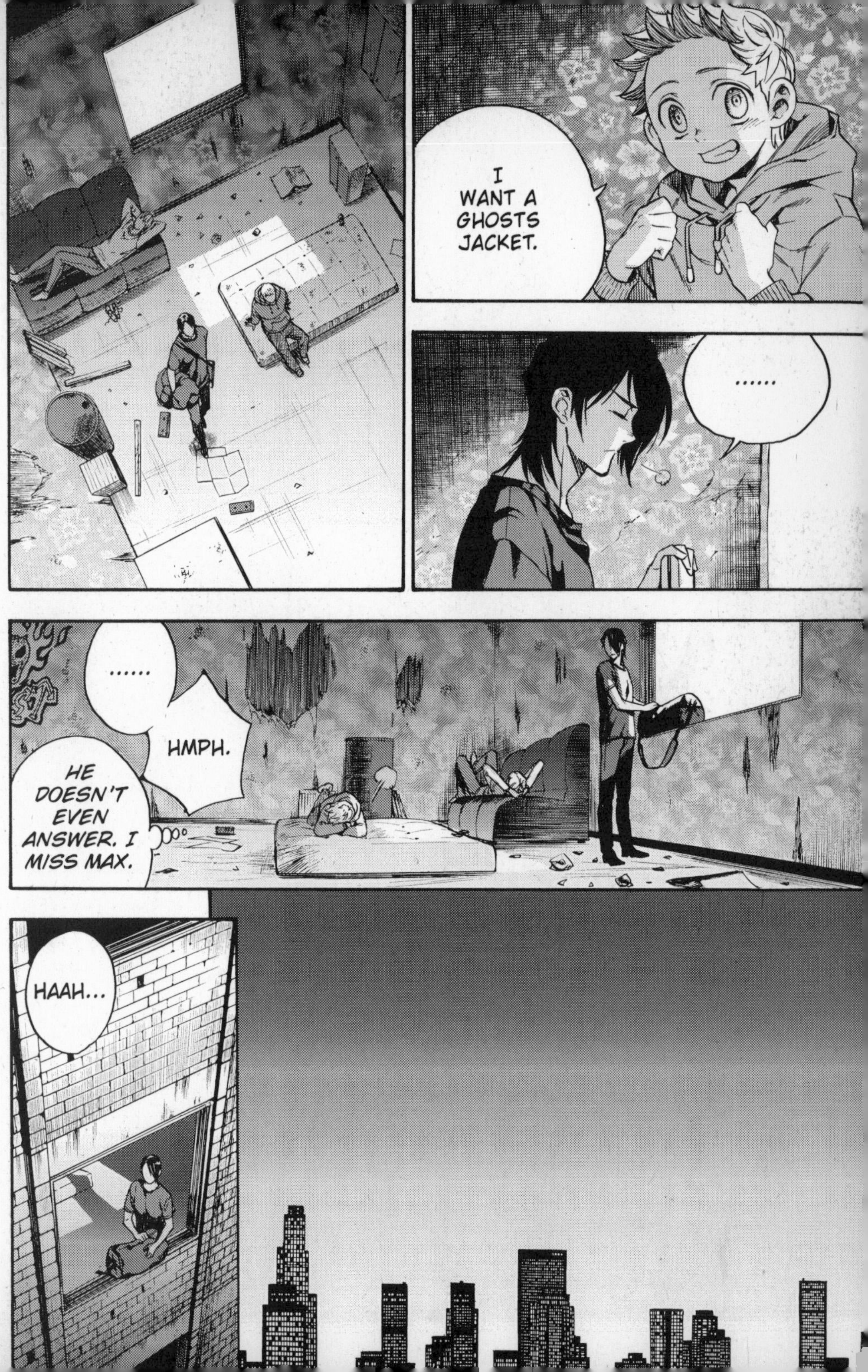
I WANT A GHOSTS JACKET.
......
......
HMPH.
HE DOESN'T EVEN ANSWER. I MISS MAX.
HAAH...

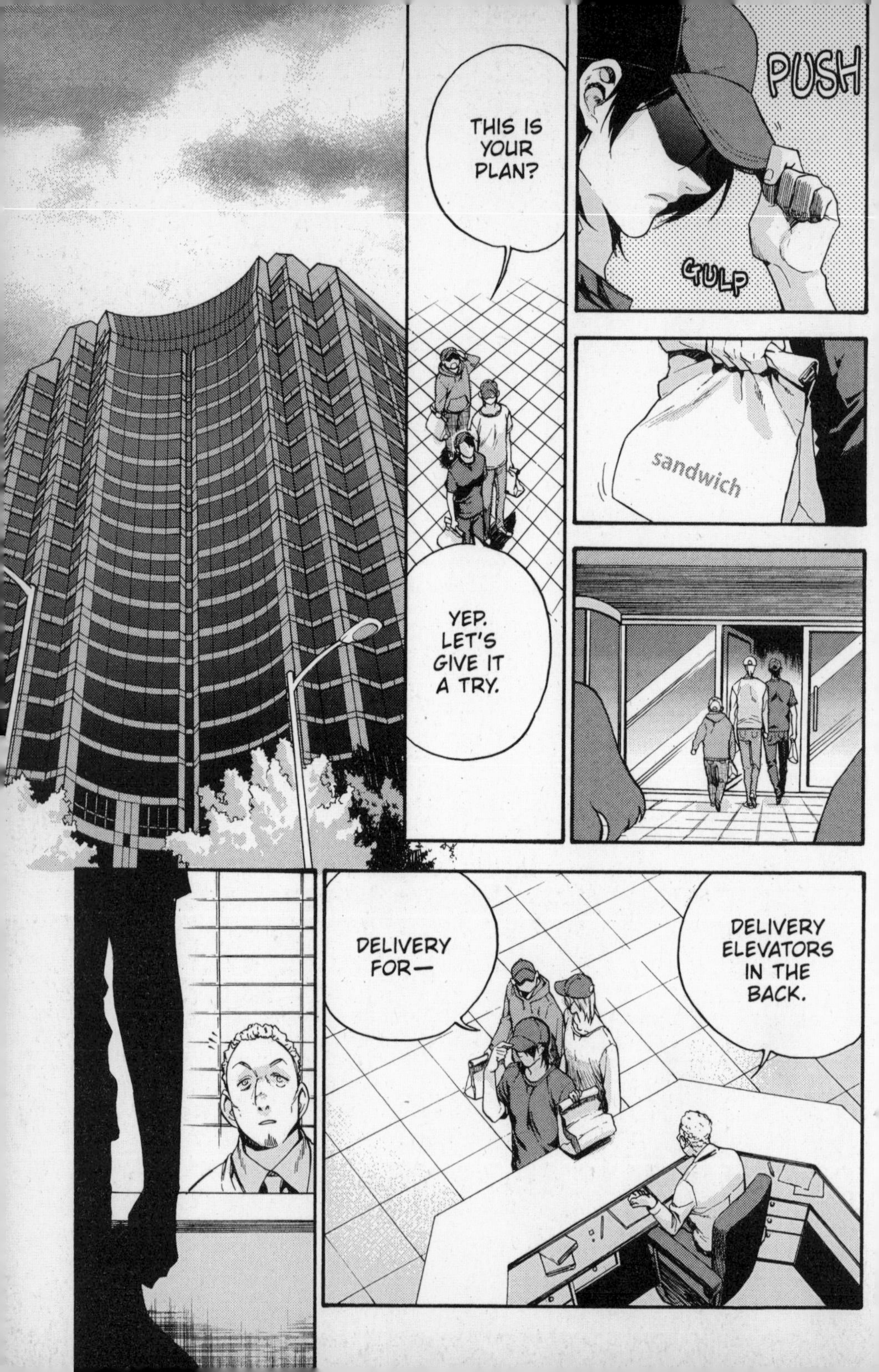
PUSH
GULP
THIS IS YOUR PLAN?
sandwich
YEP. LET'S GIVE IT A TRY.
DELIVERY ELEVATORS IN THE BACK.
DELIVERY FOR—

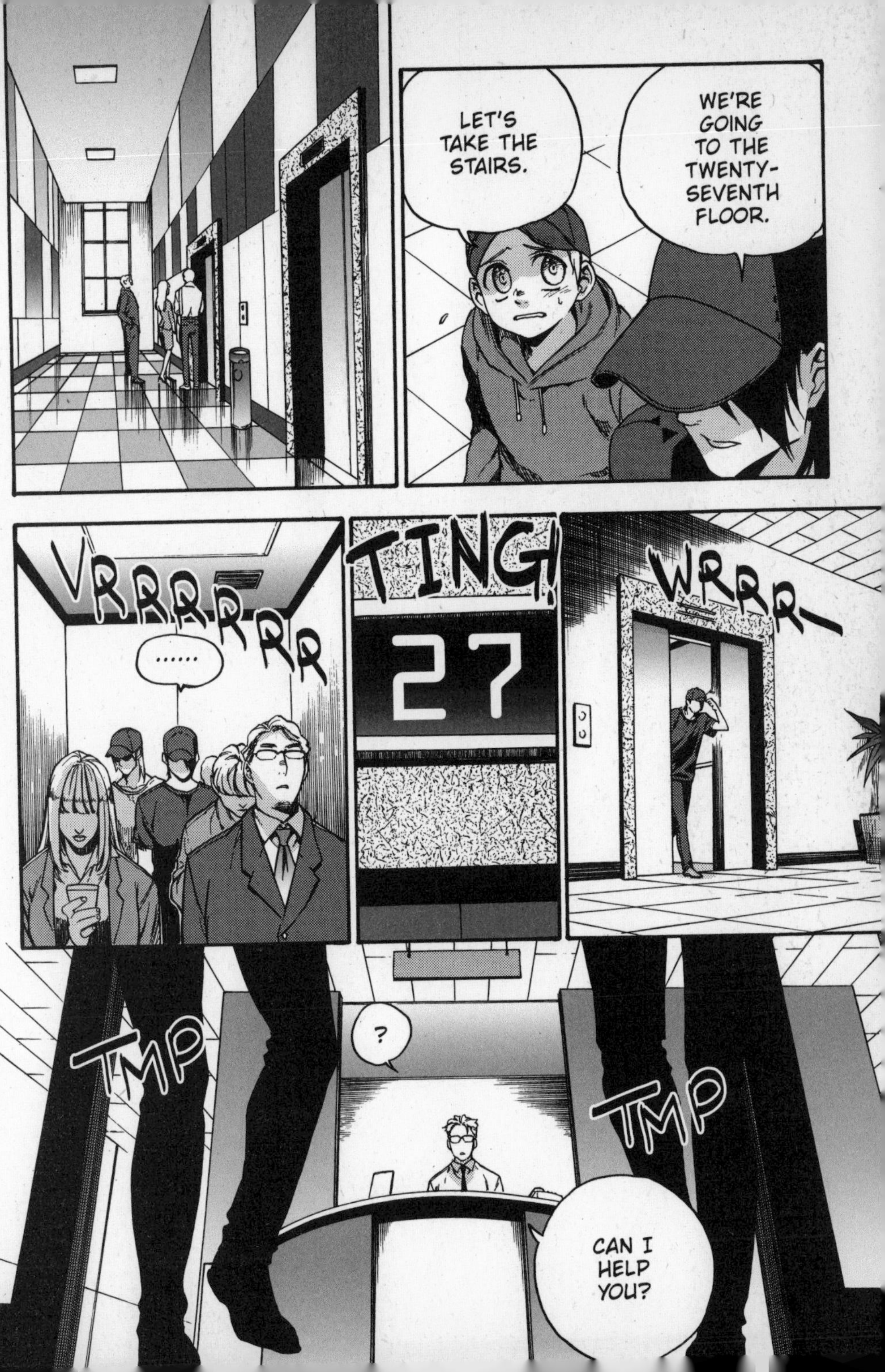
WE'RE GOING TO THE TWENTY-SEVENTH FLOOR.
LET'S TAKE THE STAIRS.
VRRRRRRR
....
TING!
27
WRRRR
TMP
?
TMP
CAN I HELP YOU?

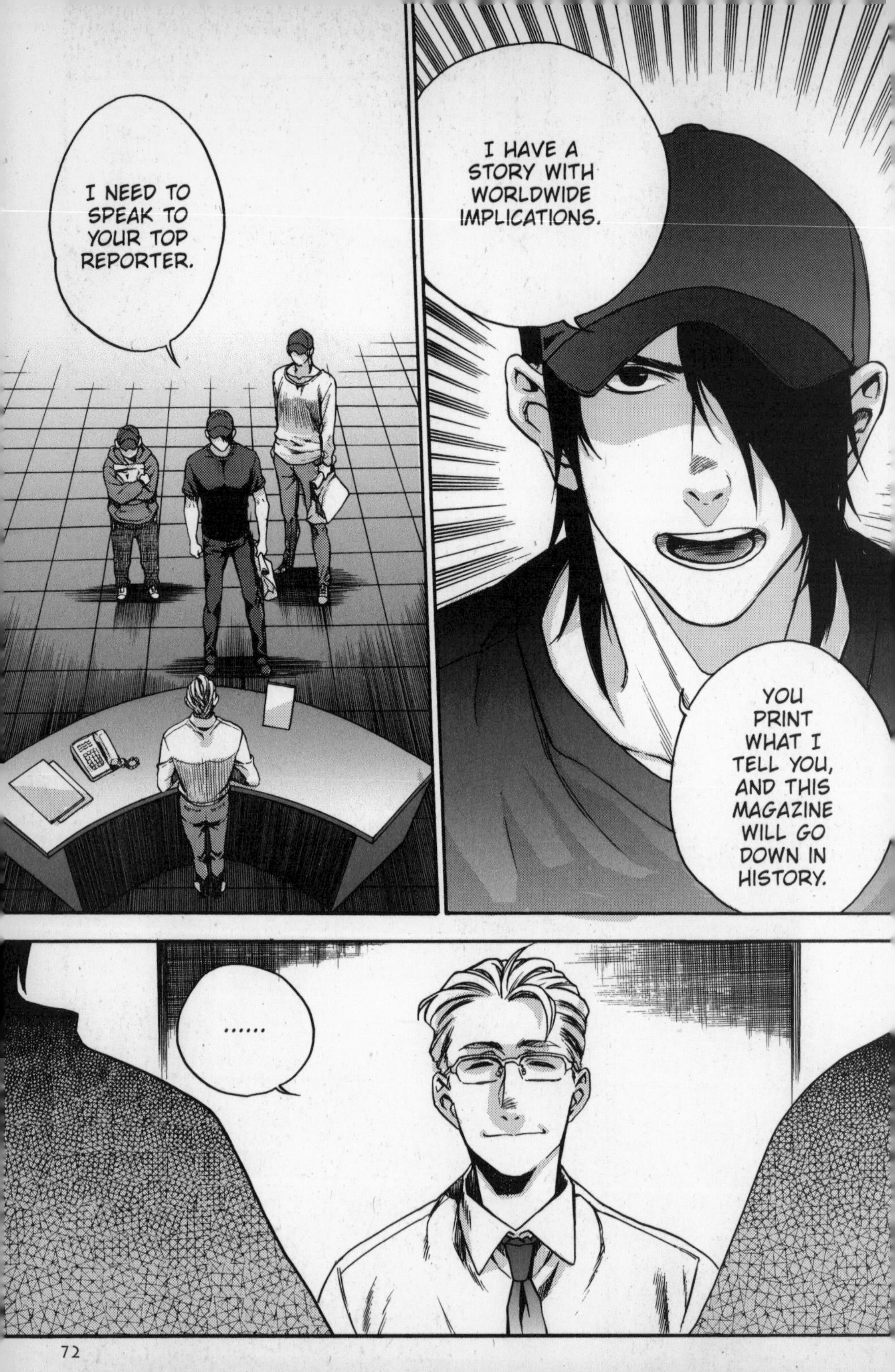

I NEED TO SPEAK TO YOUR TOP REPORTER.
I HAVE A STORY WITH WORLDWIDE IMPLICATIONS.
YOU PRINT WHAT I TELL YOU, AND THIS MAGAZINE WILL GO DOWN IN HISTORY.
......

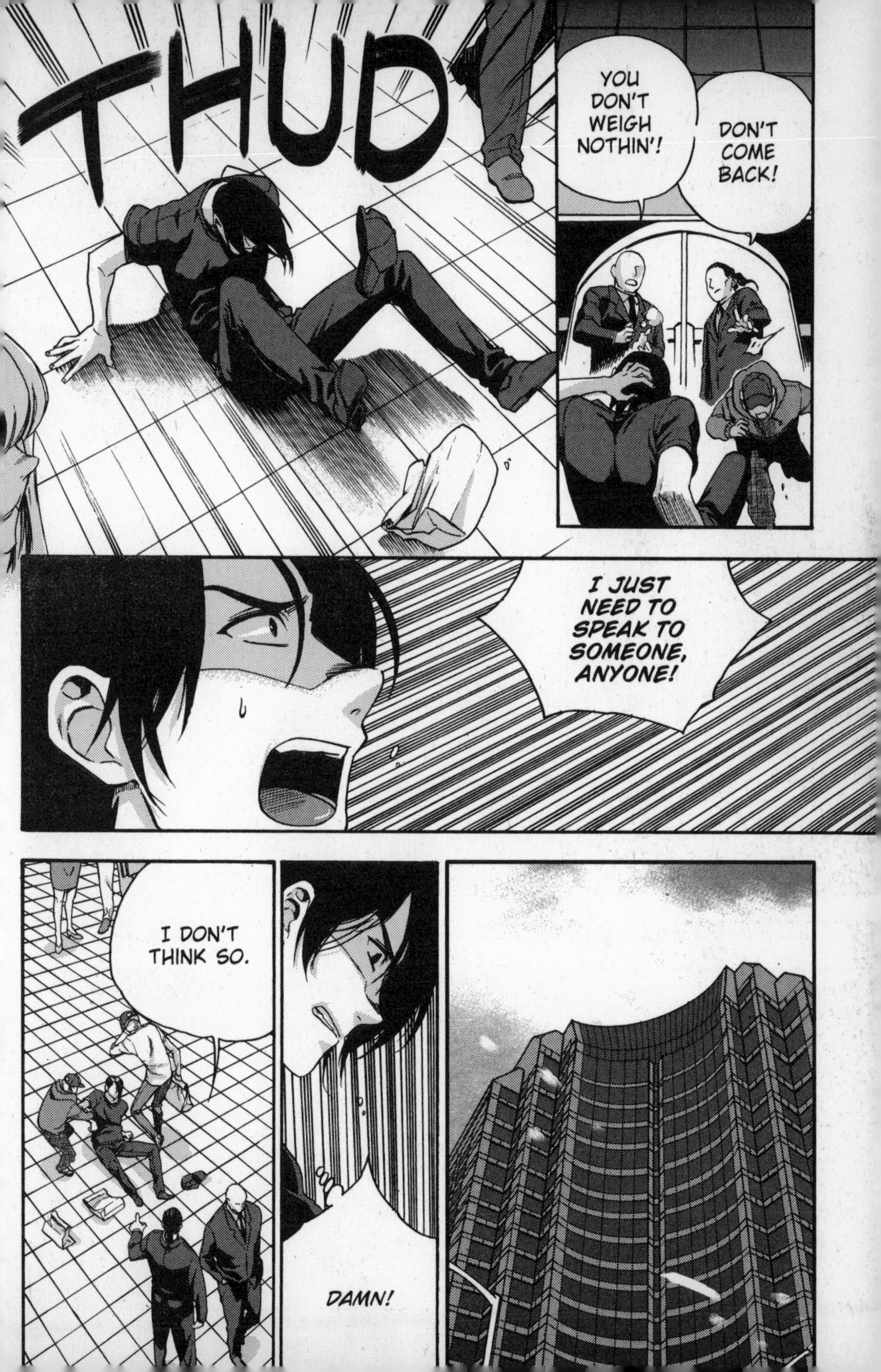
THUD
YOU DON'T WEIGH NOTHIN'!
DON'T COME BACK!
I JUST NEED TO SPEAK TO SOMEONE, ANYONE!
I DON'T THINK SO.
DAMN!

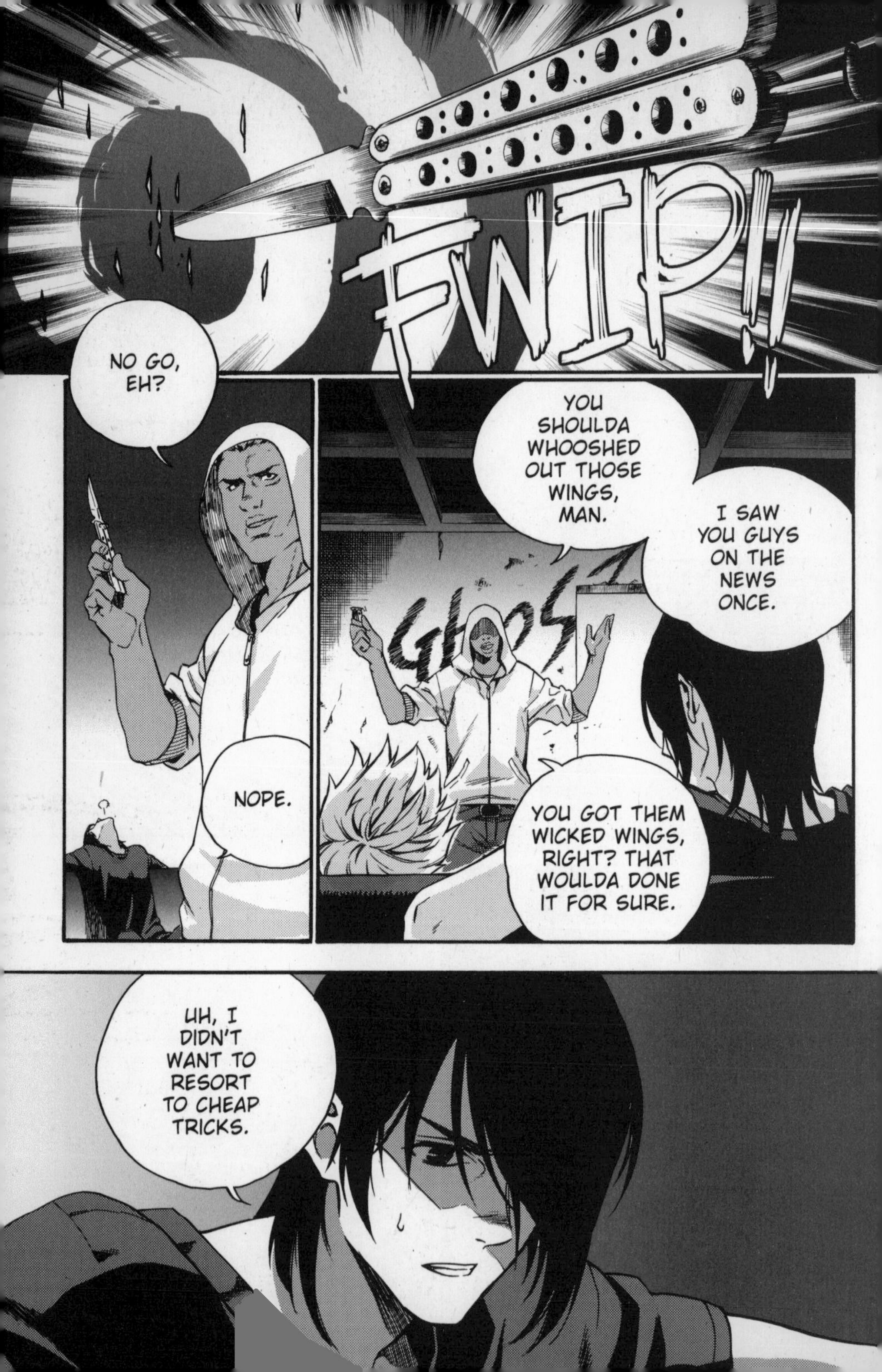
FWIP!!
NO GO, EH?
NOPE.
YOU SHOULDA WHOOSHED OUT THOSE WINGS, MAN.
I SAW YOU GUYS ON THE NEWS ONCE.
YOU GOT THEM WICKED WINGS, RIGHT? THAT WOULDA DONE IT FOR SURE.
UH, I DIDN'T WANT TO RESORT TO CHEAP TRICKS.

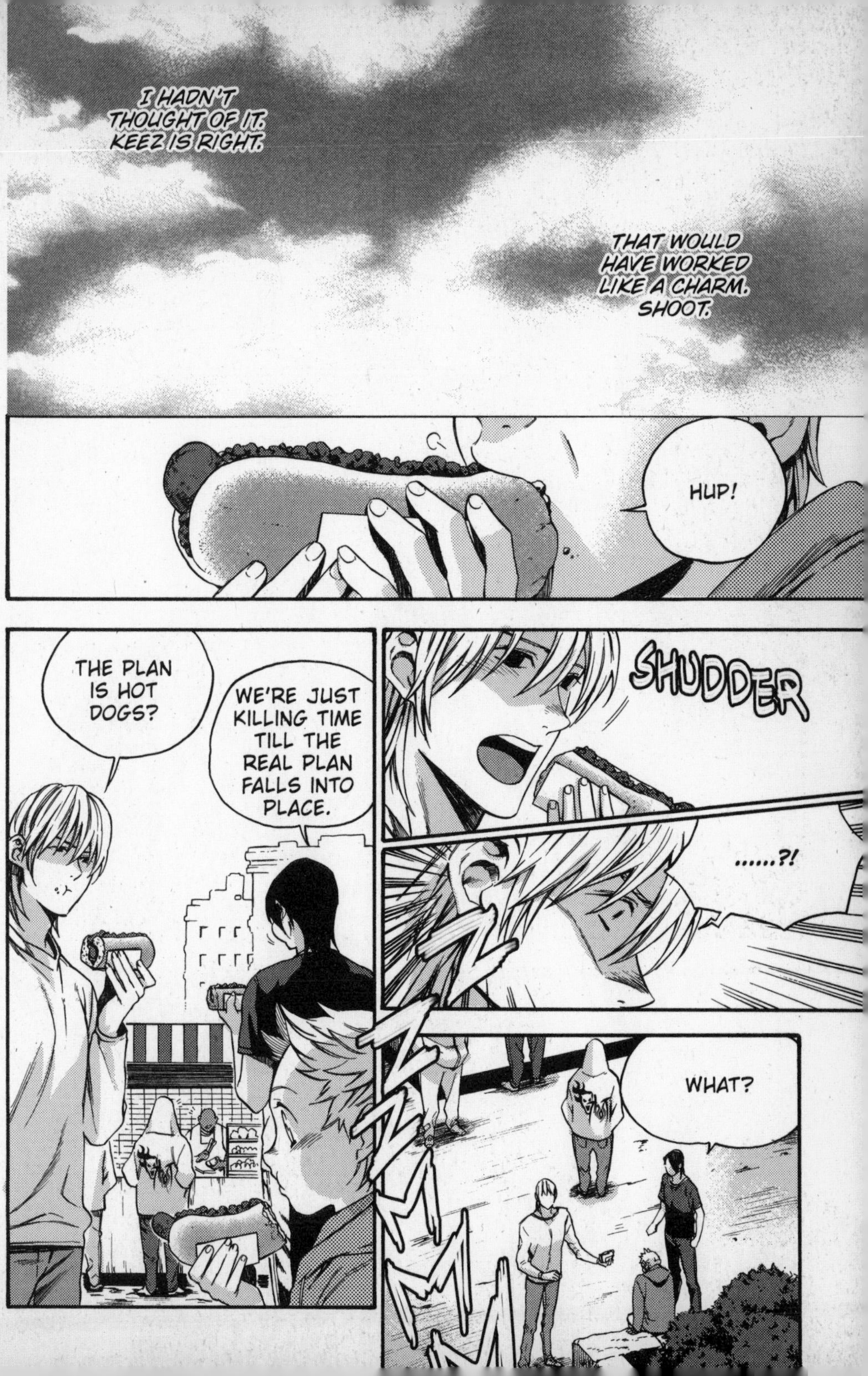
I HADN'T THOUGHT OF IT. KEEZ IS RIGHT.
THAT WOULD HAVE WORKED LIKE A CHARM. SHOOT.
HUP!
THE PLAN IS HOT DOGS?
WE'RE JUST KILLING TIME TILL THE REAL PLAN FALLS INTO PLACE.
SHUDDER
......?!
WHAT?

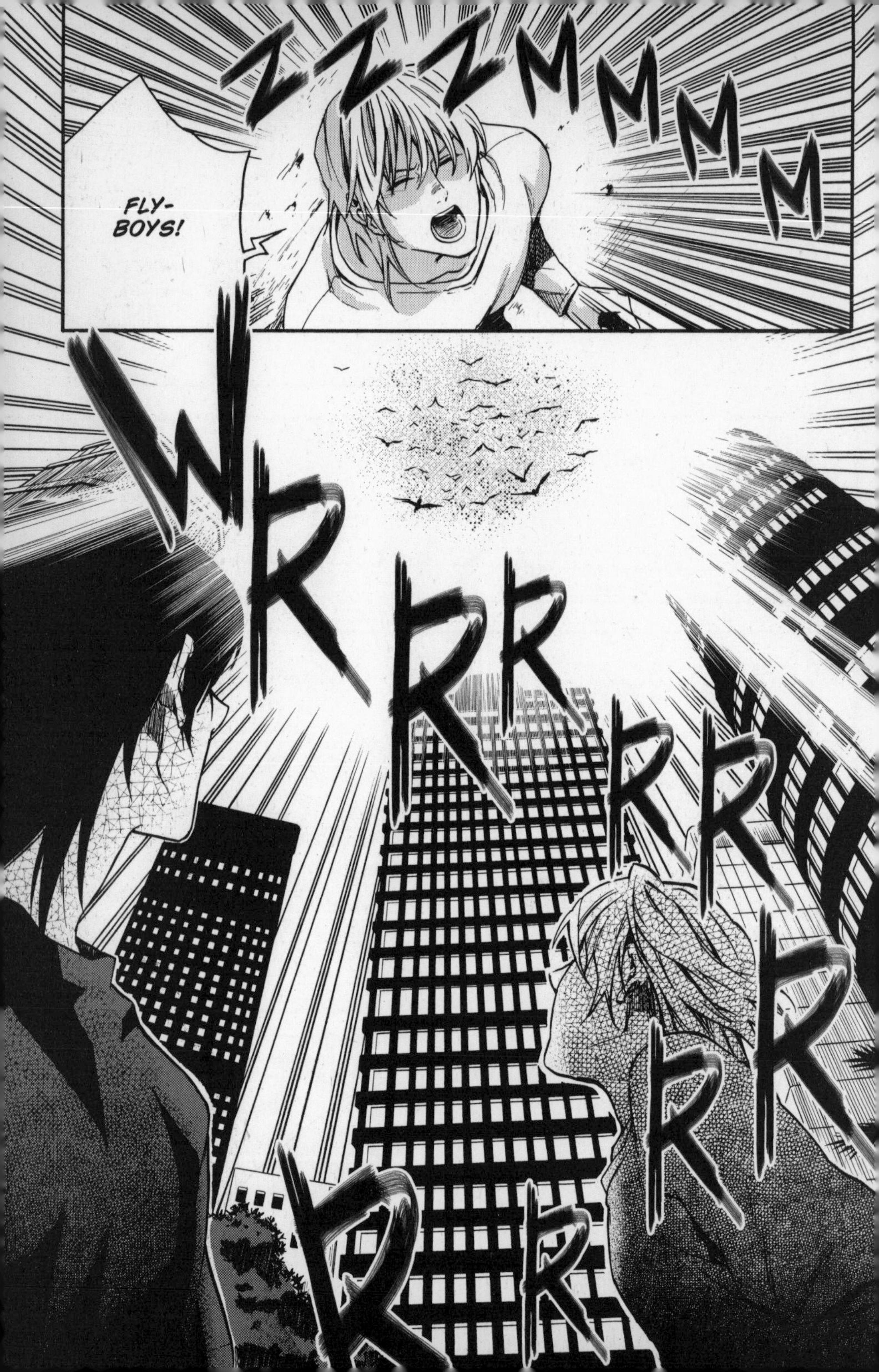
ZZZMMMMMM
FLY-BOYS!
WRRRRRRRRRRR

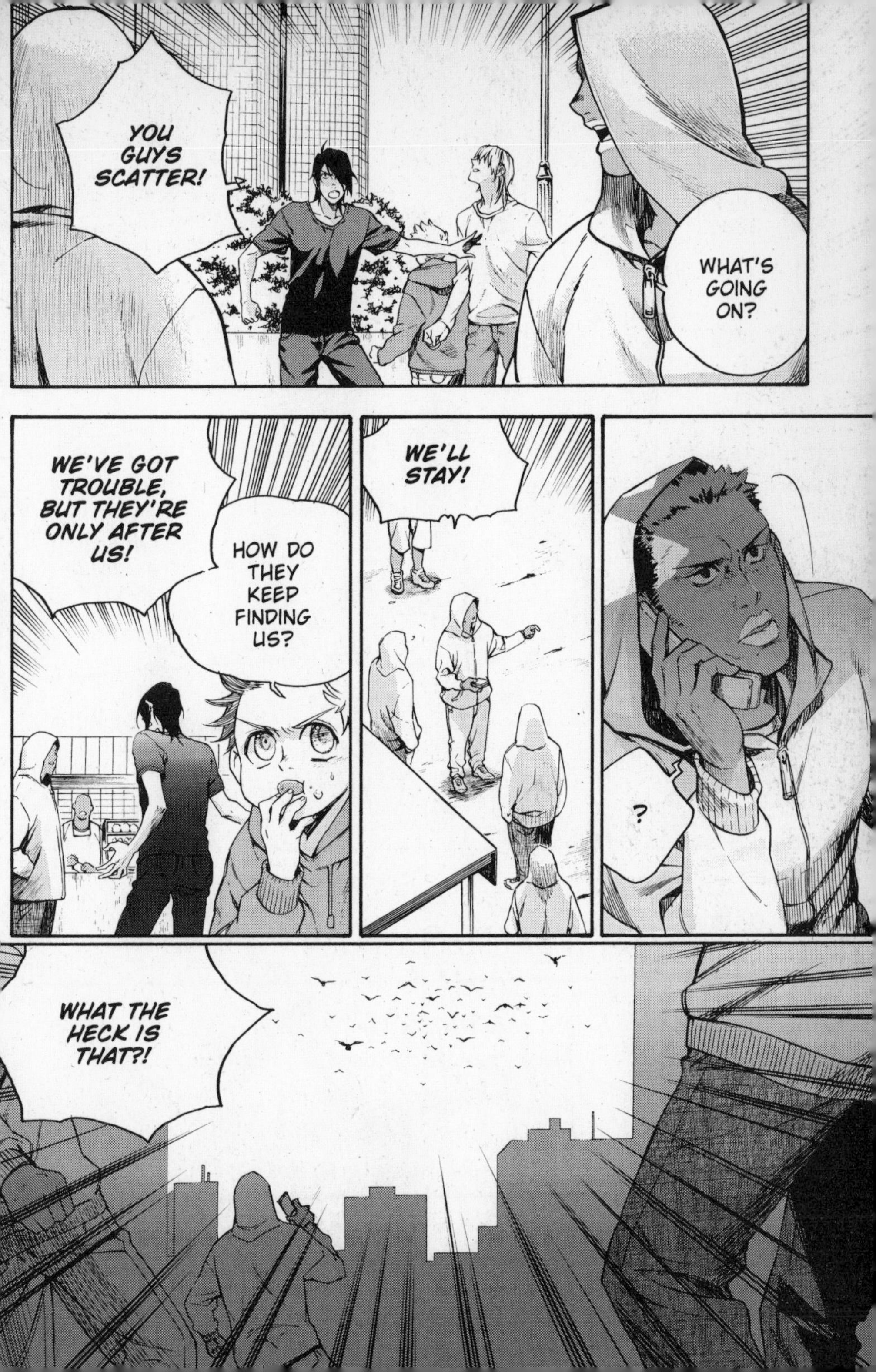
WHAT'S GOING ON?
YOU GUYS SCATTER!
WE'LL STAY!
WE'VE GOT TROUBLE, BUT THEY'RE ONLY AFTER US!
HOW DO THEY KEEP FINDING US?
?
WHAT THE HECK IS THAT?!

ROBOTS.

YOU GUYS SHOULD SPLIT!

HOLY MOTHER...

WHOA, THEY DO HAVE WINGS!

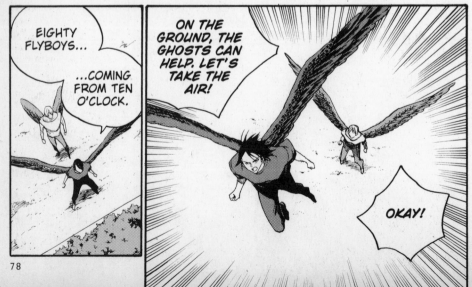

EIGHTY FLYBOYS...

...COMING FROM TEN O'CLOCK.

ON THE GROUND, THE GHOSTS CAN HELP. LET'S TAKE THE AIR!

OKAY!

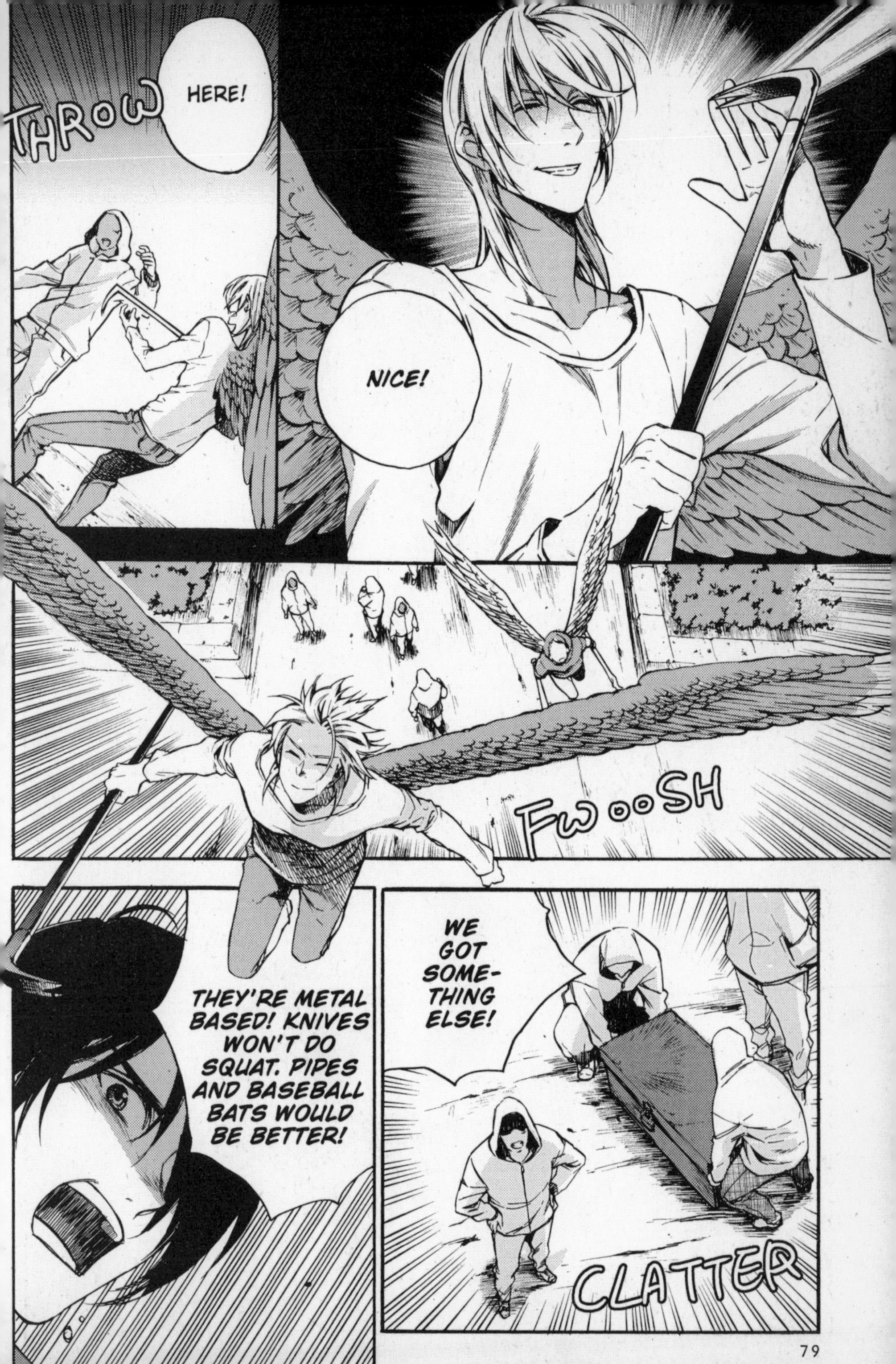
NICE!
HERE!
THROW
FWOOSH
THEY'RE METAL BASED! KNIVES WON'T DO SQUAT. PIPES AND BASEBALL BATS WOULD BE BETTER!
WE GOT SOMETHING ELSE!
CLATTER

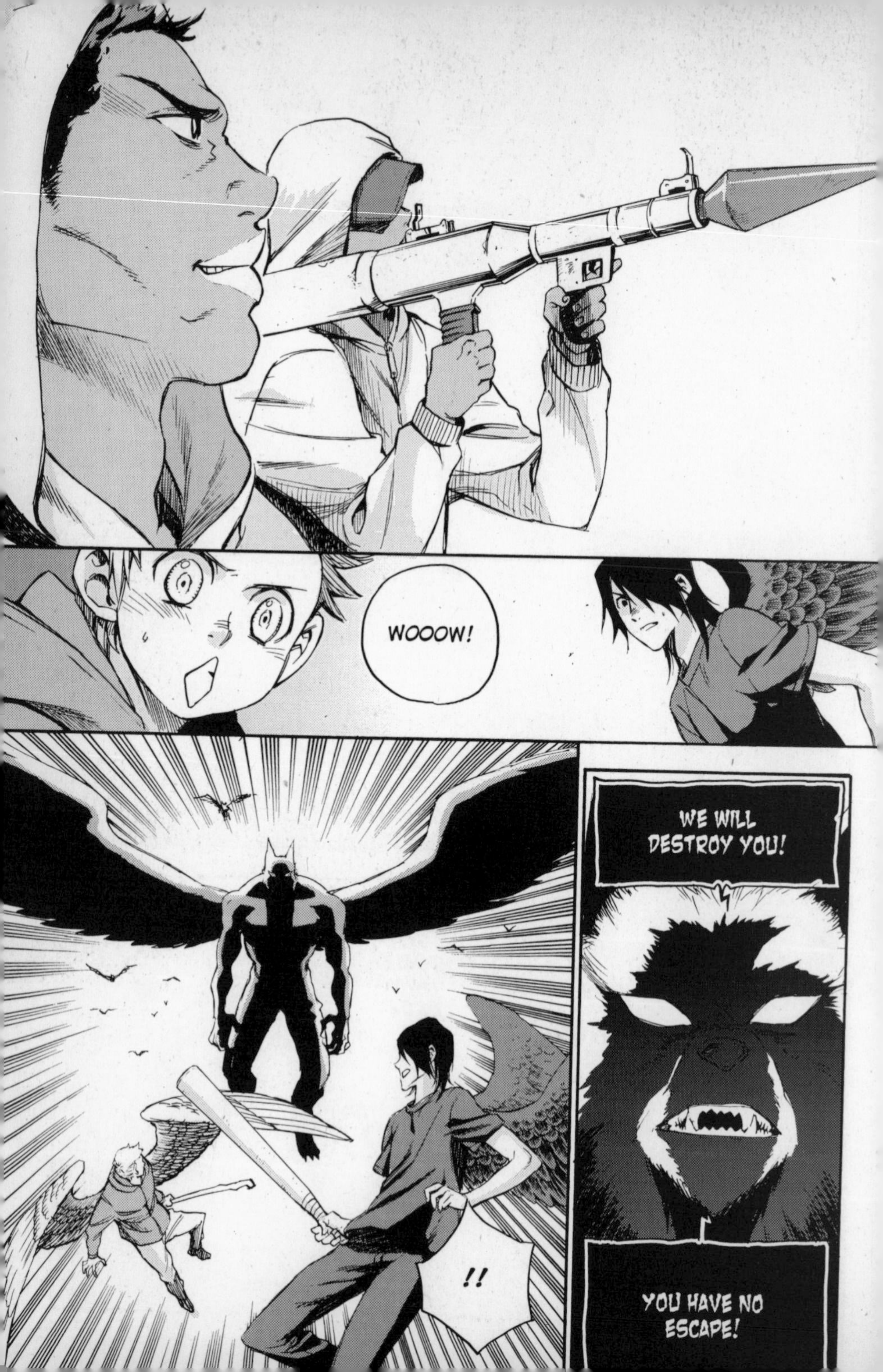
WOOOW!
WE WILL DESTROY YOU!
YOU HAVE NO ESCAPE!
!!

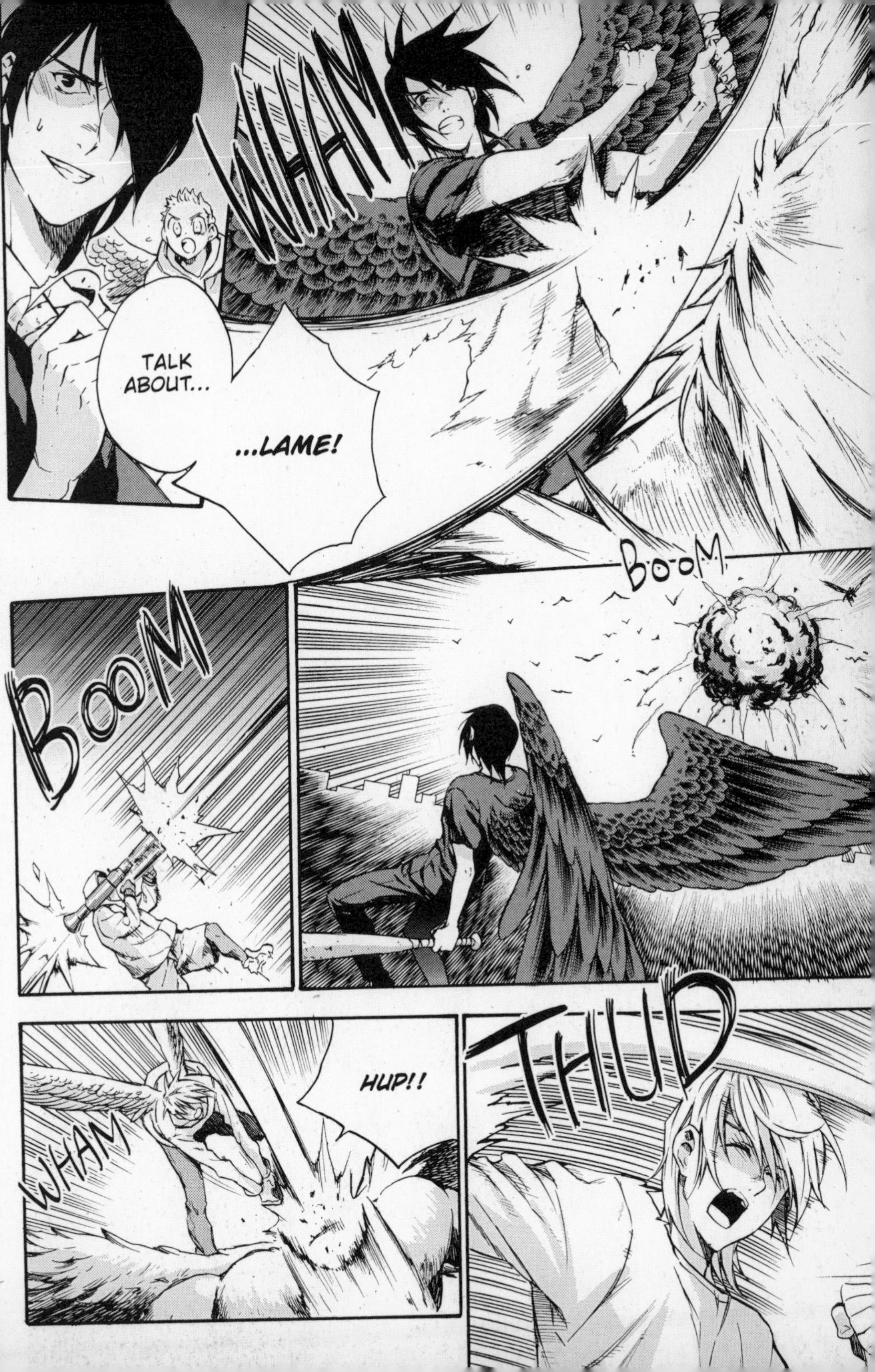
WHAM
TALK ABOUT...
...LAME!
BOOM
BOOM
HUP!!
WHAM
THUD

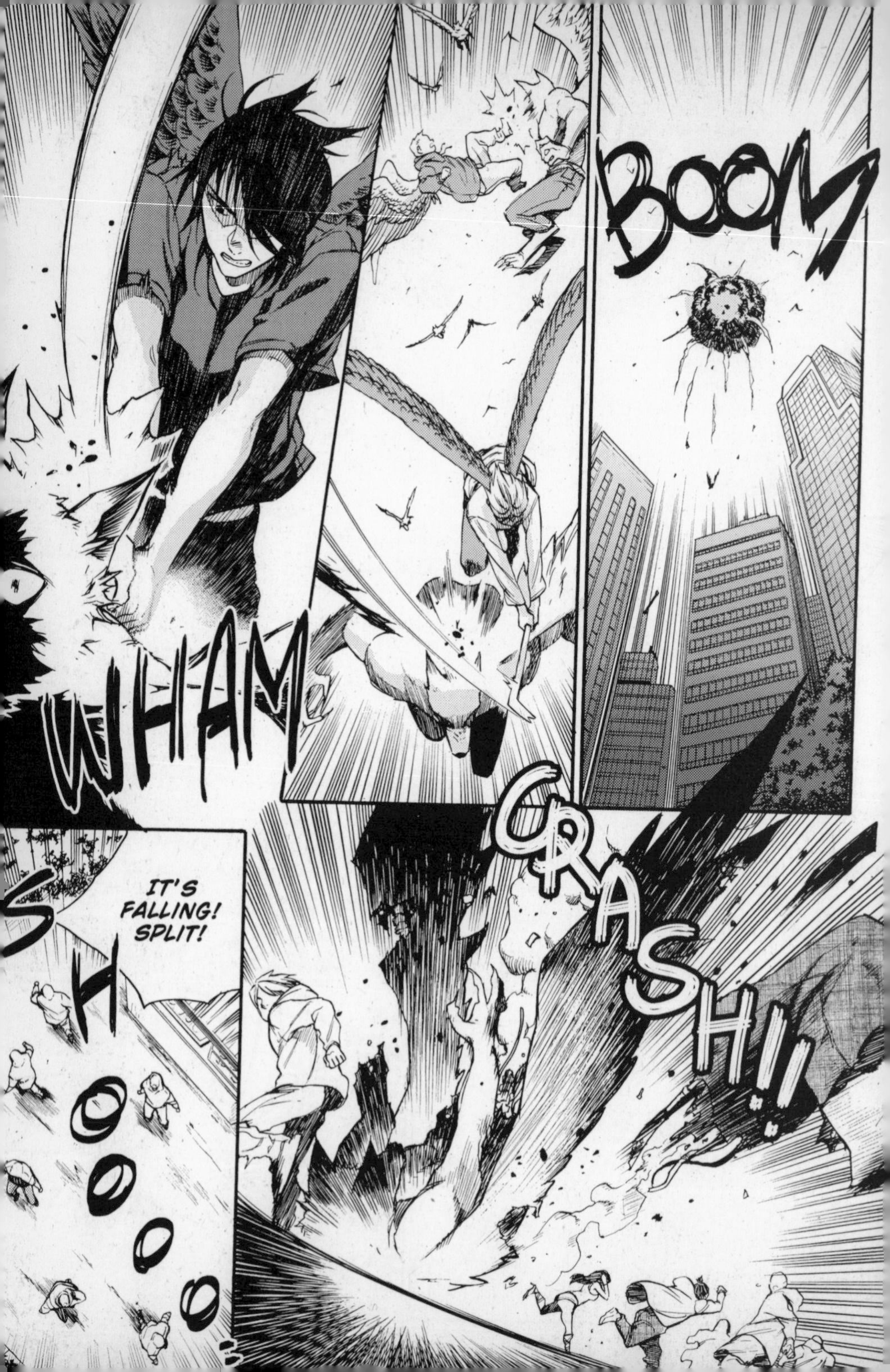
WHAM
BOOM
IT'S FALLING! SPLIT!
SHOOOOO
CRASH!!

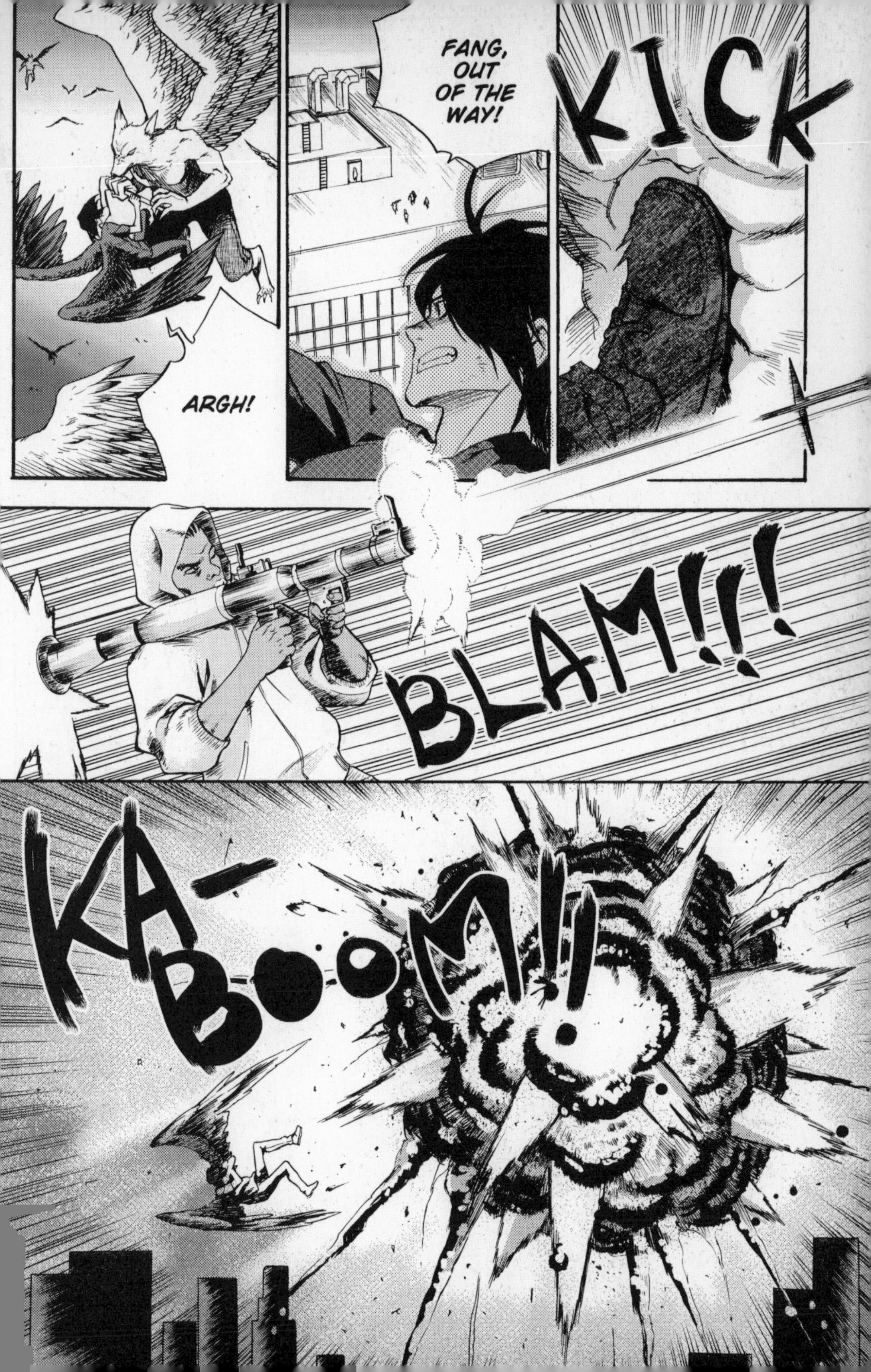
ARGH!
FANG, OUT OF THE WAY!
KICK
BLAM!!!
KA-BOOM!!

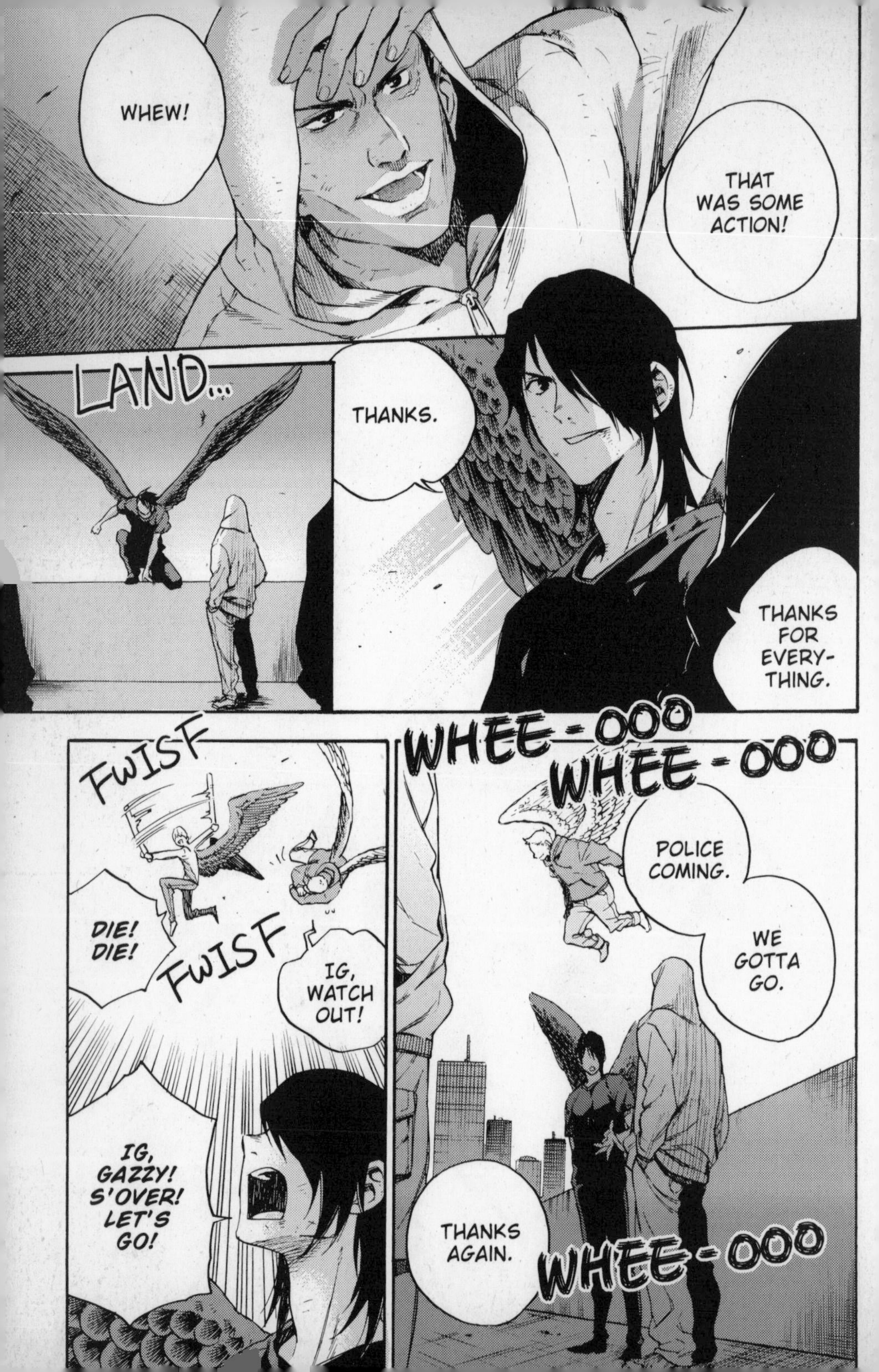
WHEW!
THAT WAS SOME ACTION!
LAND...
THANKS.
THANKS FOR EVERY-THING.
FWISF
DIE! DIE!
FWISF
IG, WATCH OUT!
IG, GAZZY! S'OVER! LET'S GO!
WHEE-OOO
WHEE-OOO
POLICE COMING.
WE GOTTA GO.
THANKS AGAIN.
WHEE-OOO

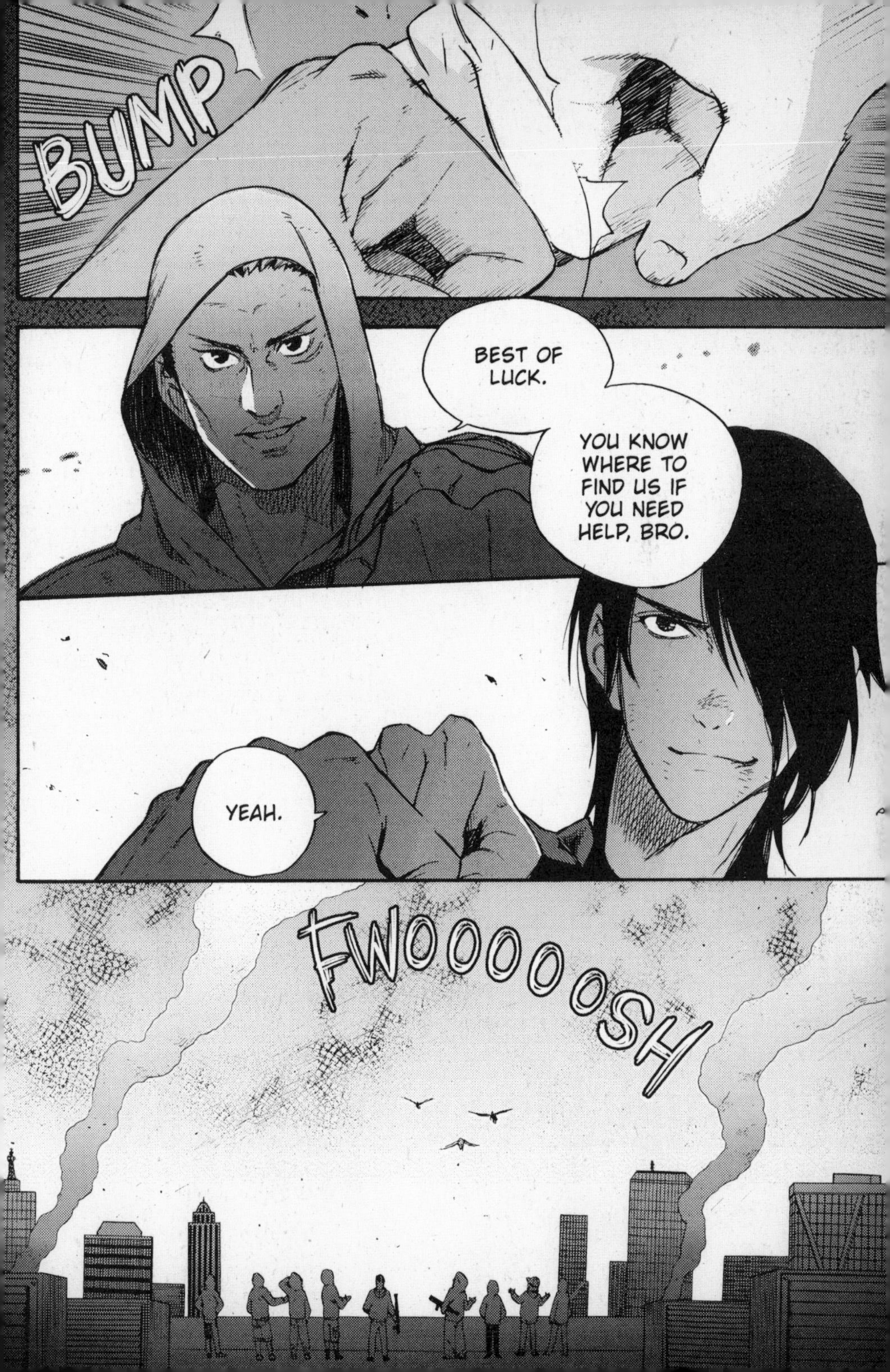
BUMP
BEST OF LUCK.
YOU KNOW WHERE TO FIND US IF YOU NEED HELP, BRO.
YEAH.
FWOOOOOSH

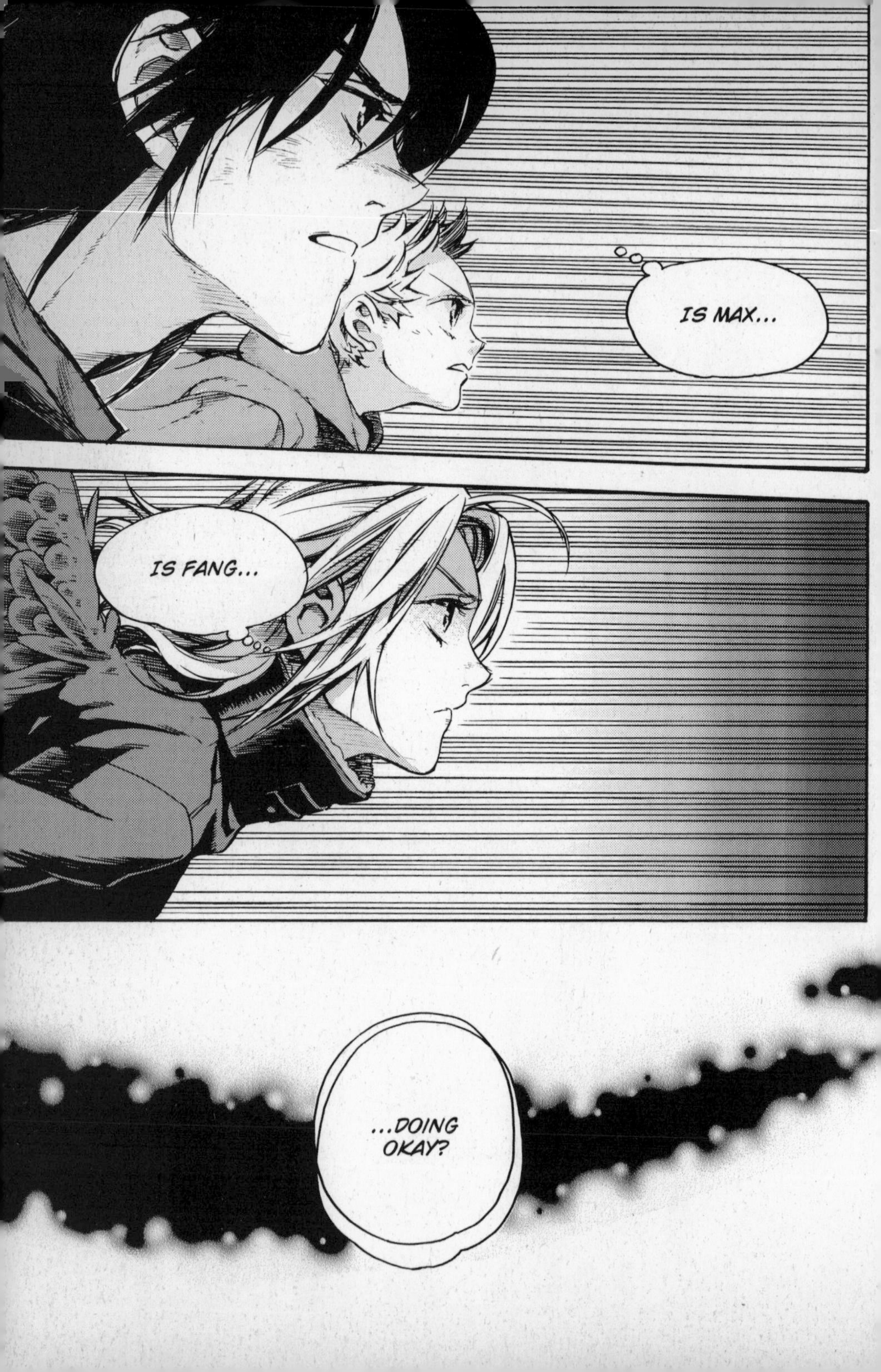
IS MAX...
IS FANG...
...DOING OKAY?

MAXIMUM
RIDE

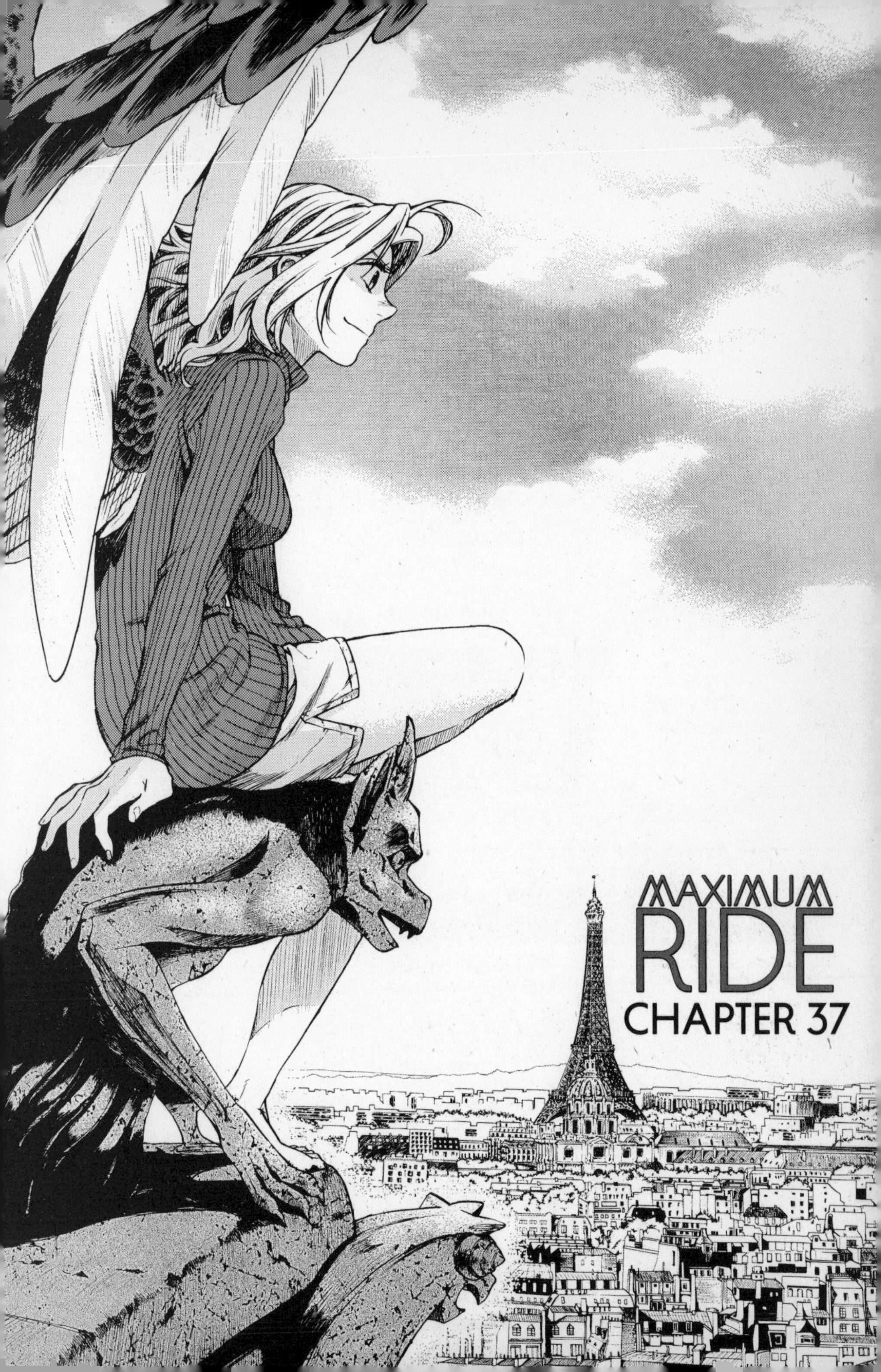
MAXIMUM
RIDE
CHAPTER 37

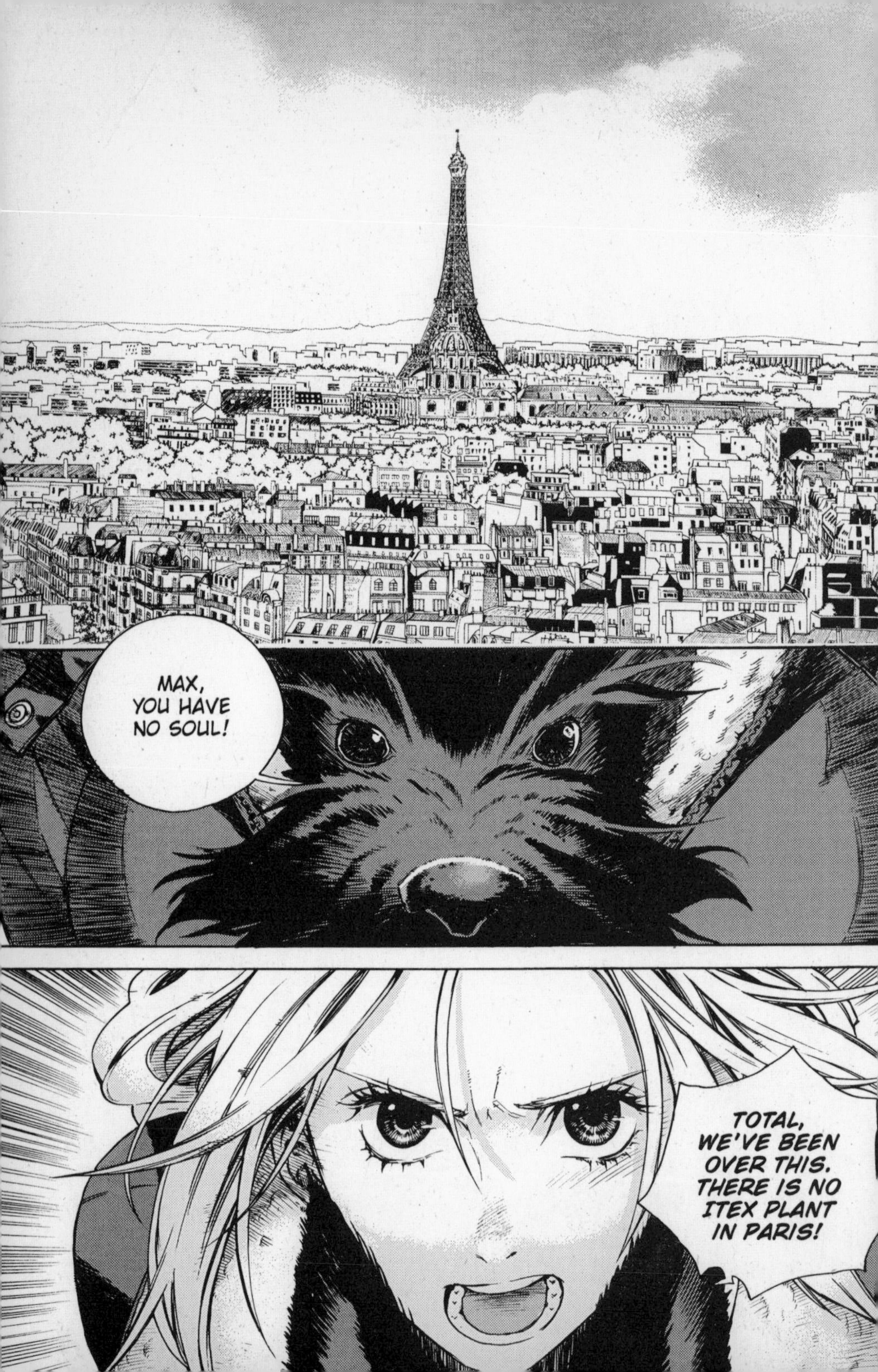
MAX, YOU HAVE NO SOUL!
TOTAL, WE'VE BEEN OVER THIS. THERE IS NO ITEX PLANT IN PARIS!

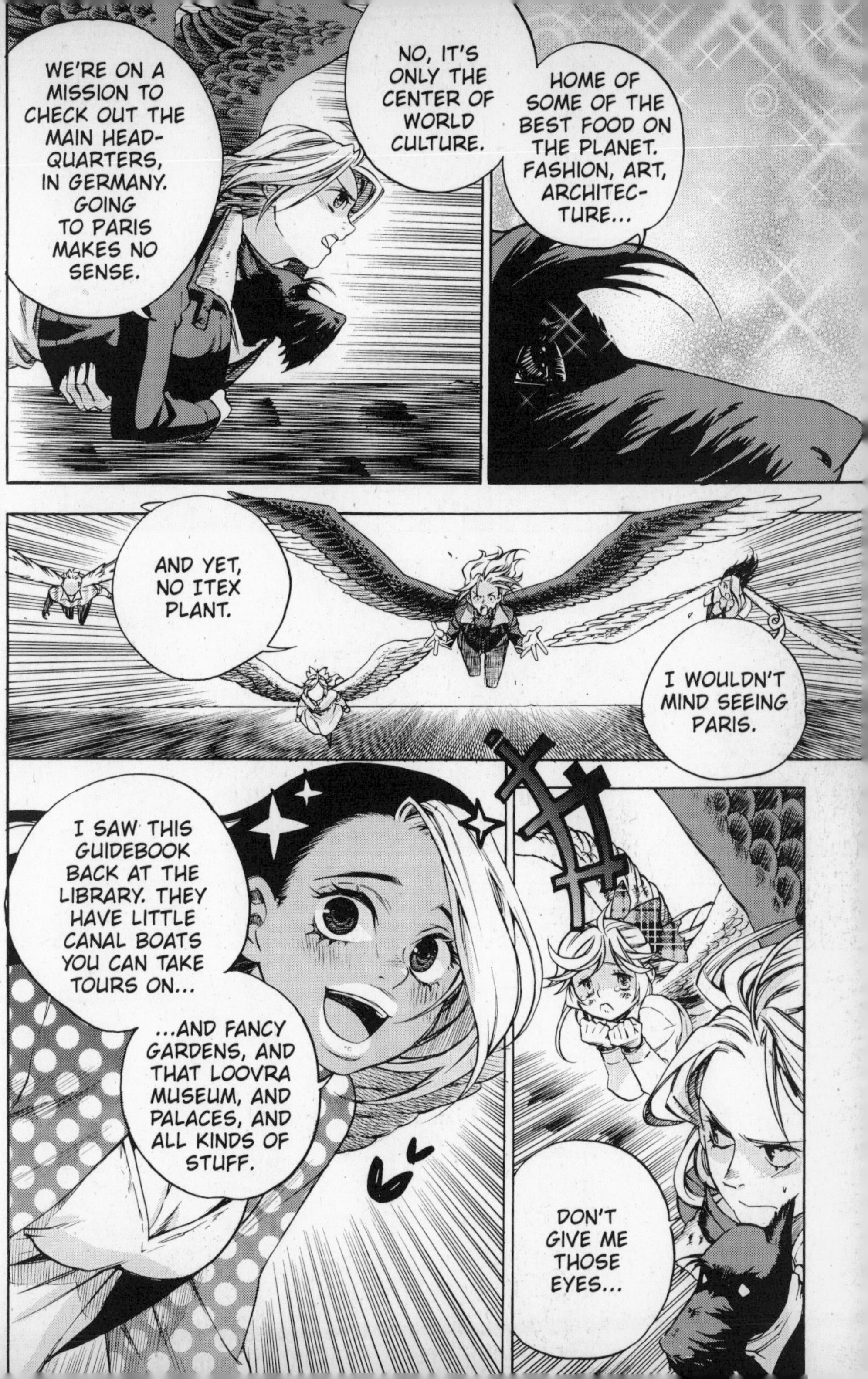
WE'RE ON A MISSION TO CHECK OUT THE MAIN HEAD-QUARTERS, IN GERMANY. GOING TO PARIS MAKES NO SENSE.
NO, IT'S ONLY THE CENTER OF WORLD CULTURE.
HOME OF SOME OF THE BEST FOOD ON THE PLANET. FASHION, ART, ARCHITEC-TURE...
AND YET, NO ITEX PLANT.
I WOULDN'T MIND SEEING PARIS.
I SAW THIS GUIDEBOOK BACK AT THE LIBRARY. THEY HAVE LITTLE CANAL BOATS YOU CAN TAKE TOURS ON...
...AND FANCY GARDENS, AND THAT LOOVRA MUSEUM, AND PALACES, AND ALL KINDS OF STUFF.
DON'T GIVE ME THOSE EYES...

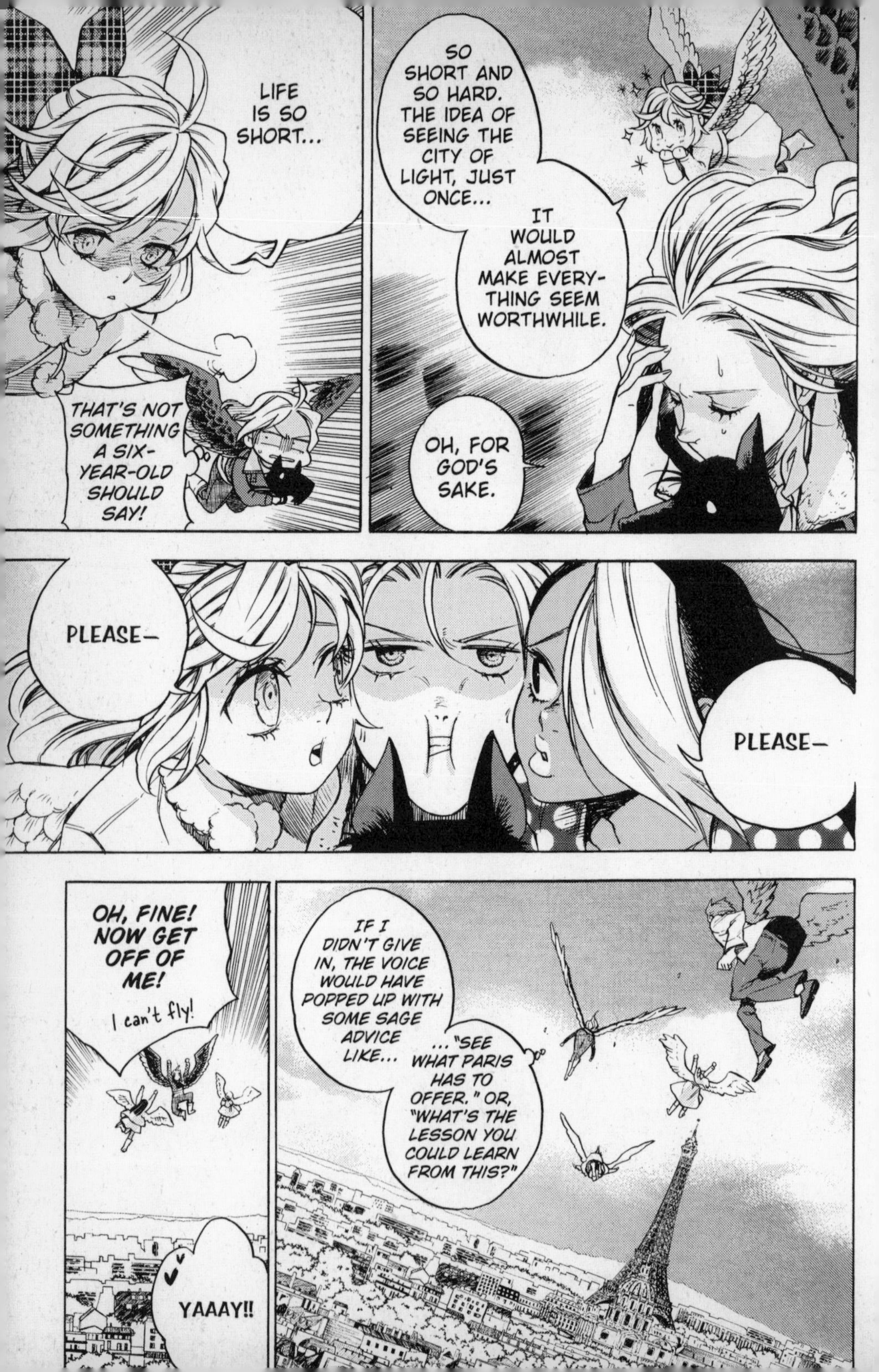
LIFE IS SO SHORT...
SO SHORT AND SO HARD. THE IDEA OF SEEING THE CITY OF LIGHT, JUST ONCE...
IT WOULD ALMOST MAKE EVERY-THING SEEM WORTHWHILE.
THAT'S NOT SOMETHING A SIX-YEAR-OLD SHOULD SAY!
OH, FOR GOD'S SAKE.
PLEASE—
PLEASE—
OH, FINE! NOW GET OFF OF ME!
I can't fly!
IF I DIDN'T GIVE IN, THE VOICE WOULD HAVE POPPED UP WITH SOME SAGE ADVICE LIKE...
..."SEE WHAT PARIS HAS TO OFFER." OR, "WHAT'S THE LESSON YOU COULD LEARN FROM THIS?"
YAAAY!!

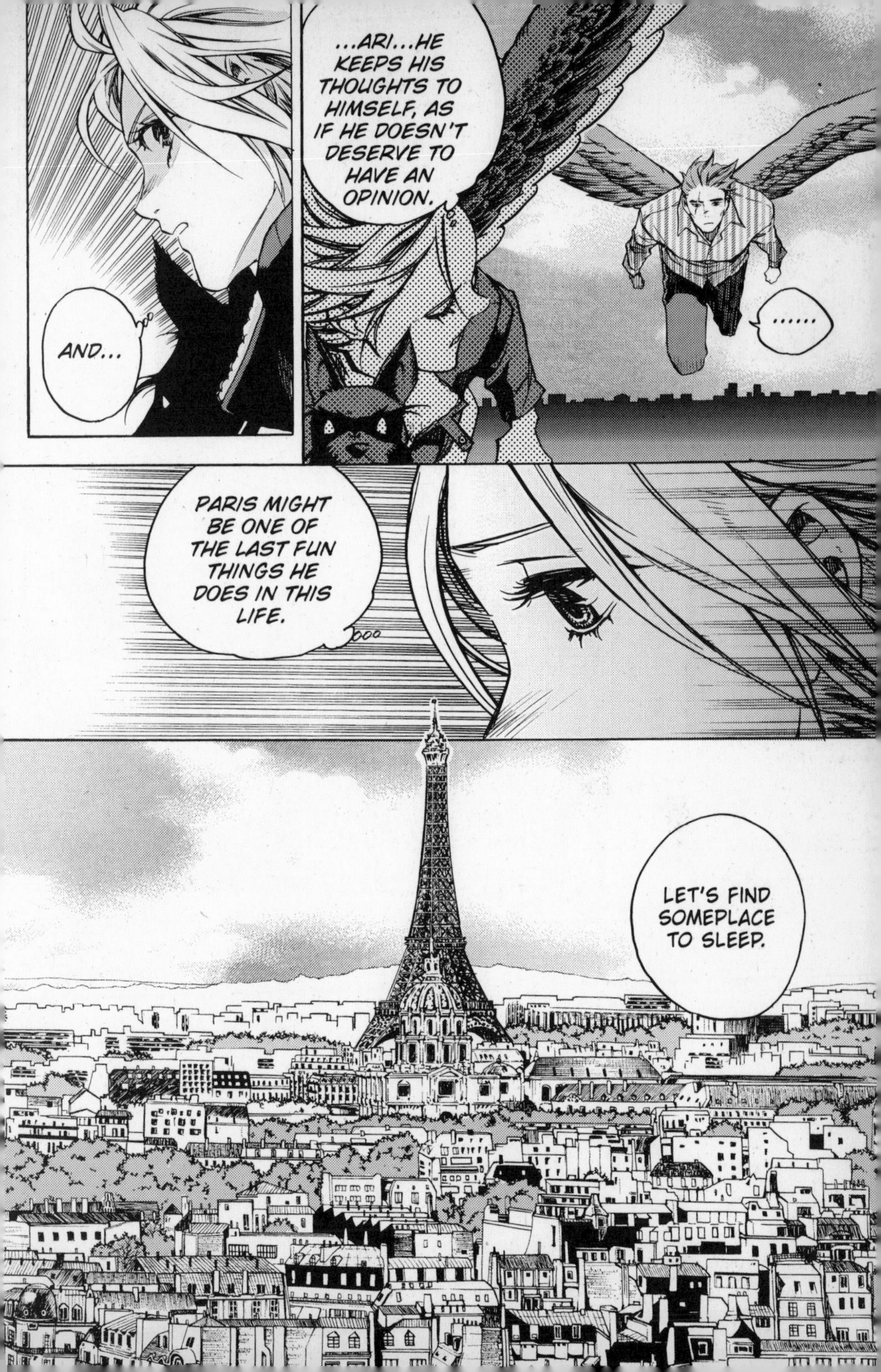
...ARI...HE KEEPS HIS THOUGHTS TO HIMSELF, AS IF HE DOESN'T DESERVE TO HAVE AN OPINION.
AND...
......
PARIS MIGHT BE ONE OF THE LAST FUN THINGS HE DOES IN THIS LIFE.
LET'S FIND SOMEPLACE TO SLEEP.

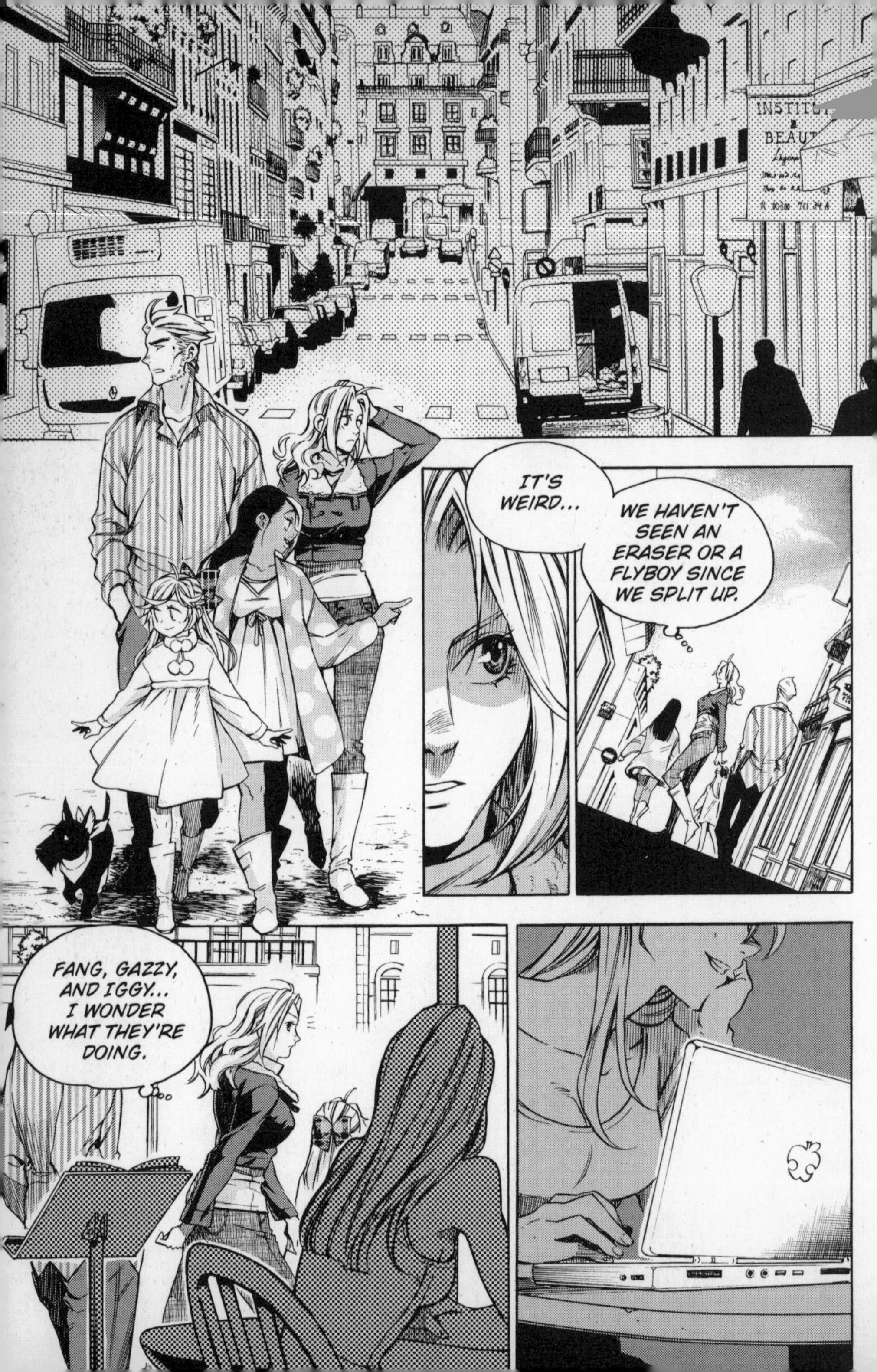
INSTITU
BEAUT
IT'S WEIRD...
WE HAVEN'T SEEN AN ERASER OR A FLYBOY SINCE WE SPLIT UP.
FANG, GAZZY, AND IGGY... I WONDER WHAT THEY'RE DOING.

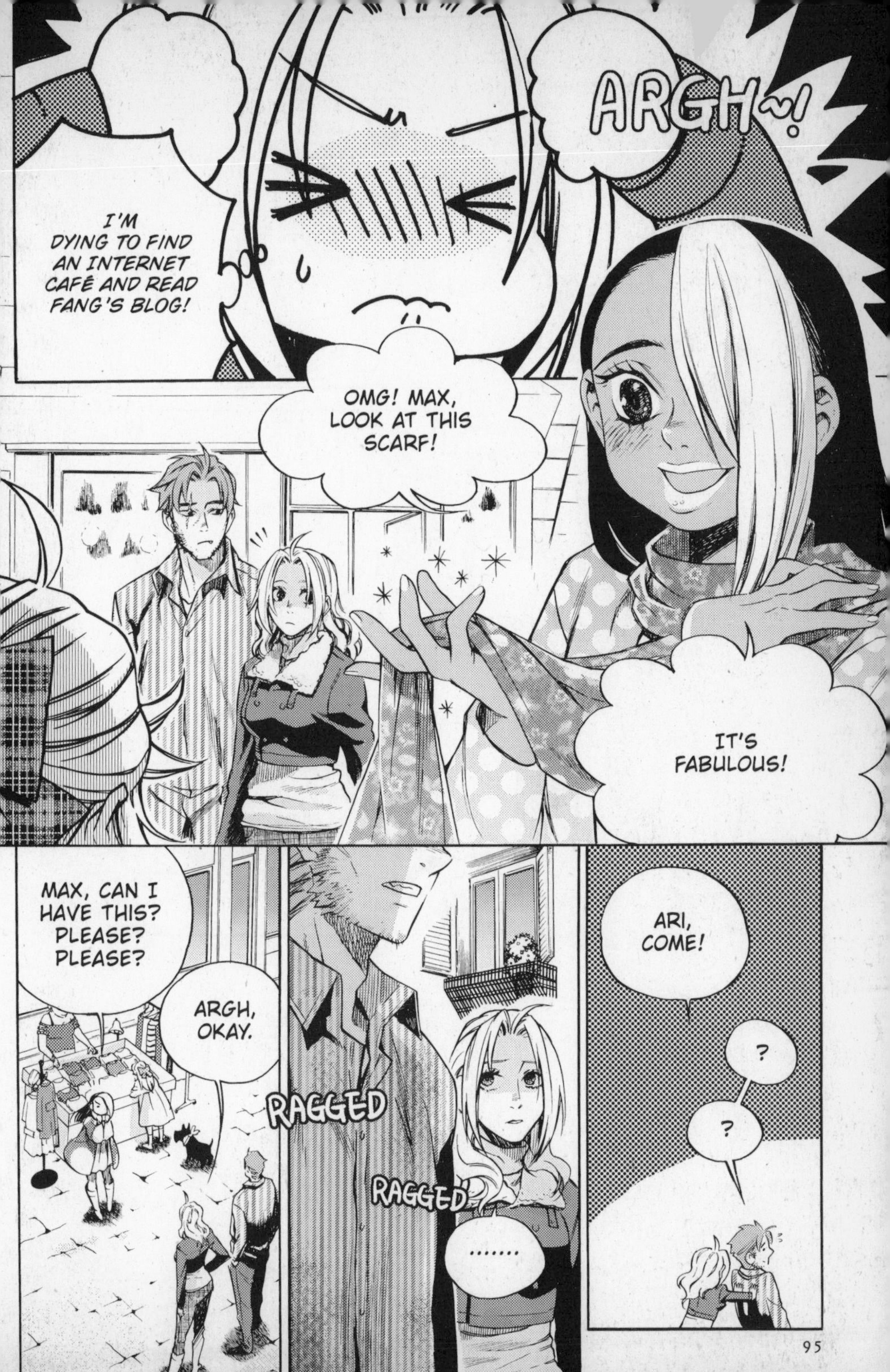
ARGH~!
I'M DYING TO FIND AN INTERNET CAFÉ AND READ FANG'S BLOG!
OMG! MAX, LOOK AT THIS SCARF!
IT'S FABULOUS!
MAX, CAN I HAVE THIS? PLEASE? PLEASE?
ARGH, OKAY.
RAGGED
RAGGED
....
ARI, COME!
?
?

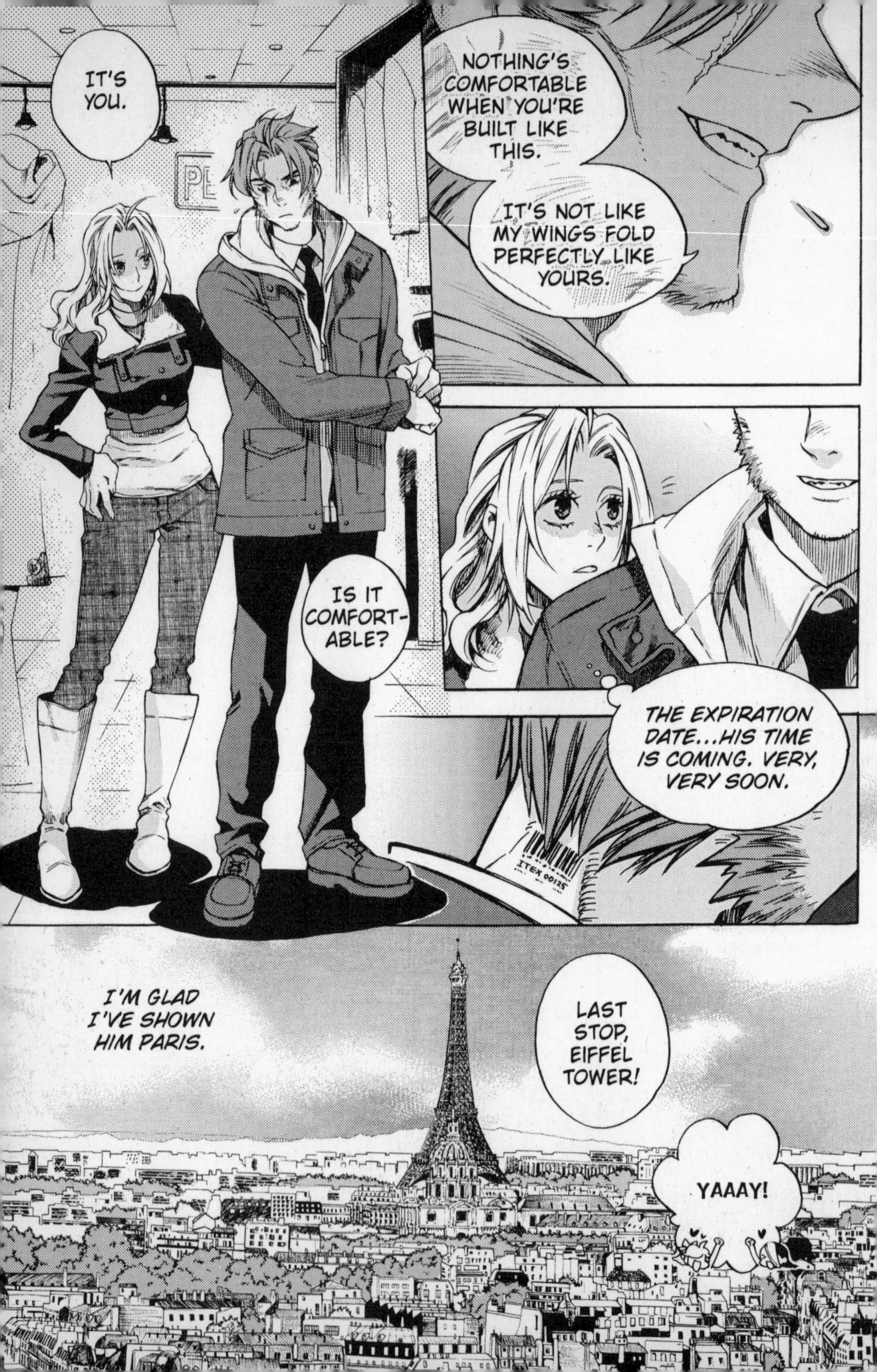
IT'S YOU.
IS IT COMFORT-ABLE?
NOTHING'S COMFORTABLE WHEN YOU'RE BUILT LIKE THIS.
IT'S NOT LIKE MY WINGS FOLD PERFECTLY LIKE YOURS.
THE EXPIRATION DATE...HIS TIME IS COMING. VERY, VERY SOON.
I'M GLAD I'VE SHOWN HIM PARIS.
LAST STOP, EIFFEL TOWER!
YAAAY!

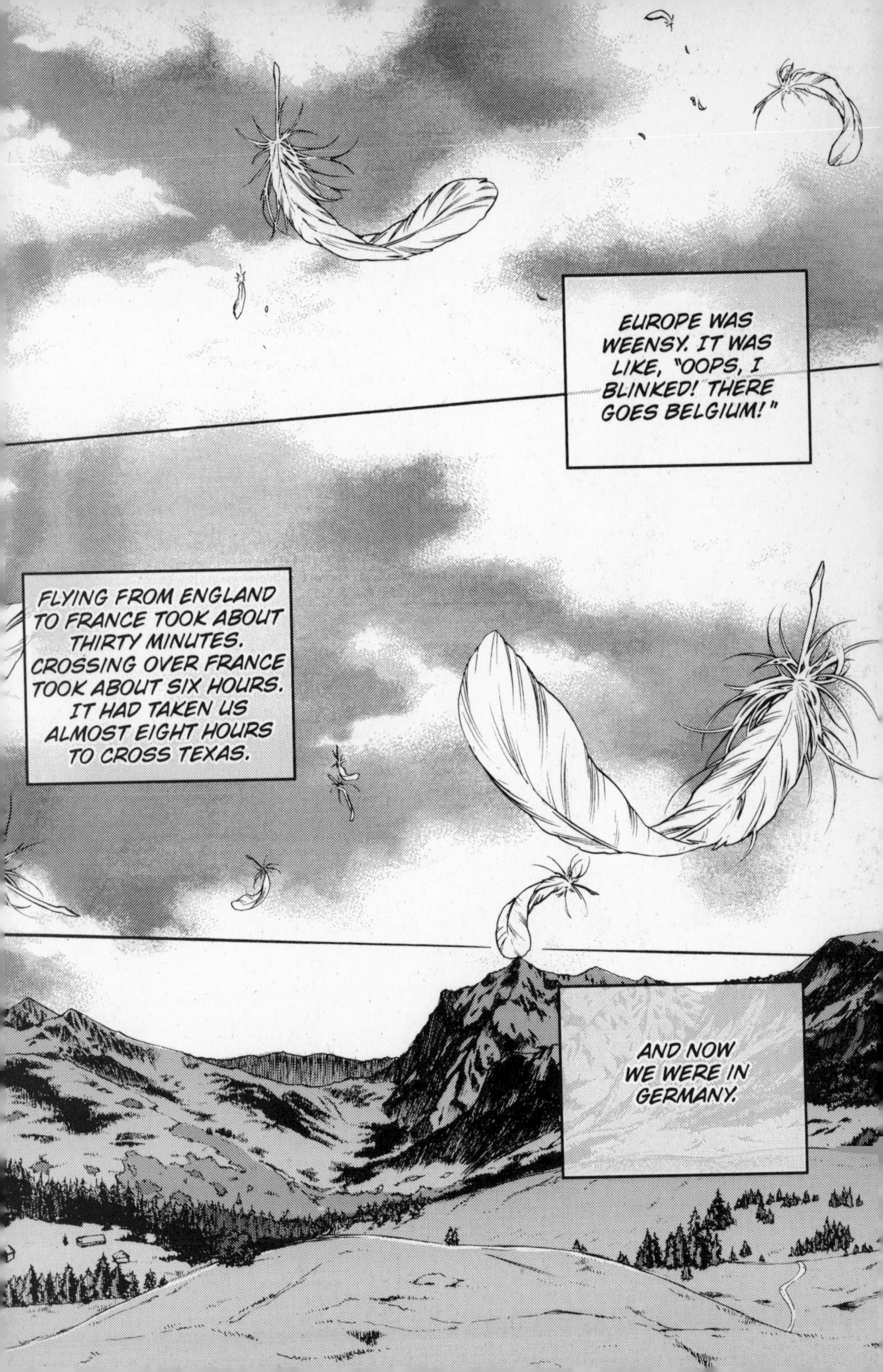
EUROPE WAS WEENSY. IT WAS LIKE, "OOPS, I BLINKED! THERE GOES BELGIUM!"
FLYING FROM ENGLAND TO FRANCE TOOK ABOUT THIRTY MINUTES. CROSSING OVER FRANCE TOOK ABOUT SIX HOURS. IT HAD TAKEN US ALMOST EIGHT HOURS TO CROSS TEXAS.
AND NOW WE WERE IN GERMANY.

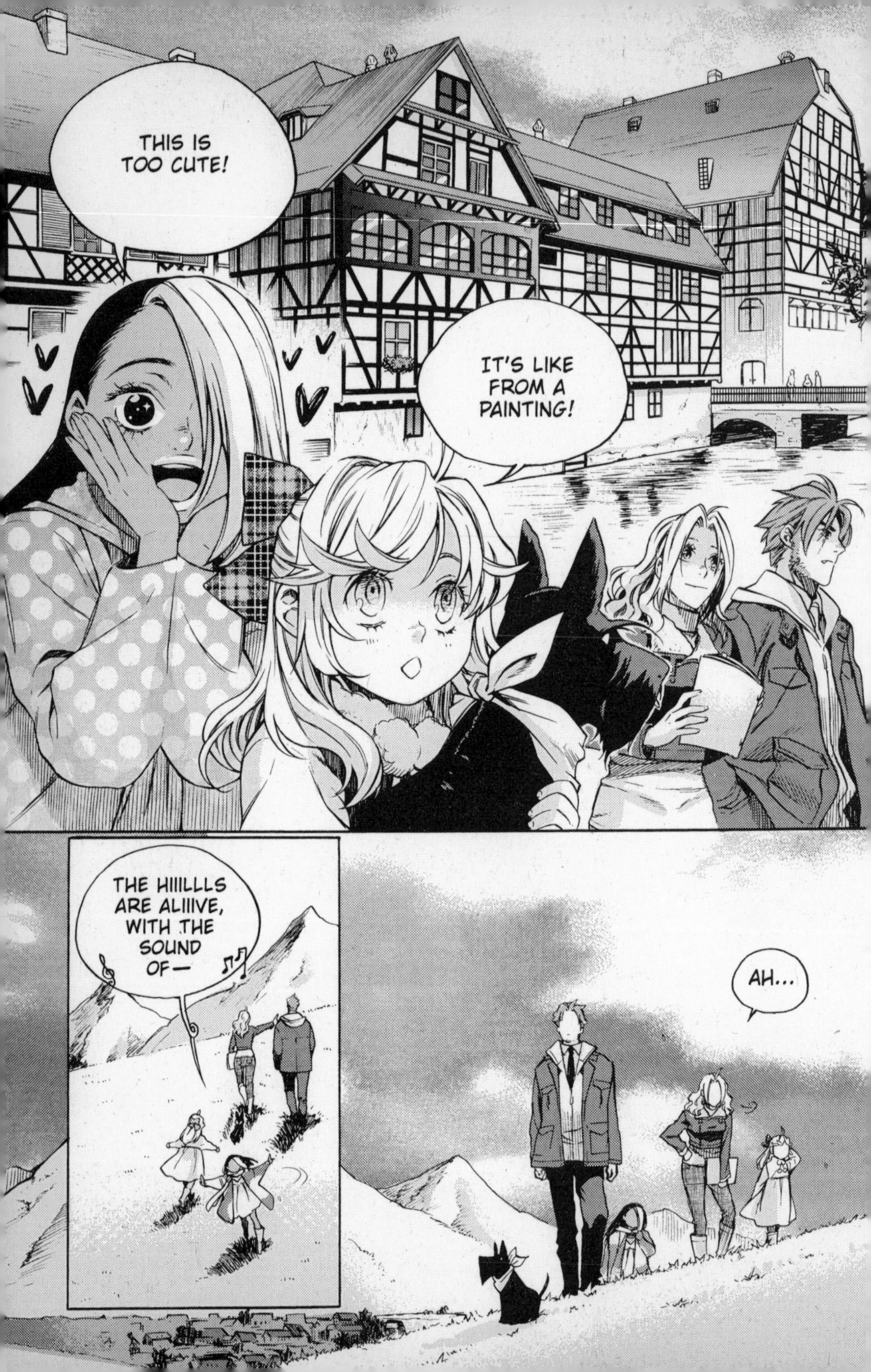
THIS IS TOO CUTE!
IT'S LIKE FROM A PAINTING!
AH...
THE HIIILLLS ARE ALIIIVE, WITH THE SOUND OF—

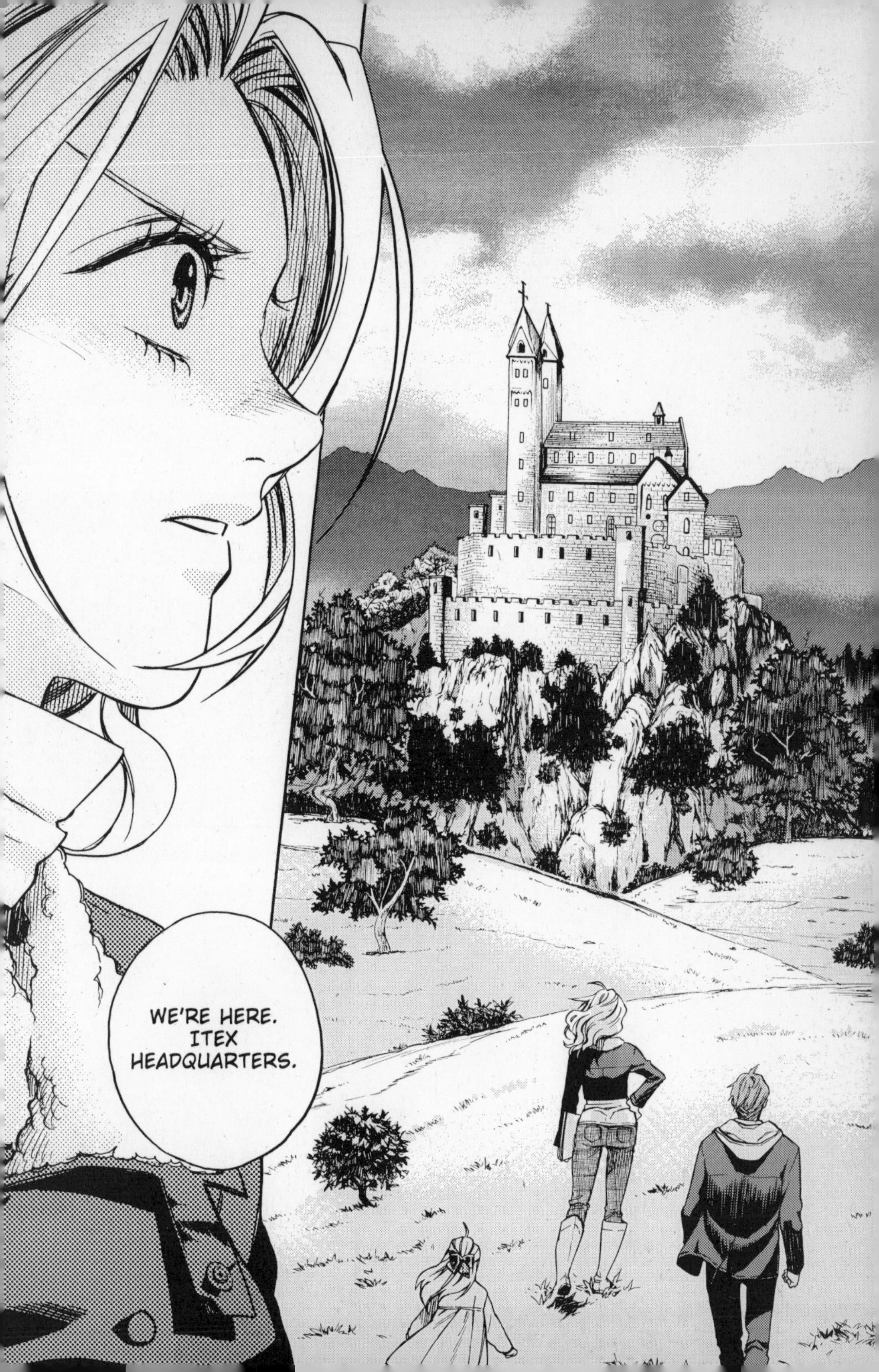
WE'RE HERE. ITEX HEADQUARTERS.

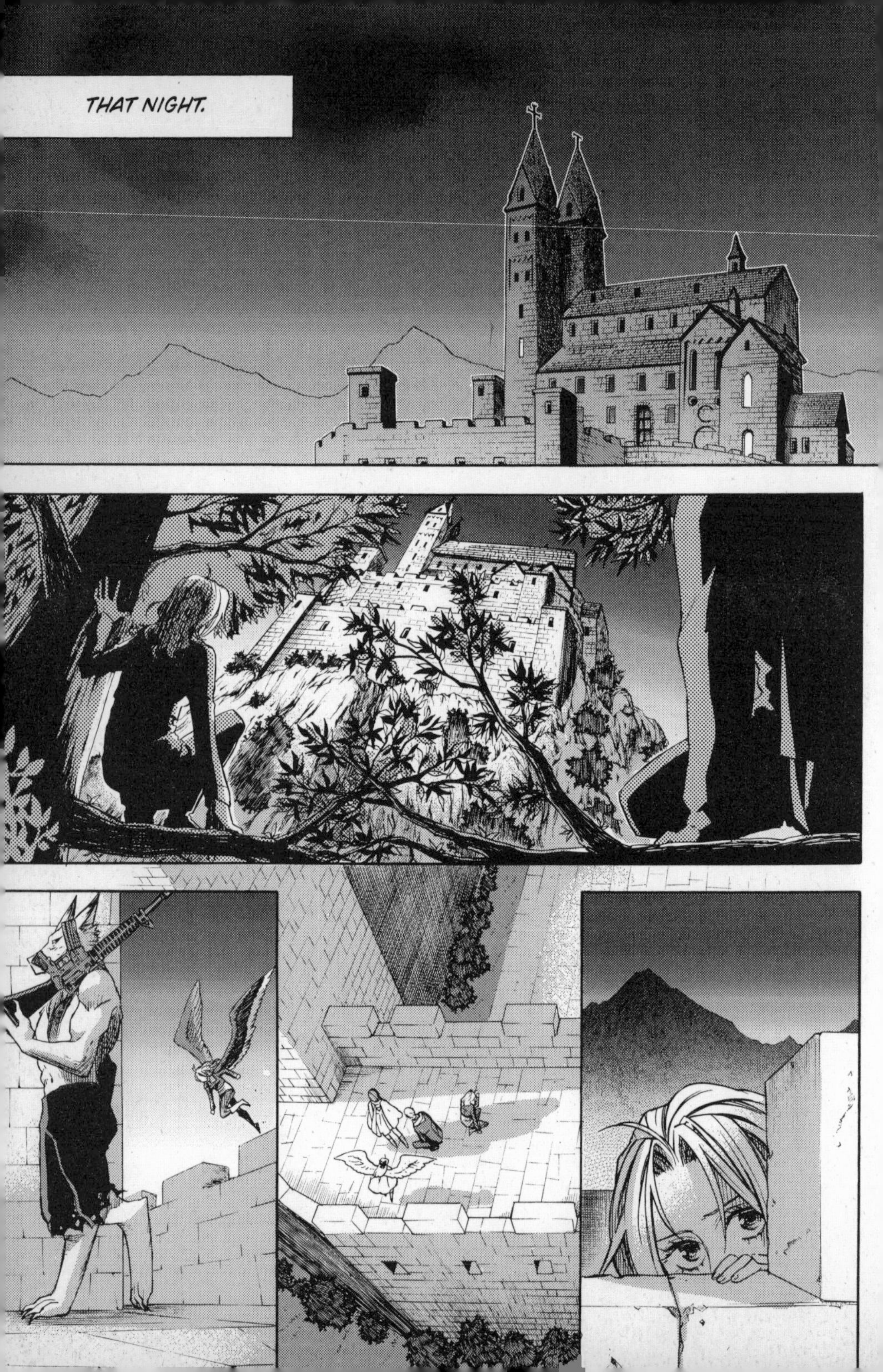
THAT NIGHT.

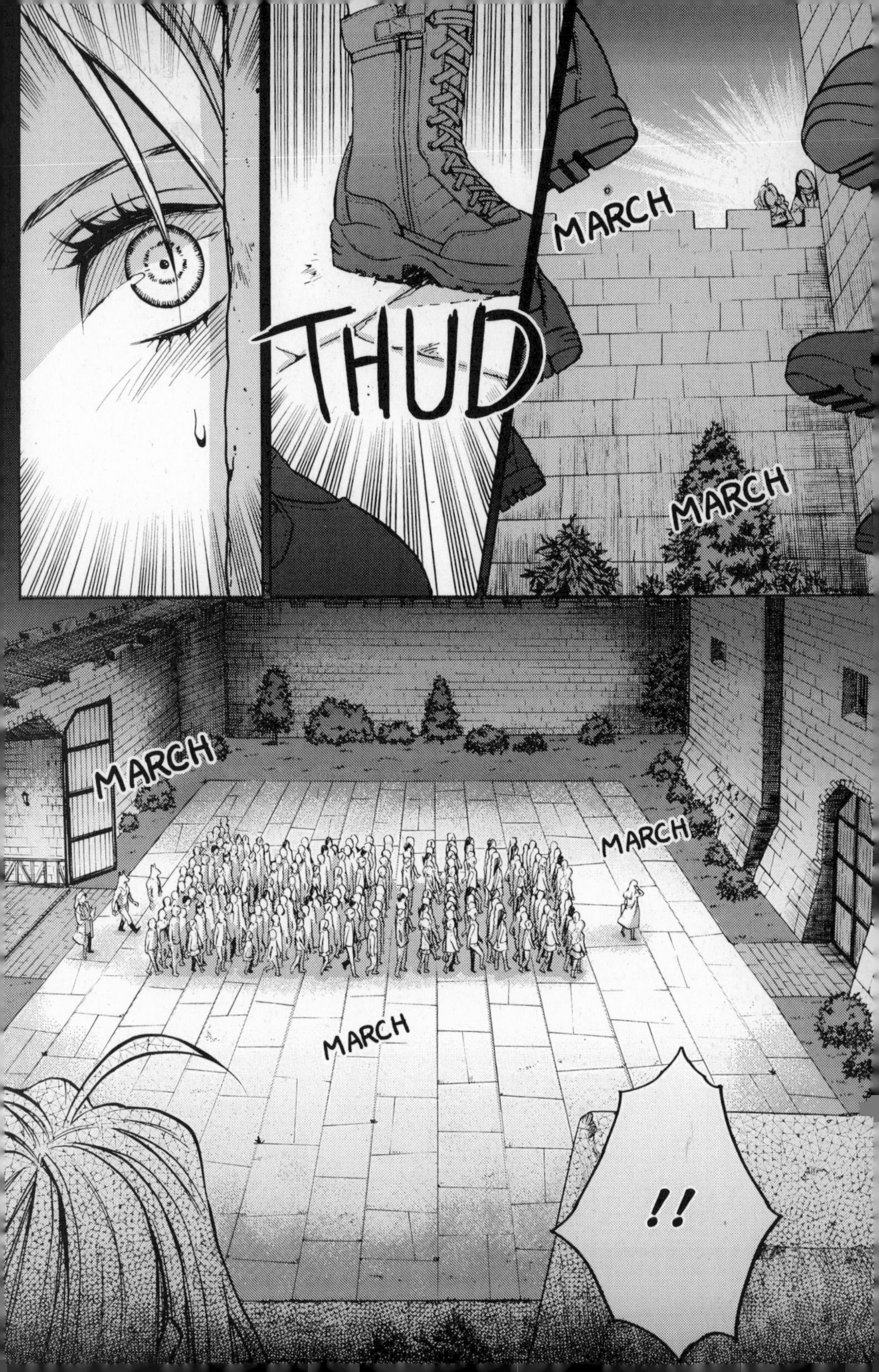
MARCH
MARCH
THUD
MARCH
MARCH
MARCH
!!

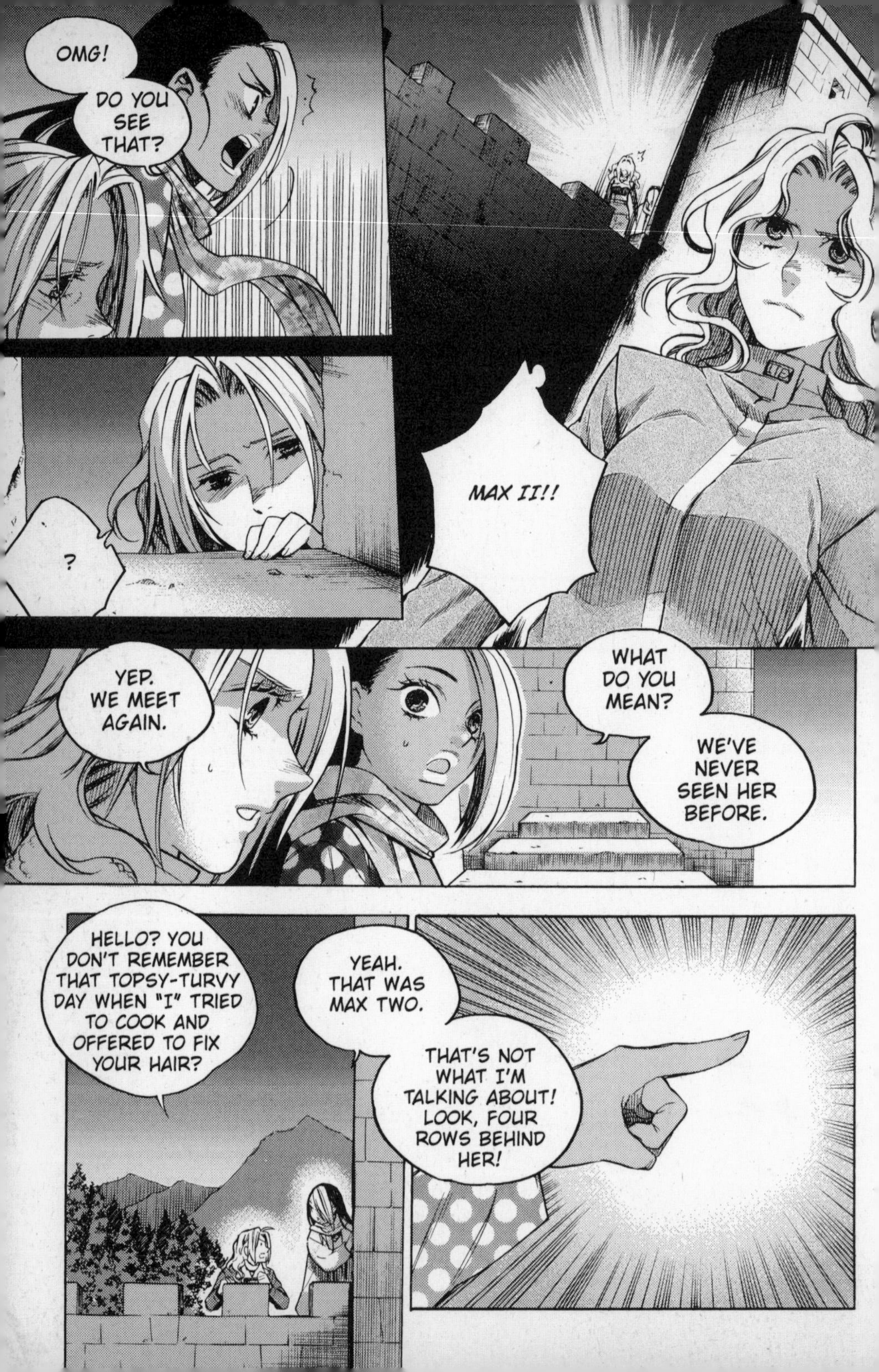
OMG!
DO YOU SEE THAT?
?
MAX II!!
YEP. WE MEET AGAIN.
WHAT DO YOU MEAN?
WE'VE NEVER SEEN HER BEFORE.
HELLO? YOU DON'T REMEMBER THAT TOPSY-TURVY DAY WHEN "I" TRIED TO COOK AND OFFERED TO FIX YOUR HAIR?
YEAH. THAT WAS MAX TWO.
THAT'S NOT WHAT I'M TALKING ABOUT! LOOK, FOUR ROWS BEHIND HER!

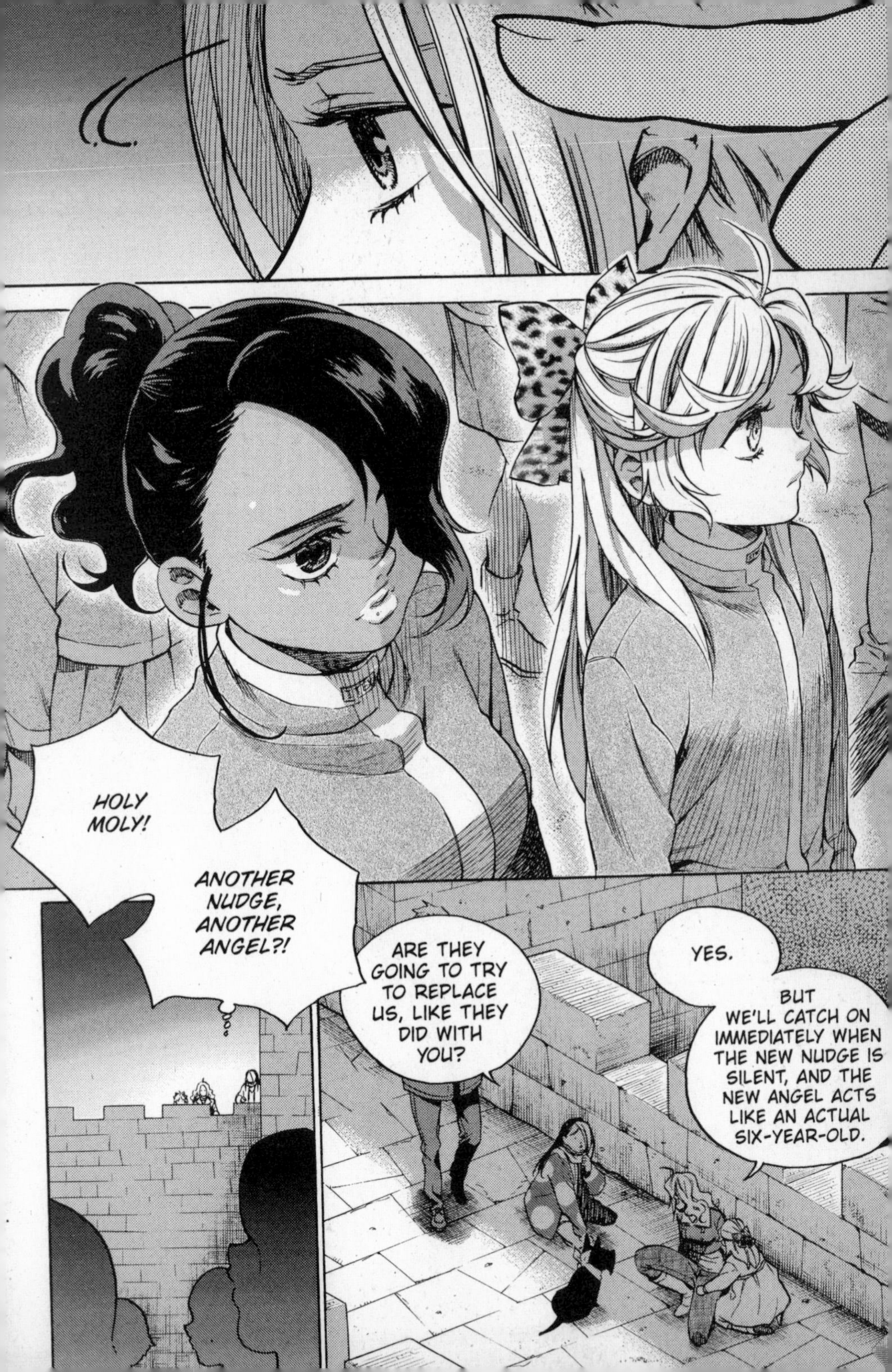
HOLY MOLY!
ANOTHER NUDGE, ANOTHER ANGEL?!
YES.
BUT WE'LL CATCH ON IMMEDIATELY WHEN THE NEW NUDGE IS SILENT, AND THE NEW ANGEL ACTS LIKE AN ACTUAL SIX-YEAR-OLD.
ARE THEY GOING TO TRY TO REPLACE US, LIKE THEY DID WITH YOU?

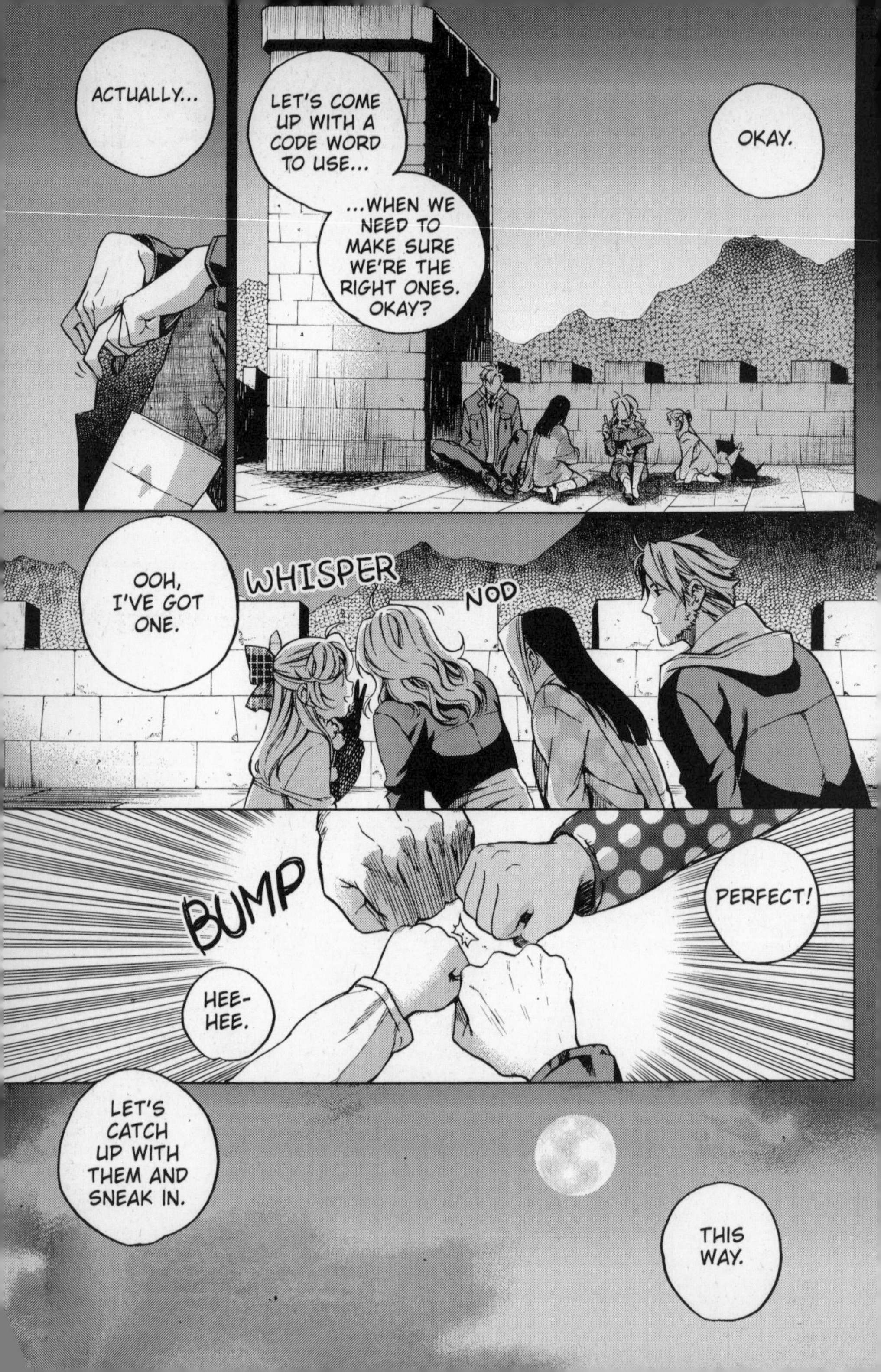
ACTUALLY...
LET'S COME UP WITH A CODE WORD TO USE...
...WHEN WE NEED TO MAKE SURE WE'RE THE RIGHT ONES. OKAY?
OKAY.
OOH, I'VE GOT ONE.
WHISPER
NOD
BUMP
PERFECT!
HEE-HEE.
LET'S CATCH UP WITH THEM AND SNEAK IN.
THIS WAY.

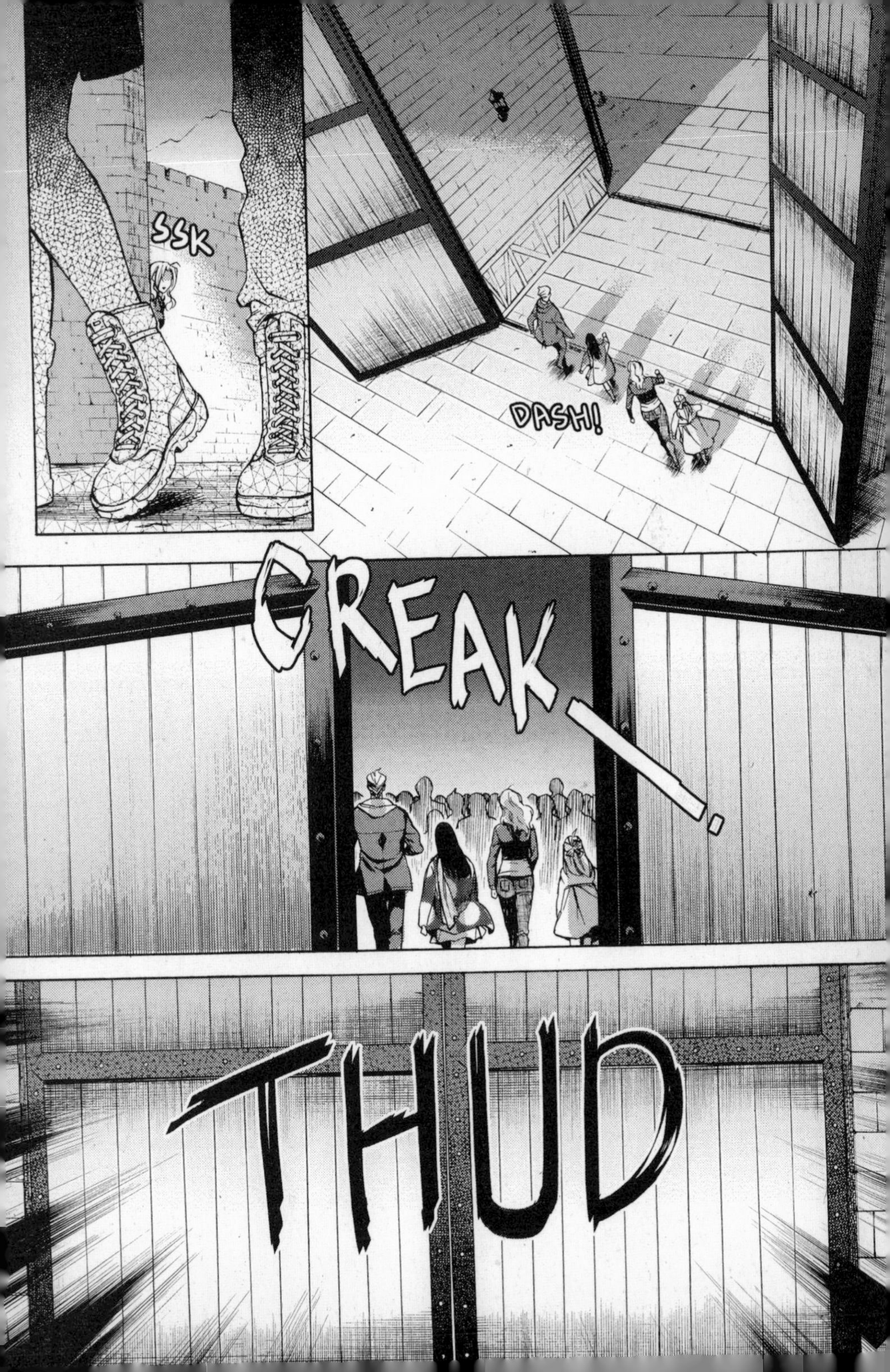
SSK
DASH!
CREAK...
THUD

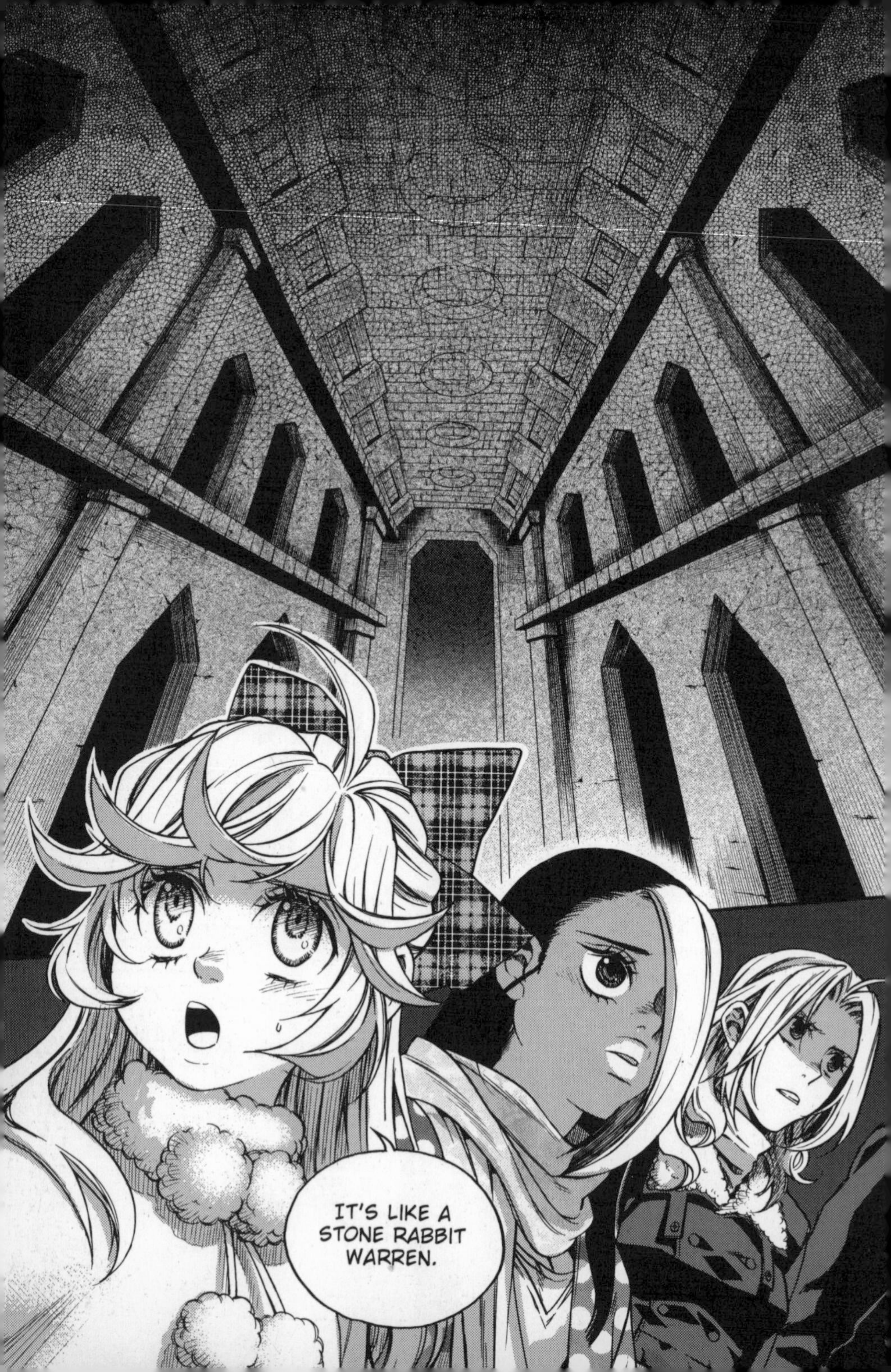
IT'S LIKE A STONE RABBIT WARREN.

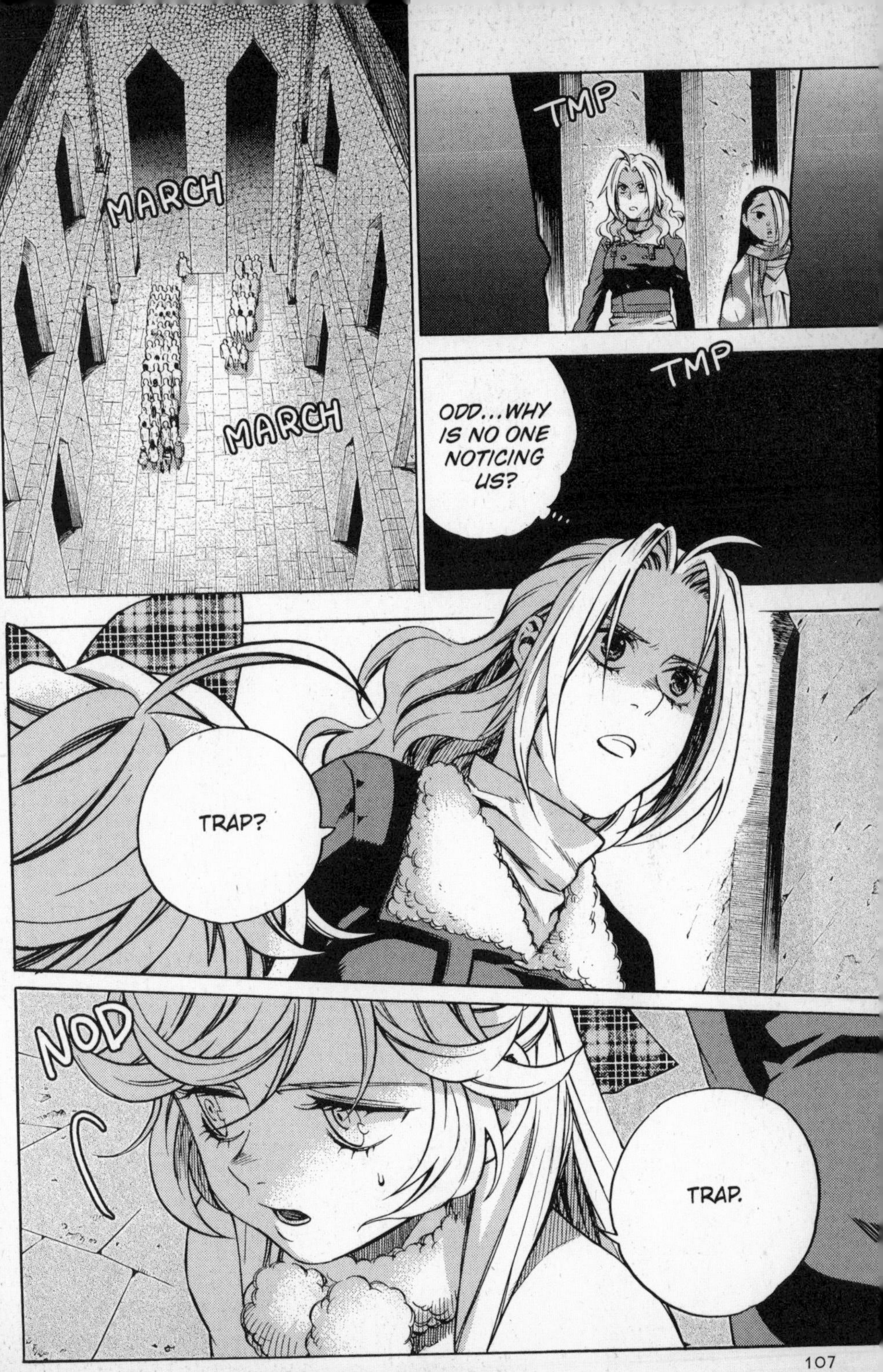
MARCH
MARCH
TMP
TMP
ODD...WHY IS NO ONE NOTICING US?
TRAP?
NOD
TRAP.

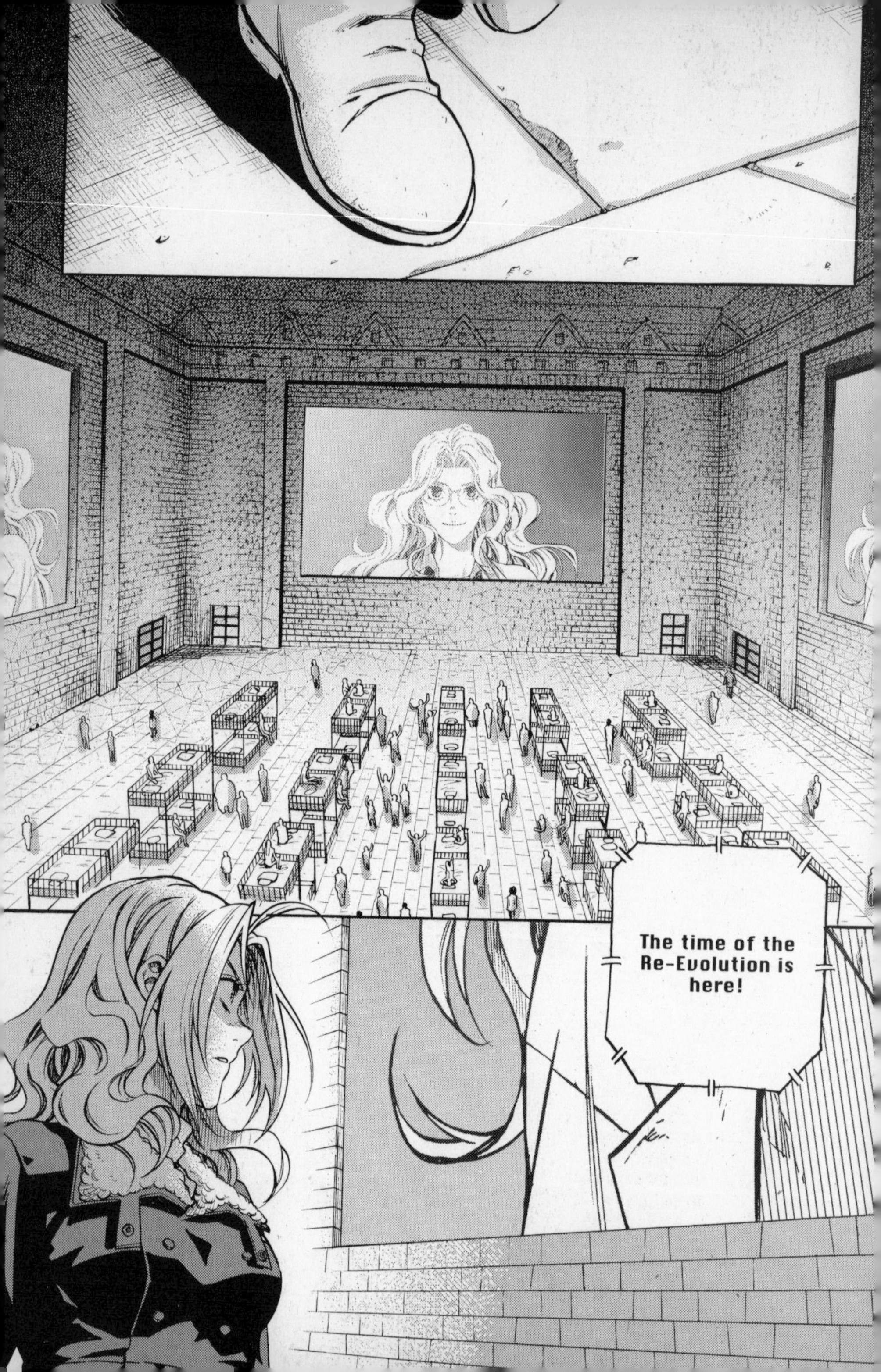
The time of the
Re-Evolution is
here!

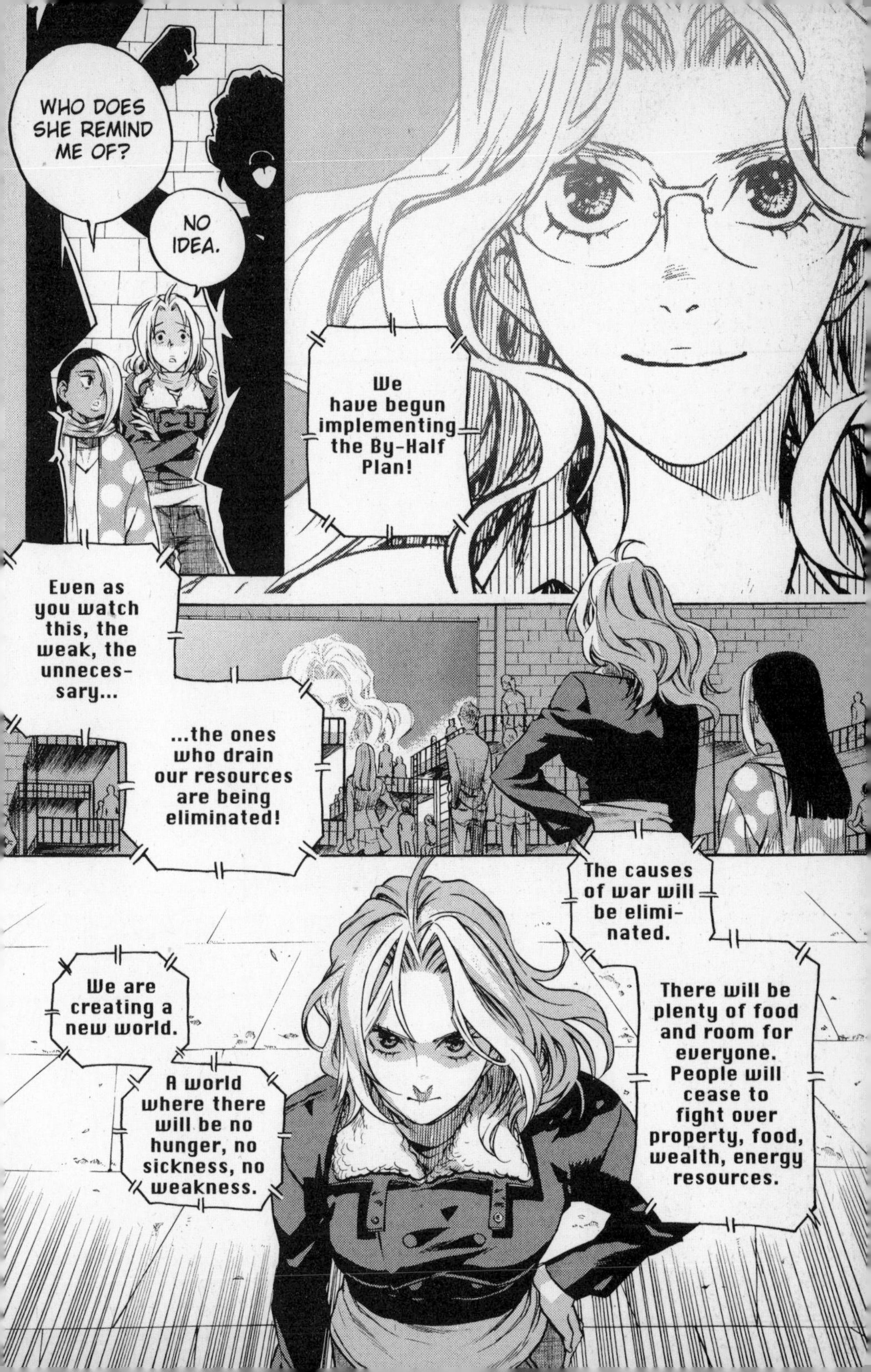
WHO DOES SHE REMIND ME OF?
NO IDEA.
We have begun implementing the By-Half Plan!
Even as you watch this, the weak, the unneces-sary...
...the ones who drain our resources are being eliminated!
The causes of war will be elimi-nated.
We are creating a new world.
A world where there will be no hunger, no sickness, no weakness.
There will be plenty of food and room for everyone. People will cease to fight over property, food, wealth, energy resources.

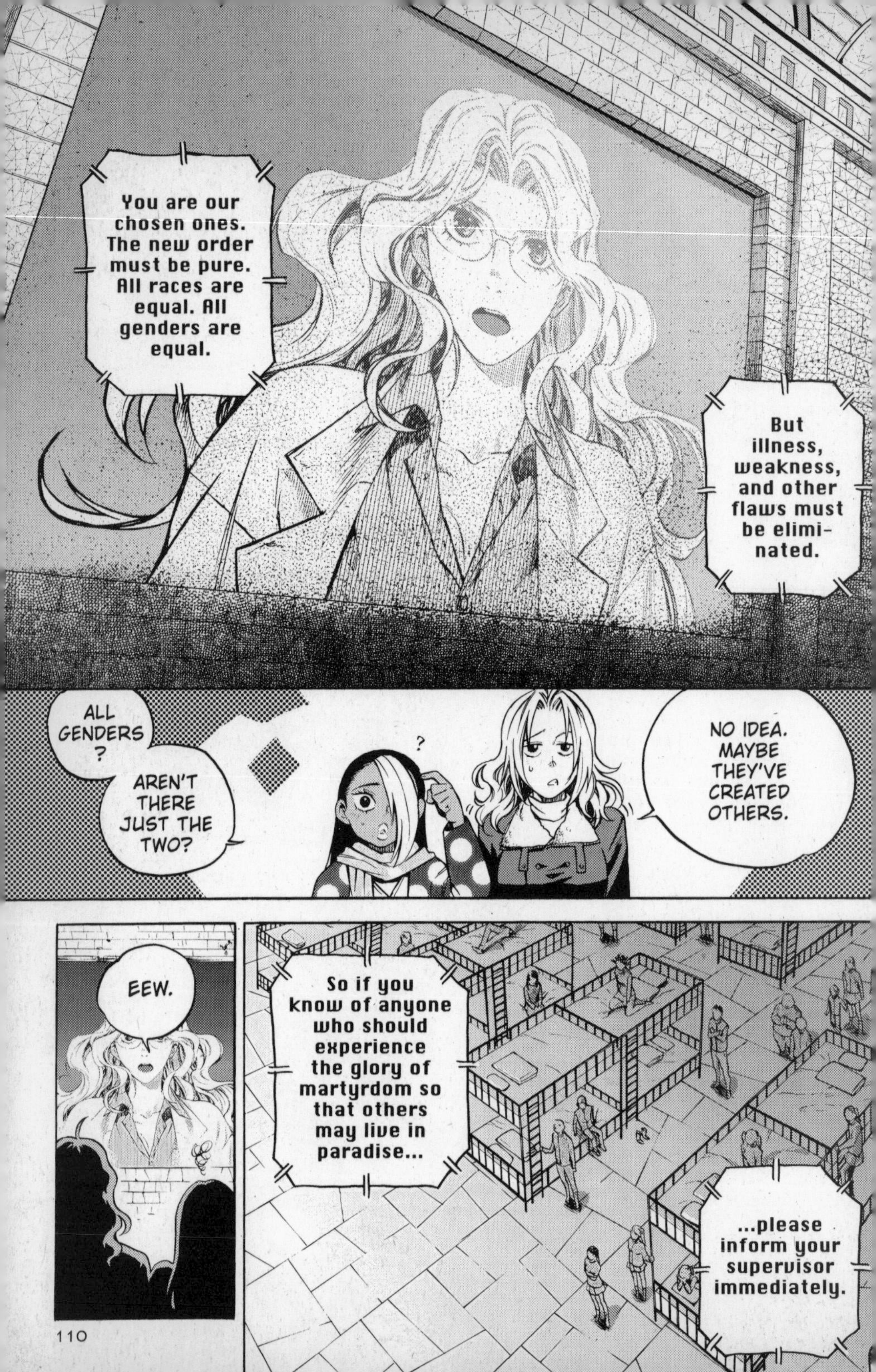
You are our chosen ones. The new order must be pure. All races are equal. All genders are equal.
But illness, weakness, and other flaws must be elimi- nated.
ALL GENDERS ?
AREN'T THERE JUST THE TWO?
?
NO IDEA. MAYBE THEY'VE CREATED OTHERS.
EEW.
So if you know of anyone who should experience the glory of martyrdom so that others may live in paradise...
...please inform your supervisor immediately.

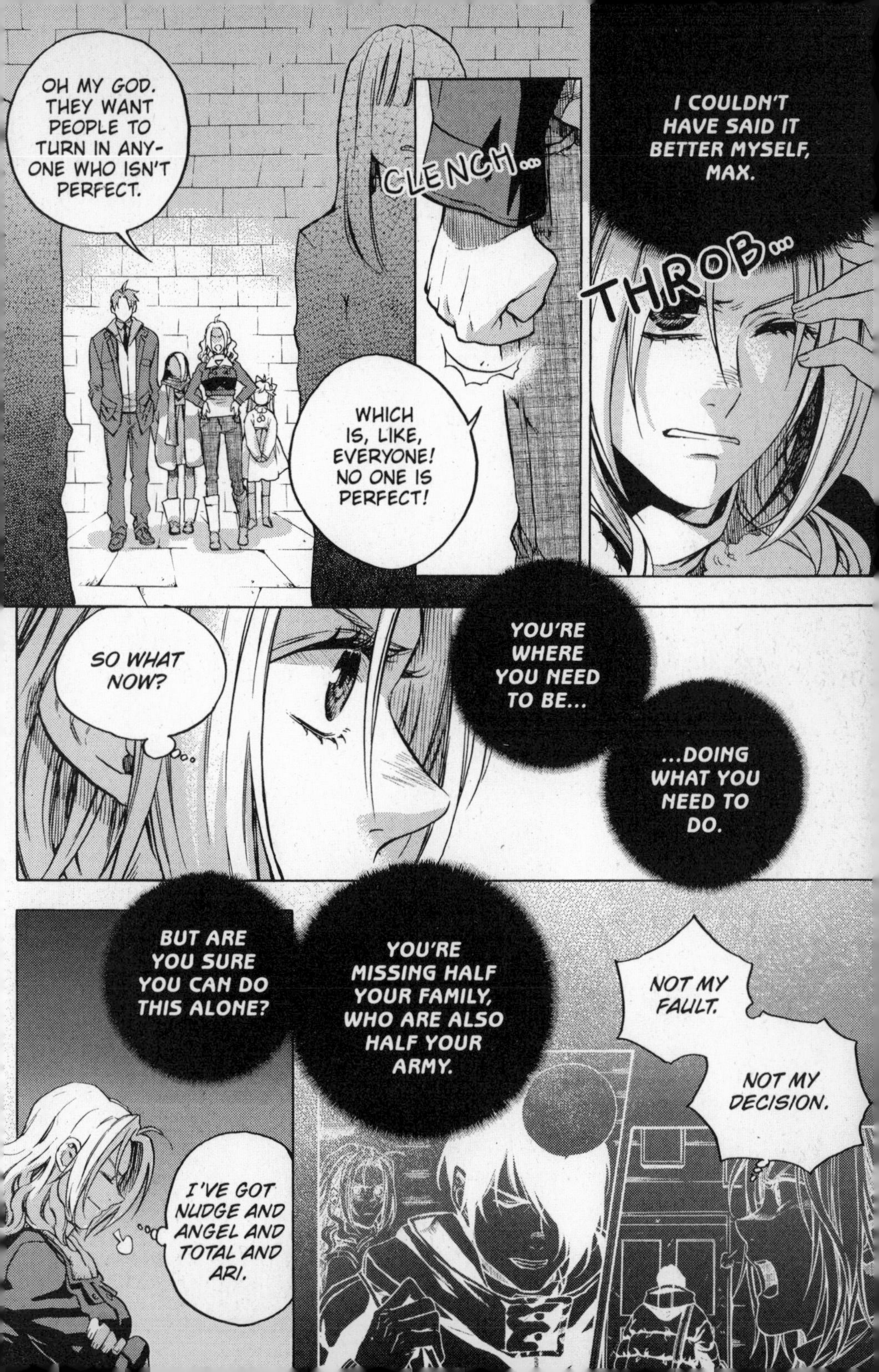

OH MY GOD. THEY WANT PEOPLE TO TURN IN ANY-ONE WHO ISN'T PERFECT.
CLENCH...
WHICH IS, LIKE, EVERYONE! NO ONE IS PERFECT!
I COULDN'T HAVE SAID IT BETTER MYSELF, MAX.
THROB...
SO WHAT NOW?
YOU'RE WHERE YOU NEED TO BE...
...DOING WHAT YOU NEED TO DO.
BUT ARE YOU SURE YOU CAN DO THIS ALONE?
YOU'RE MISSING HALF YOUR FAMILY, WHO ARE ALSO HALF YOUR ARMY.
NOT MY FAULT.
NOT MY DECISION.
I'VE GOT NUDGE AND ANGEL AND TOTAL AND ARI.

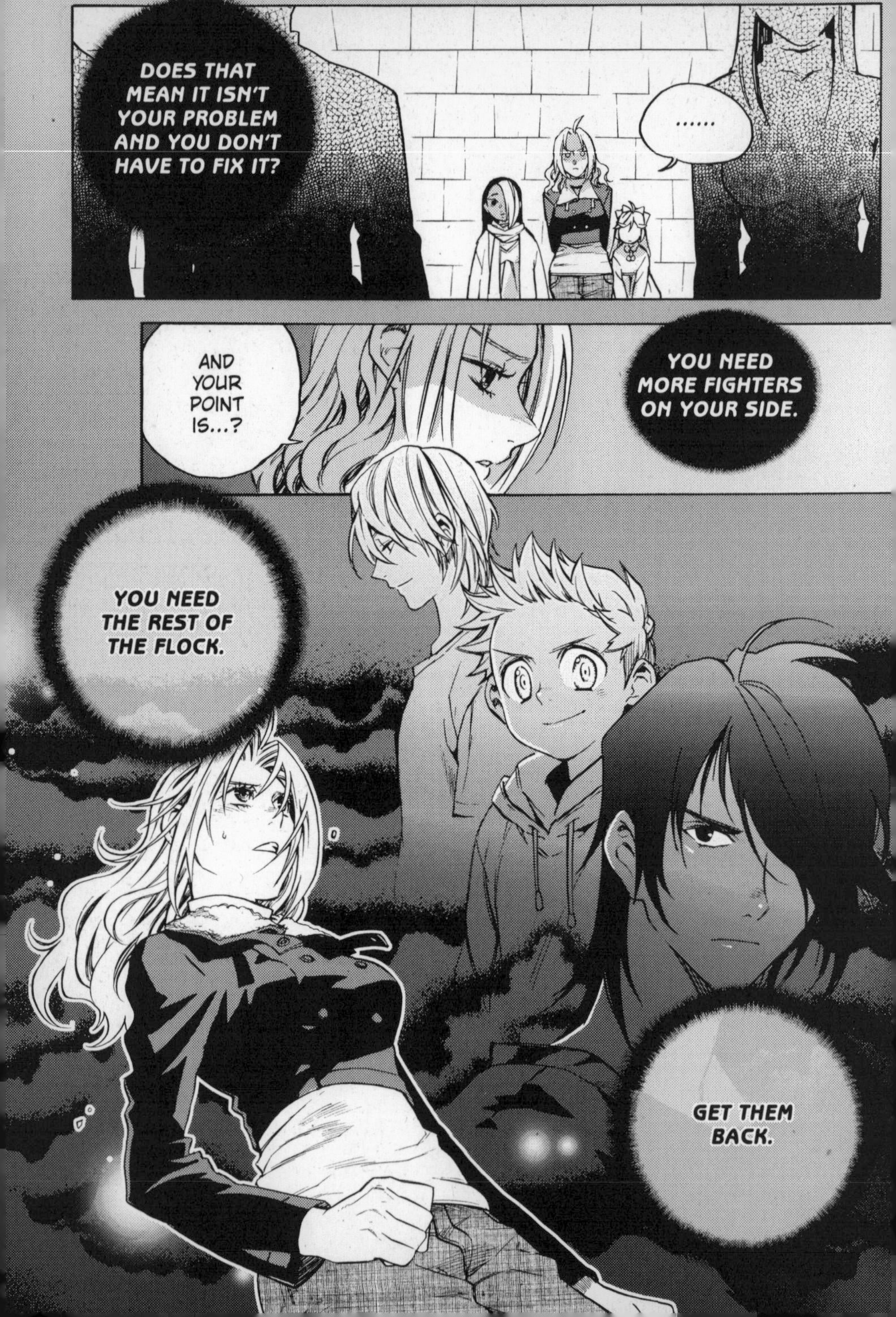
DOES THAT MEAN IT ISN'T YOUR PROBLEM AND YOU DON'T HAVE TO FIX IT?
......
AND YOUR POINT IS...?
YOU NEED MORE FIGHTERS ON YOUR SIDE.
YOU NEED THE REST OF THE FLOCK.
GET THEM BACK.

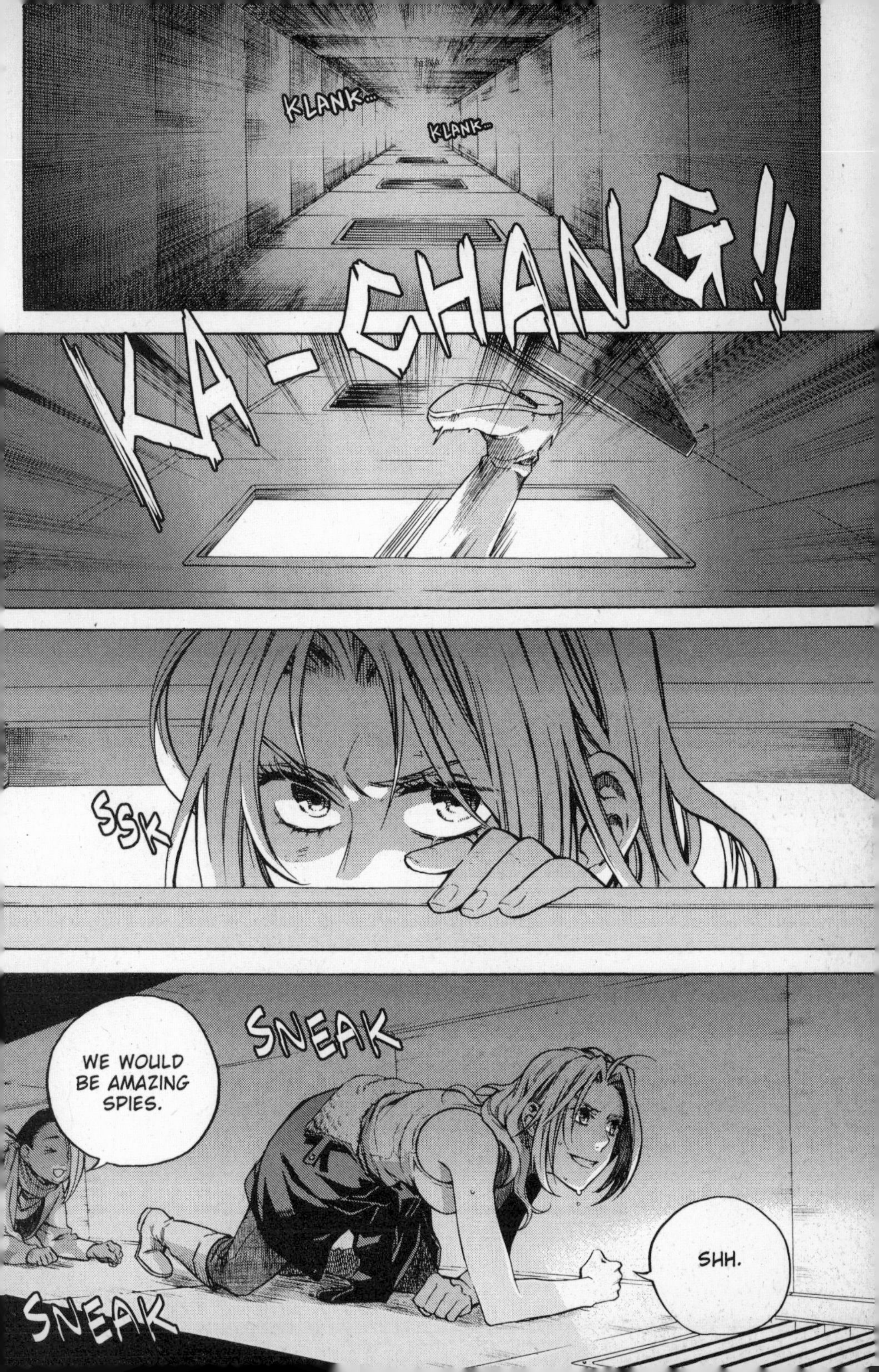
KLANK...
KLANK...
KA-CHANG!!
SSK
SNEAK
WE WOULD BE AMAZING SPIES.
SHH.
SNEAK

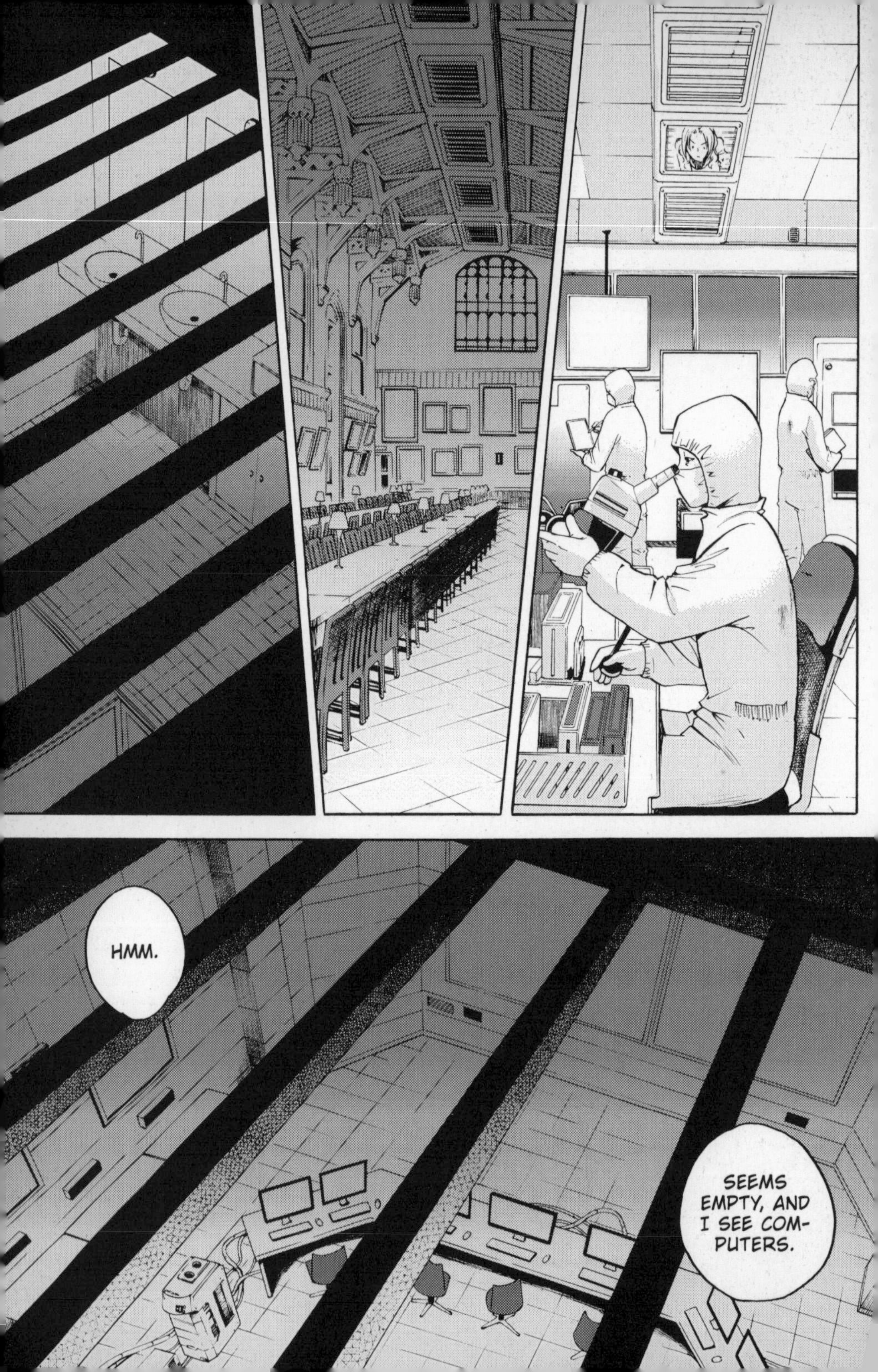
HMM.
SEEMS EMPTY, AND I SEE COM-PUTERS.

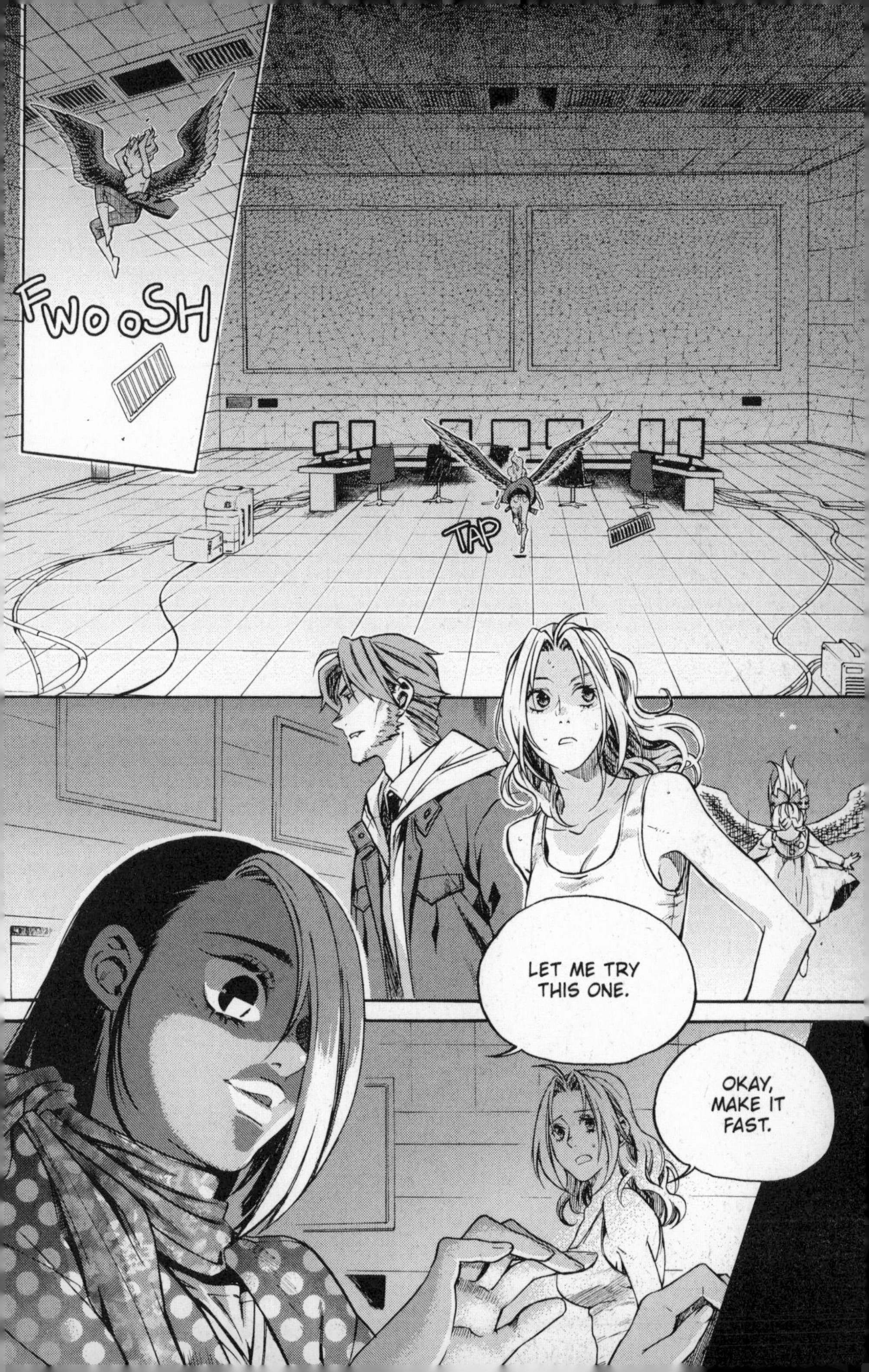
FWOOSH
TAP
LET ME TRY THIS ONE.
OKAY, MAKE IT FAST.

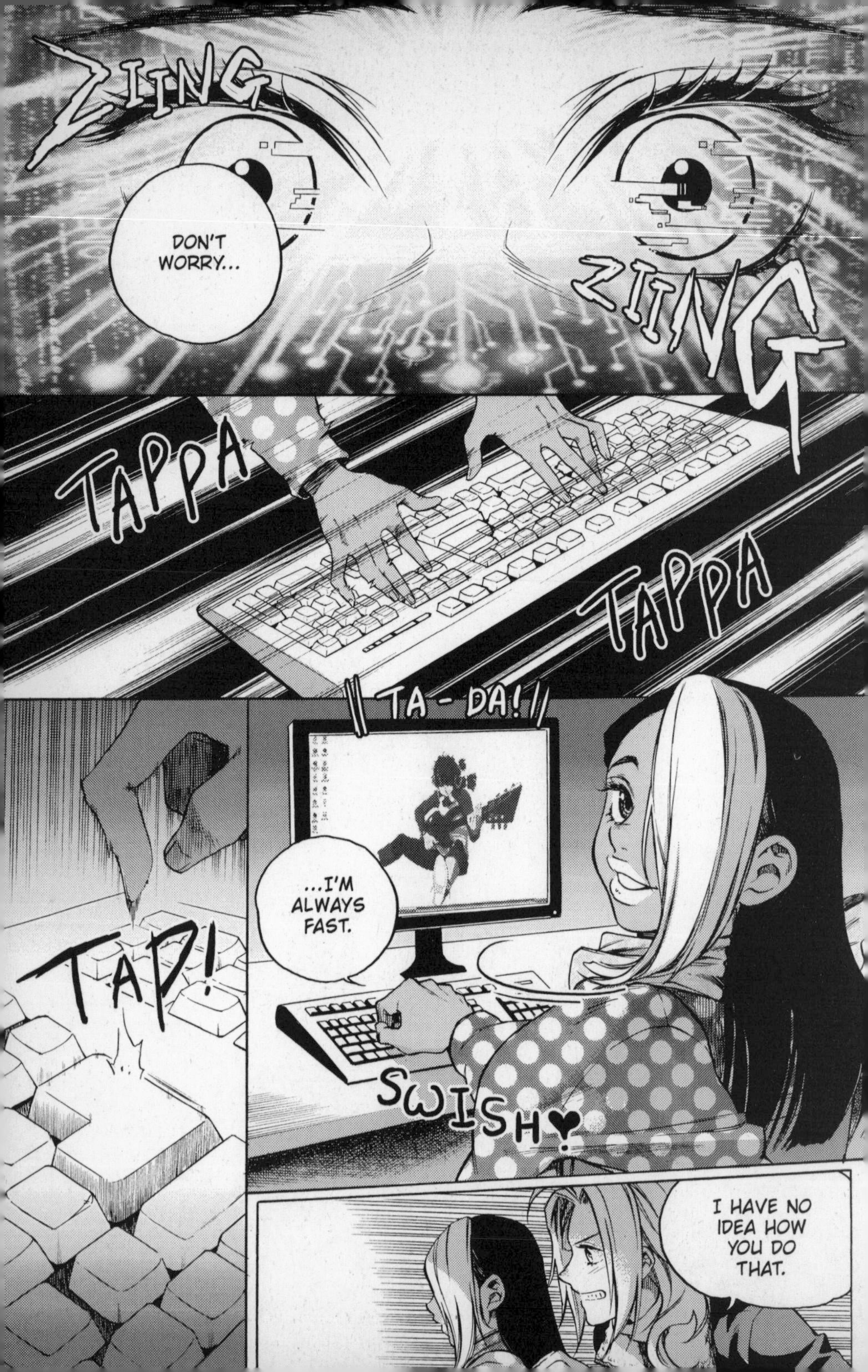
ZIING
DON'T WORRY...
ZIING
TAPPA
TAPPA
TAP!
TA-DA!
...I'M ALWAYS FAST.
SWISH♥
I HAVE NO IDEA HOW YOU DO THAT.

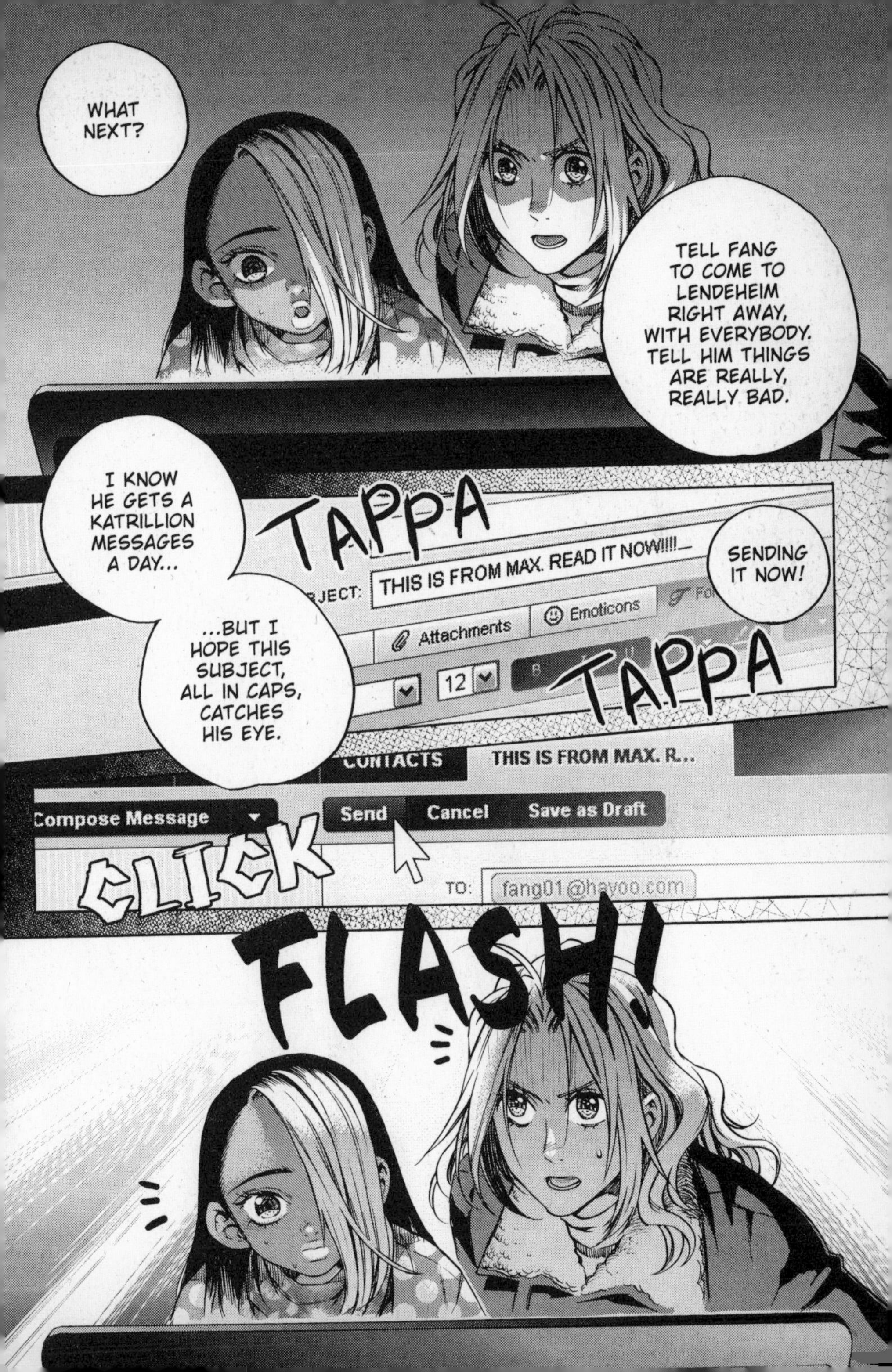
WHAT NEXT?
TELL FANG TO COME TO LENDEHEIM RIGHT AWAY, WITH EVERYBODY. TELL HIM THINGS ARE REALLY, REALLY BAD.
I KNOW HE GETS A KATRILLION MESSAGES A DAY...
TAPPA
THIS IS FROM MAX. READ IT NOW!!!!_
Attachments
Emoticons
...BUT I HOPE THIS SUBJECT, ALL IN CAPS, CATCHES HIS EYE.
SENDING IT NOW!
TAPPA
CONTACTS
THIS IS FROM MAX. R...
Compose Message
Send
Cancel
Save as Draft
CLICK
TO:
fang01@hayoo.com
FLASH!

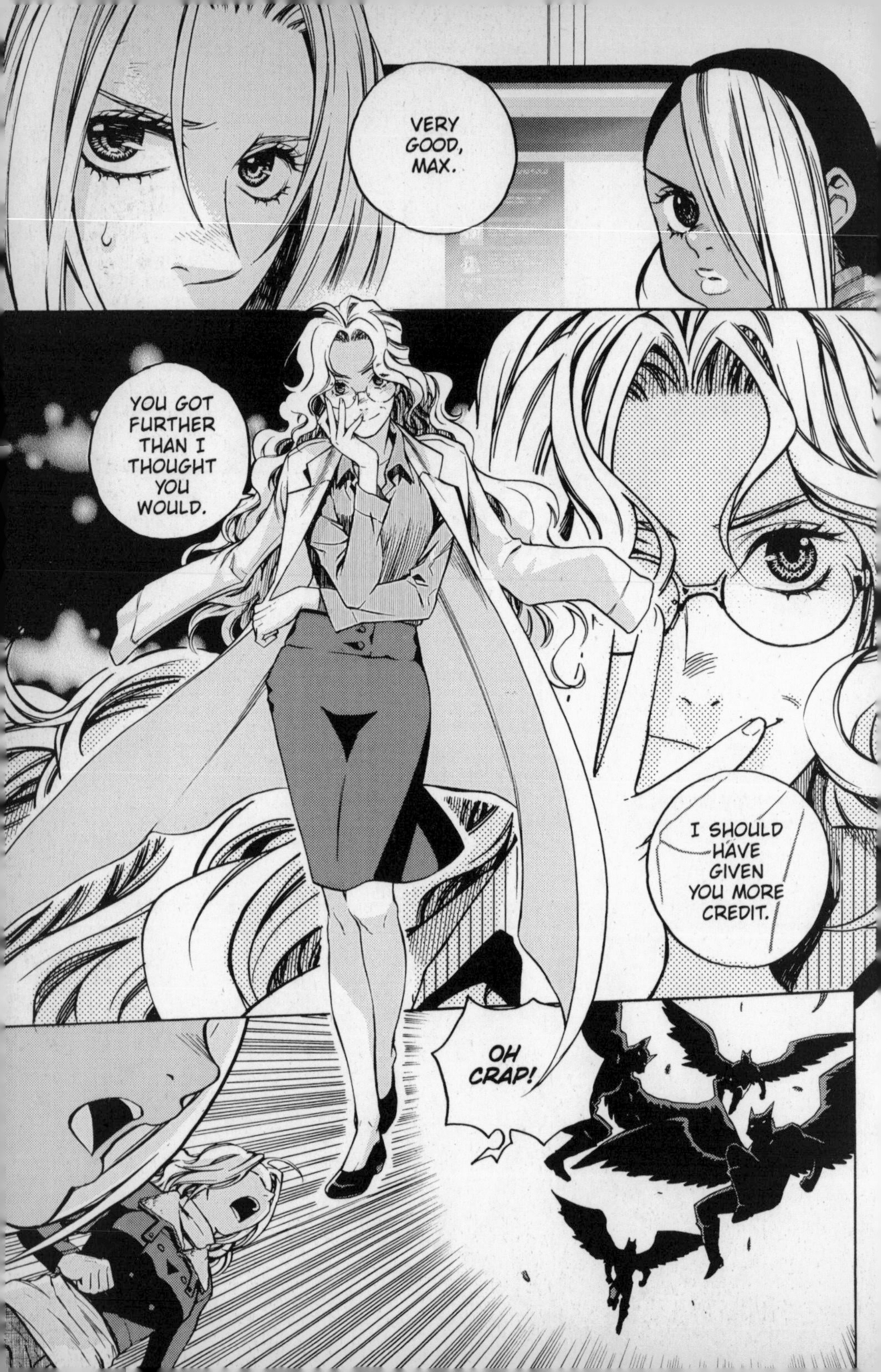
VERY GOOD, MAX.
YOU GOT FURTHER THAN I THOUGHT YOU WOULD.
I SHOULD HAVE GIVEN YOU MORE CREDIT.
OH CRAP!

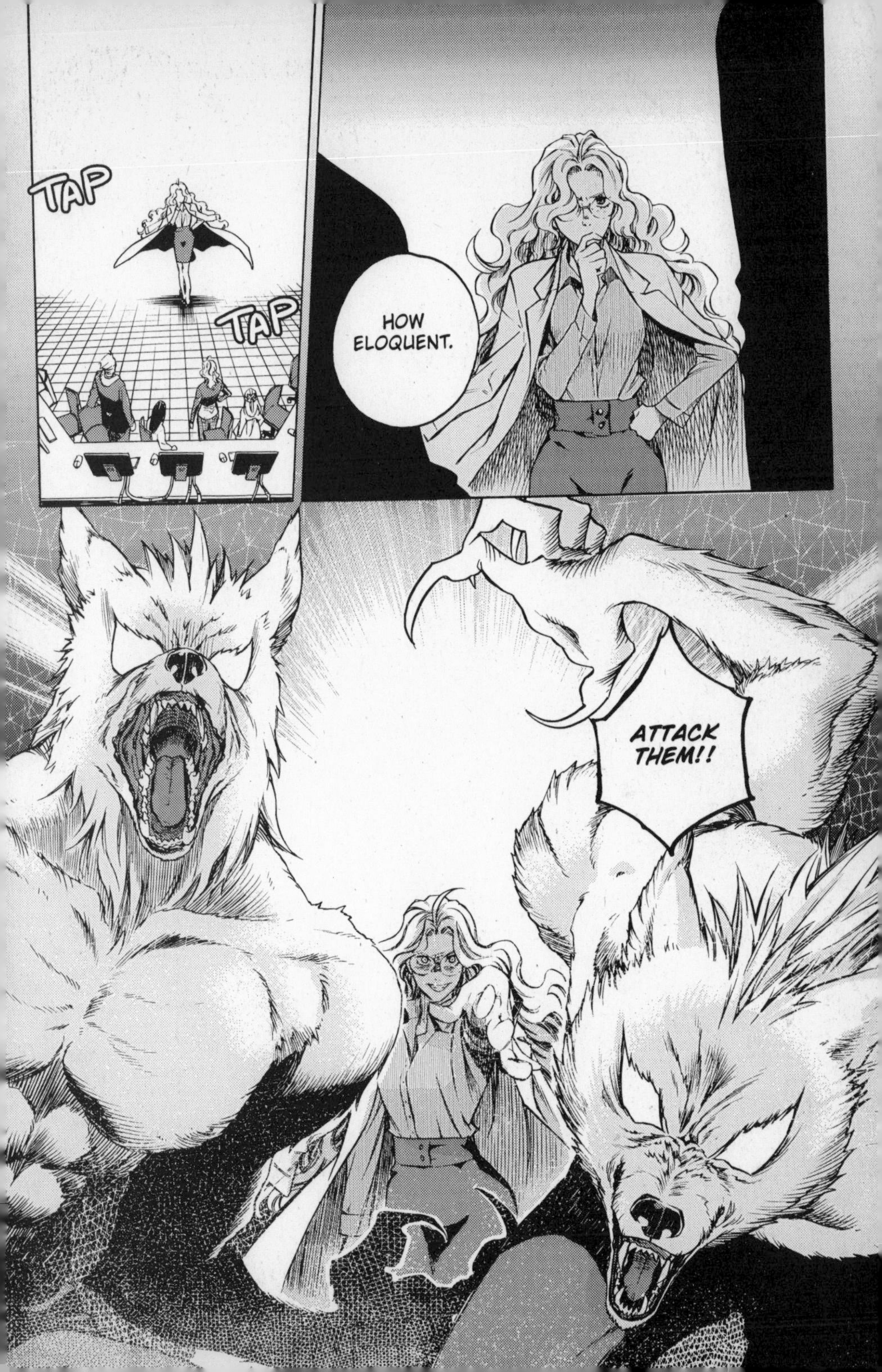
HOW ELOQUENT.
TAP
TAP
ATTACK THEM!!

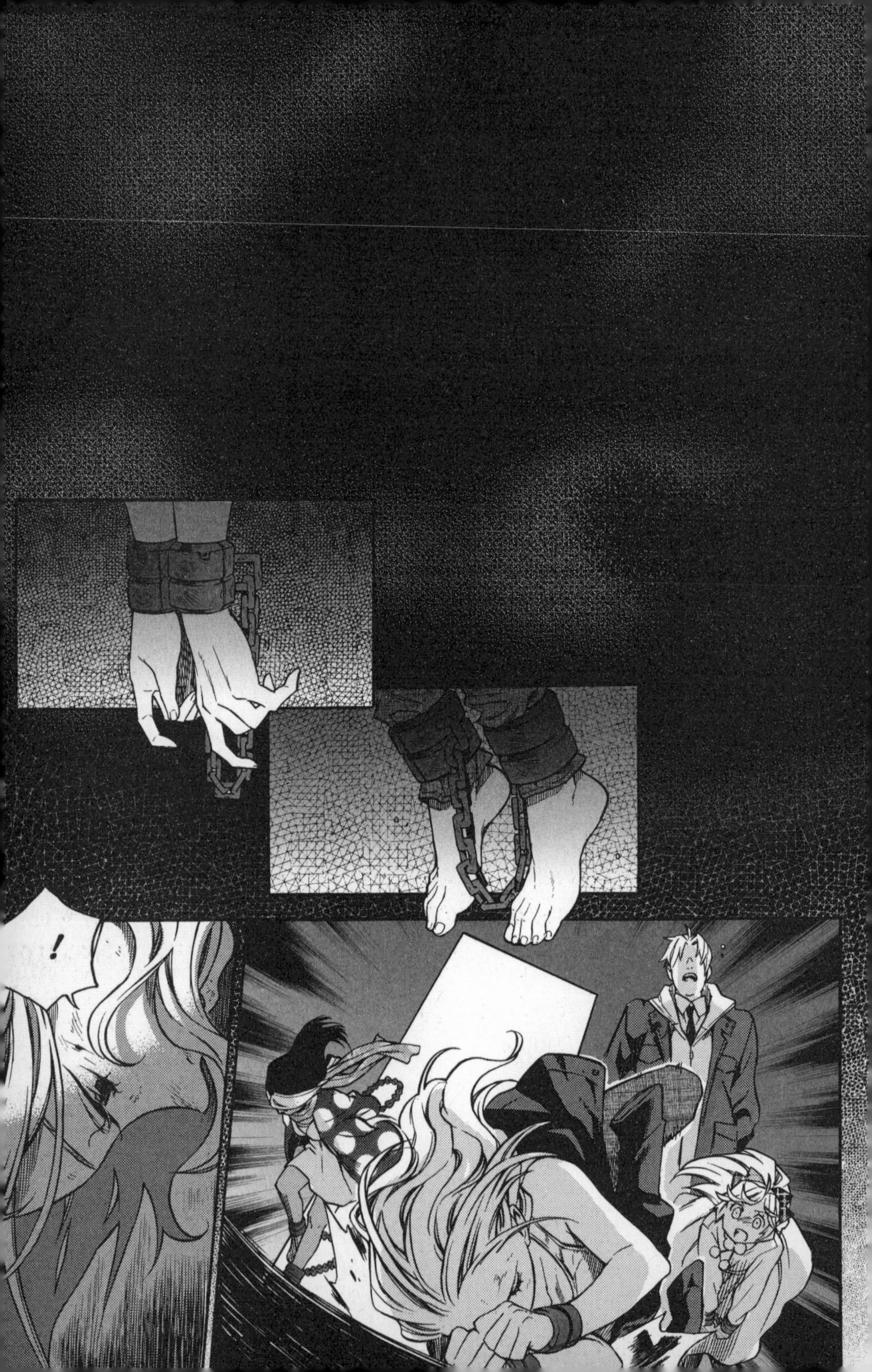
!

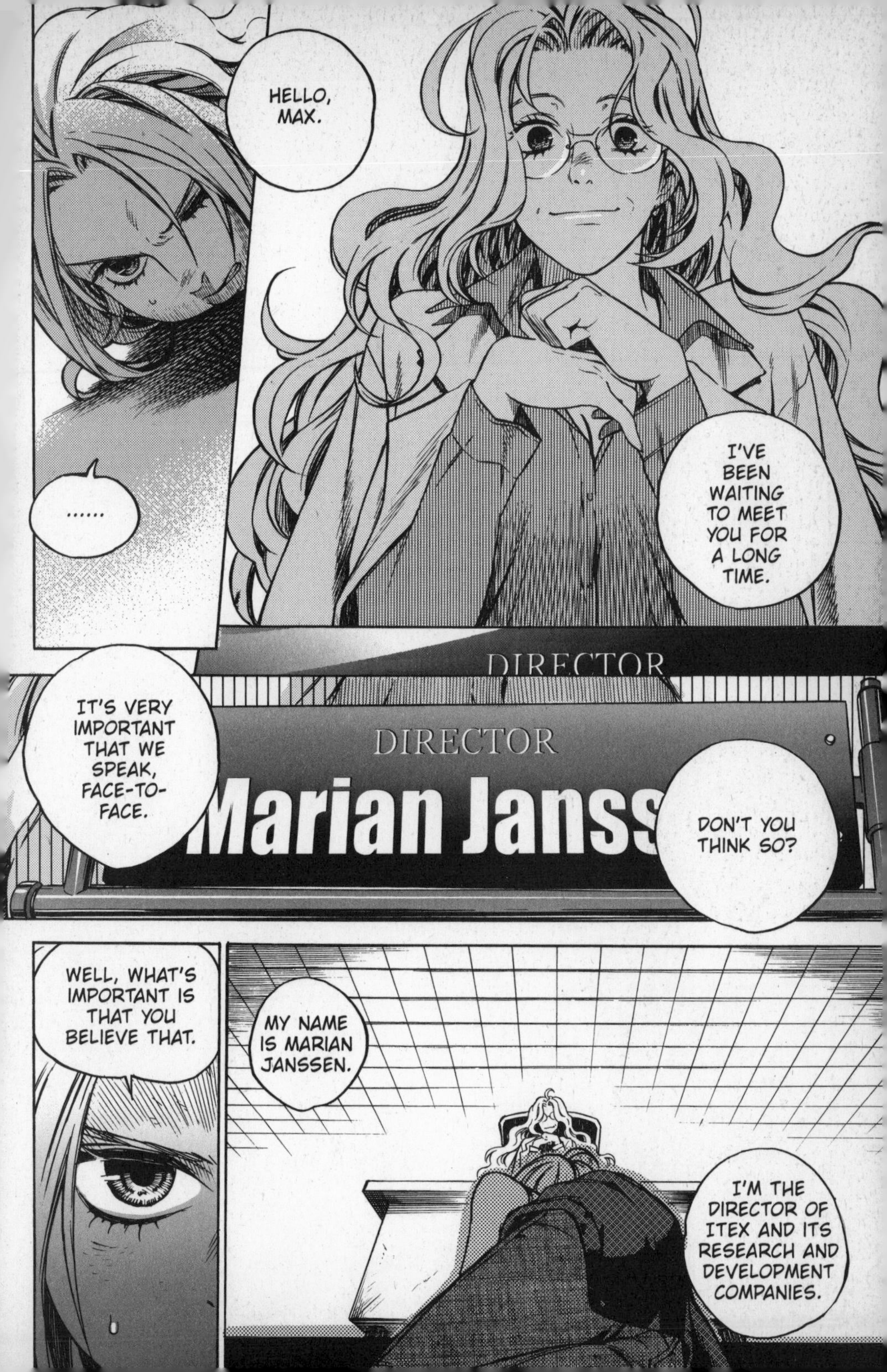
HELLO, MAX.
......
I'VE BEEN WAITING TO MEET YOU FOR A LONG TIME.
DIRECTOR
DIRECTOR
Marian Janss
IT'S VERY IMPORTANT THAT WE SPEAK, FACE-TO-FACE.
DON'T YOU THINK SO?
WELL, WHAT'S IMPORTANT IS THAT YOU BELIEVE THAT.
MY NAME IS MARIAN JANSSEN.
I'M THE DIRECTOR OF ITEX AND ITS RESEARCH AND DEVELOPMENT COMPANIES.

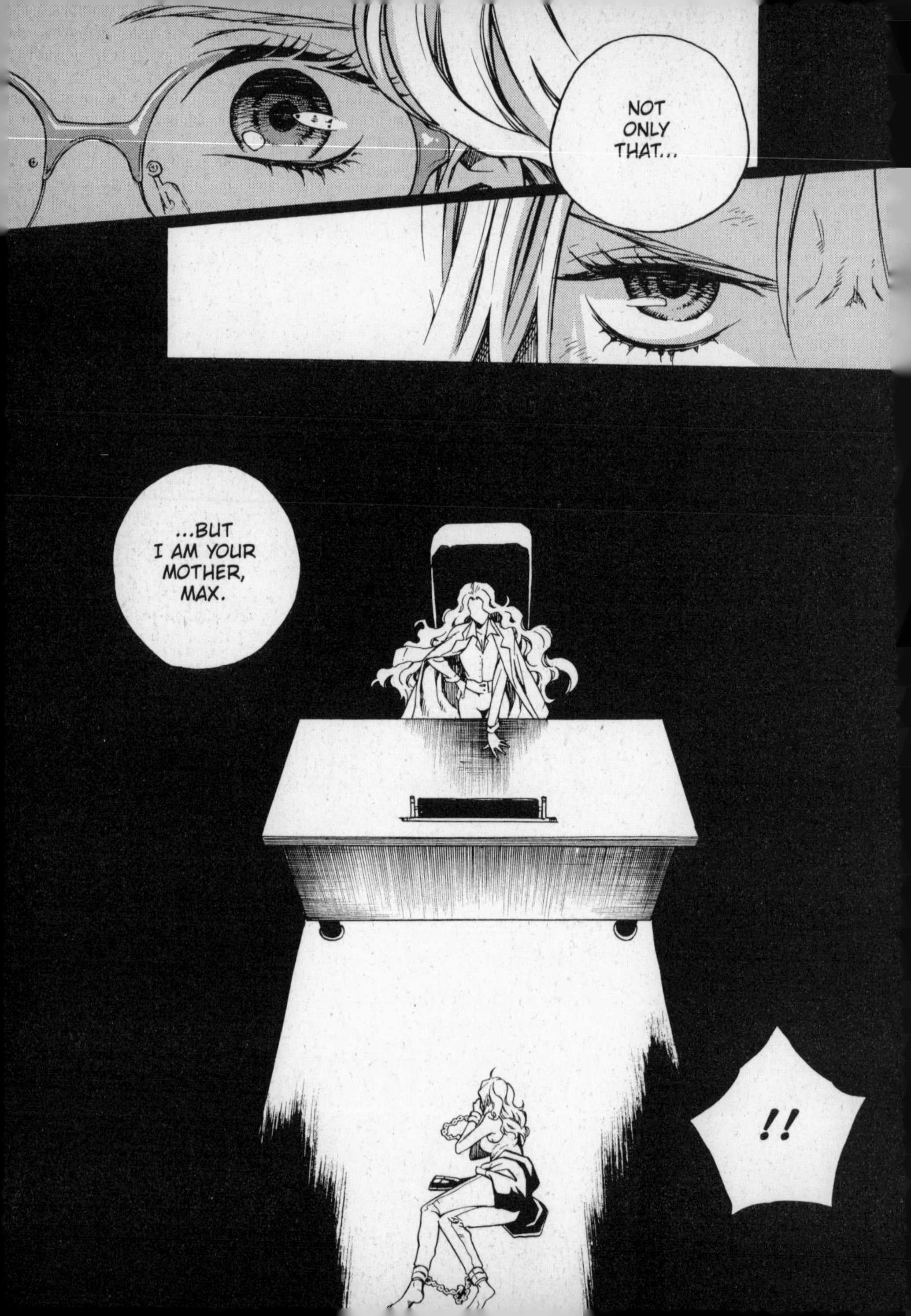
NOT ONLY THAT...
...BUT I AM YOUR MOTHER, MAX.
!!

MAXIMUM
RIDE

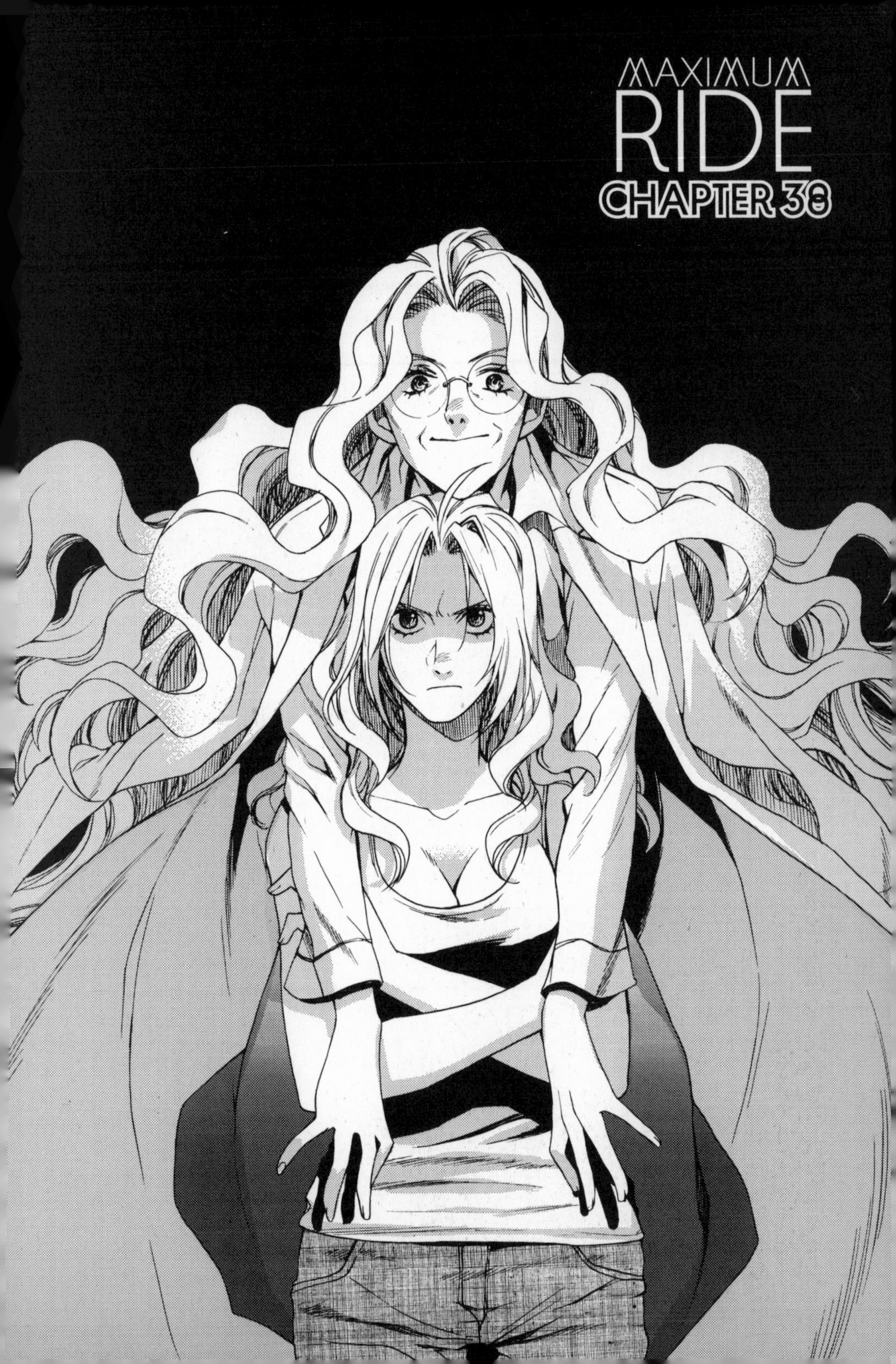
MAXIMUM
RIDE
CHAPTER 38

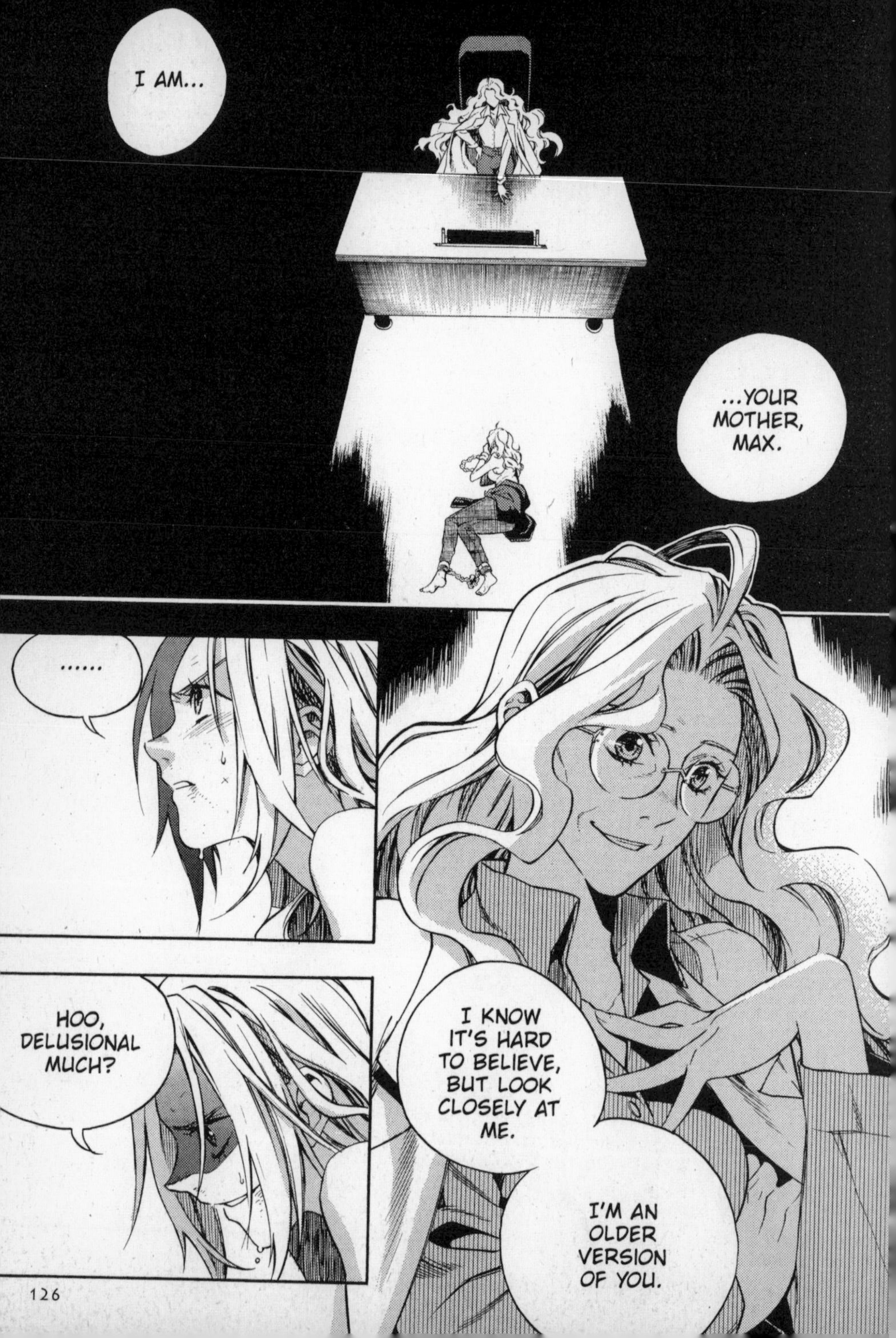
I AM...
...YOUR MOTHER, MAX.
......
I KNOW IT'S HARD TO BELIEVE, BUT LOOK CLOSELY AT ME.
I'M AN OLDER VERSION OF YOU.
HOO, DELUSIONAL MUCH?

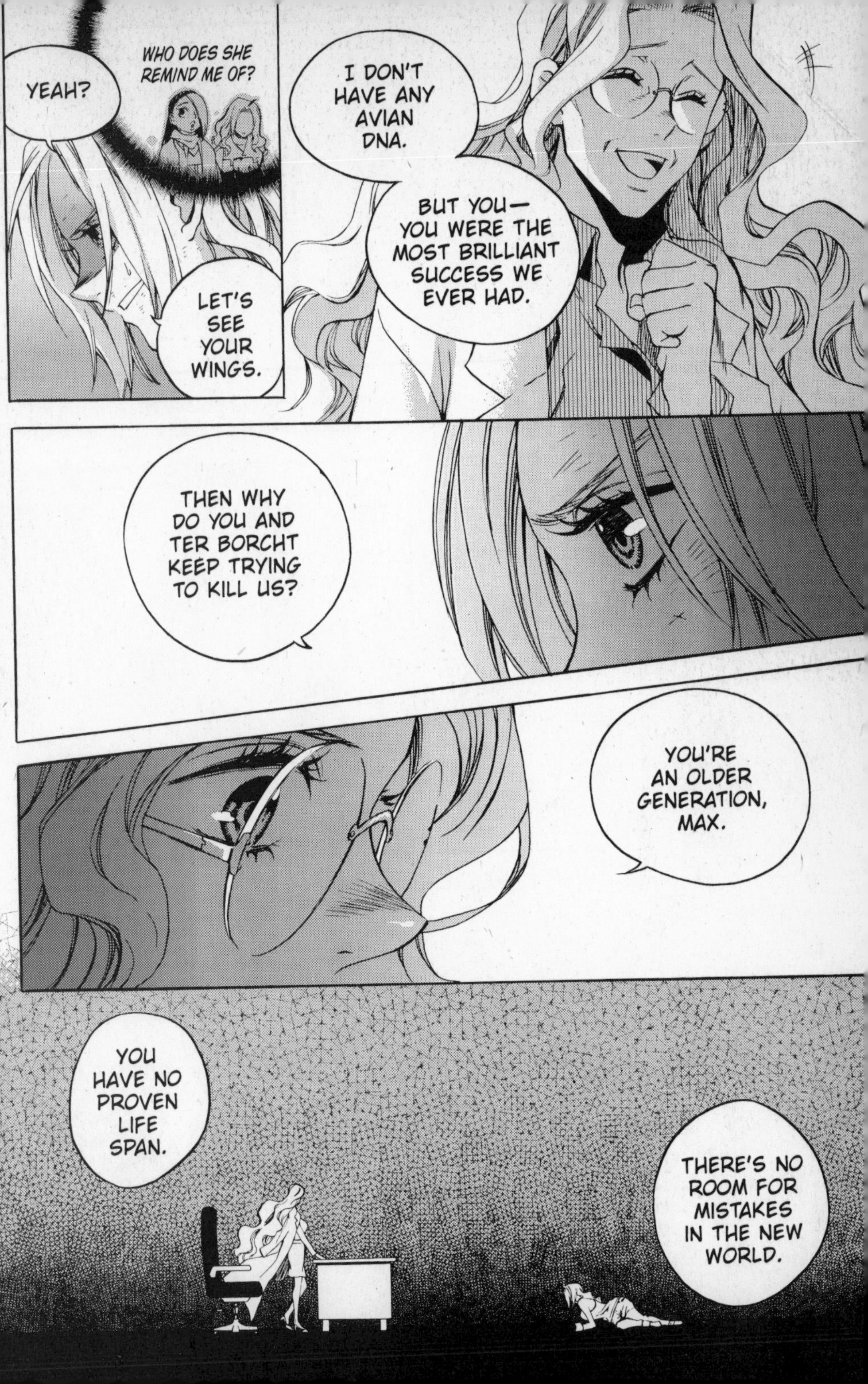
YEAH?
WHO DOES SHE REMIND ME OF?
LET'S SEE YOUR WINGS.
I DON'T HAVE ANY AVIAN DNA.
BUT YOU— YOU WERE THE MOST BRILLIANT SUCCESS WE EVER HAD.
THEN WHY DO YOU AND TER BORCHT KEEP TRYING TO KILL US?
YOU'RE AN OLDER GENERATION, MAX.
YOU HAVE NO PROVEN LIFE SPAN.
THERE'S NO ROOM FOR MISTAKES IN THE NEW WORLD.

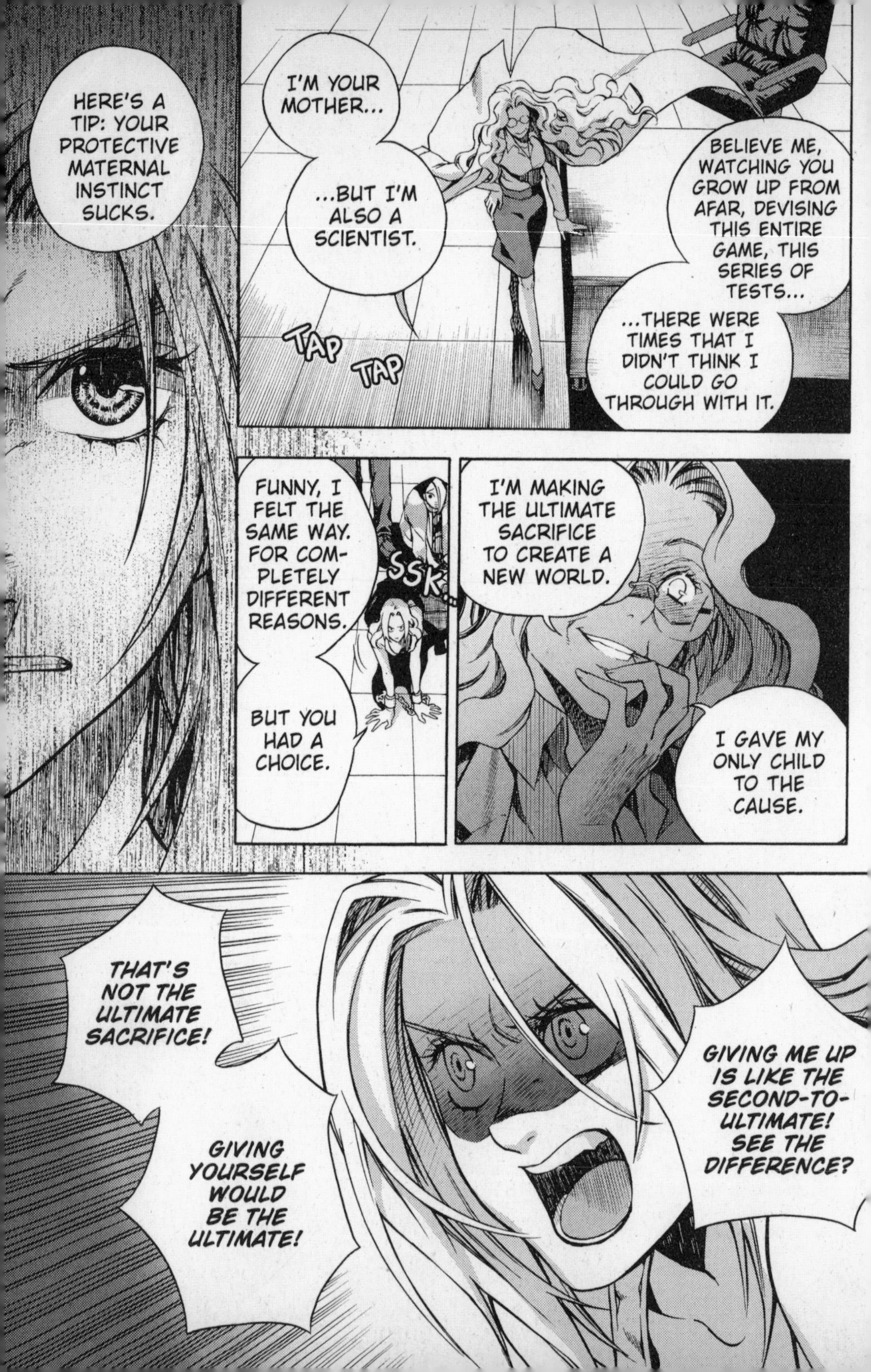
HERE'S A TIP: YOUR PROTECTIVE MATERNAL INSTINCT SUCKS.
I'M YOUR MOTHER...
...BUT I'M ALSO A SCIENTIST.
TAP TAP
BELIEVE ME, WATCHING YOU GROW UP FROM AFAR, DEVISING THIS ENTIRE GAME, THIS SERIES OF TESTS...
...THERE WERE TIMES THAT I DIDN'T THINK I COULD GO THROUGH WITH IT.
FUNNY, I FELT THE SAME WAY. FOR COMPLETELY DIFFERENT REASONS.
SSK
BUT YOU HAD A CHOICE.
I'M MAKING THE ULTIMATE SACRIFICE TO CREATE A NEW WORLD.
I GAVE MY ONLY CHILD TO THE CAUSE.
THAT'S NOT THE ULTIMATE SACRIFICE!
GIVING YOURSELF WOULD BE THE ULTIMATE!
GIVING ME UP IS LIKE THE SECOND-TO-ULTIMATE! SEE THE DIFFERENCE?

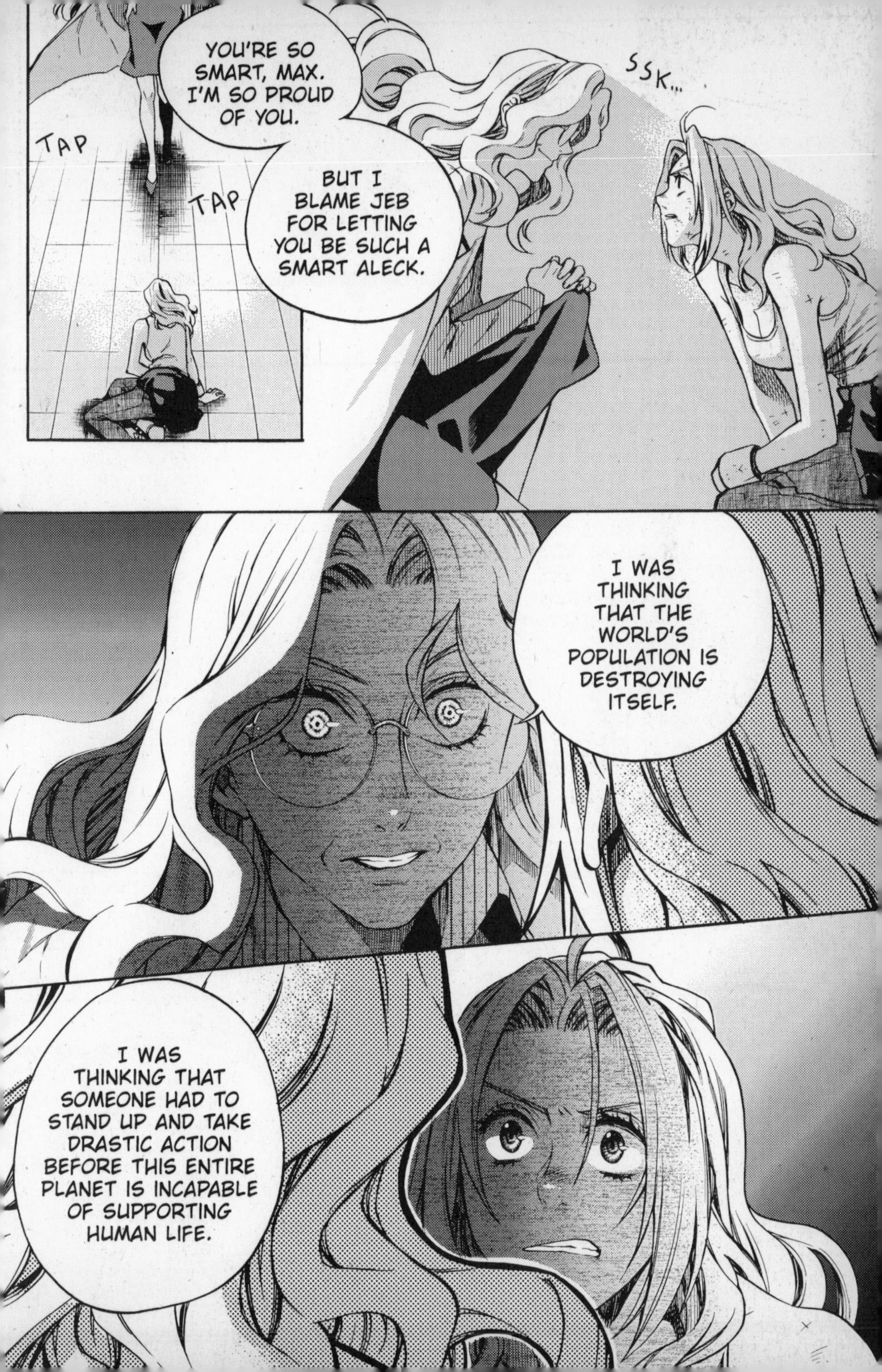
YOU'RE SO SMART, MAX. I'M SO PROUD OF YOU.
SSK...
TAP
TAP
BUT I BLAME JEB FOR LETTING YOU BE SUCH A SMART ALECK.
I WAS THINKING THAT THE WORLD'S POPULATION IS DESTROYING ITSELF.
I WAS THINKING THAT SOMEONE HAD TO STAND UP AND TAKE DRASTIC ACTION BEFORE THIS ENTIRE PLANET IS INCAPABLE OF SUPPORTING HUMAN LIFE.

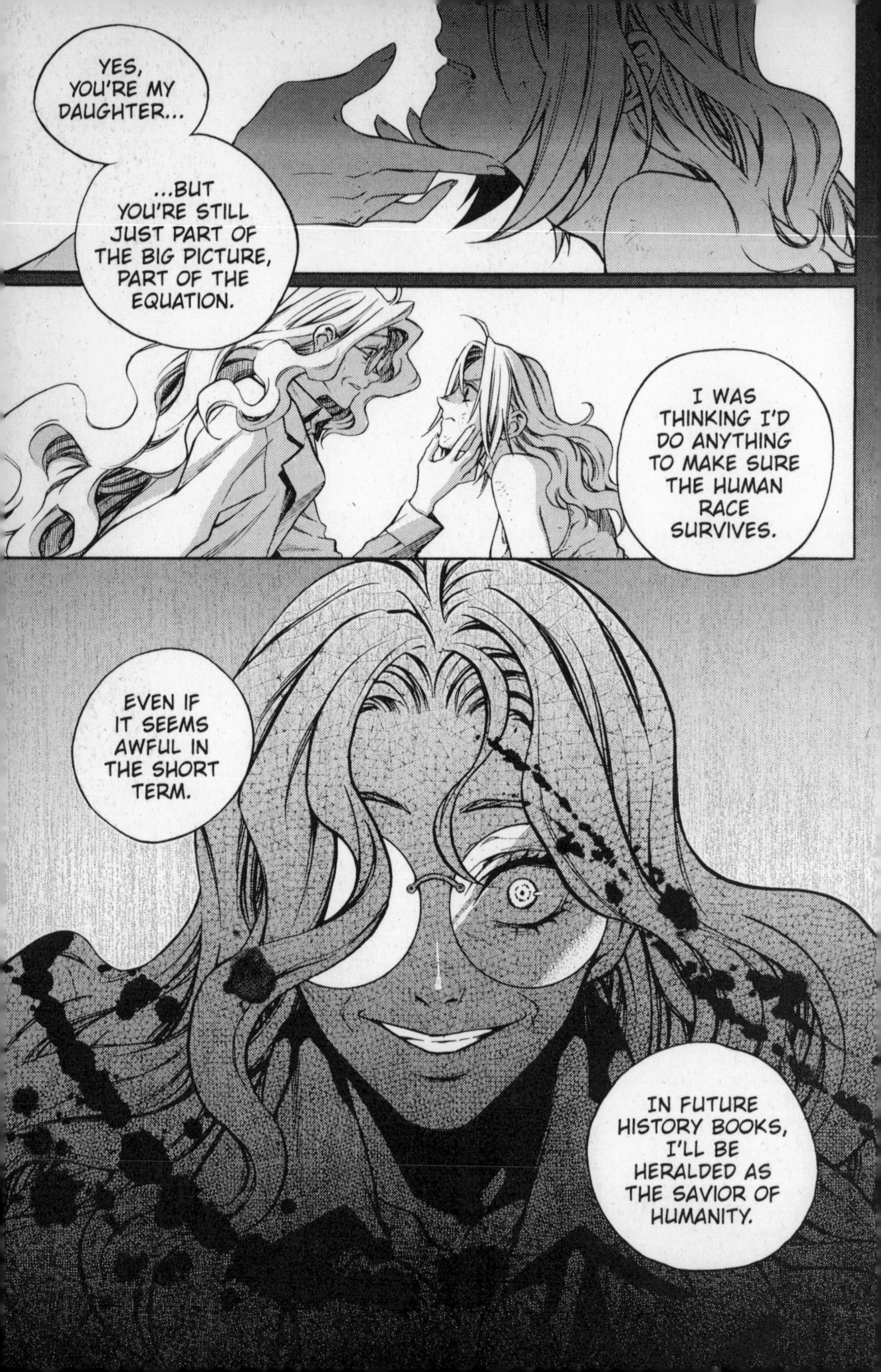
YES, YOU'RE MY DAUGHTER...
...BUT YOU'RE STILL JUST PART OF THE BIG PICTURE, PART OF THE EQUATION.
I WAS THINKING I'D DO ANYTHING TO MAKE SURE THE HUMAN RACE SURVIVES.
EVEN IF IT SEEMS AWFUL IN THE SHORT TERM.
IN FUTURE HISTORY BOOKS, I'LL BE HERALDED AS THE SAVIOR OF HUMANITY.

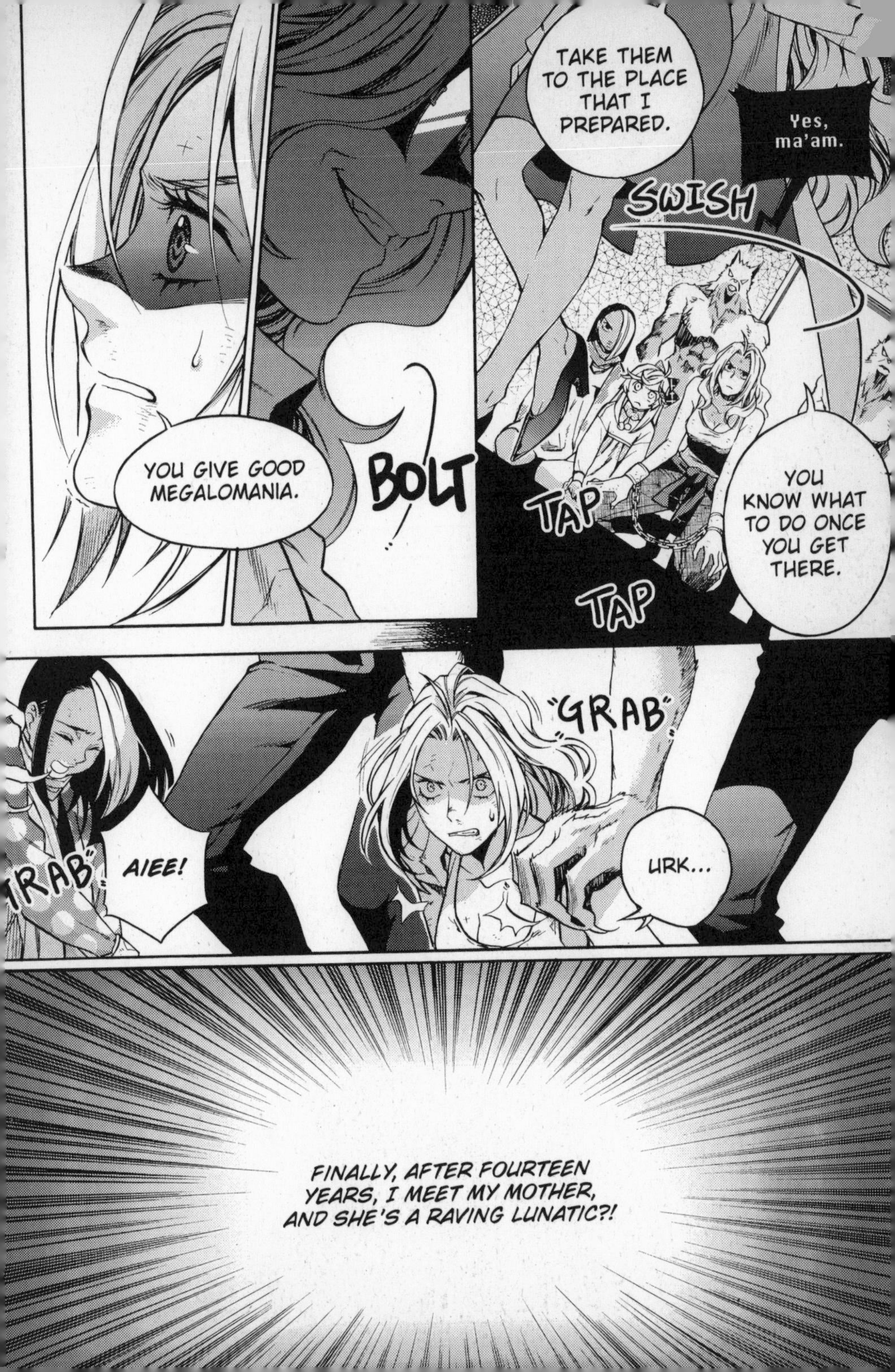

TAKE THEM TO THE PLACE THAT I PREPARED.
Yes, ma'am.
SWISH
YOU KNOW WHAT TO DO ONCE YOU GET THERE.
TAP
TAP
BOLT
YOU GIVE GOOD MEGALOMANIA.
GRAB
URK...
GRAB
AIEE!
FINALLY, AFTER FOURTEEN YEARS, I MEET MY MOTHER, AND SHE'S A RAVING LUNATIC?!

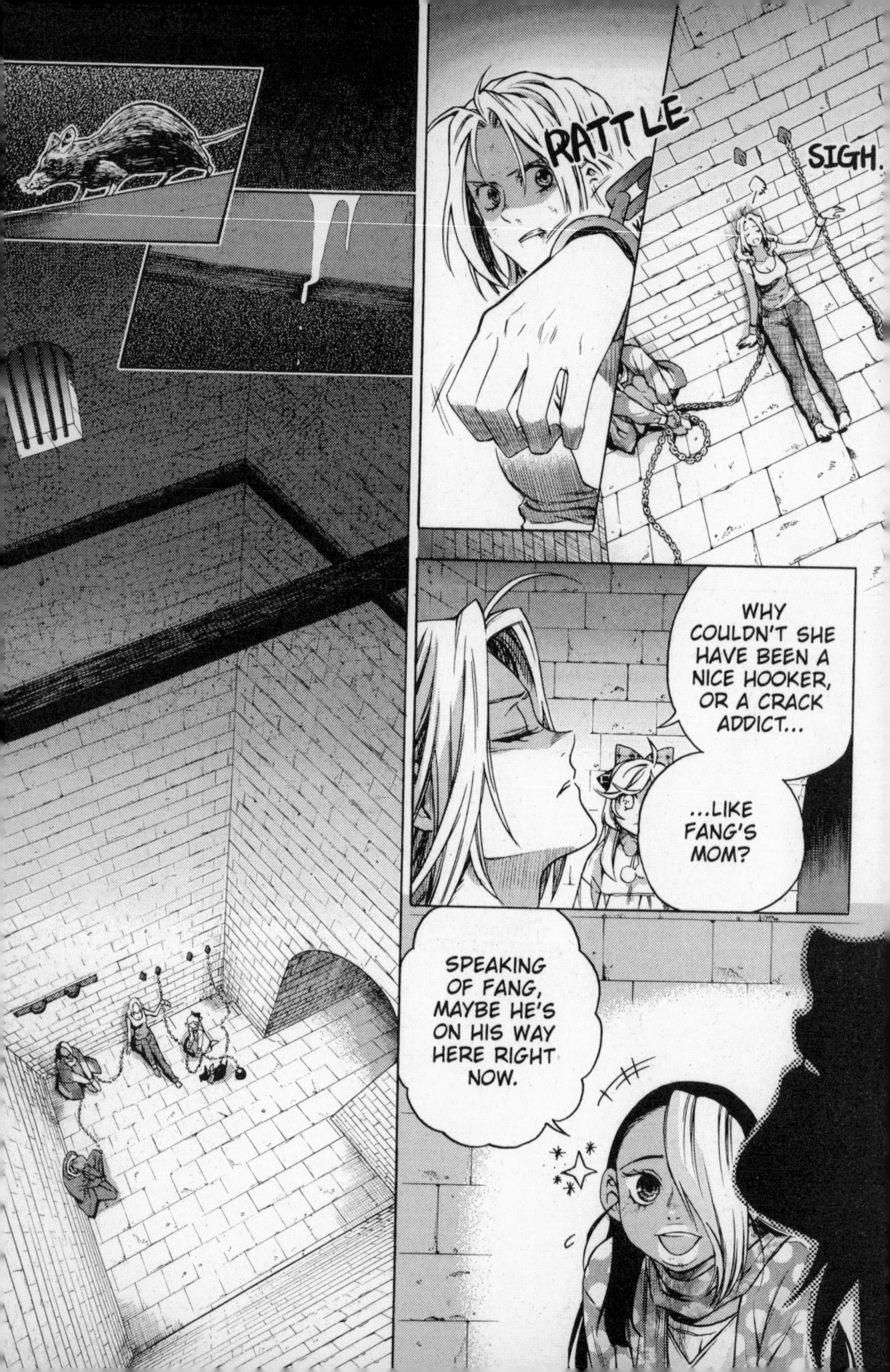
RATTLE
SIGH.
WHY COULDN'T SHE HAVE BEEN A NICE HOOKER, OR A CRACK ADDICT...
...LIKE FANG'S MOM?
SPEAKING OF FANG, MAYBE HE'S ON HIS WAY HERE RIGHT NOW.

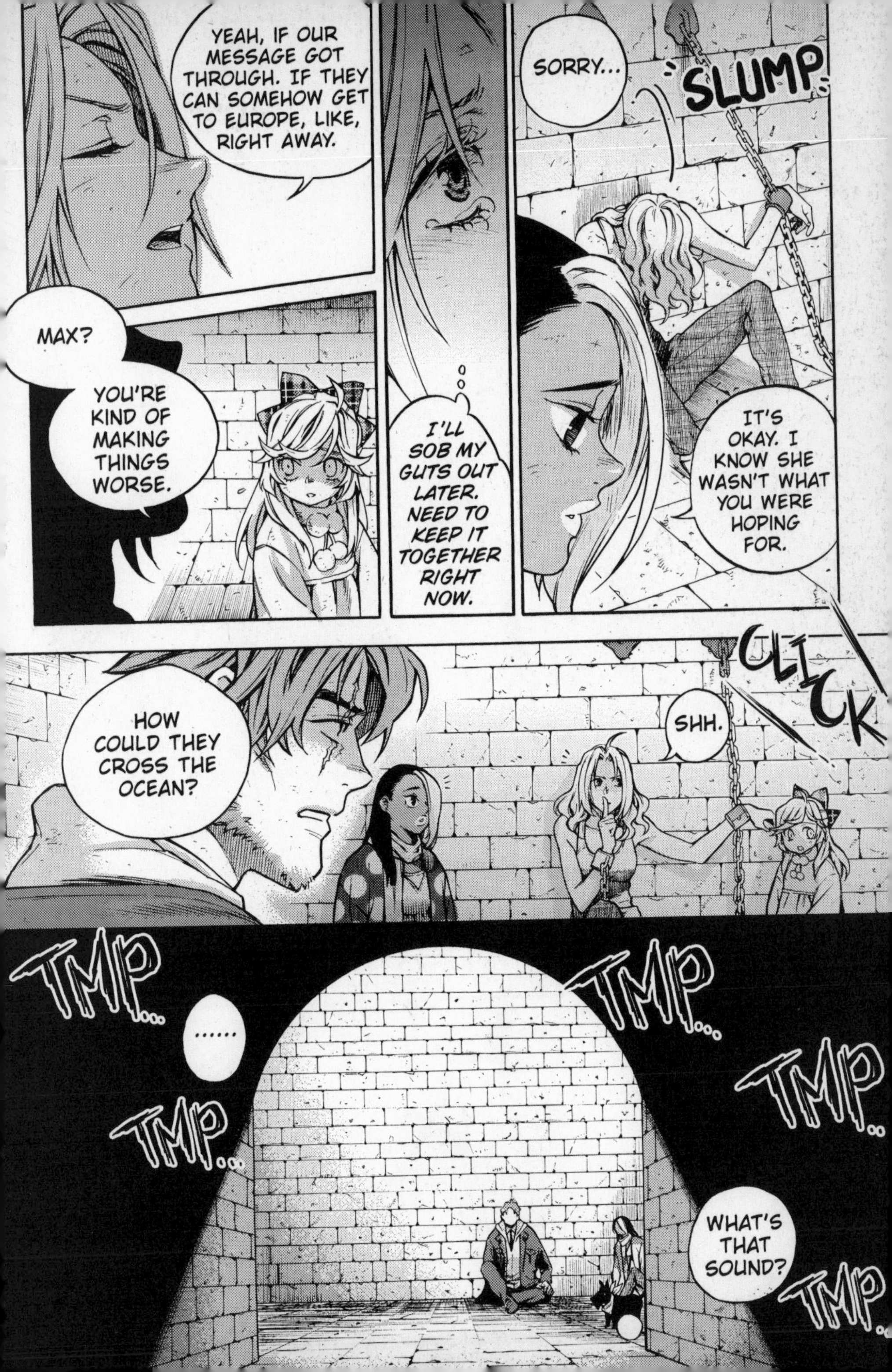
YEAH, IF OUR MESSAGE GOT THROUGH. IF THEY CAN SOMEHOW GET TO EUROPE, LIKE, RIGHT AWAY.
SORRY...
SLUMP
MAX?
YOU'RE KIND OF MAKING THINGS WORSE.
I'LL SOB MY GUTS OUT LATER. NEED TO KEEP IT TOGETHER RIGHT NOW.
IT'S OKAY. I KNOW SHE WASN'T WHAT YOU WERE HOPING FOR.
CLICK
HOW COULD THEY CROSS THE OCEAN?
SHH.
TMP...
......
TMP...
TMP...
TMP..
WHAT'S THAT SOUND?
TMP..

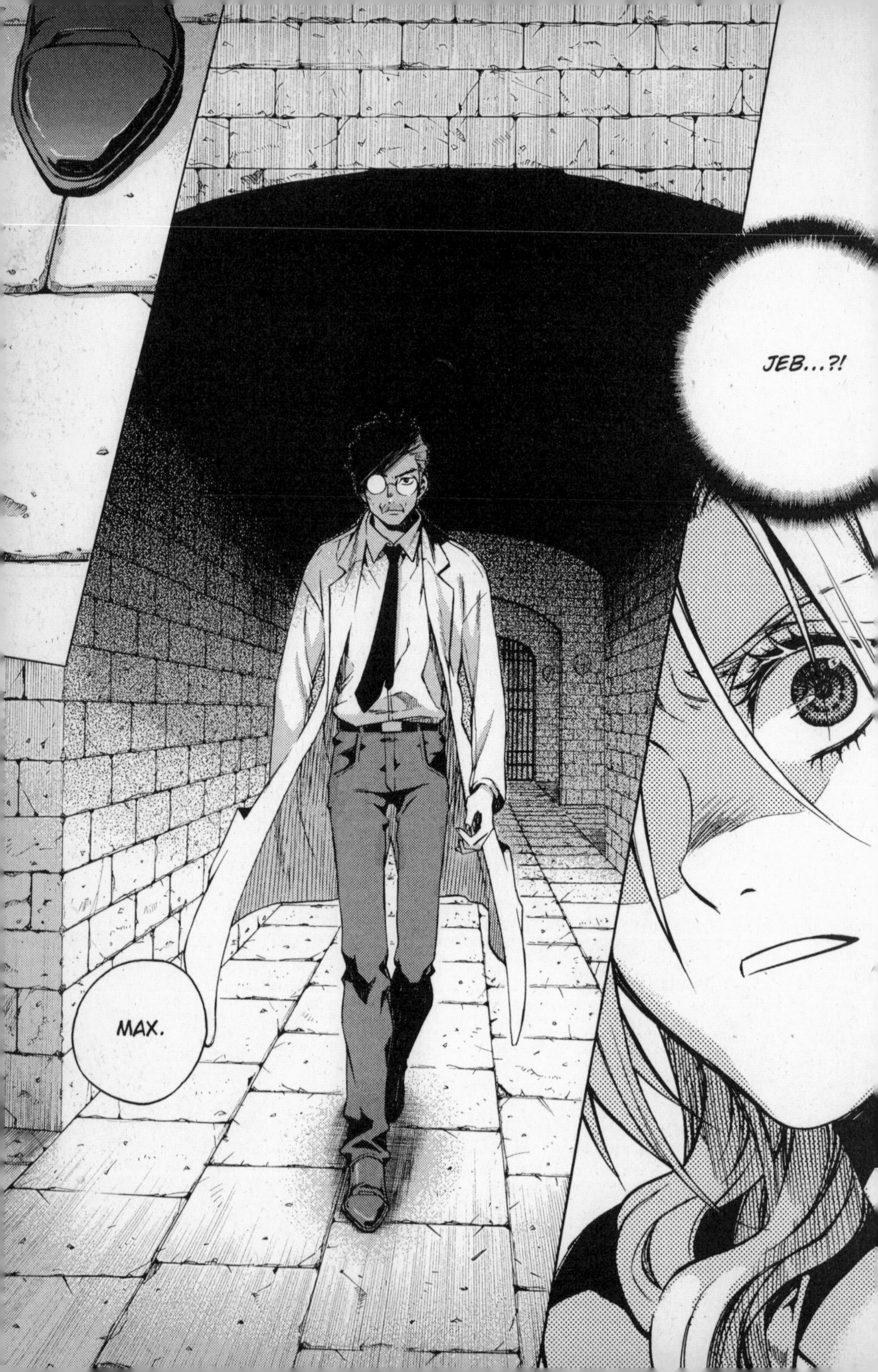
JEB...?!
MAX.

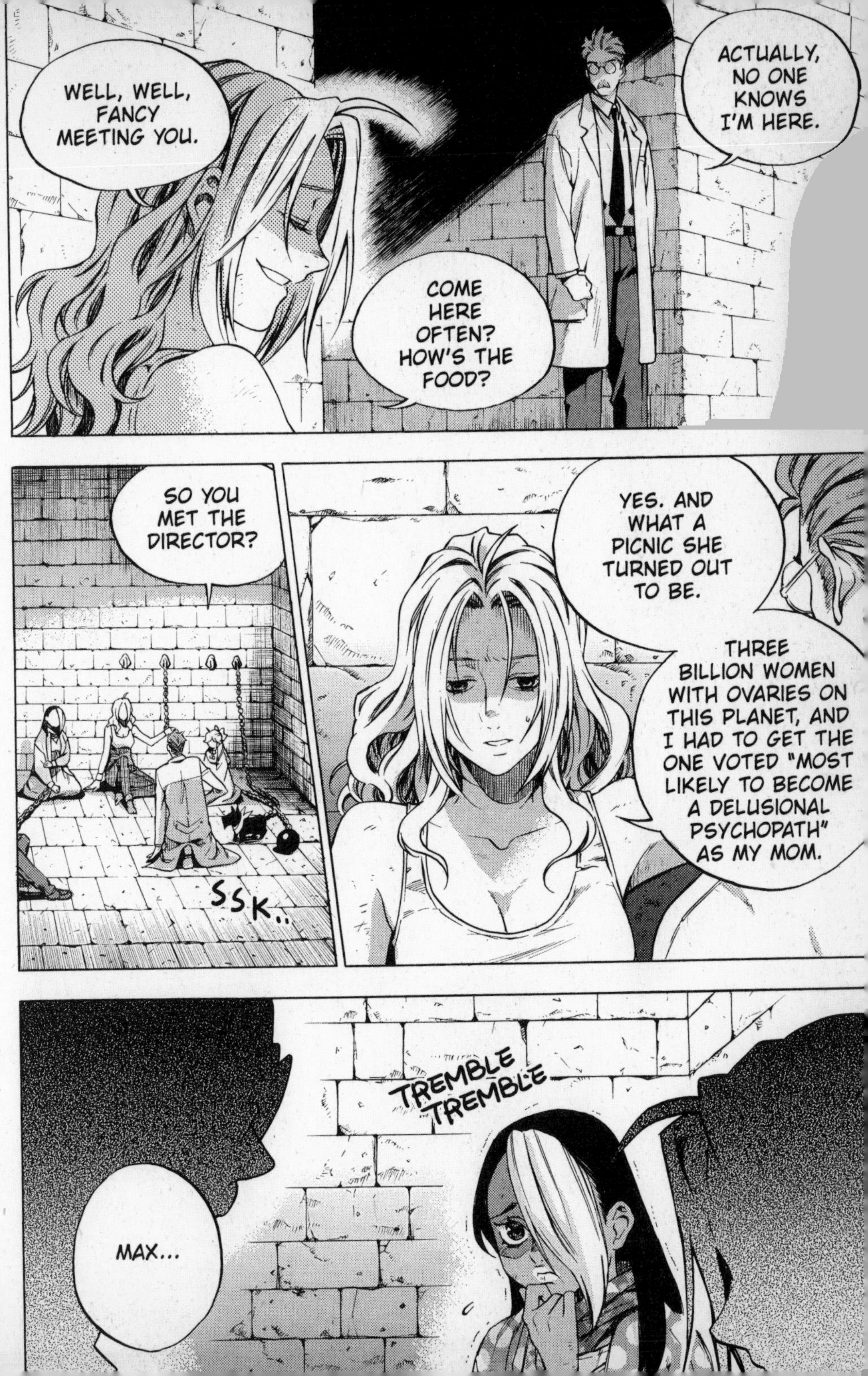
WELL, WELL, FANCY MEETING YOU.
COME HERE OFTEN? HOW'S THE FOOD?
ACTUALLY, NO ONE KNOWS I'M HERE.
YES. AND WHAT A PICNIC SHE TURNED OUT TO BE.
THREE BILLION WOMEN WITH OVARIES ON THIS PLANET, AND I HAD TO GET THE ONE VOTED "MOST LIKELY TO BECOME A DELUSIONAL PSYCHOPATH" AS MY MOM.
SO YOU MET THE DIRECTOR?
SSK..
TREMBLE TREMBLE
MAX...

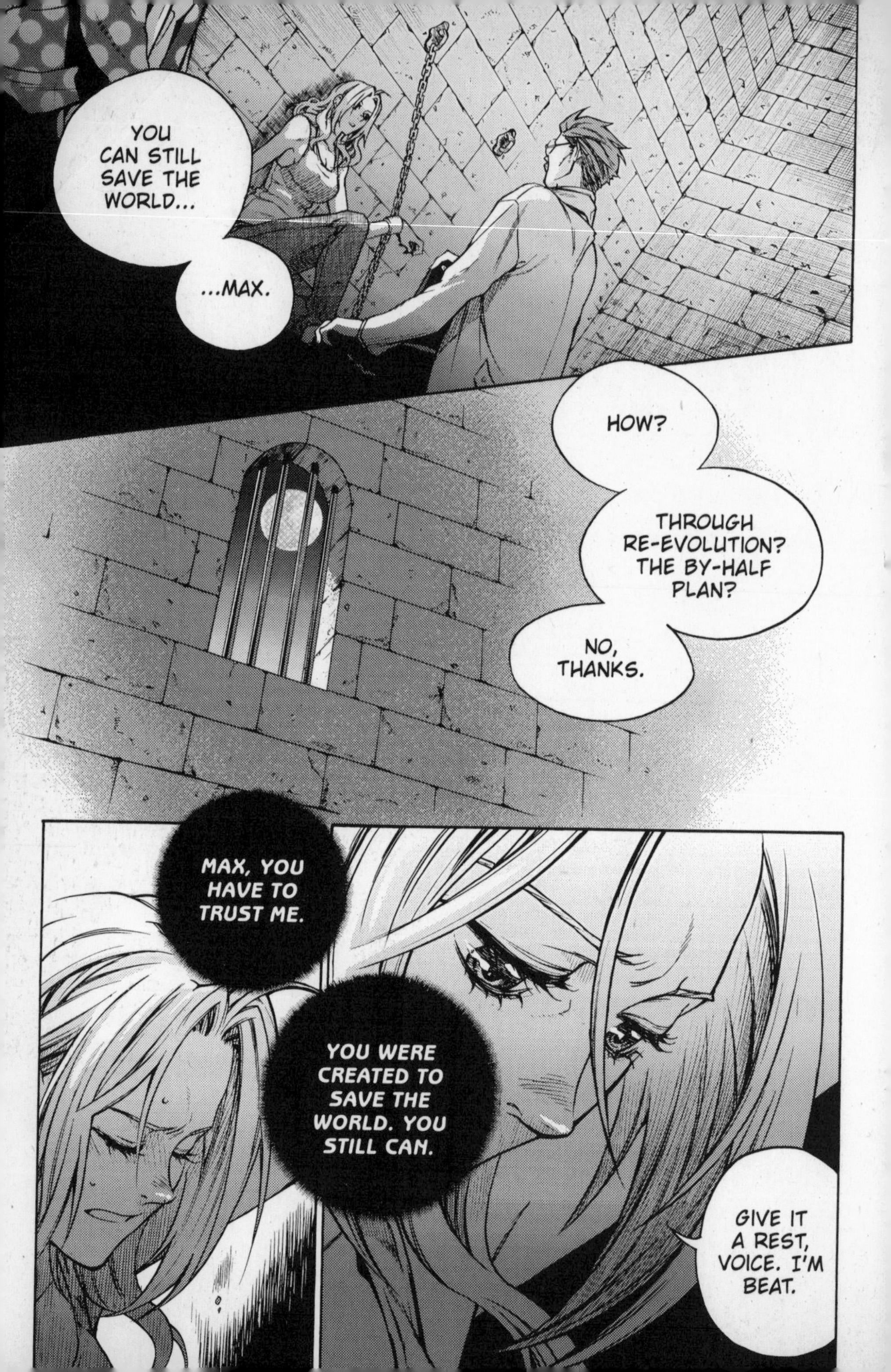
YOU CAN STILL SAVE THE WORLD...
...MAX.
HOW?
THROUGH RE-EVOLUTION? THE BY-HALF PLAN?
NO, THANKS.
MAX, YOU HAVE TO TRUST ME.
YOU WERE CREATED TO SAVE THE WORLD. YOU STILL CAN.
GIVE IT A REST, VOICE. I'M BEAT.

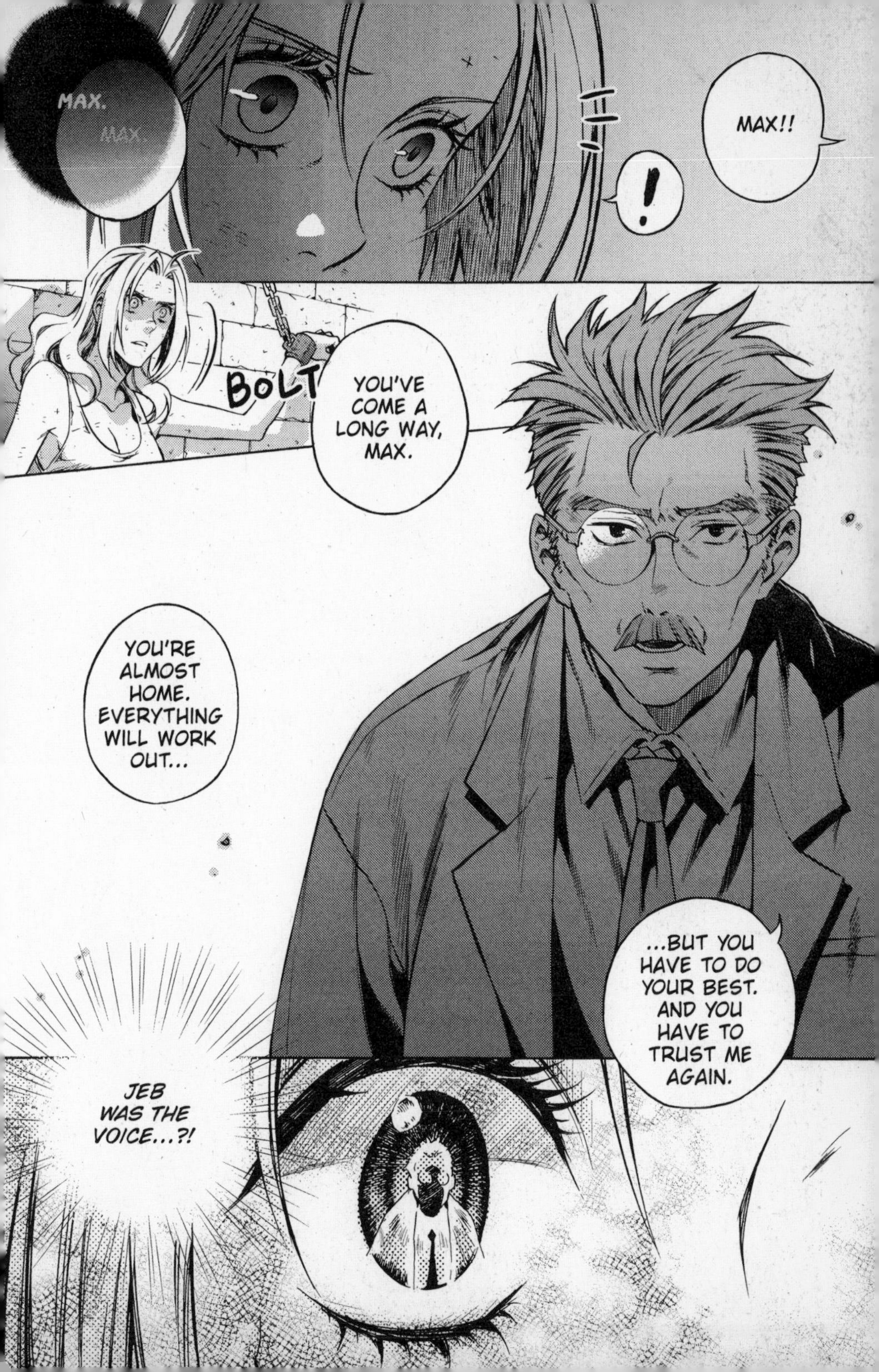
MAX.
MAX.
MAX!!
!
BOLT
YOU'VE COME A LONG WAY, MAX.
YOU'RE ALMOST HOME. EVERYTHING WILL WORK OUT...
...BUT YOU HAVE TO DO YOUR BEST. AND YOU HAVE TO TRUST ME AGAIN.
JEB WAS THE VOICE...?!

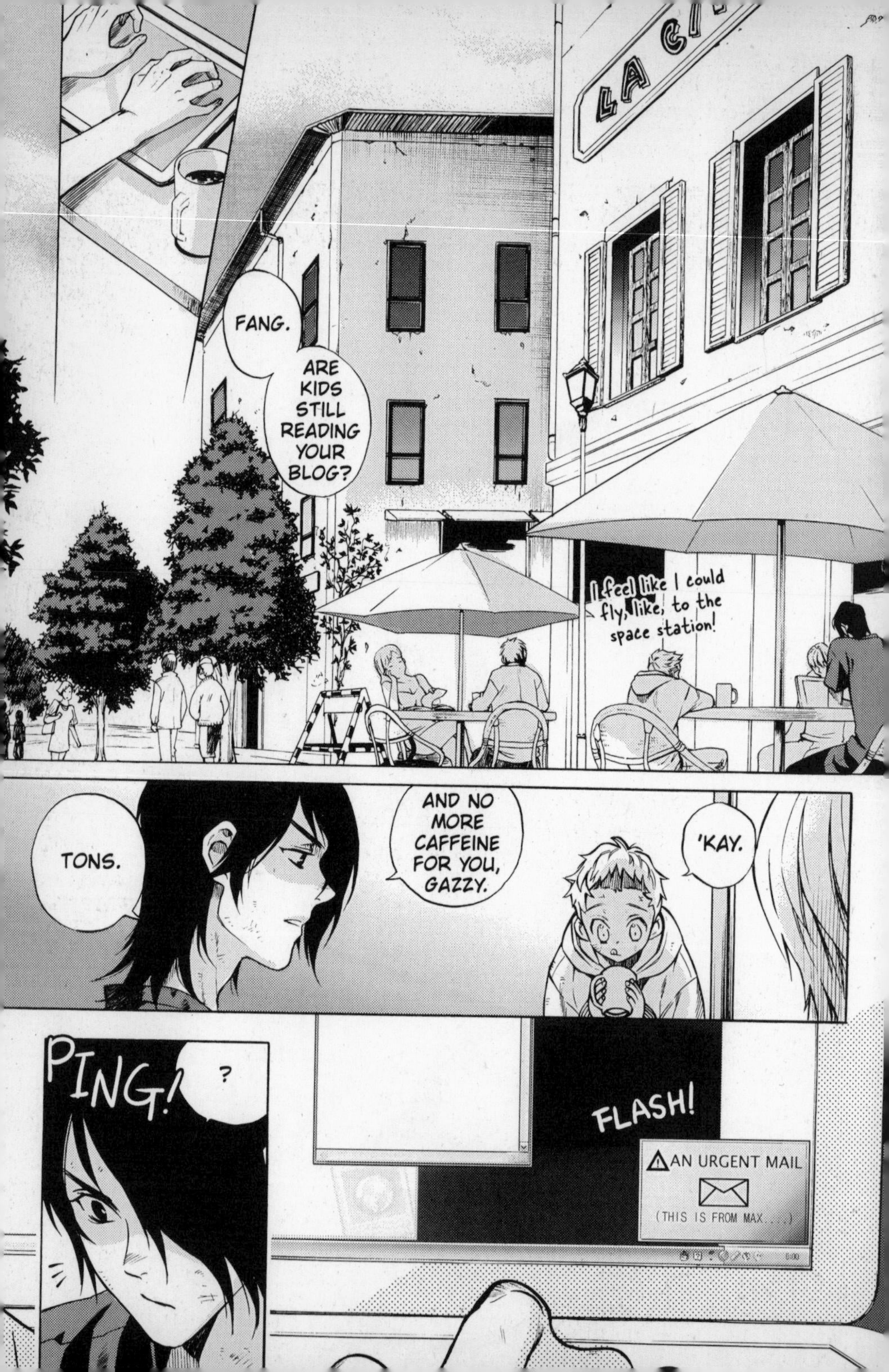
FANG.
ARE KIDS STILL READING YOUR BLOG?
I feel like I could fly, like, to the space station!
TONS.
AND NO MORE CAFFEINE FOR YOU, GAZZY.
'KAY.
PING!
?
FLASH!
AN URGENT MAIL
(THIS IS FROM MAX....)

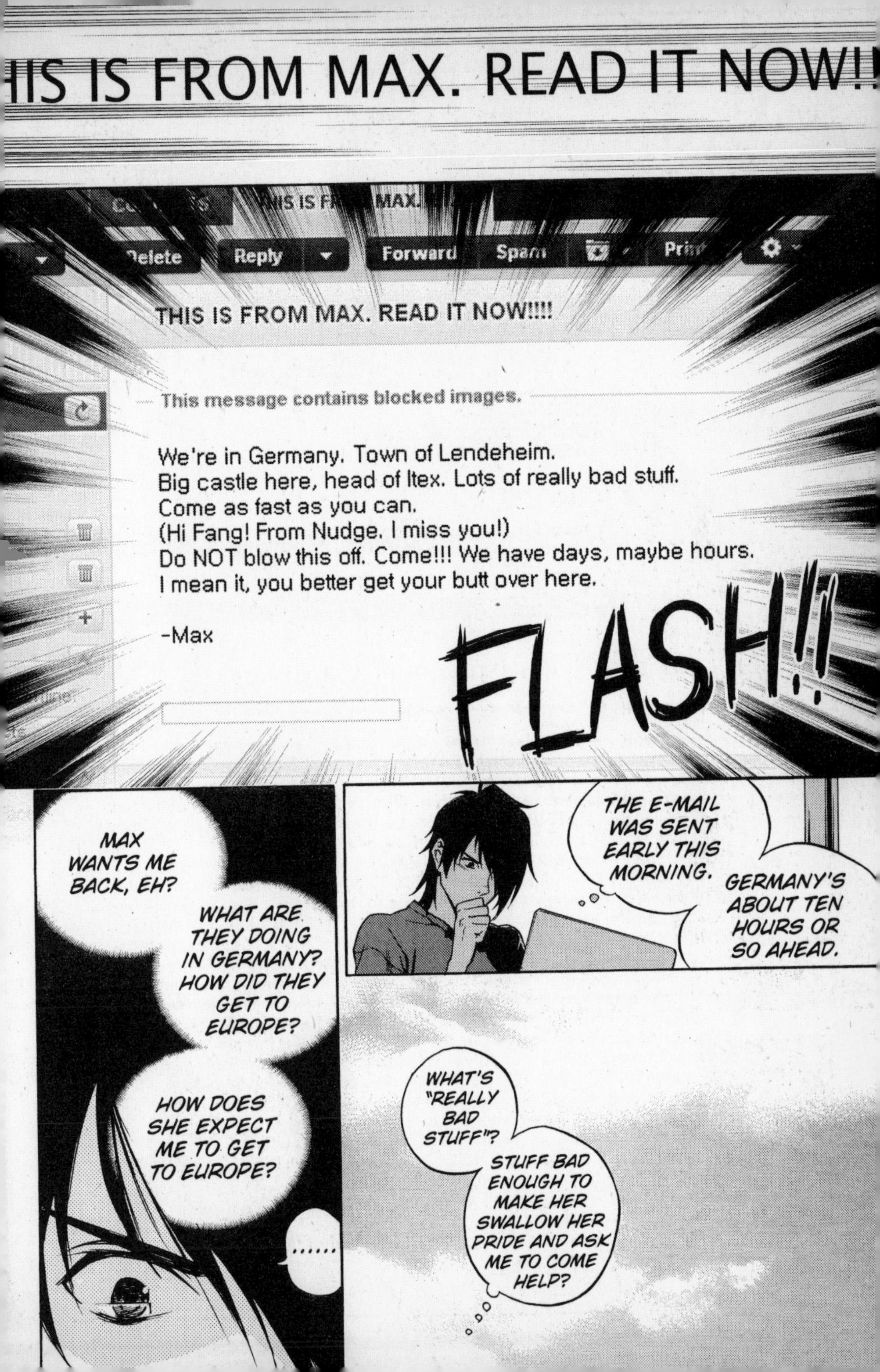
THIS IS FROM MAX. READ IT NOW!!
Delete
Reply
Forward
Spam
THIS IS FROM MAX. READ IT NOW!!!!
This message contains blocked images.
We're in Germany. Town of Lendeheim.
Big castle here, head of Itex. Lots of really bad stuff.
Come as fast as you can.
(Hi Fang! From Nudge. I miss you!)
Do NOT blow this off. Come!!! We have days, maybe hours.
I mean it, you better get your butt over here.
-Max
FLASH!!
THE E-MAIL WAS SENT EARLY THIS MORNING.
GERMANY'S ABOUT TEN HOURS OR SO AHEAD.
MAX WANTS ME BACK, EH?
WHAT ARE THEY DOING IN GERMANY? HOW DID THEY GET TO EUROPE?
HOW DOES SHE EXPECT ME TO GET TO EUROPE?
......
WHAT'S "REALLY BAD STUFF"?
STUFF BAD ENOUGH TO MAKE HER SWALLOW HER PRIDE AND ASK ME TO COME HELP?

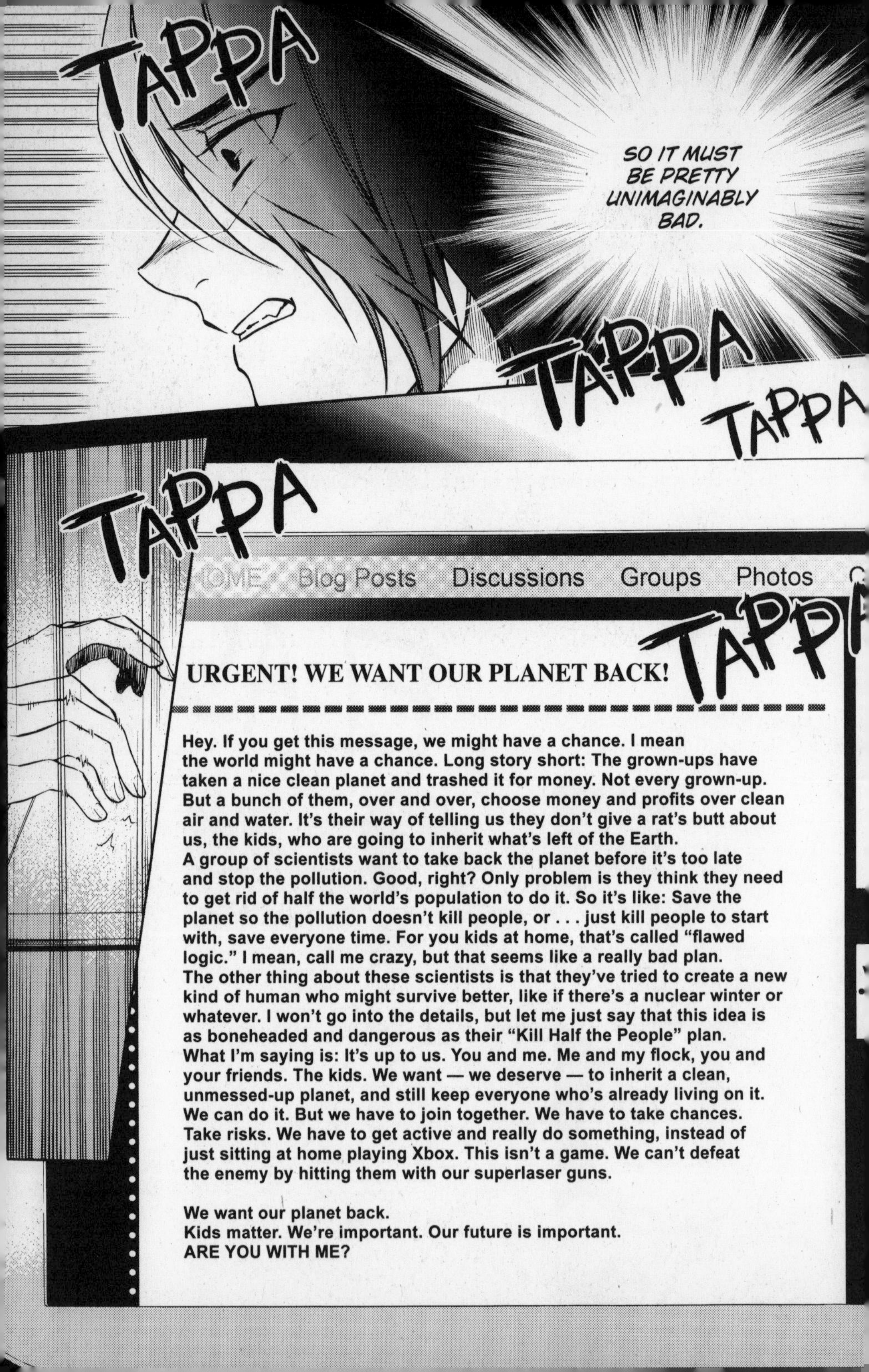
TAPPA
SO IT MUST BE PRETTY UNIMAGINABLY BAD.
TAPPA
TAPPA
TAPPA
Blog Posts
Discussions
Groups
Photos
URGENT! WE WANT OUR PLANET BACK!
Hey. If you get this message, we might have a chance. I mean the world might have a chance. Long story short: The grown-ups have taken a nice clean planet and trashed it for money. Not every grown-up. But a bunch of them, over and over, choose money and profits over clean air and water. It's their way of telling us they don't give a rat's butt about us, the kids, who are going to inherit what's left of the Earth.
A group of scientists want to take back the planet before it's too late and stop the pollution. Good, right? Only problem is they think they need to get rid of half the world's population to do it. So it's like: Save the planet so the pollution doesn't kill people, or . . . just kill people to start with, save everyone time. For you kids at home, that's called "flawed logic." I mean, call me crazy, but that seems like a really bad plan.
The other thing about these scientists is that they've tried to create a new kind of human who might survive better, like if there's a nuclear winter or whatever. I won't go into the details, but let me just say that this idea is as boneheaded and dangerous as their "Kill Half the People" plan.
What I'm saying is: It's up to us. You and me. Me and my flock, you and your friends. The kids. We want — we deserve — to inherit a clean, unmessed-up planet, and still keep everyone who's already living on it.
We can do it. But we have to join together. We have to take chances. Take risks. We have to get active and really do something, instead of just sitting at home playing Xbox. This isn't a game. We can't defeat the enemy by hitting them with our superlaser guns.
We want our planet back.
Kids matter. We're important. Our future is important.
ARE YOU WITH ME?

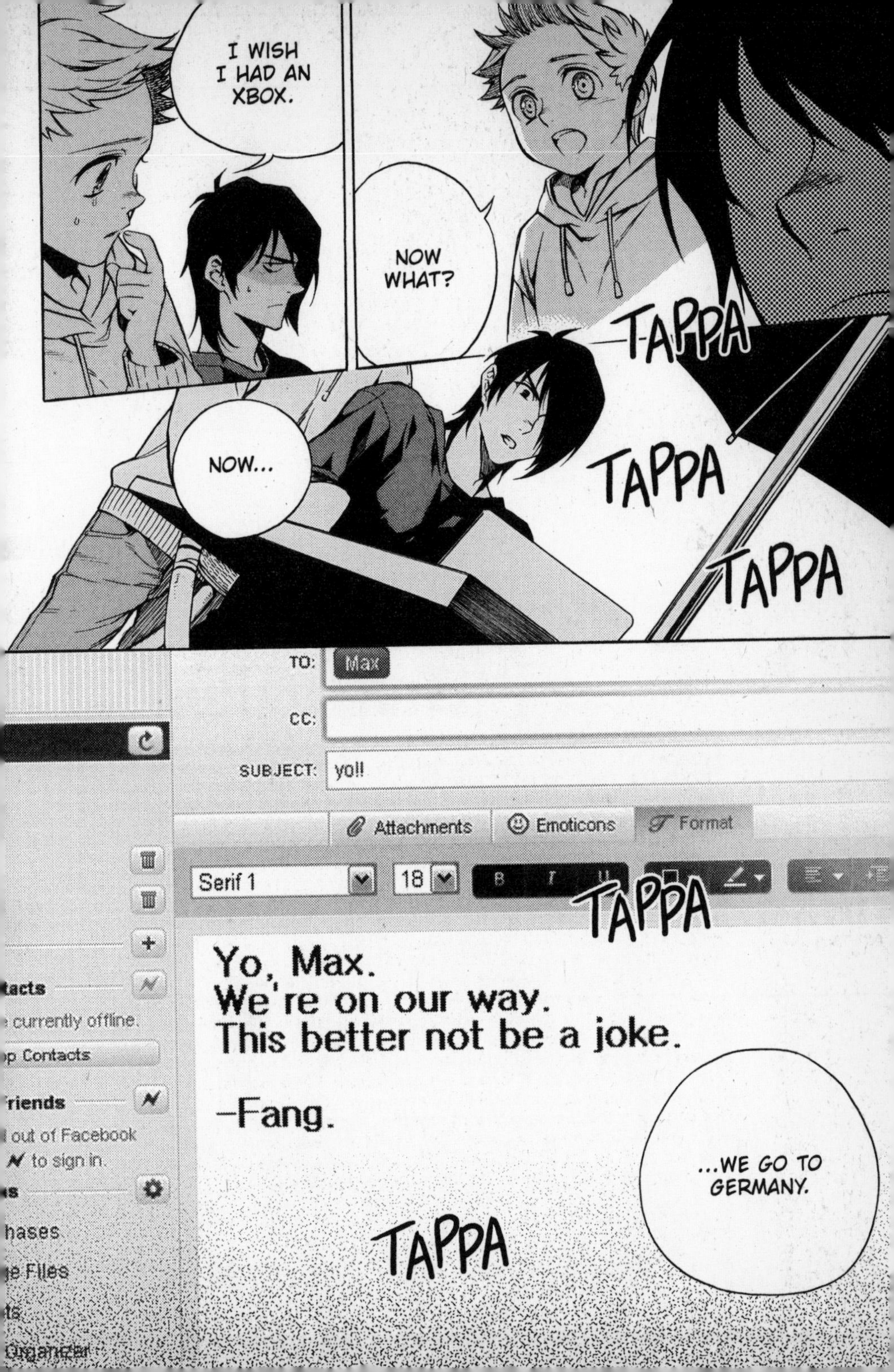
I WISH I HAD AN XBOX.
NOW WHAT?
TAPPA
NOW...
TAPPA
TAPPA
TO:
Max
CC:
SUBJECT:
yo!!
Attachments
Emoticons
Format
Serif 1
18
TAPPA
Yo, Max.
We're on our way.
This better not be a joke.
–Fang.
TAPPA
...WE GO TO GERMANY.

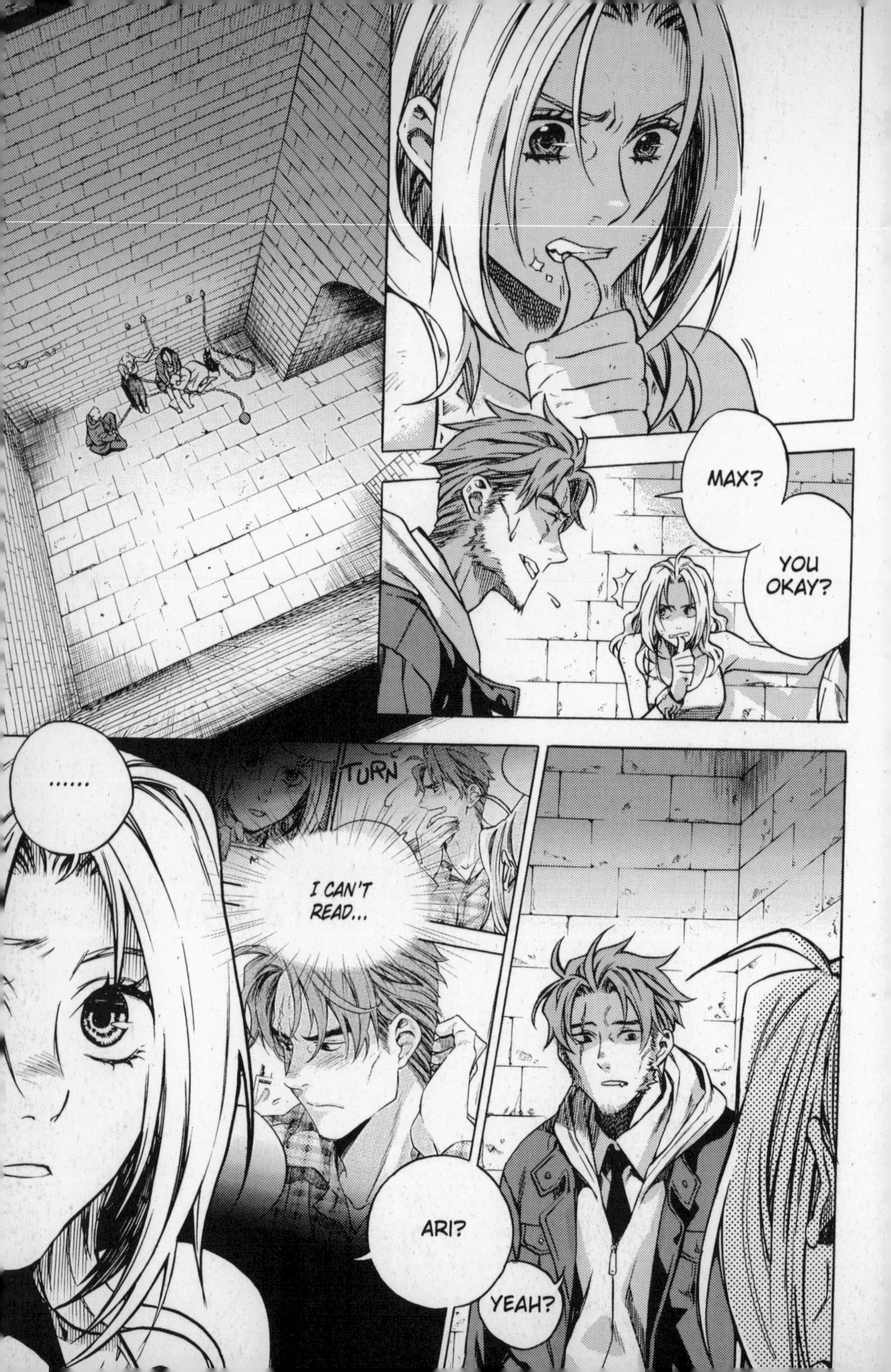
MAX?
YOU OKAY?
......
TURN
I CAN'T READ...
ARI?
YEAH?

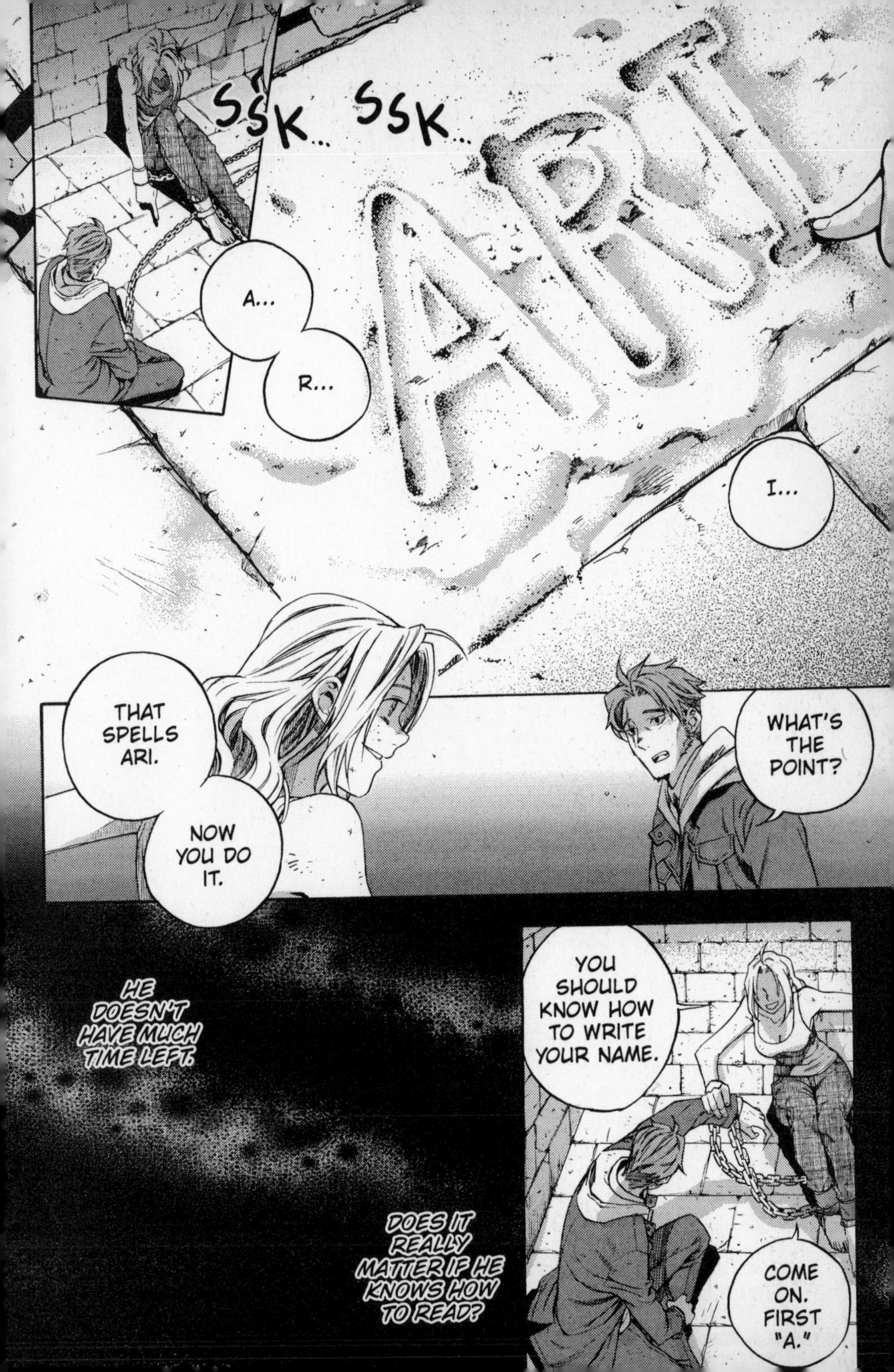
SSK... SSK...
A...
R...
I...
THAT SPELLS ARI.
NOW YOU DO IT.
WHAT'S THE POINT?
YOU SHOULD KNOW HOW TO WRITE YOUR NAME.
HE DOESN'T HAVE MUCH TIME LEFT.
DOES IT REALLY MATTER IF HE KNOWS HOW TO READ?
COME ON. FIRST "A."

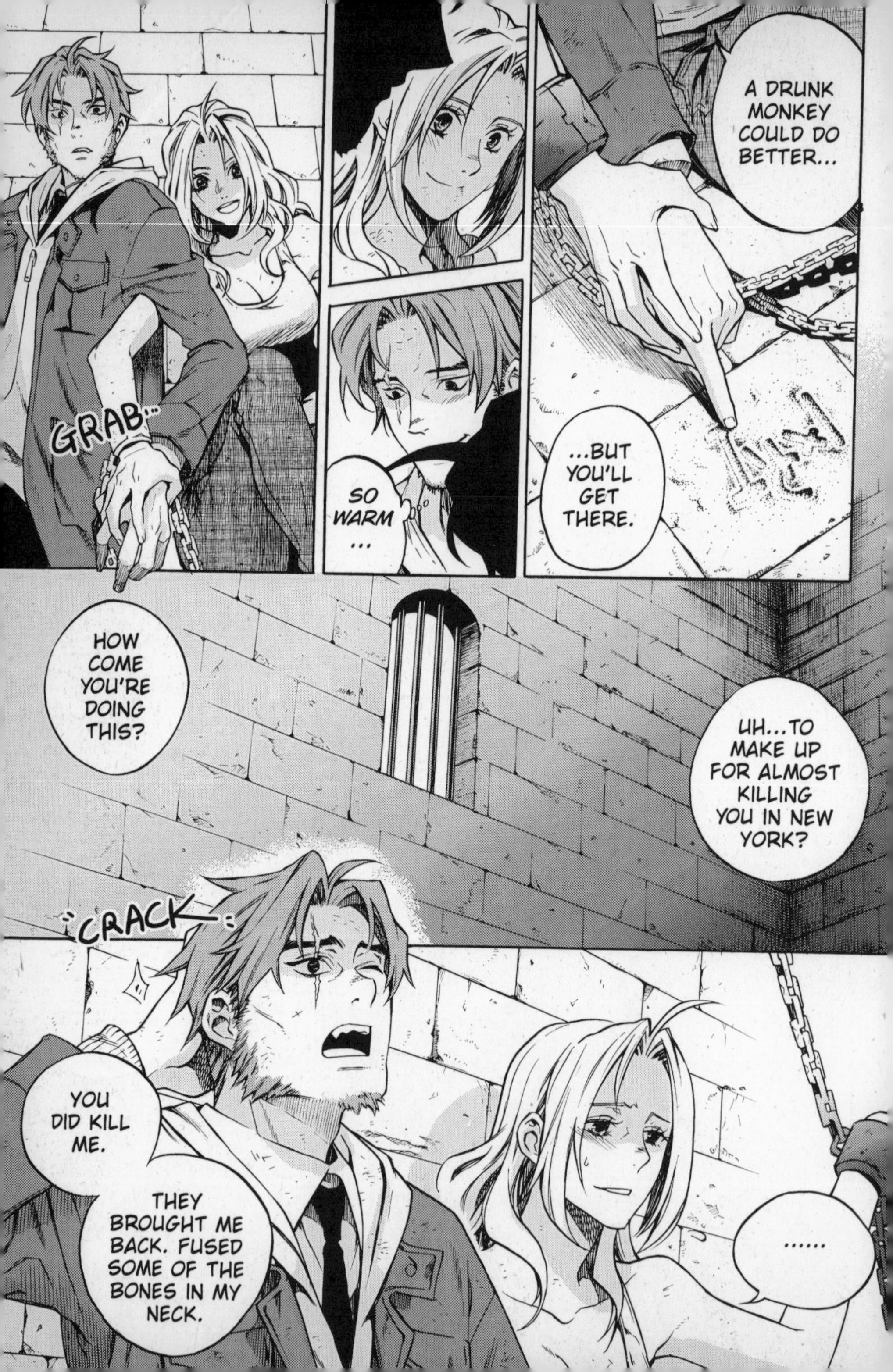
GRAB...
A DRUNK MONKEY COULD DO BETTER...
...BUT YOU'LL GET THERE.
SO WARM...
HOW COME YOU'RE DOING THIS?
UH...TO MAKE UP FOR ALMOST KILLING YOU IN NEW YORK?
CRACK
YOU DID KILL ME.
THEY BROUGHT ME BACK. FUSED SOME OF THE BONES IN MY NECK.
......

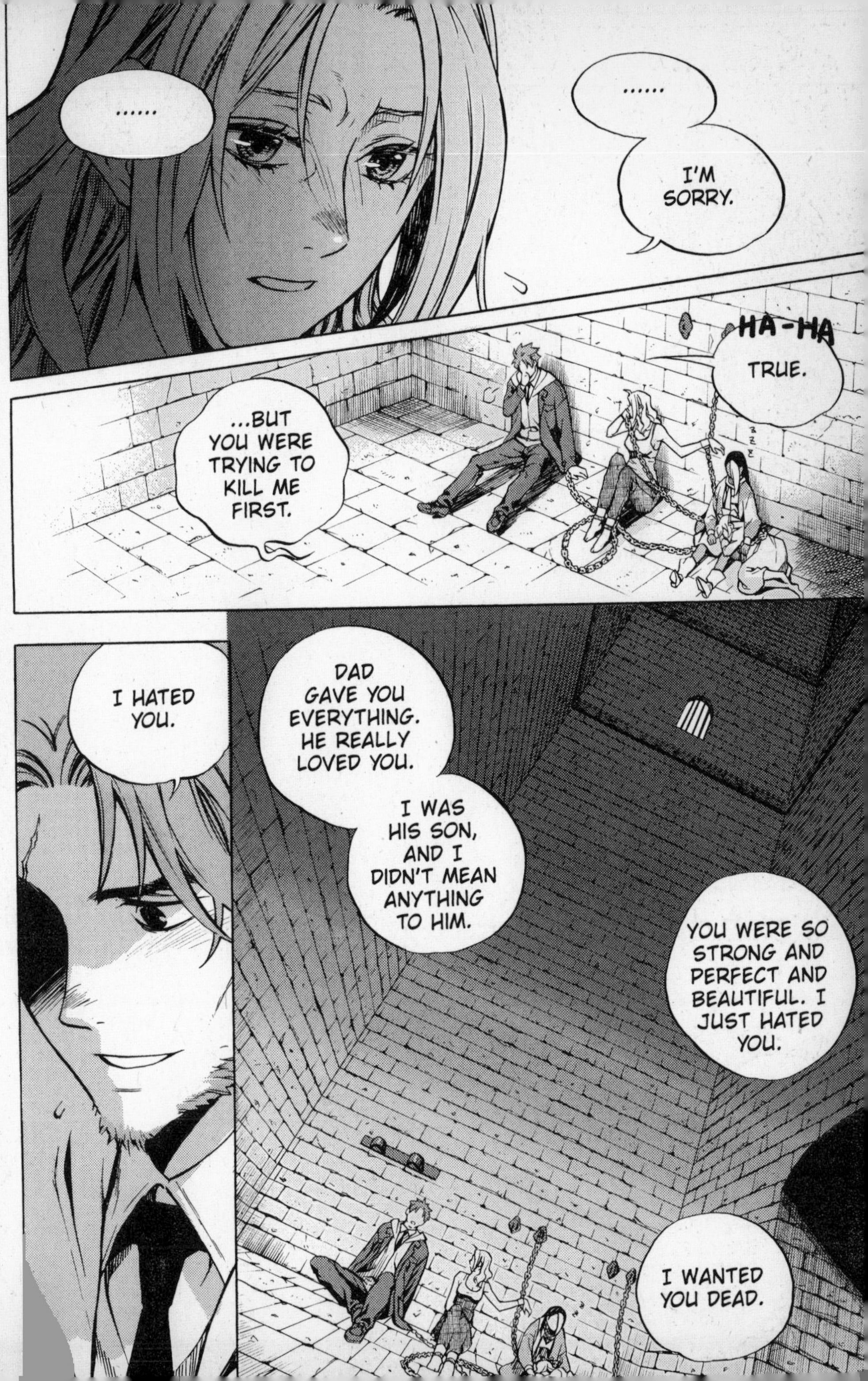
......
I'M SORRY.
......
HA-HA
TRUE.
...BUT YOU WERE TRYING TO KILL ME FIRST.
I HATED YOU.
DAD GAVE YOU EVERYTHING. HE REALLY LOVED YOU.
I WAS HIS SON, AND I DIDN'T MEAN ANYTHING TO HIM.
YOU WERE SO STRONG AND PERFECT AND BEAUTIFUL. I JUST HATED YOU.
I WANTED YOU DEAD.

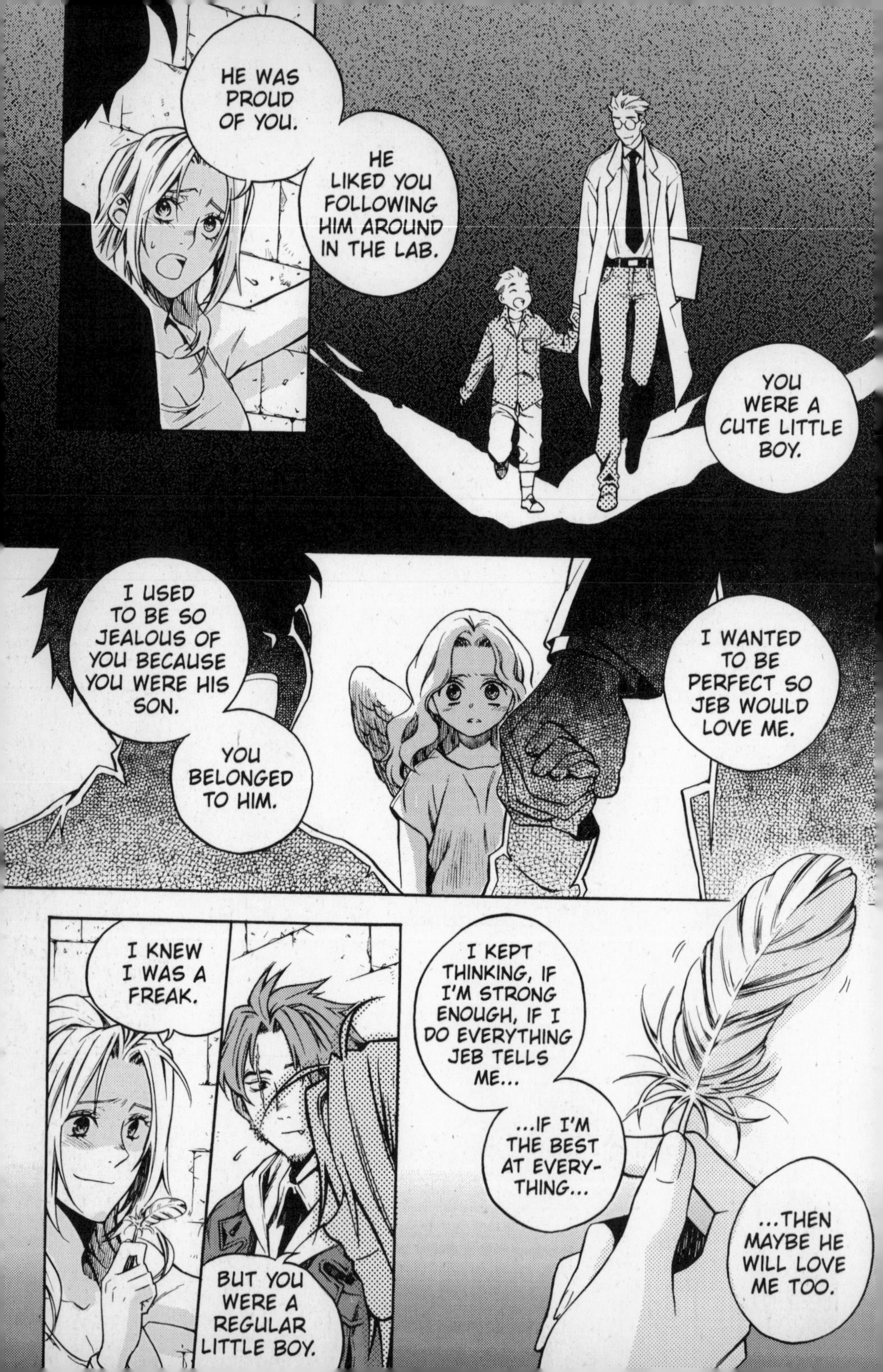
HE WAS PROUD OF YOU.
HE LIKED YOU FOLLOWING HIM AROUND IN THE LAB.
YOU WERE A CUTE LITTLE BOY.
I USED TO BE SO JEALOUS OF YOU BECAUSE YOU WERE HIS SON.
YOU BELONGED TO HIM.
I WANTED TO BE PERFECT SO JEB WOULD LOVE ME.
I KNEW I WAS A FREAK.
BUT YOU WERE A REGULAR LITTLE BOY.
I KEPT THINKING, IF I'M STRONG ENOUGH, IF I DO EVERYTHING JEB TELLS ME...
...IF I'M THE BEST AT EVERY-THING...
...THEN MAYBE HE WILL LOVE ME TOO.

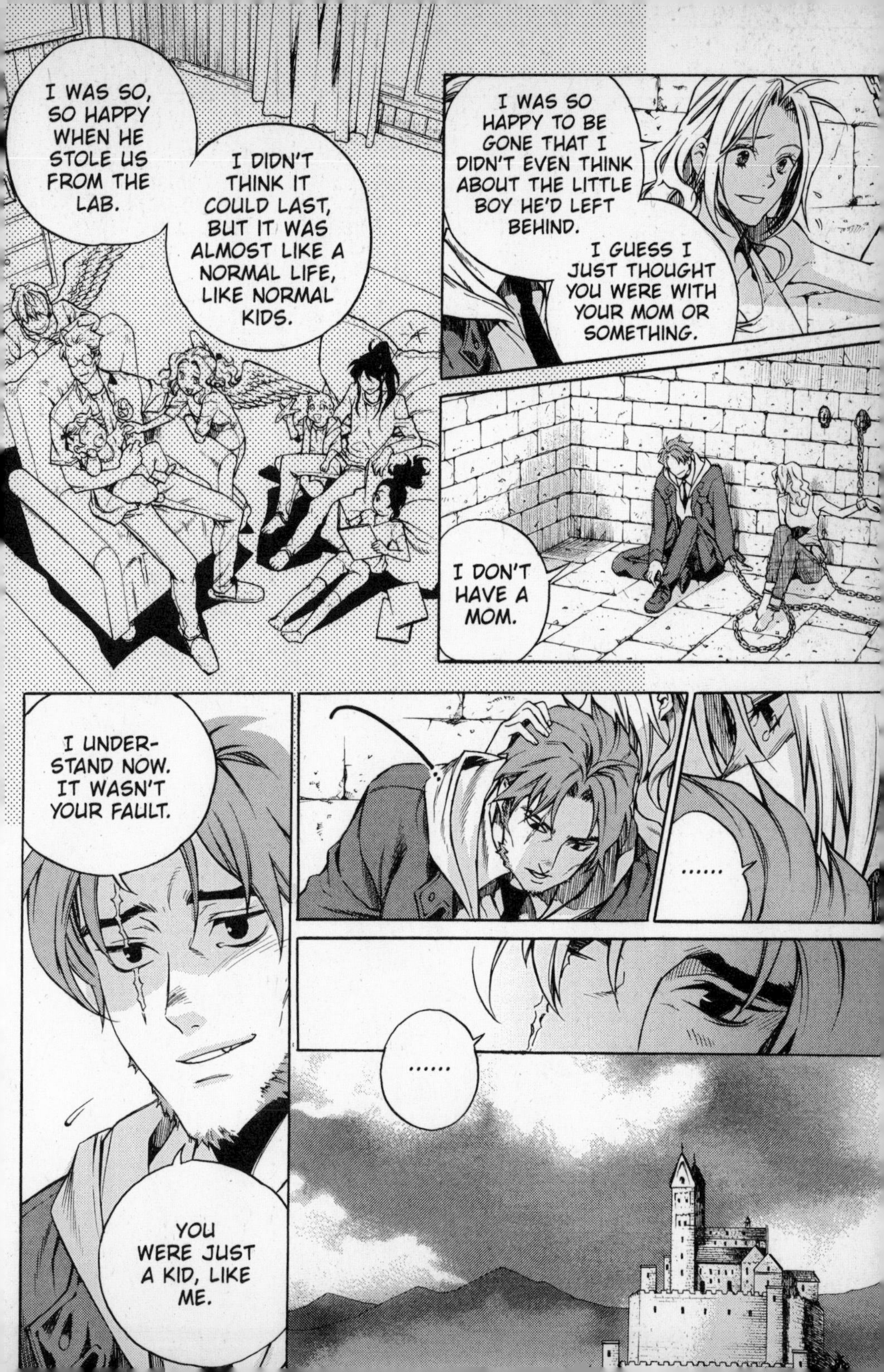

I WAS SO, SO HAPPY WHEN HE STOLE US FROM THE LAB.
I DIDN'T THINK IT COULD LAST, BUT IT WAS ALMOST LIKE A NORMAL LIFE, LIKE NORMAL KIDS.
I WAS SO HAPPY TO BE GONE THAT I DIDN'T EVEN THINK ABOUT THE LITTLE BOY HE'D LEFT BEHIND.
I GUESS I JUST THOUGHT YOU WERE WITH YOUR MOM OR SOMETHING.
I DON'T HAVE A MOM.
I UNDER-STAND NOW. IT WASN'T YOUR FAULT.
......
......
YOU WERE JUST A KID, LIKE ME.

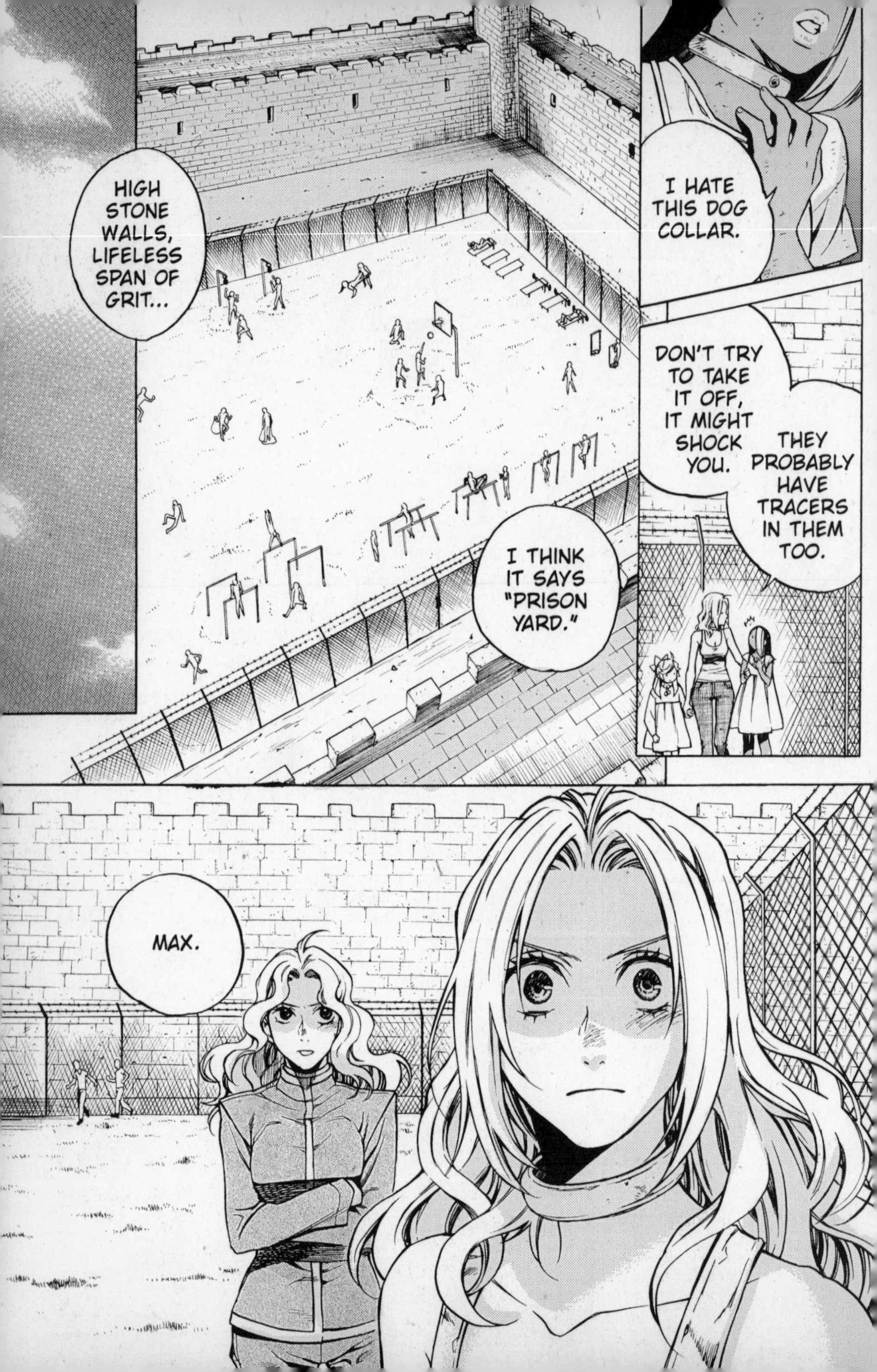
HIGH STONE WALLS, LIFELESS SPAN OF GRIT...
I HATE THIS DOG COLLAR.
DON'T TRY TO TAKE IT OFF, IT MIGHT SHOCK YOU.
THEY PROBABLY HAVE TRACERS IN THEM TOO.
I THINK IT SAYS "PRISON YARD."
MAX.

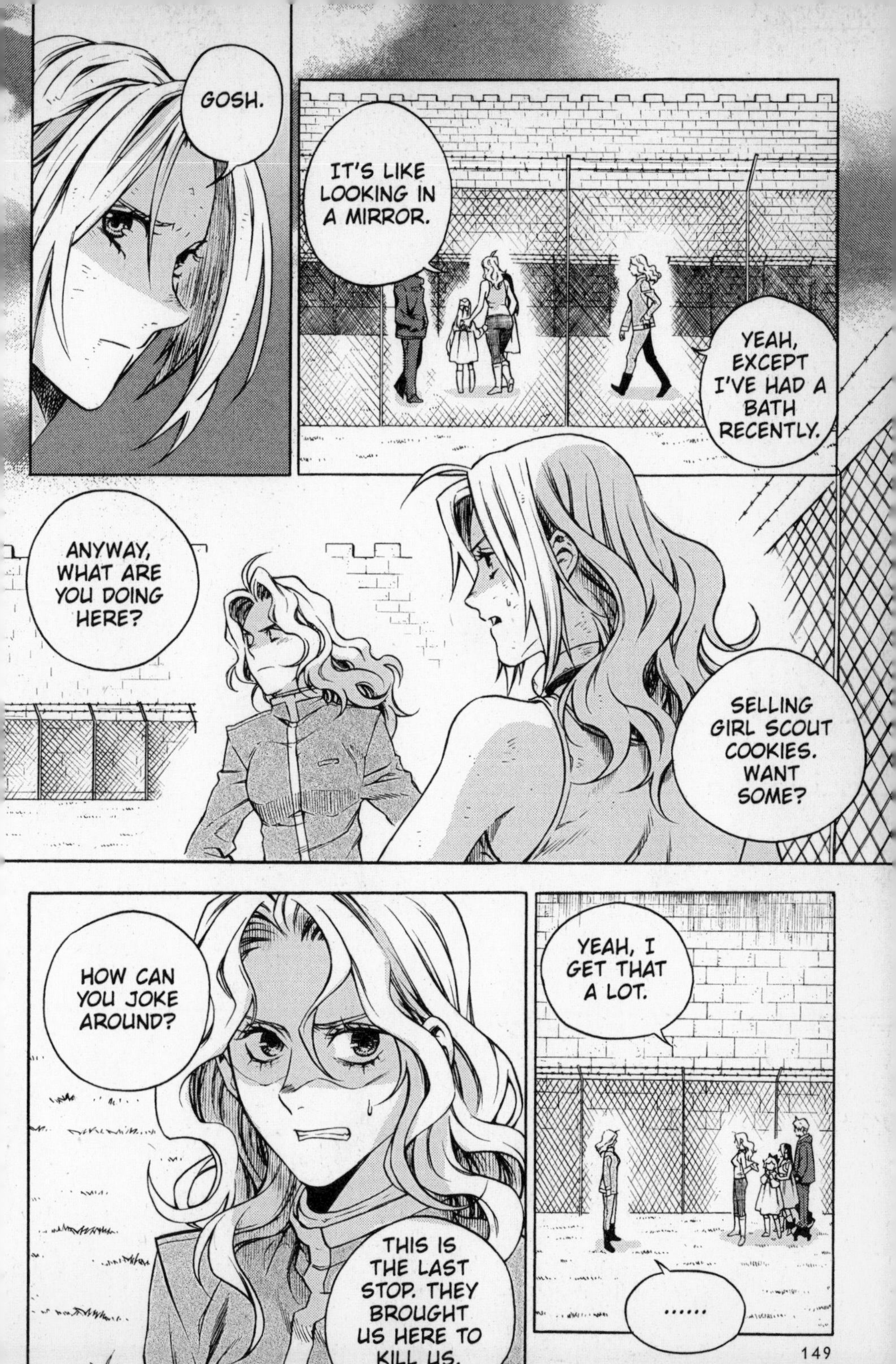
GOSH.
IT'S LIKE LOOKING IN A MIRROR.
YEAH, EXCEPT I'VE HAD A BATH RECENTLY.
ANYWAY, WHAT ARE YOU DOING HERE?
SELLING GIRL SCOUT COOKIES. WANT SOME?
HOW CAN YOU JOKE AROUND?
THIS IS THE LAST STOP. THEY BROUGHT US HERE TO KILL US.
YEAH, I GET THAT A LOT.
......

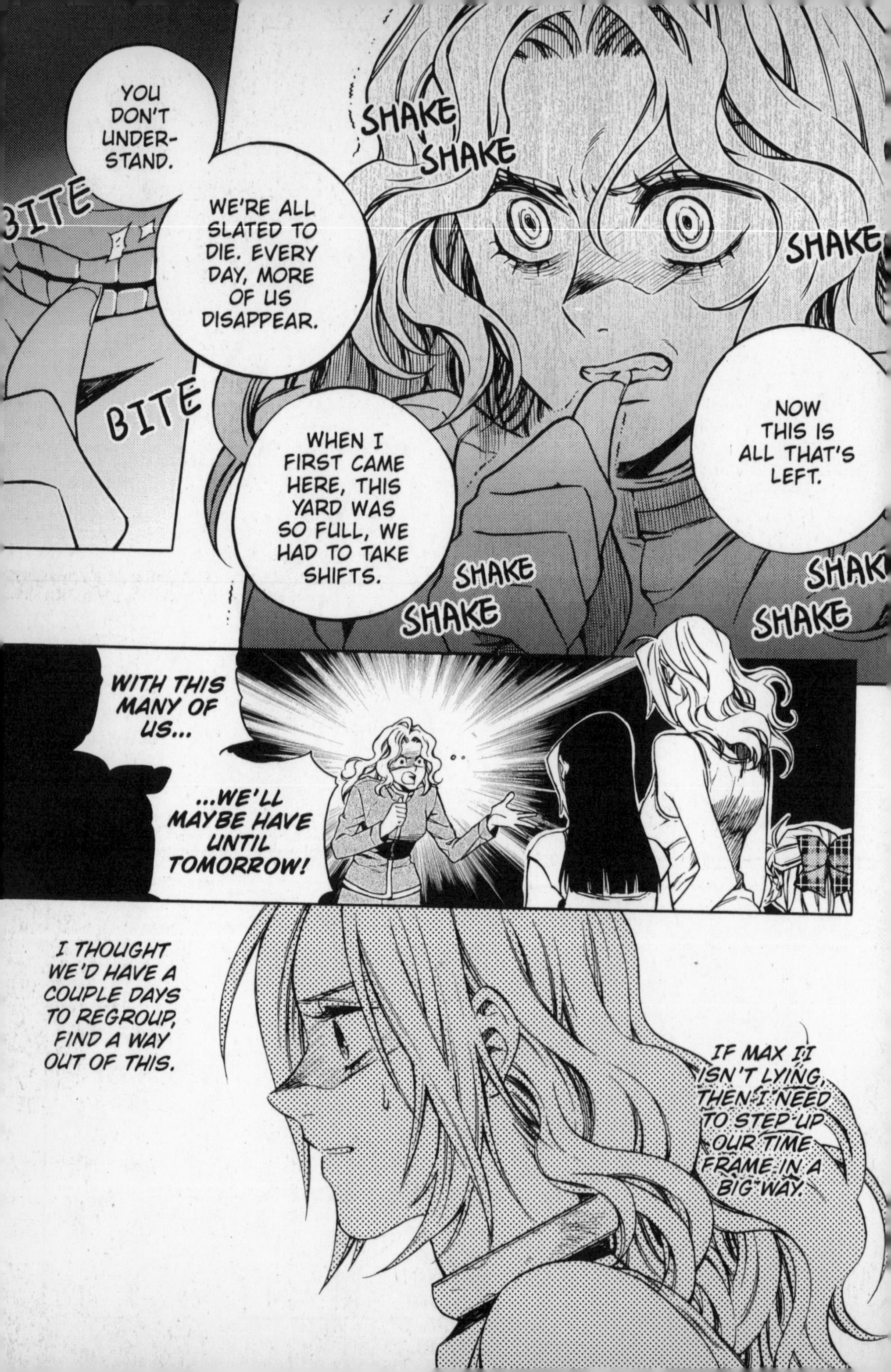
YOU DON'T UNDER-STAND.
BITE
BITE
WE'RE ALL SLATED TO DIE. EVERY DAY, MORE OF US DISAPPEAR.
SHAKE
SHAKE
SHAKE
WHEN I FIRST CAME HERE, THIS YARD WAS SO FULL, WE HAD TO TAKE SHIFTS.
NOW THIS IS ALL THAT'S LEFT.
SHAKE
SHAKE
SHAKE
WITH THIS MANY OF US...
...WE'LL MAYBE HAVE UNTIL TOMORROW!
I THOUGHT WE'D HAVE A COUPLE DAYS TO REGROUP, FIND A WAY OUT OF THIS.
IF MAX II ISN'T LYING, THEN I NEED TO STEP UP OUR TIME FRAME IN A BIG WAY.

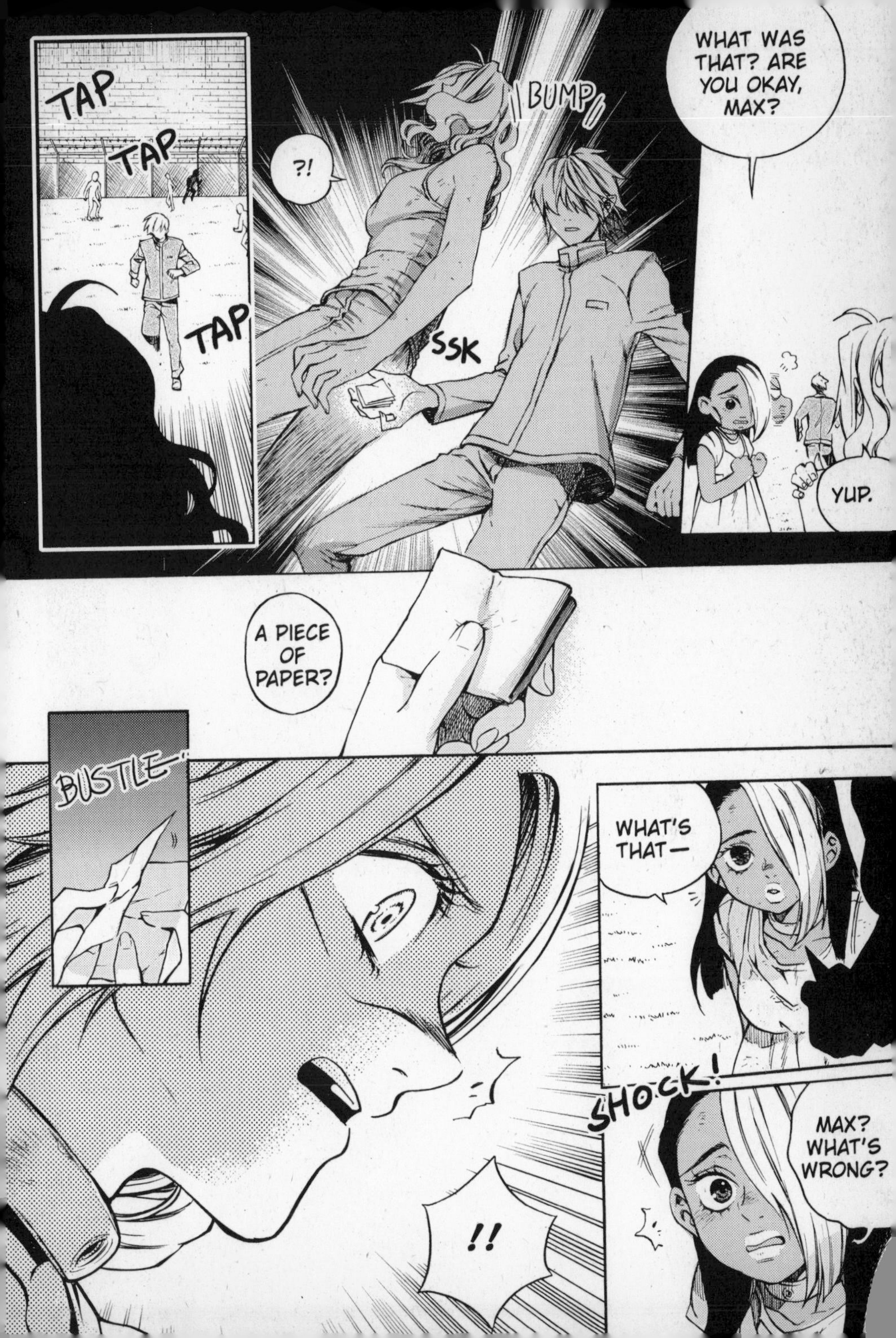
WHAT WAS THAT? ARE YOU OKAY, MAX?
BUMP
?!
TAP
TAP
TAP
SSK
YUP.
A PIECE OF PAPER?
BUSTLE
WHAT'S THAT—
SHOCK!
MAX? WHAT'S WRONG?
!!

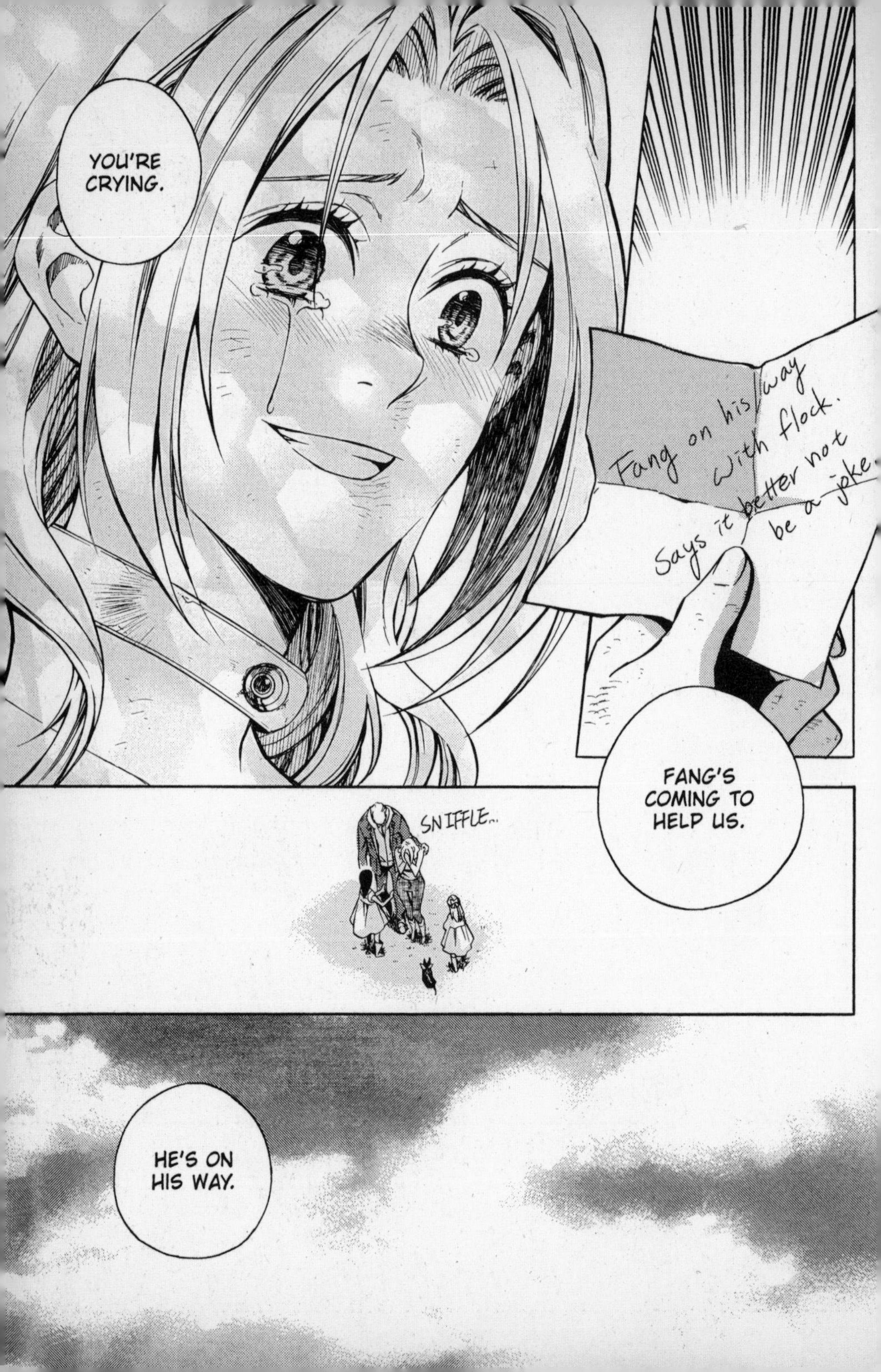

YOU'RE CRYING.
Fang on his way with flock. Says it better not be a joke
FANG'S COMING TO HELP US.
SNIFFLE..
HE'S ON HIS WAY.

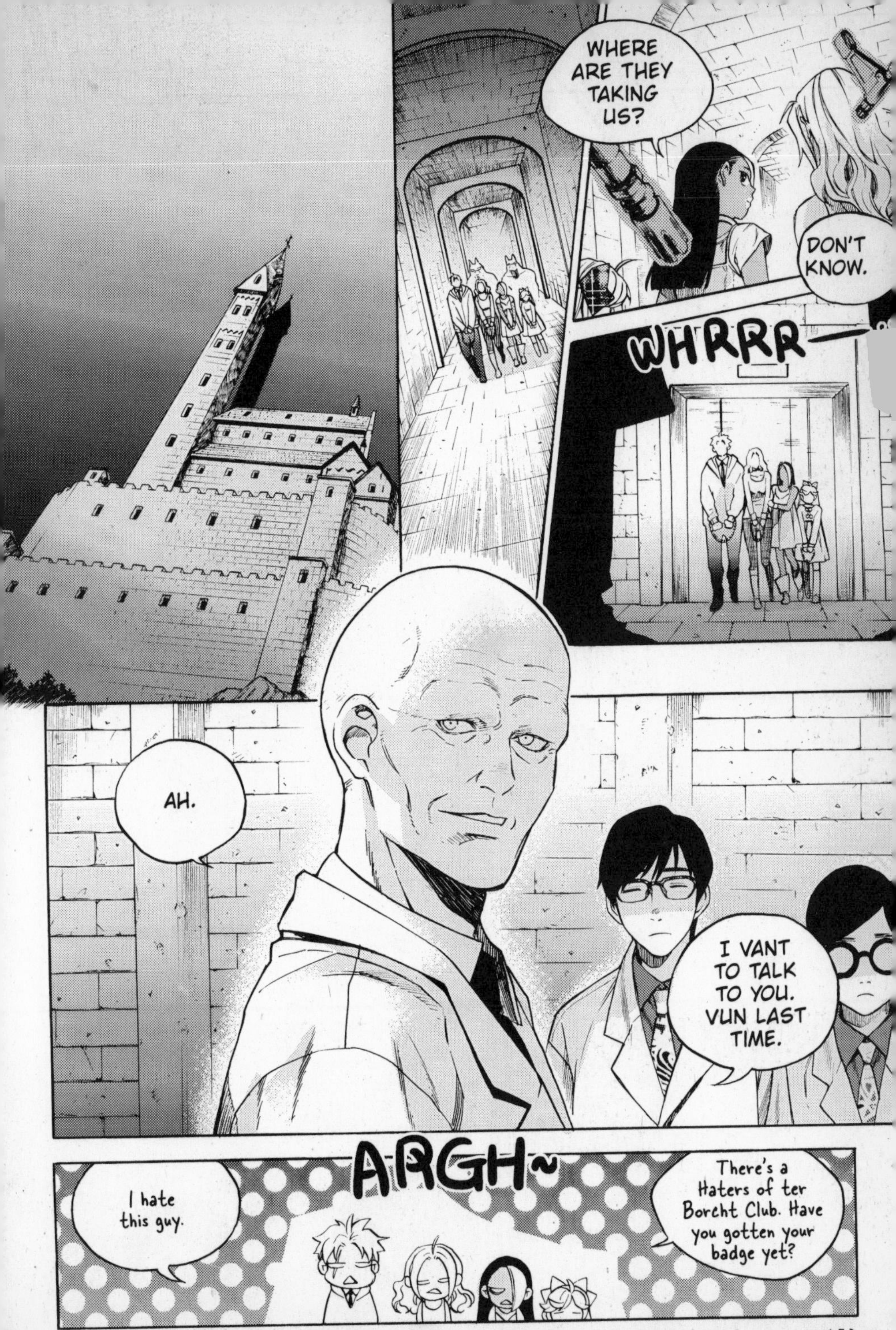

WHERE ARE THEY TAKING US?
DON'T KNOW.
WHRRR
AH.
I VANT TO TALK TO YOU. VUN LAST TIME.
ARGH~
I hate this guy.
There's a Haters of ter Borcht Club. Have you gotten your badge yet?

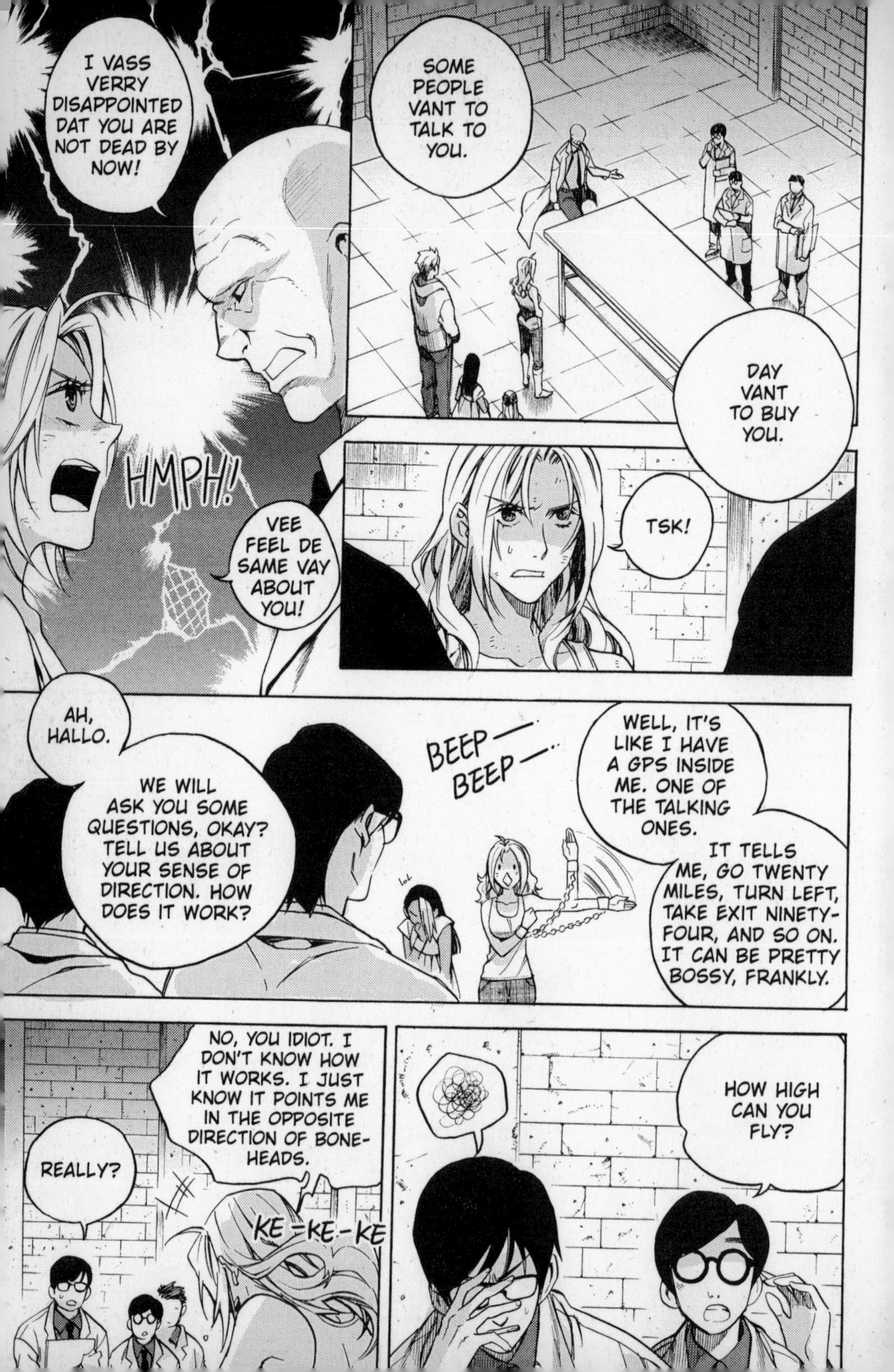
I VASS VERRY DISAPPOINTED DAT YOU ARE NOT DEAD BY NOW!
HMPH!
VEE FEEL DE SAME VAY ABOUT YOU!
SOME PEOPLE VANT TO TALK TO YOU.
DAY VANT TO BUY YOU.
TSK!
AH, HALLO.
WE WILL ASK YOU SOME QUESTIONS, OKAY? TELL US ABOUT YOUR SENSE OF DIRECTION. HOW DOES IT WORK?
BEEP— BEEP—...
WELL, IT'S LIKE I HAVE A GPS INSIDE ME. ONE OF THE TALKING ONES.
IT TELLS ME, GO TWENTY MILES, TURN LEFT, TAKE EXIT NINETY-FOUR, AND SO ON. IT CAN BE PRETTY BOSSY, FRANKLY.
REALLY?
NO, YOU IDIOT. I DON'T KNOW HOW IT WORKS. I JUST KNOW IT POINTS ME IN THE OPPOSITE DIRECTION OF BONE-HEADS.
KE-KE-KE
HOW HIGH CAN YOU FLY?

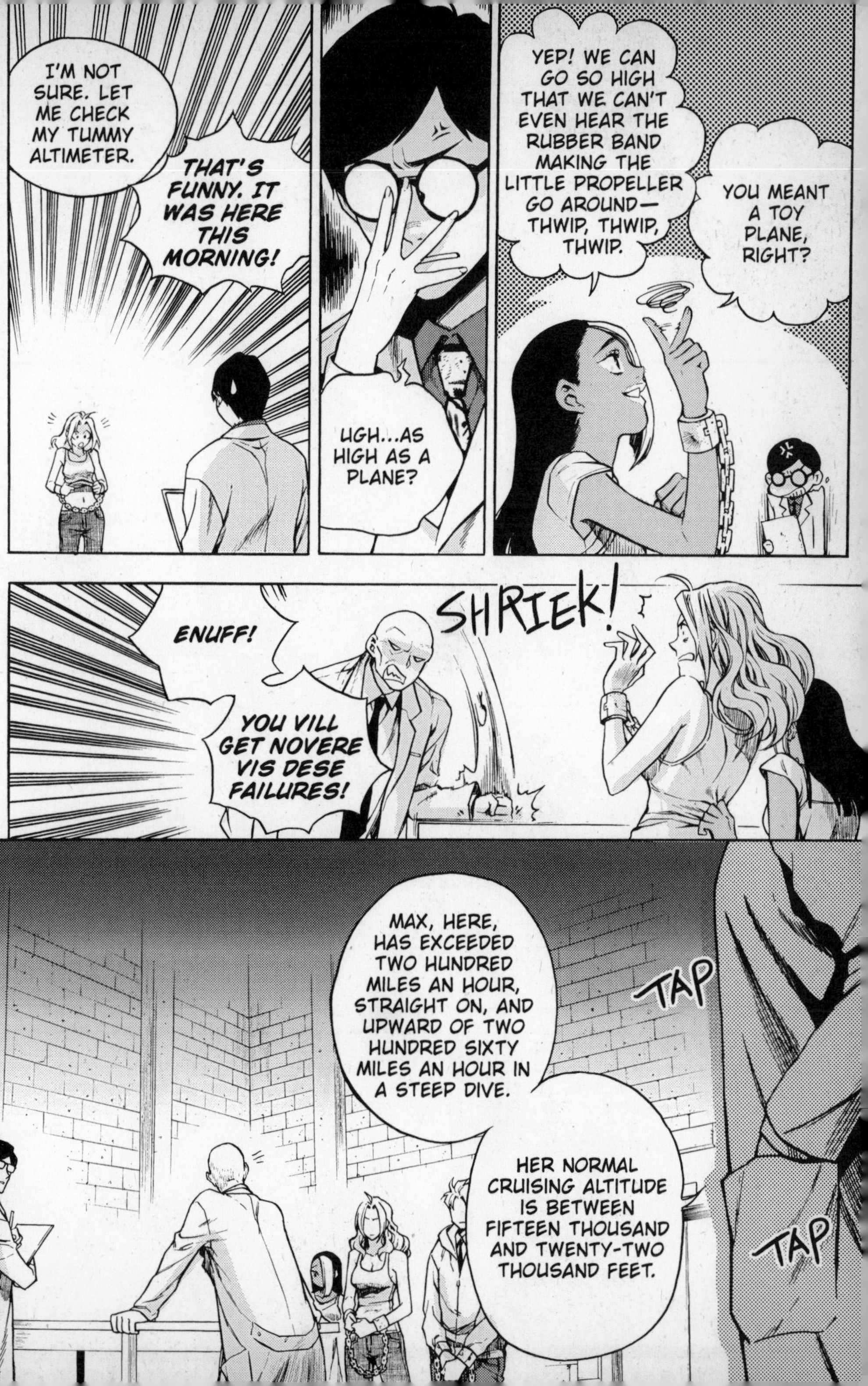
I'M NOT SURE. LET ME CHECK MY TUMMY ALTIMETER.
THAT'S FUNNY. IT WAS HERE THIS MORNING!
UGH...AS HIGH AS A PLANE?
YEP! WE CAN GO SO HIGH THAT WE CAN'T EVEN HEAR THE RUBBER BAND MAKING THE LITTLE PROPELLER GO AROUND—THWIP, THWIP, THWIP.
YOU MEANT A TOY PLANE, RIGHT?
ENUFF!
YOU VILL GET NOVERE VIS DESE FAILURES!
SHRIEK!
MAX, HERE, HAS EXCEEDED TWO HUNDRED MILES AN HOUR, STRAIGHT ON, AND UPWARD OF TWO HUNDRED SIXTY MILES AN HOUR IN A STEEP DIVE.
TAP
HER NORMAL CRUISING ALTITUDE IS BETWEEN FIFTEEN THOUSAND AND TWENTY-TWO THOUSAND FEET.
TAP

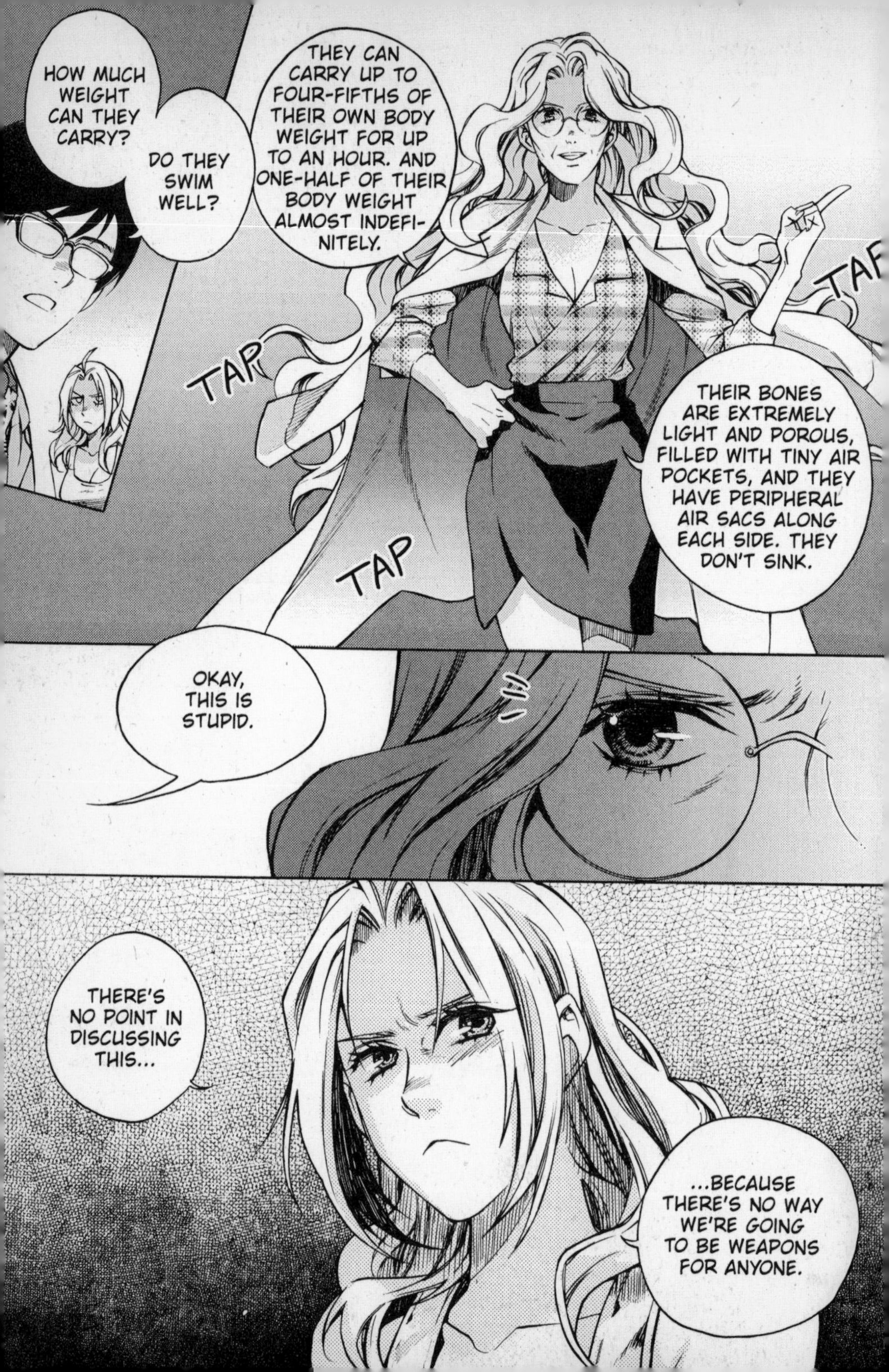
HOW MUCH WEIGHT CAN THEY CARRY?
DO THEY SWIM WELL?
THEY CAN CARRY UP TO FOUR-FIFTHS OF THEIR OWN BODY WEIGHT FOR UP TO AN HOUR. AND ONE-HALF OF THEIR BODY WEIGHT ALMOST INDEFI-NITELY.
TAP
TAP
TAP
THEIR BONES ARE EXTREMELY LIGHT AND POROUS, FILLED WITH TINY AIR POCKETS, AND THEY HAVE PERIPHERAL AIR SACS ALONG EACH SIDE. THEY DON'T SINK.
OKAY, THIS IS STUPID.
THERE'S NO POINT IN DISCUSSING THIS...
...BECAUSE THERE'S NO WAY WE'RE GOING TO BE WEAPONS FOR ANYONE.

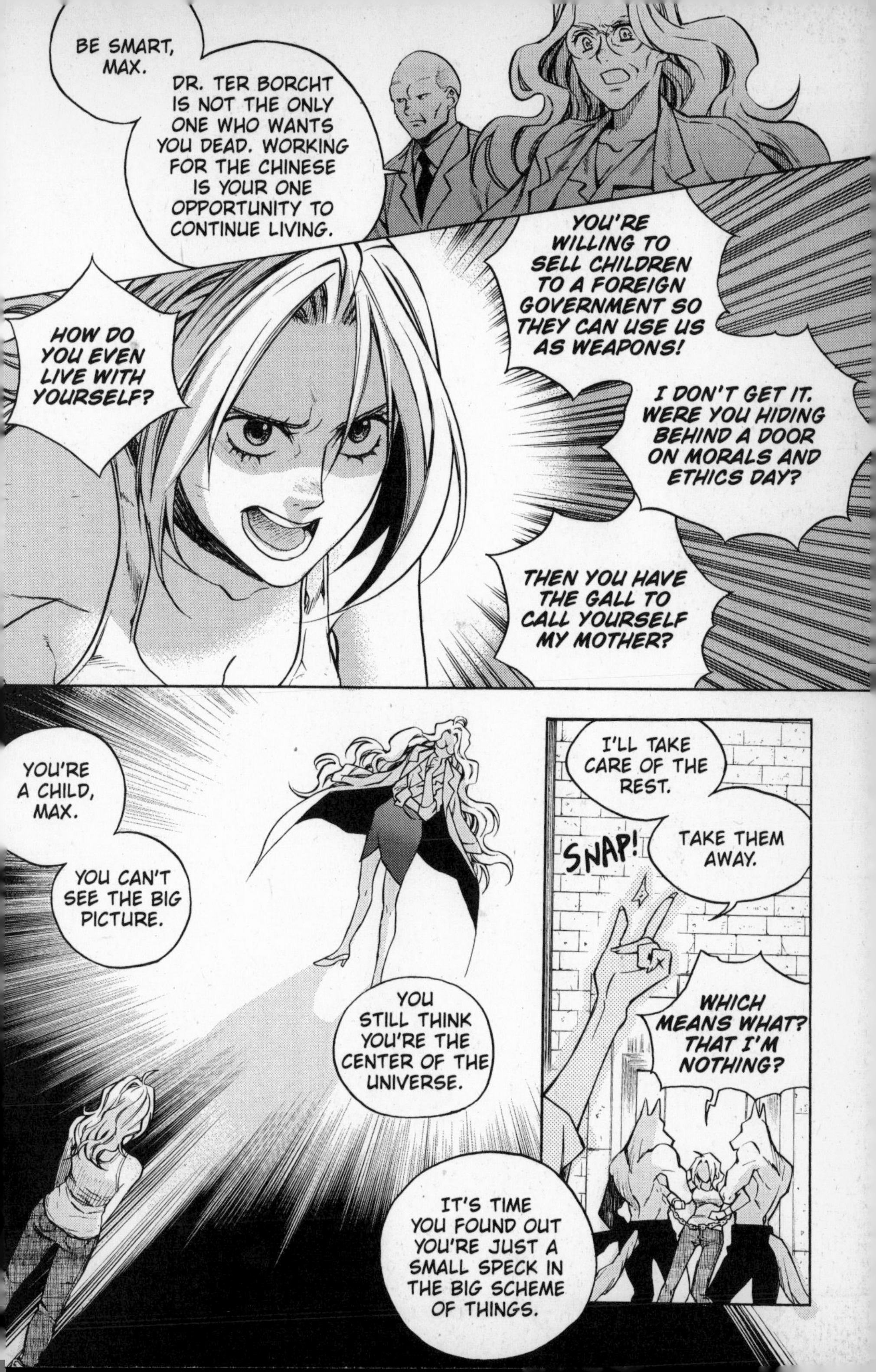
BE SMART, MAX.
DR. TER BORCHT IS NOT THE ONLY ONE WHO WANTS YOU DEAD. WORKING FOR THE CHINESE IS YOUR ONE OPPORTUNITY TO CONTINUE LIVING.
YOU'RE WILLING TO SELL CHILDREN TO A FOREIGN GOVERNMENT SO THEY CAN USE US AS WEAPONS!
HOW DO YOU EVEN LIVE WITH YOURSELF?
I DON'T GET IT. WERE YOU HIDING BEHIND A DOOR ON MORALS AND ETHICS DAY?
THEN YOU HAVE THE GALL TO CALL YOURSELF MY MOTHER?
YOU'RE A CHILD, MAX.
YOU CAN'T SEE THE BIG PICTURE.
YOU STILL THINK YOU'RE THE CENTER OF THE UNIVERSE.
IT'S TIME YOU FOUND OUT YOU'RE JUST A SMALL SPECK IN THE BIG SCHEME OF THINGS.
I'LL TAKE CARE OF THE REST.
SNAP!
TAKE THEM AWAY.
WHICH MEANS WHAT? THAT I'M NOTHING?

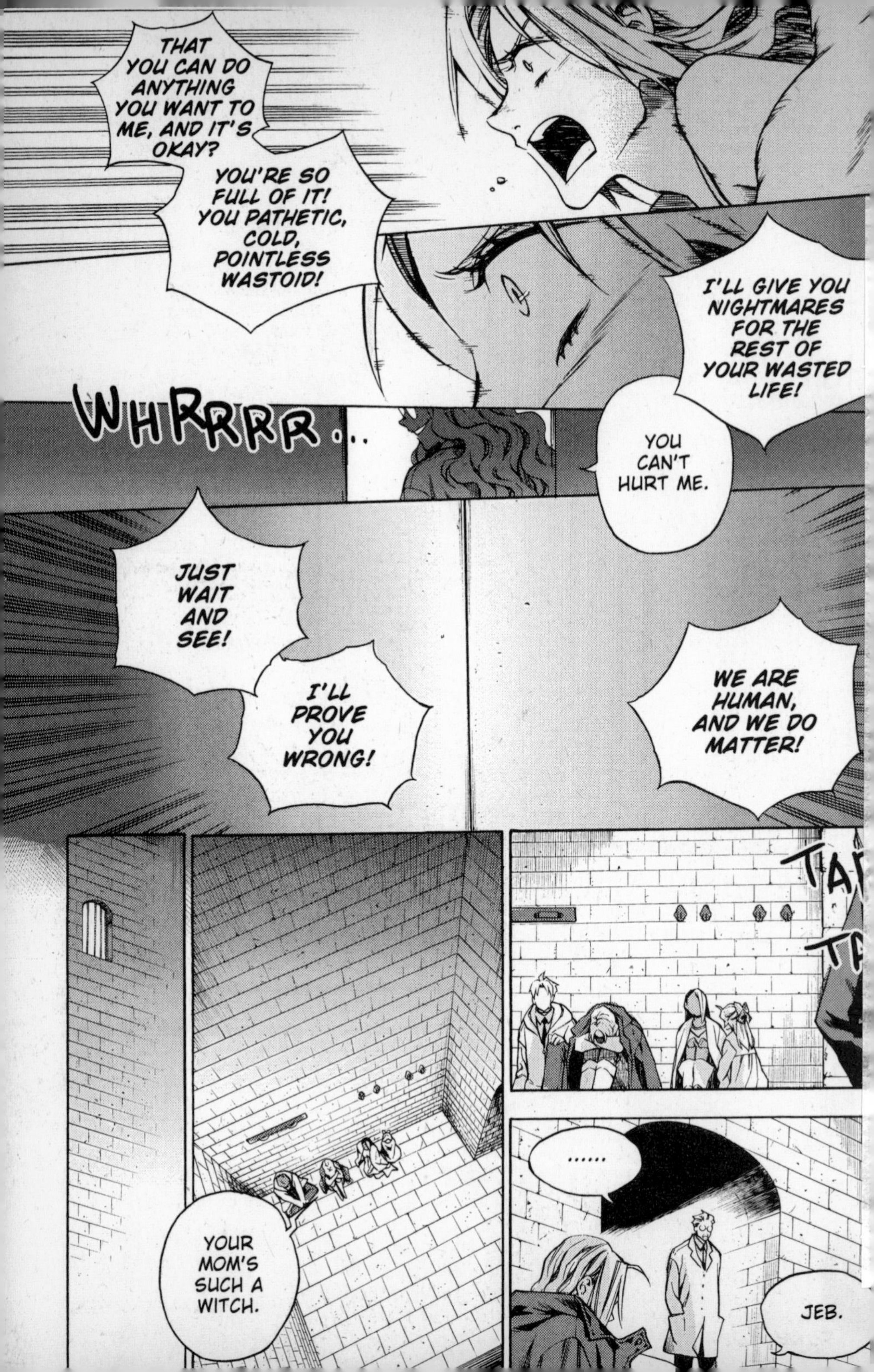

THAT YOU CAN DO ANYTHING YOU WANT TO ME, AND IT'S OKAY?
YOU'RE SO FULL OF IT! YOU PATHETIC, COLD, POINTLESS WASTOID!
I'LL GIVE YOU NIGHTMARES FOR THE REST OF YOUR WASTED LIFE!
WHRRRRR...
YOU CAN'T HURT ME.
JUST WAIT AND SEE!
I'LL PROVE YOU WRONG!
WE ARE HUMAN, AND WE DO MATTER!
TA
TA
......
YOUR MOM'S SUCH A WITCH.
JEB.

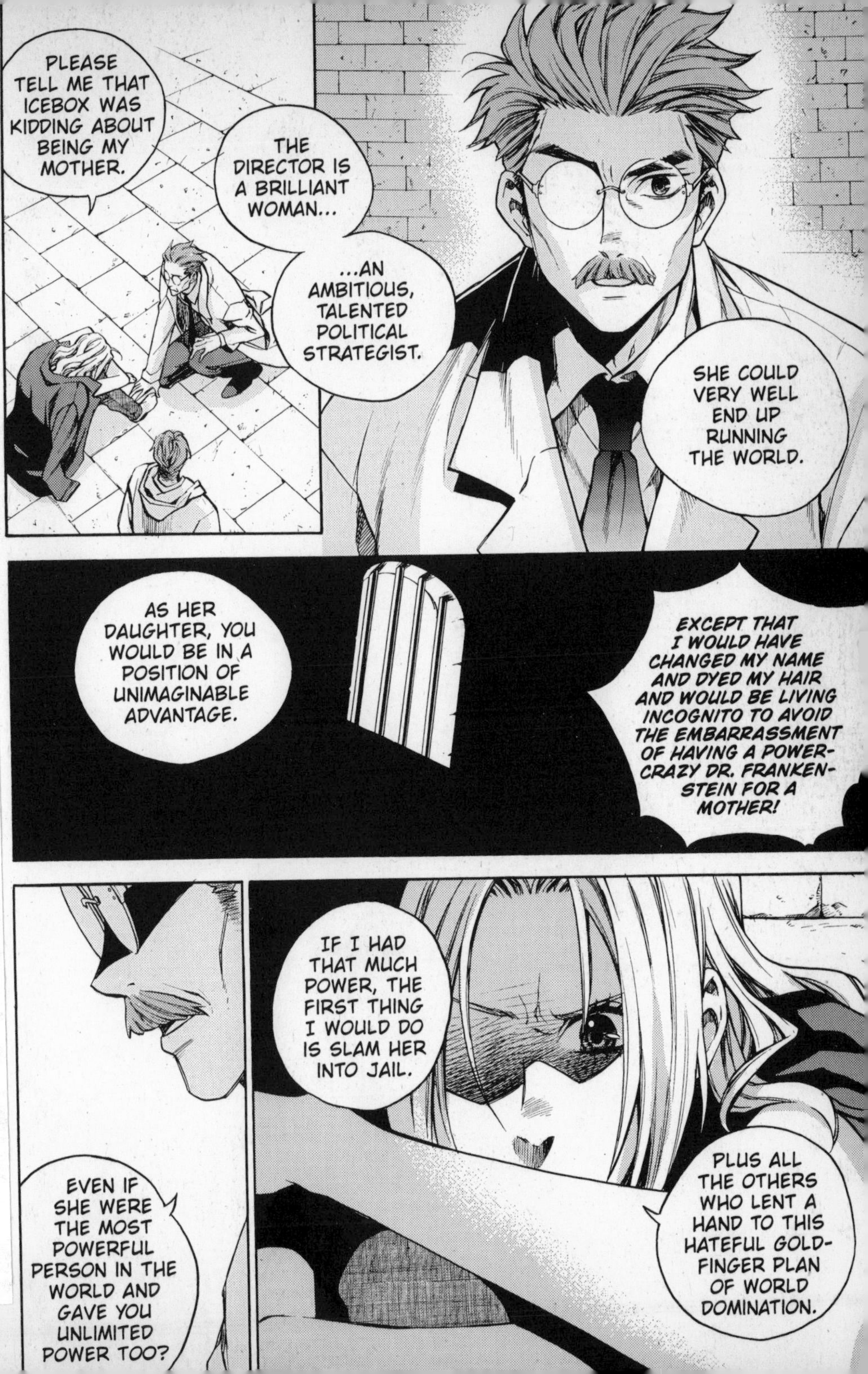
PLEASE TELL ME THAT ICEBOX WAS KIDDING ABOUT BEING MY MOTHER.
THE DIRECTOR IS A BRILLIANT WOMAN...
...AN AMBITIOUS, TALENTED POLITICAL STRATEGIST.
SHE COULD VERY WELL END UP RUNNING THE WORLD.
AS HER DAUGHTER, YOU WOULD BE IN A POSITION OF UNIMAGINABLE ADVANTAGE.
EXCEPT THAT I WOULD HAVE CHANGED MY NAME AND DYED MY HAIR AND WOULD BE LIVING INCOGNITO TO AVOID THE EMBARRASSMENT OF HAVING A POWER-CRAZY DR. FRANKEN-STEIN FOR A MOTHER!
IF I HAD THAT MUCH POWER, THE FIRST THING I WOULD DO IS SLAM HER INTO JAIL.
PLUS ALL THE OTHERS WHO LENT A HAND TO THIS HATEFUL GOLD-FINGER PLAN OF WORLD DOMINATION.
EVEN IF SHE WERE THE MOST POWERFUL PERSON IN THE WORLD AND GAVE YOU UNLIMITED POWER TOO?

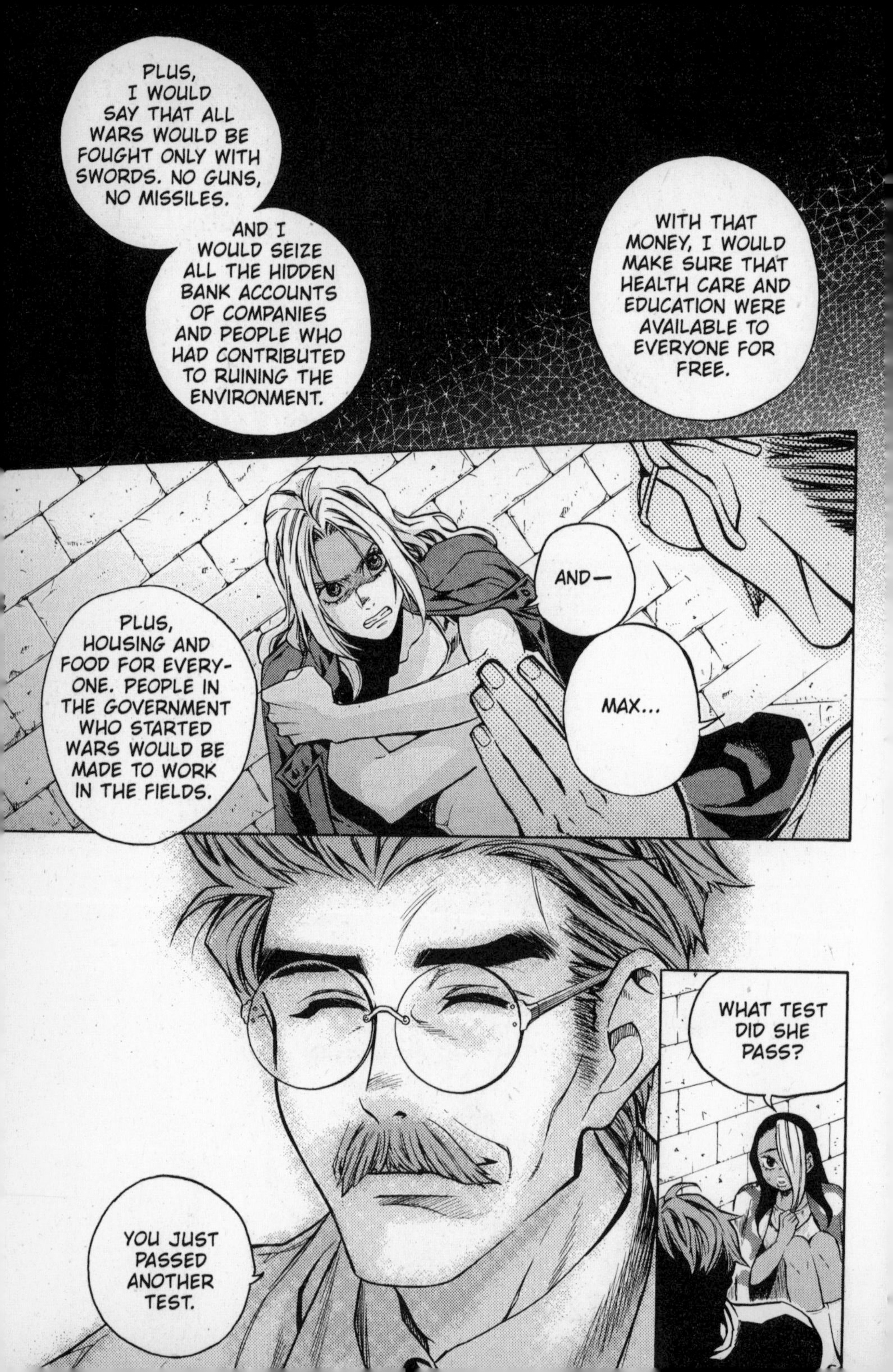
PLUS, I WOULD SAY THAT ALL WARS WOULD BE FOUGHT ONLY WITH SWORDS. NO GUNS, NO MISSILES.
AND I WOULD SEIZE ALL THE HIDDEN BANK ACCOUNTS OF COMPANIES AND PEOPLE WHO HAD CONTRIBUTED TO RUINING THE ENVIRONMENT.
WITH THAT MONEY, I WOULD MAKE SURE THAT HEALTH CARE AND EDUCATION WERE AVAILABLE TO EVERYONE FOR FREE.
PLUS, HOUSING AND FOOD FOR EVERY-ONE. PEOPLE IN THE GOVERNMENT WHO STARTED WARS WOULD BE MADE TO WORK IN THE FIELDS.
AND—
MAX...
WHAT TEST DID SHE PASS?
YOU JUST PASSED ANOTHER TEST.

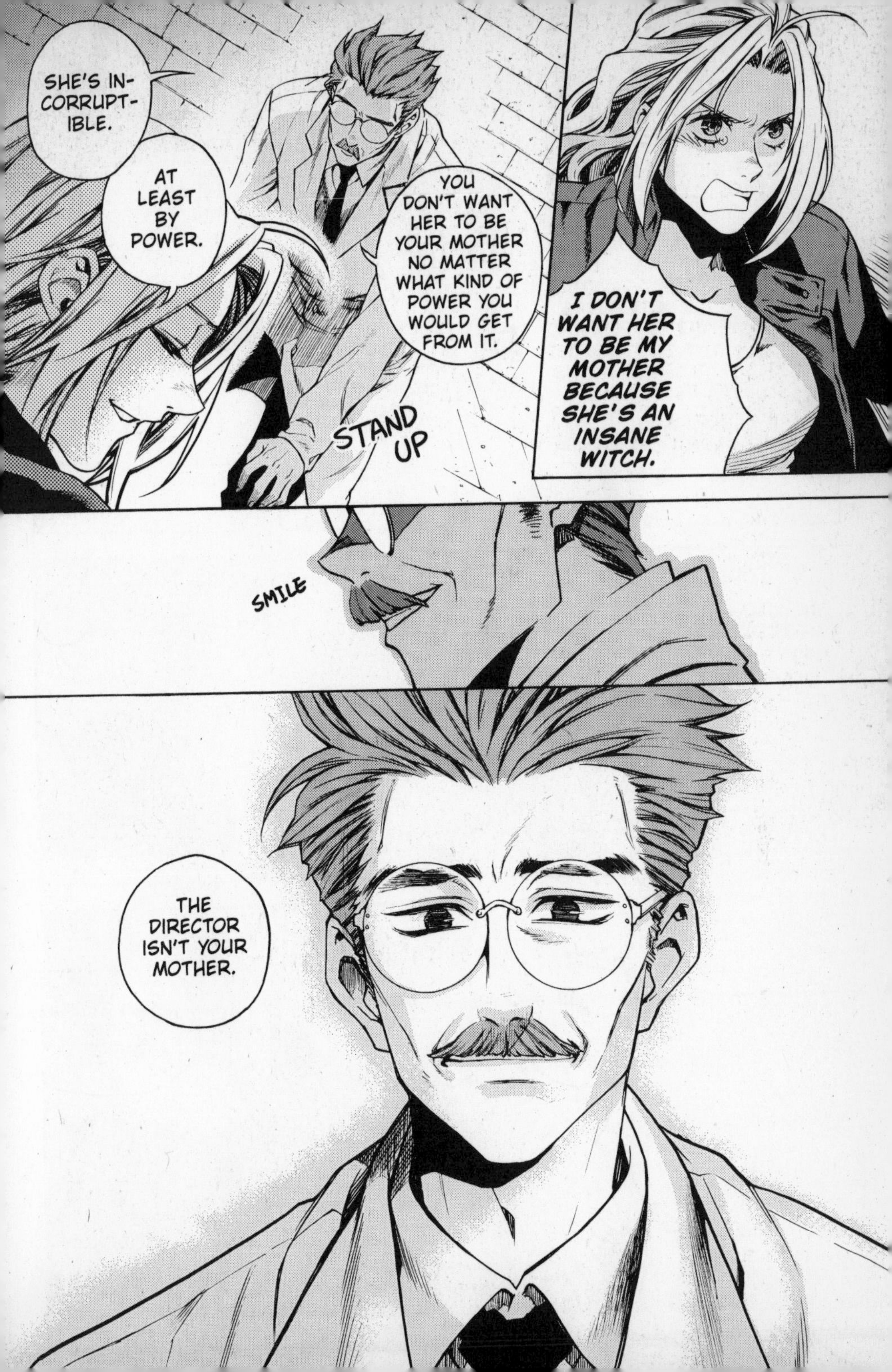
I DON'T WANT HER TO BE MY MOTHER BECAUSE SHE'S AN INSANE WITCH.
YOU DON'T WANT HER TO BE YOUR MOTHER NO MATTER WHAT KIND OF POWER YOU WOULD GET FROM IT.
SHE'S IN-CORRUPT-IBLE.
AT LEAST BY POWER.
STAND UP
SMILE
THE DIRECTOR ISN'T YOUR MOTHER.

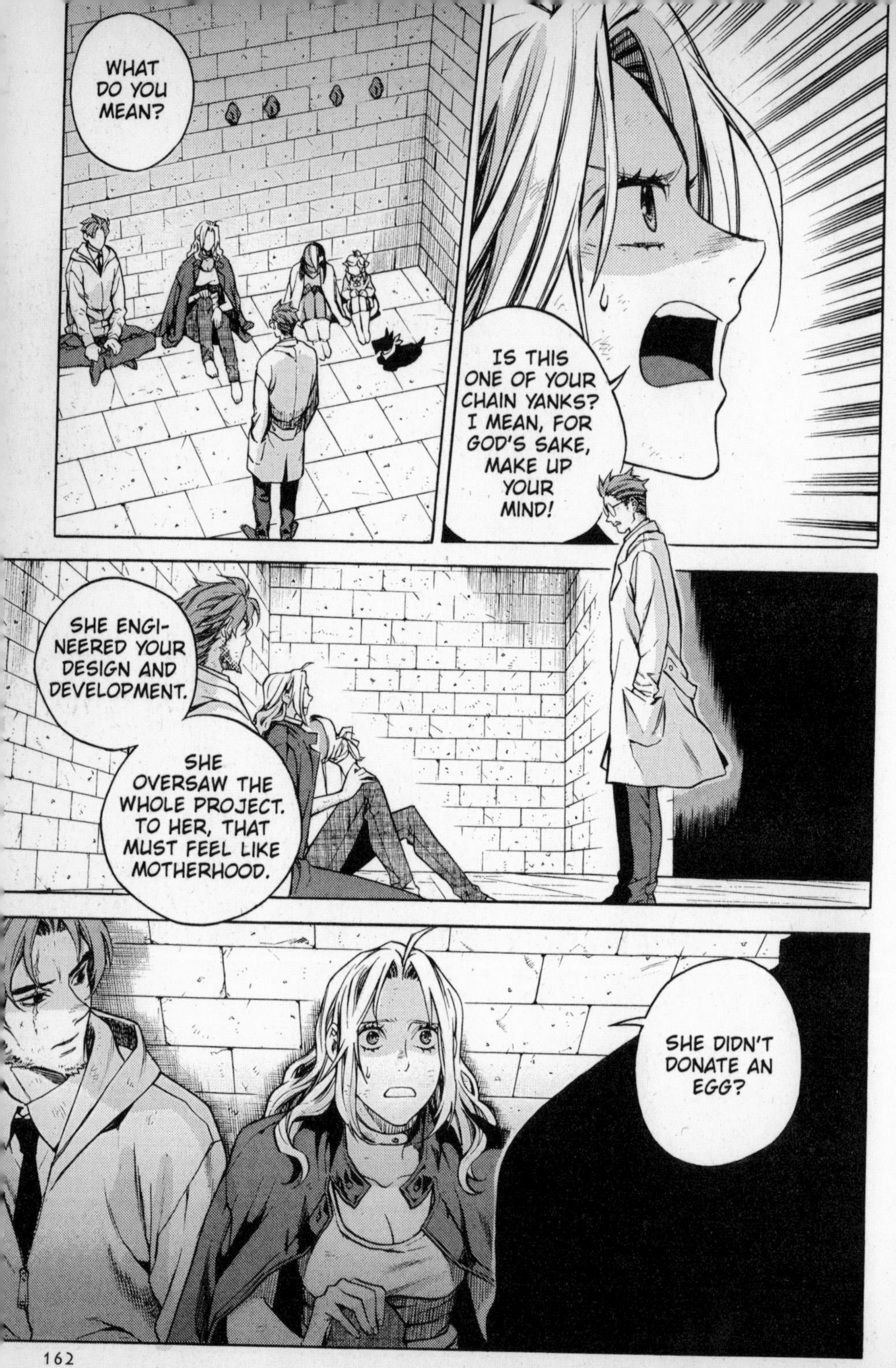
WHAT DO YOU MEAN?
IS THIS ONE OF YOUR CHAIN YANKS? I MEAN, FOR GOD'S SAKE, MAKE UP YOUR MIND!
SHE ENGI-NEERED YOUR DESIGN AND DEVELOPMENT.
SHE OVERSAW THE WHOLE PROJECT. TO HER, THAT MUST FEEL LIKE MOTHERHOOD.
SHE DIDN'T DONATE AN EGG?

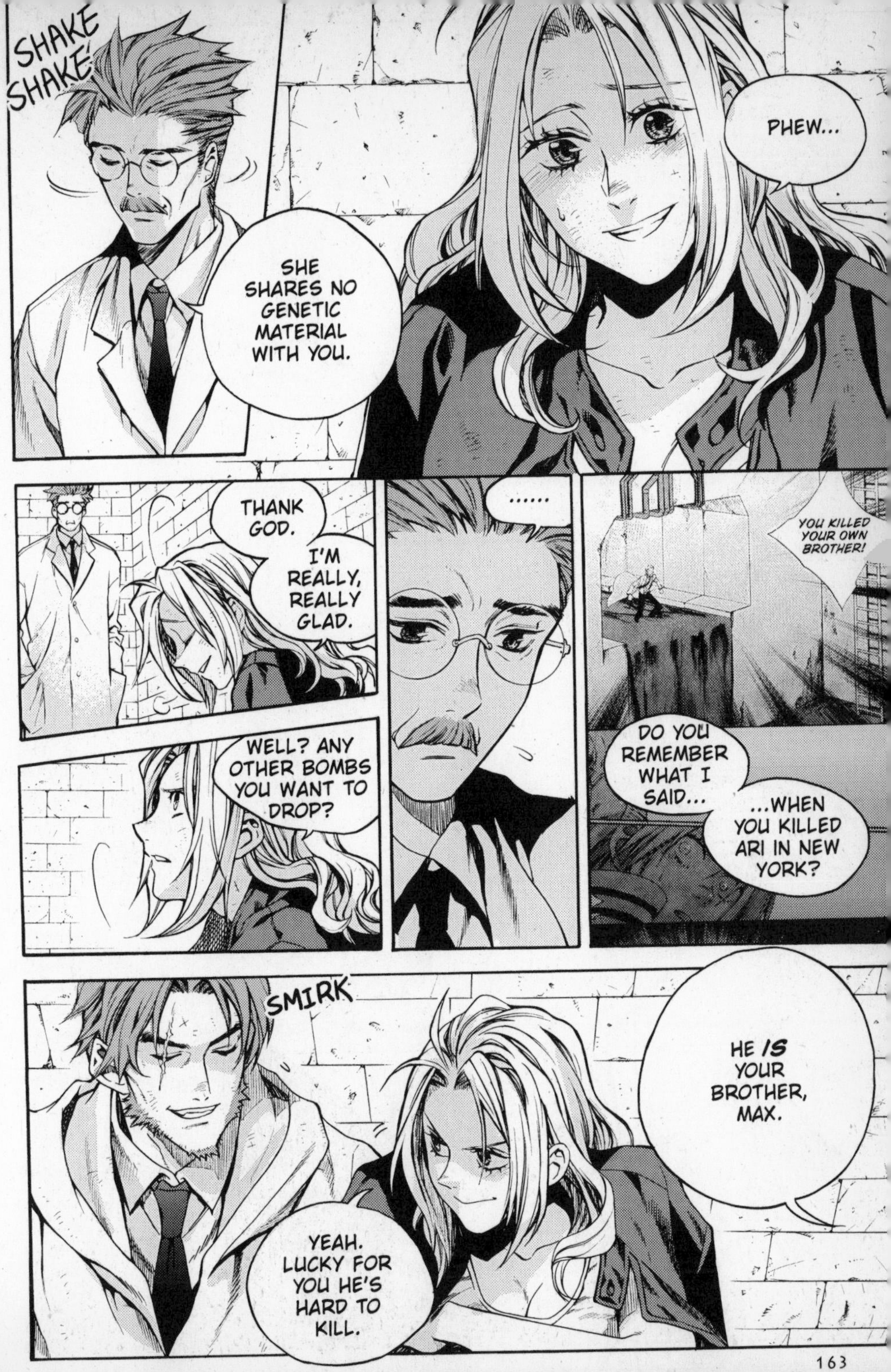
SHAKE SHAKE
PHEW...
SHE SHARES NO GENETIC MATERIAL WITH YOU.
THANK GOD.
I'M REALLY, REALLY GLAD.
......
YOU KILLED YOUR OWN BROTHER!
WELL? ANY OTHER BOMBS YOU WANT TO DROP?
DO YOU REMEMBER WHAT I SAID...
...WHEN YOU KILLED ARI IN NEW YORK?
SMIRK
HE IS YOUR BROTHER, MAX.
YEAH. LUCKY FOR YOU HE'S HARD TO KILL.

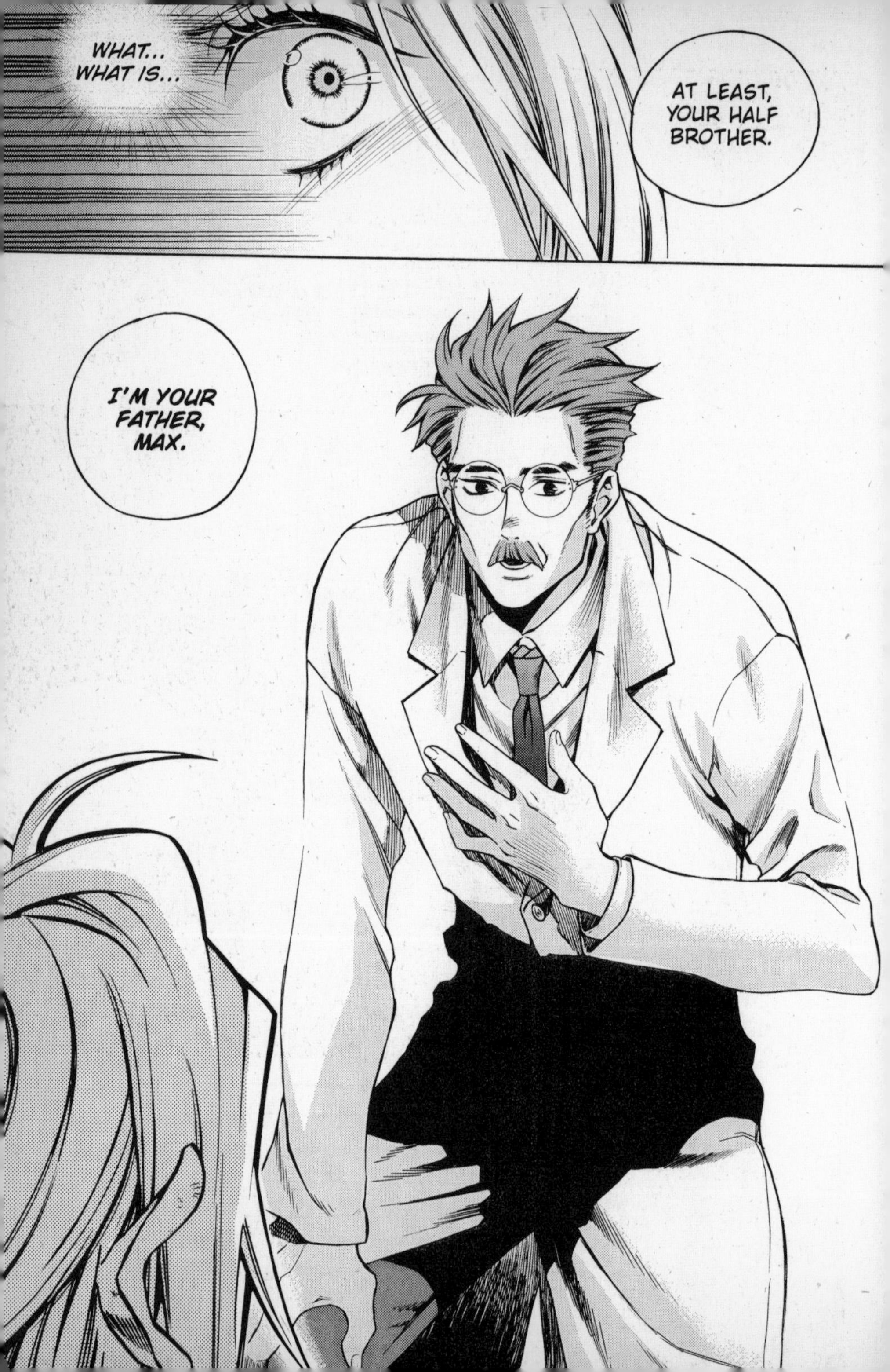
AT LEAST, YOUR HALF BROTHER.
WHAT... WHAT IS...
I'M YOUR FATHER, MAX.

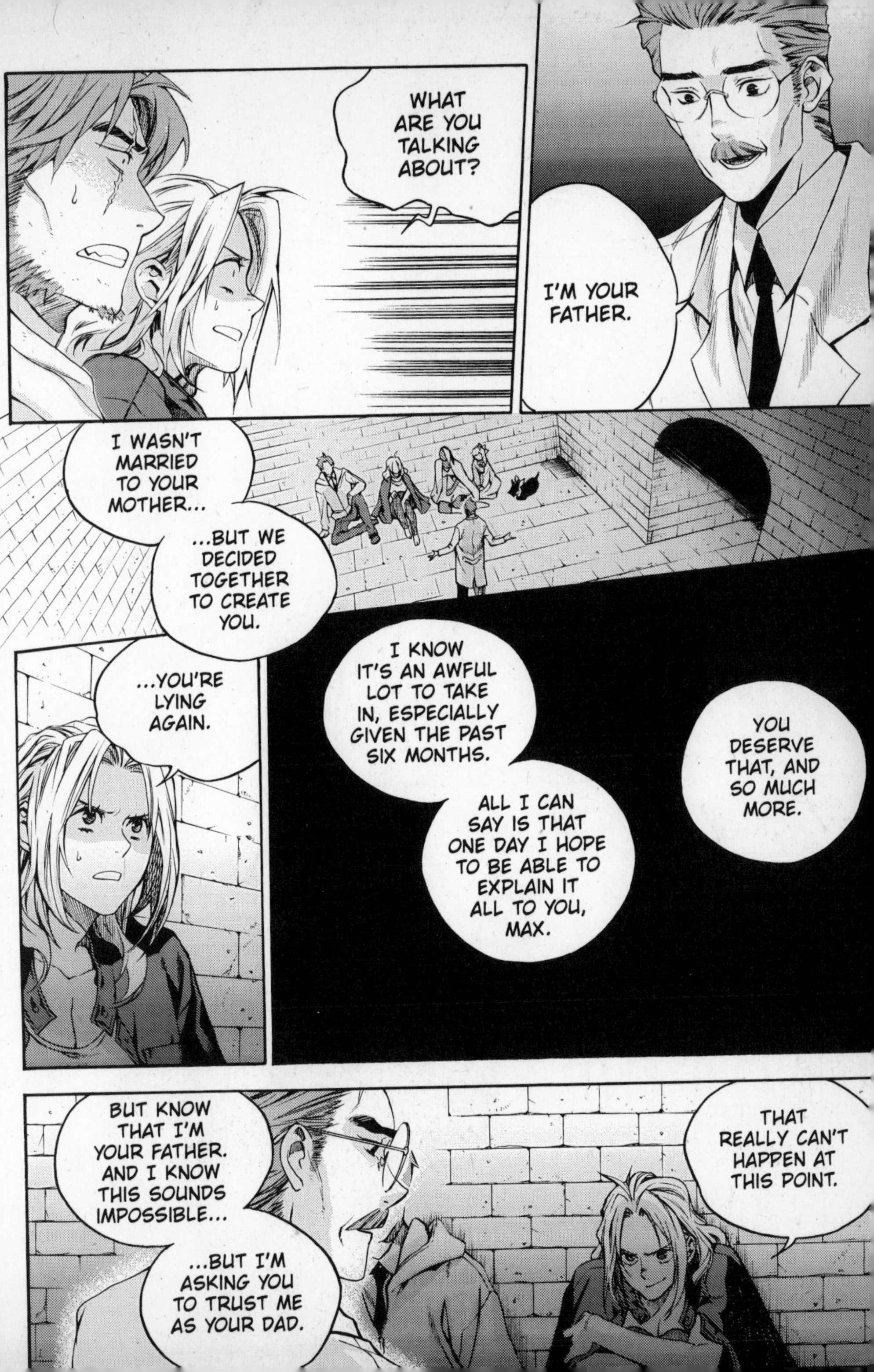
WHAT ARE YOU TALKING ABOUT?
I'M YOUR FATHER.
I WASN'T MARRIED TO YOUR MOTHER...
...BUT WE DECIDED TOGETHER TO CREATE YOU.
...YOU'RE LYING AGAIN.
I KNOW IT'S AN AWFUL LOT TO TAKE IN, ESPECIALLY GIVEN THE PAST SIX MONTHS.
ALL I CAN SAY IS THAT ONE DAY I HOPE TO BE ABLE TO EXPLAIN IT ALL TO YOU, MAX.
YOU DESERVE THAT, AND SO MUCH MORE.
BUT KNOW THAT I'M YOUR FATHER. AND I KNOW THIS SOUNDS IMPOSSIBLE...
...BUT I'M ASKING YOU TO TRUST ME AS YOUR DAD.
THAT REALLY CAN'T HAPPEN AT THIS POINT.

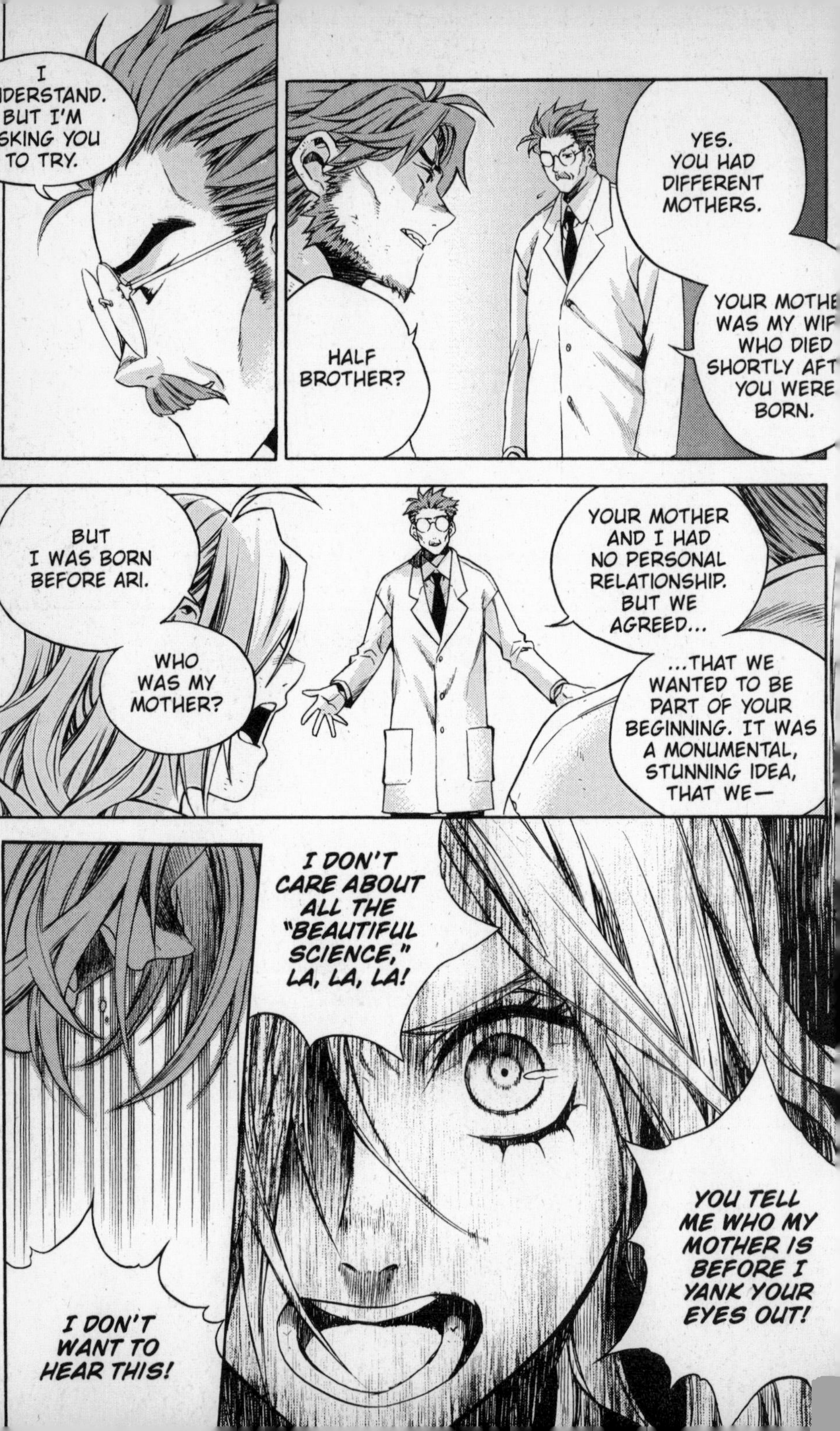
I UNDERSTAND. BUT I'M ASKING YOU TO TRY.
YES. YOU HAD DIFFERENT MOTHERS.
HALF BROTHER?
YOUR MOTHE WAS MY WIF WHO DIED SHORTLY AFT YOU WERE BORN.
BUT I WAS BORN BEFORE ARI.
WHO WAS MY MOTHER?
YOUR MOTHER AND I HAD NO PERSONAL RELATIONSHIP. BUT WE AGREED...
...THAT WE WANTED TO BE PART OF YOUR BEGINNING. IT WAS A MONUMENTAL, STUNNING IDEA, THAT WE—
I DON'T CARE ABOUT ALL THE "BEAUTIFUL SCIENCE," LA, LA, LA!
YOU TELL ME WHO MY MOTHER IS BEFORE I YANK YOUR EYES OUT!
I DON'T WANT TO HEAR THIS!

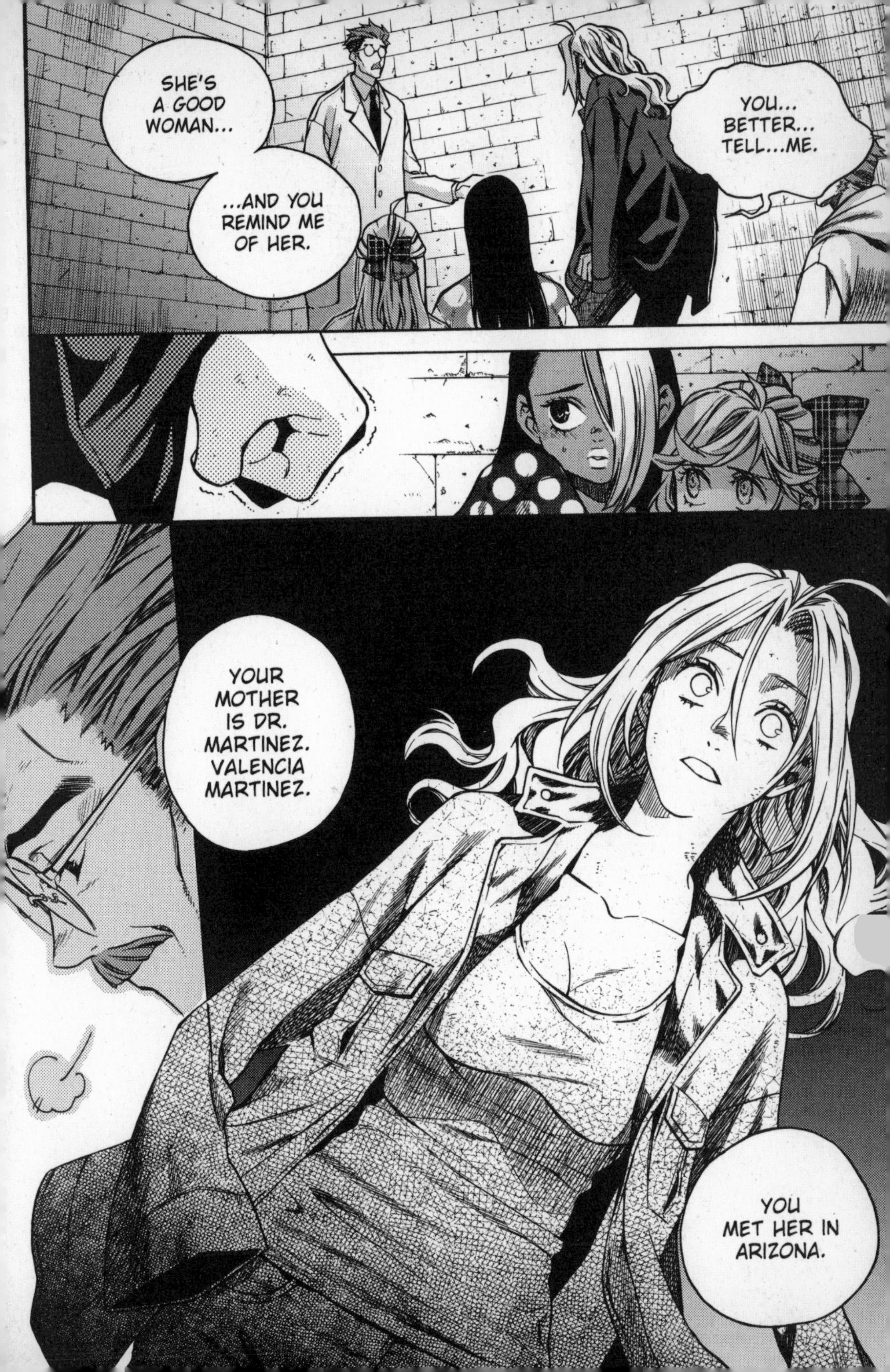
SHE'S A GOOD WOMAN...
...AND YOU REMIND ME OF HER.
YOU... BETTER... TELL...ME.
YOUR MOTHER IS DR. MARTINEZ. VALENCIA MARTINEZ.
YOU MET HER IN ARIZONA.

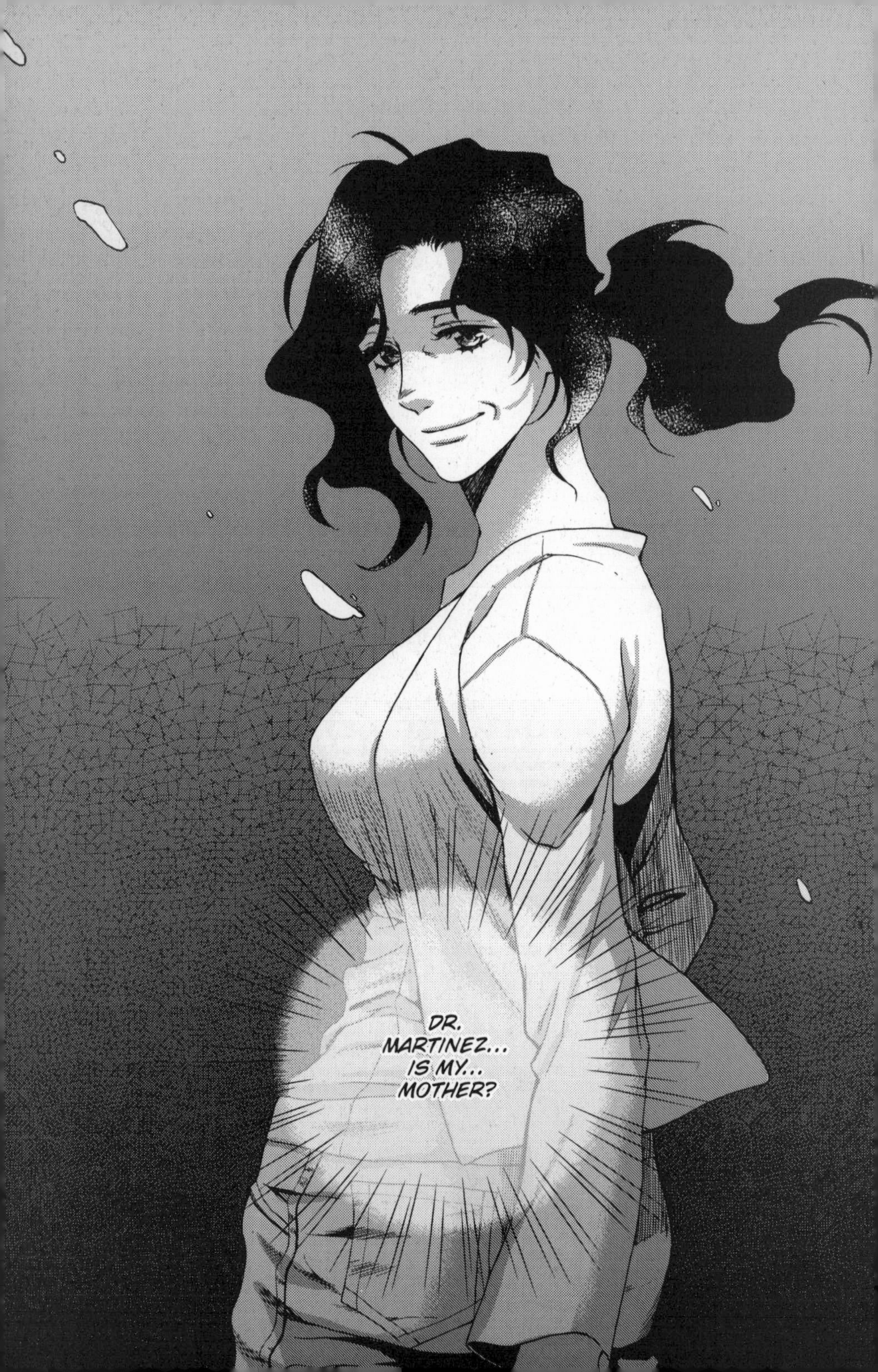
DR. MARTINEZ... IS MY... MOTHER?

MAXIMUM
RIDE

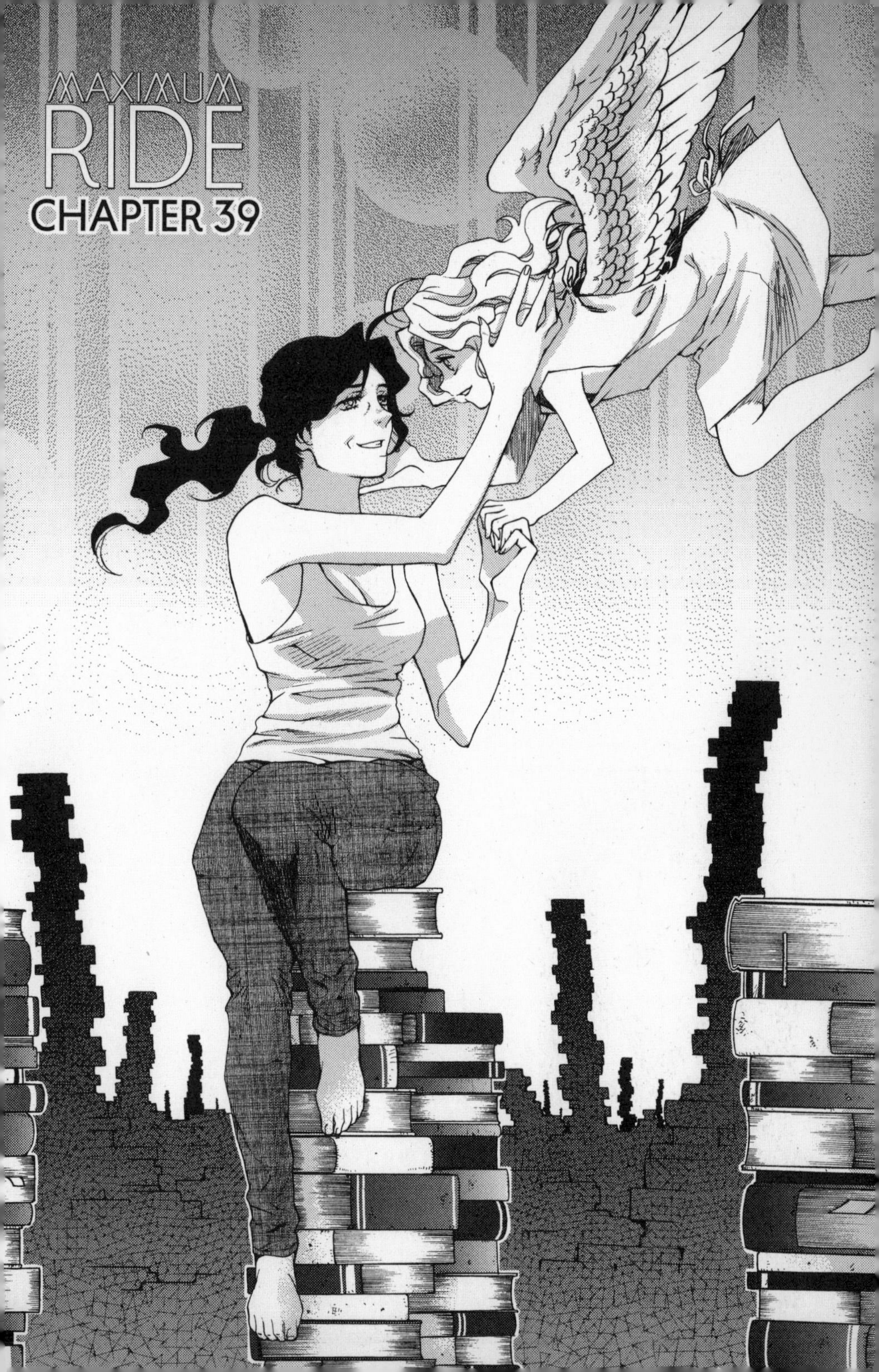
MAXIMUM
RIDE
CHAPTER 39

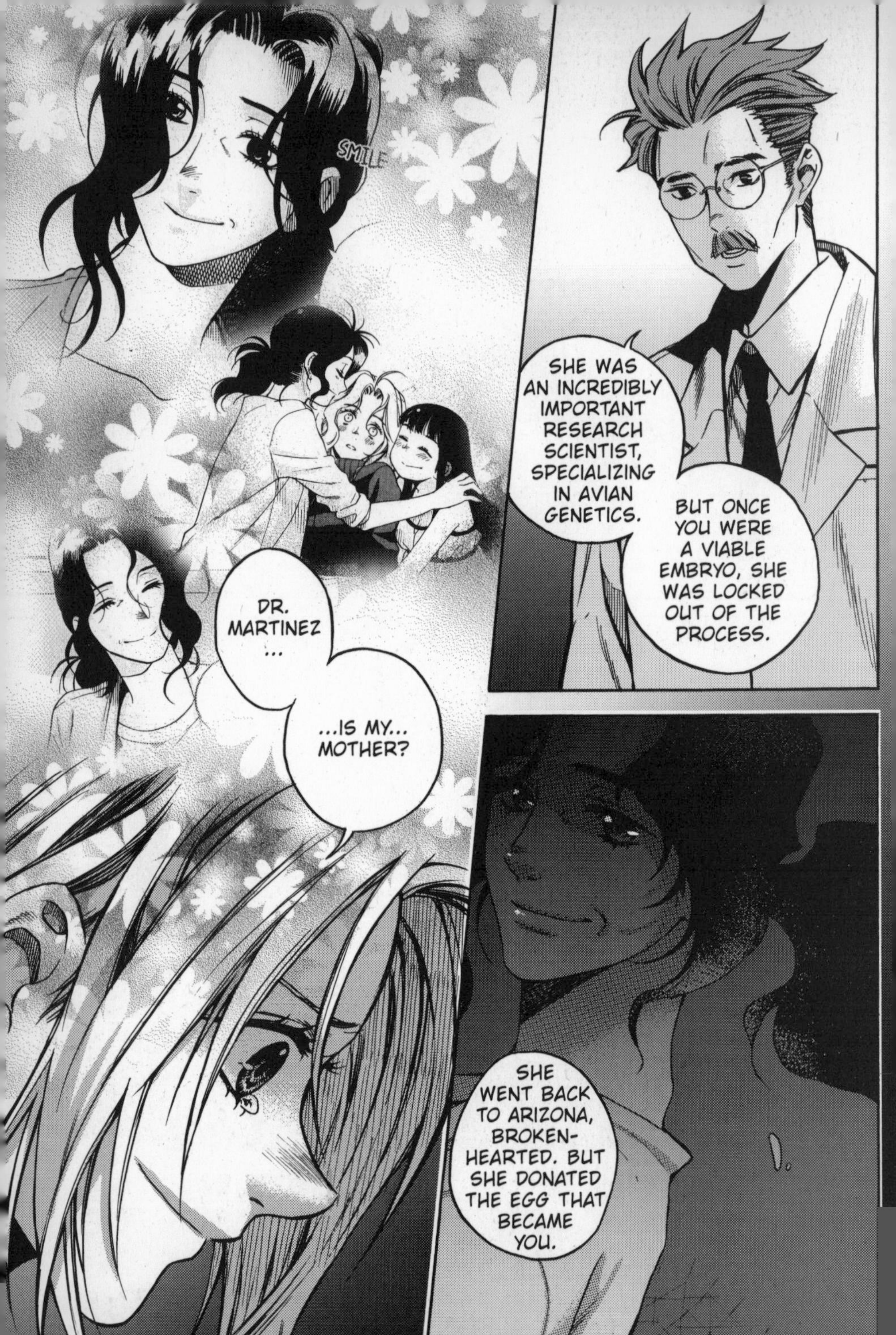
SMILE
SHE WAS AN INCREDIBLY IMPORTANT RESEARCH SCIENTIST, SPECIALIZING IN AVIAN GENETICS.
BUT ONCE YOU WERE A VIABLE EMBRYO, SHE WAS LOCKED OUT OF THE PROCESS.
DR. MARTINEZ ...
...IS MY... MOTHER?
SHE WENT BACK TO ARIZONA, BROKEN-HEARTED. BUT SHE DONATED THE EGG THAT BECAME YOU.

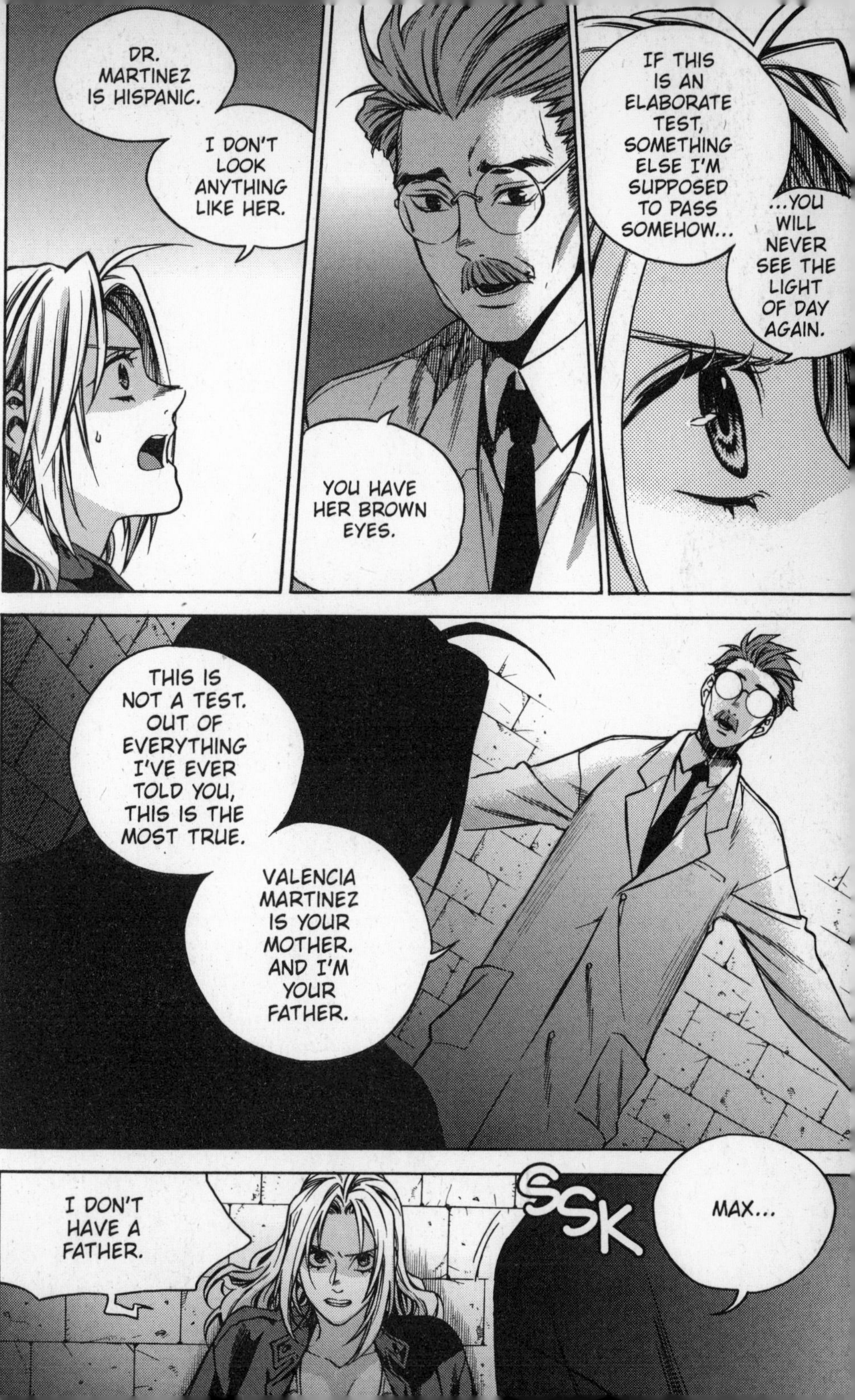
DR. MARTINEZ IS HISPANIC.
I DON'T LOOK ANYTHING LIKE HER.
YOU HAVE HER BROWN EYES.
IF THIS IS AN ELABORATE TEST, SOMETHING ELSE I'M SUPPOSED TO PASS SOMEHOW...
...YOU WILL NEVER SEE THE LIGHT OF DAY AGAIN.
THIS IS NOT A TEST. OUT OF EVERYTHING I'VE EVER TOLD YOU, THIS IS THE MOST TRUE.
VALENCIA MARTINEZ IS YOUR MOTHER. AND I'M YOUR FATHER.
I DON'T HAVE A FATHER.
SSK
MAX...

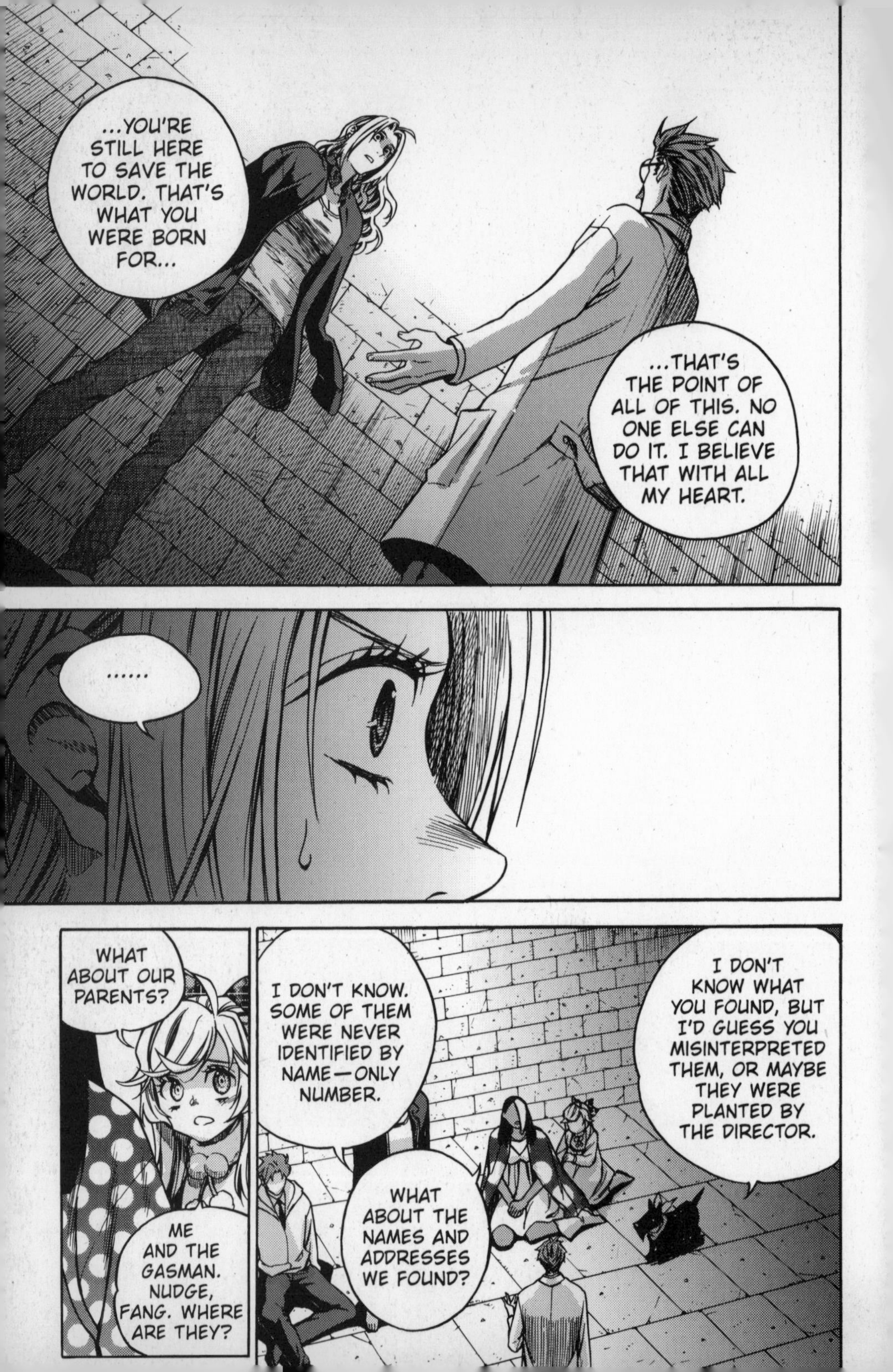
...YOU'RE STILL HERE TO SAVE THE WORLD. THAT'S WHAT YOU WERE BORN FOR...
...THAT'S THE POINT OF ALL OF THIS. NO ONE ELSE CAN DO IT. I BELIEVE THAT WITH ALL MY HEART.
......
WHAT ABOUT OUR PARENTS?
ME AND THE GASMAN. NUDGE, FANG. WHERE ARE THEY?
I DON'T KNOW. SOME OF THEM WERE NEVER IDENTIFIED BY NAME—ONLY NUMBER.
WHAT ABOUT THE NAMES AND ADDRESSES WE FOUND?
I DON'T KNOW WHAT YOU FOUND, BUT I'D GUESS YOU MISINTERPRETED THEM, OR MAYBE THEY WERE PLANTED BY THE DIRECTOR.

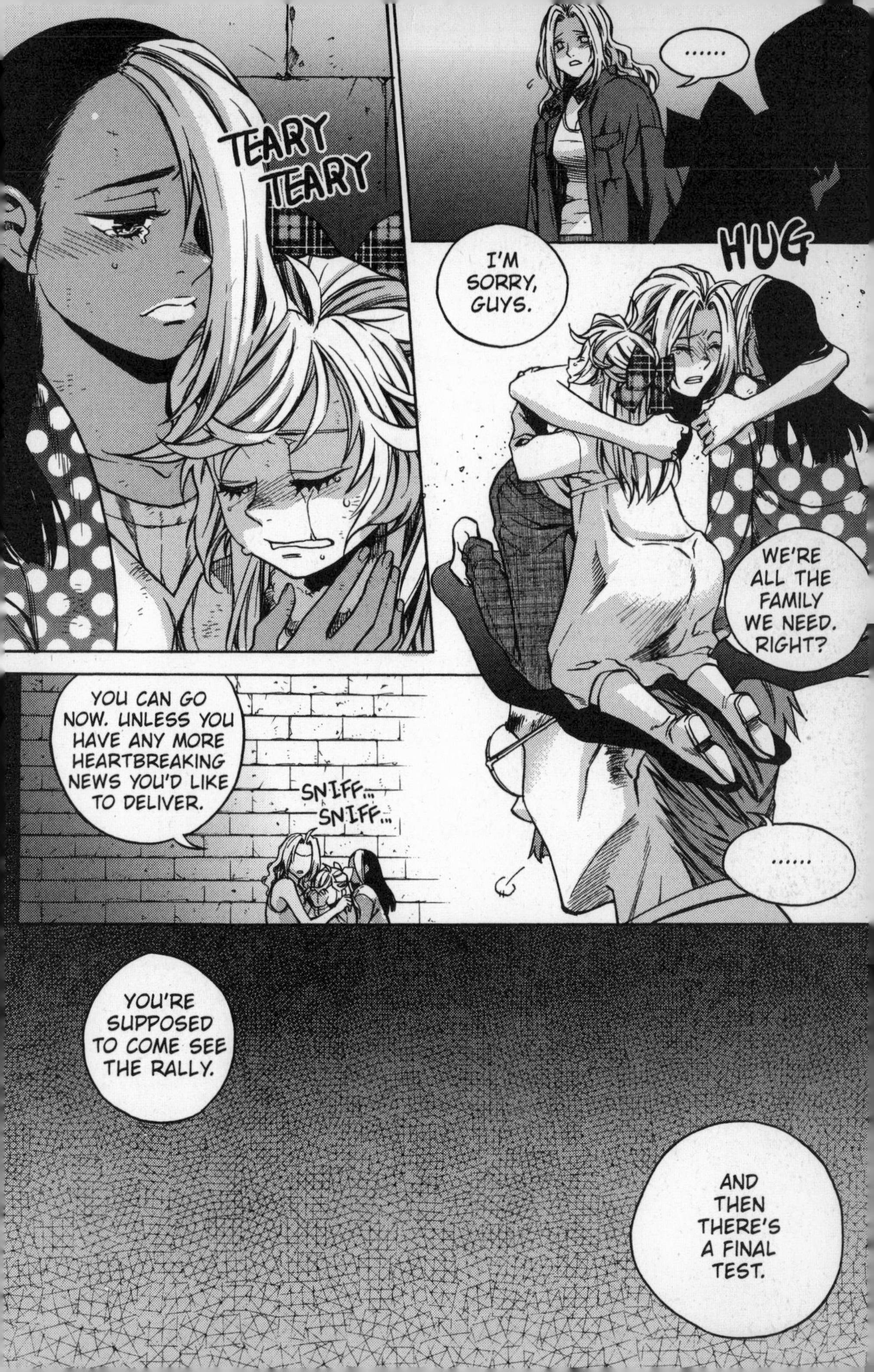
......
TEARY TEARY
HUG
I'M SORRY, GUYS.
WE'RE ALL THE FAMILY WE NEED. RIGHT?
......
YOU CAN GO NOW. UNLESS YOU HAVE ANY MORE HEARTBREAKING NEWS YOU'D LIKE TO DELIVER.
SNIFF... SNIFF...
YOU'RE SUPPOSED TO COME SEE THE RALLY.
AND THEN THERE'S A FINAL TEST.

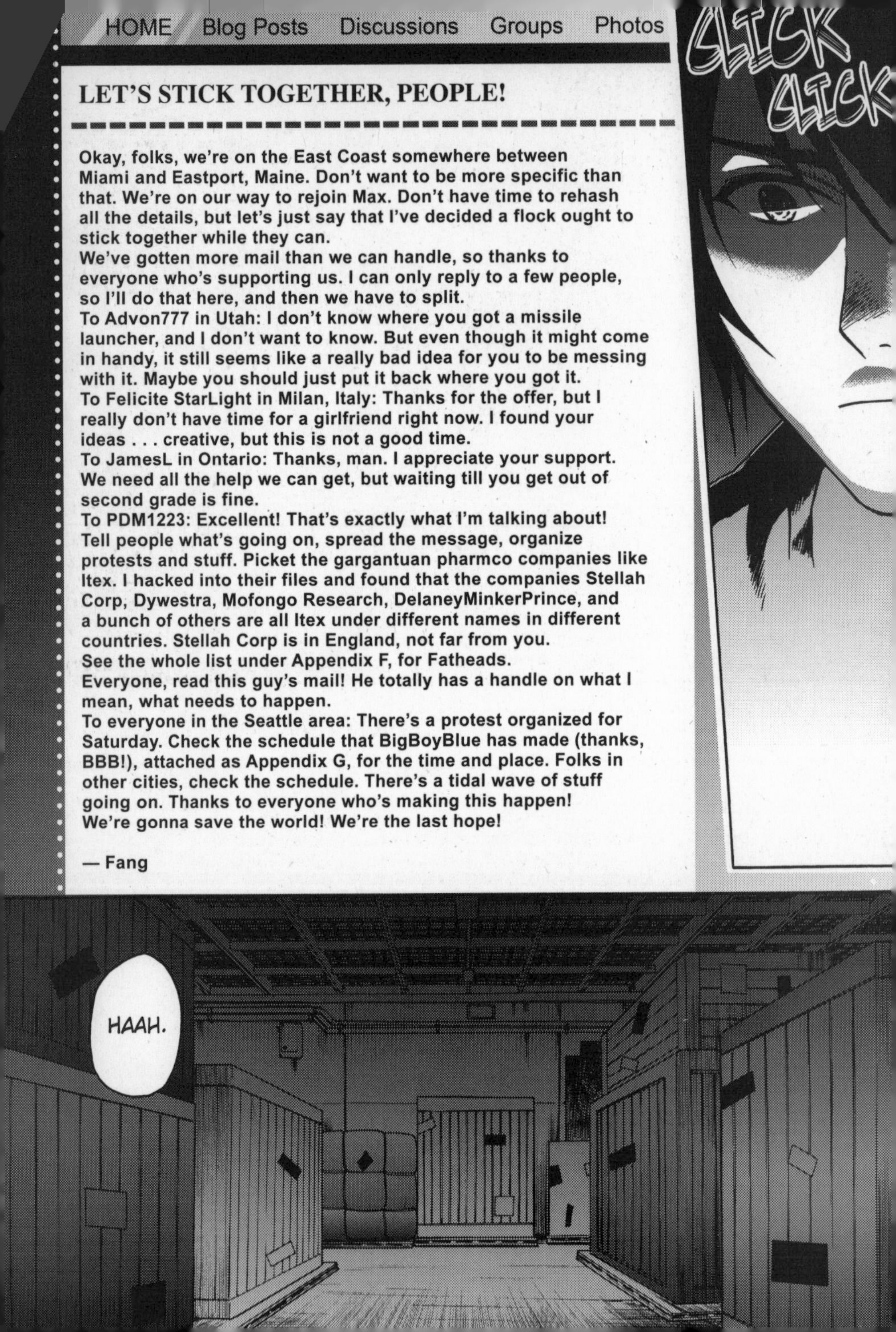

HOME Blog Posts Discussions Groups Photos
CLICK CLICK
LET'S STICK TOGETHER, PEOPLE!
Okay, folks, we're on the East Coast somewhere between Miami and Eastport, Maine. Don't want to be more specific than that. We're on our way to rejoin Max. Don't have time to rehash all the details, but let's just say that I've decided a flock ought to stick together while they can.
We've gotten more mail than we can handle, so thanks to everyone who's supporting us. I can only reply to a few people, so I'll do that here, and then we have to split.
To Advon777 in Utah: I don't know where you got a missile launcher, and I don't want to know. But even though it might come in handy, it still seems like a really bad idea for you to be messing with it. Maybe you should just put it back where you got it.
To Felicite StarLight in Milan, Italy: Thanks for the offer, but I really don't have time for a girlfriend right now. I found your ideas . . . creative, but this is not a good time.
To JamesL in Ontario: Thanks, man. I appreciate your support. We need all the help we can get, but waiting till you get out of second grade is fine.
To PDM1223: Excellent! That's exactly what I'm talking about! Tell people what's going on, spread the message, organize protests and stuff. Picket the gargantuan pharmco companies like Itex. I hacked into their files and found that the companies Stellah Corp, Dywestra, Mofongo Research, DelaneyMinkerPrince, and a bunch of others are all Itex under different names in different countries. Stellah Corp is in England, not far from you.
See the whole list under Appendix F, for Fatheads.
Everyone, read this guy's mail! He totally has a handle on what I mean, what needs to happen.
To everyone in the Seattle area: There's a protest organized for Saturday. Check the schedule that BigBoyBlue has made (thanks, BBB!), attached as Appendix G, for the time and place. Folks in other cities, check the schedule. There's a tidal wave of stuff going on. Thanks to everyone who's making this happen!
We're gonna save the world! We're the last hope!
— Fang
HAAH.

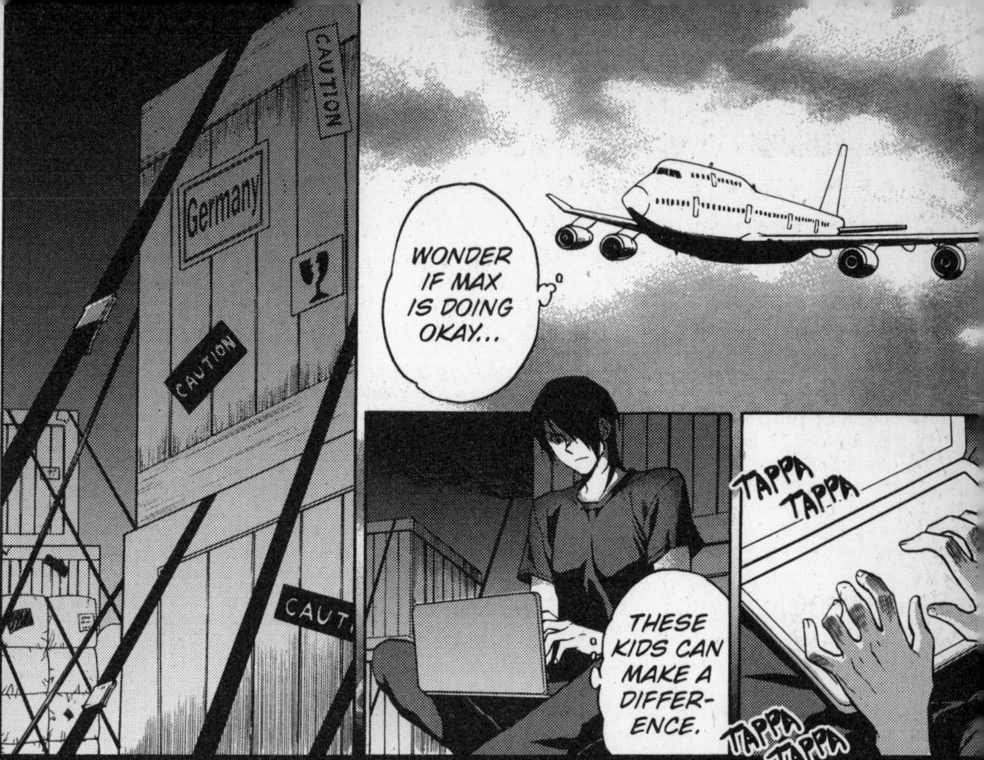
CAUTION
Germany
CAUTION
CAUT
WONDER IF MAX IS DOING OKAY...
TAPPA TAPPA
THESE KIDS CAN MAKE A DIFFER-ENCE.
TAPPA TAPPA

HOME Blog Posts Discussions Groups Photos Ch

WATCH OUT, GUYS, HERE WE COME

It's about five a.m. We should be sneaking on board the cargo plane soon. I've let the others sleep as much as they can — and of course now I'm so wiped I can't think straight. I'll try to grab some zzz's on the plane. Once it's up in the air, we're golden. We're probably the only people in the world who don't worry about plane crashes. If something happens to this plane and we start going down, I'll be like, later!
I hope Max is okay. Any of you guys — if you're around Lendeheim, Germany, go to the castle there and raise heck, okay?

— Fang

Vi
9

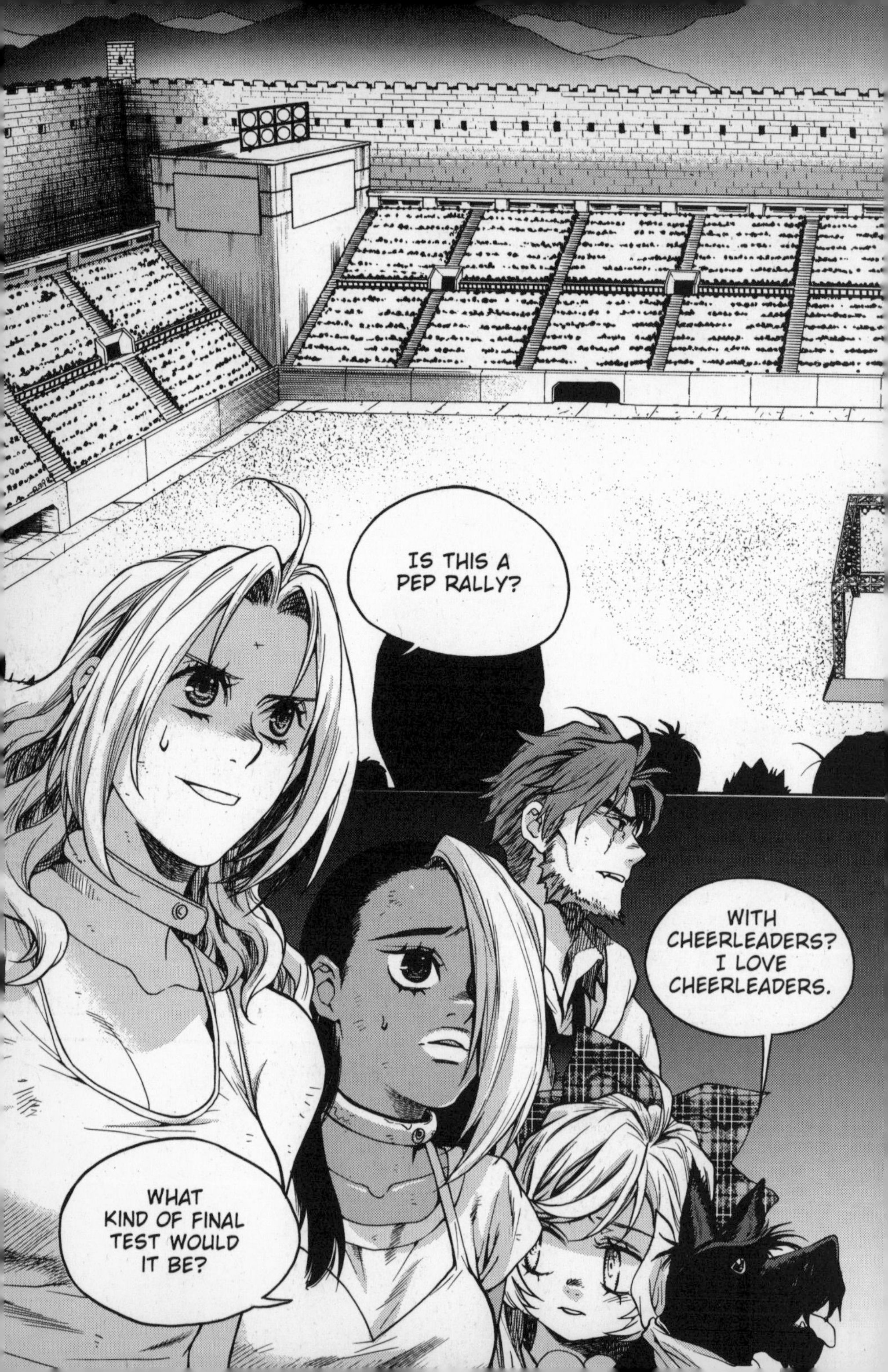
IS THIS A PEP RALLY?
WITH CHEERLEADERS? I LOVE CHEERLEADERS.
WHAT KIND OF FINAL TEST WOULD IT BE?

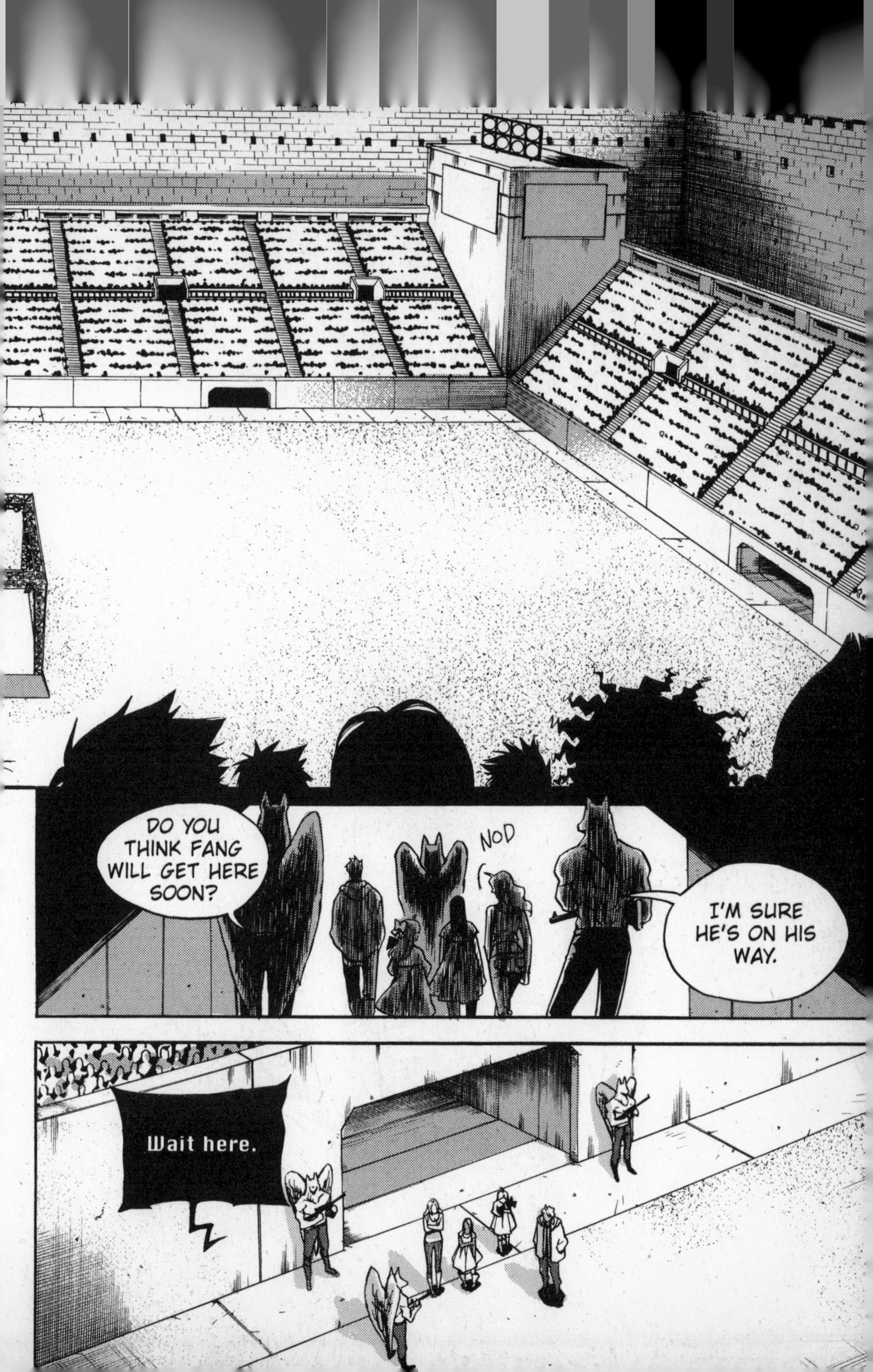
DO YOU THINK FANG WILL GET HERE SOON?
NOD
I'M SURE HE'S ON HIS WAY.
Wait here.

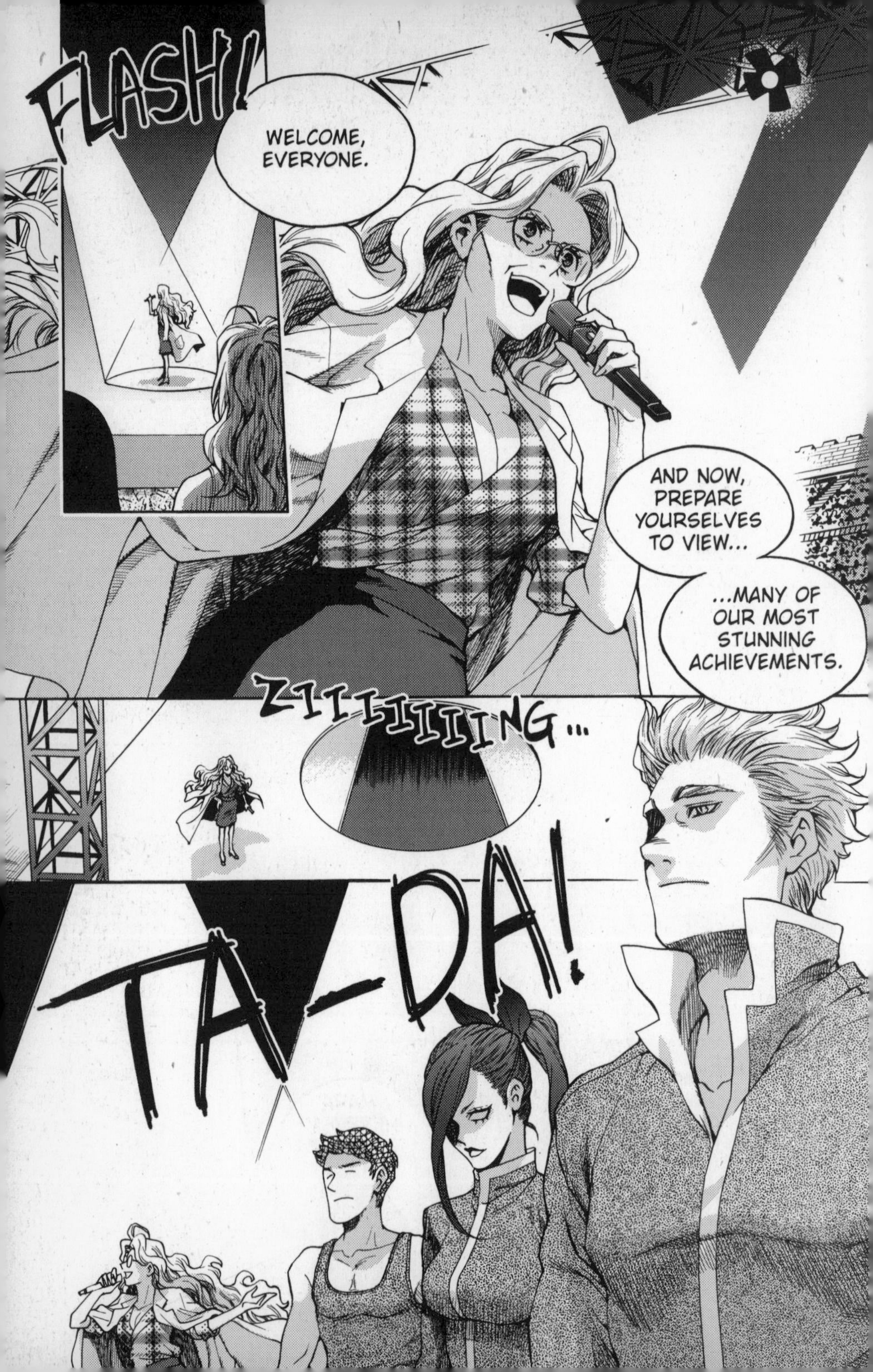
FLASH!
WELCOME, EVERYONE.
AND NOW, PREPARE YOURSELVES TO VIEW...
...MANY OF OUR MOST STUNNING ACHIEVEMENTS.
ZIIIIIIING...
TA-DA!

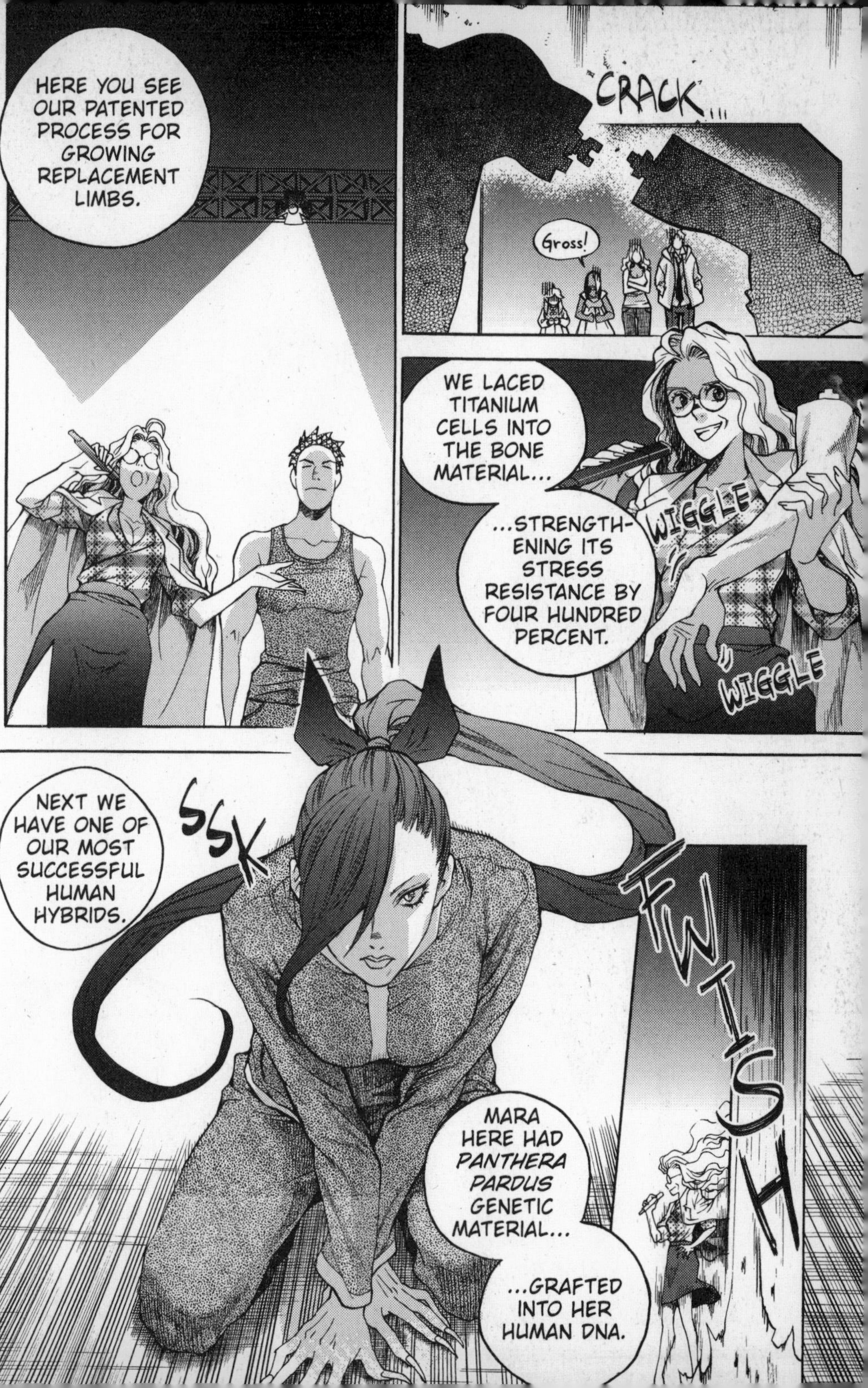
HERE YOU SEE OUR PATENTED PROCESS FOR GROWING REPLACEMENT LIMBS.
CRACK
Gross!
WE LACED TITANIUM CELLS INTO THE BONE MATERIAL...
...STRENGTH-ENING ITS STRESS RESISTANCE BY FOUR HUNDRED PERCENT.
WIGGLE
WIGGLE
NEXT WE HAVE ONE OF OUR MOST SUCCESSFUL HUMAN HYBRIDS.
SSK
FWISH
MARA HERE HAD *PANTHERA PARDUS* GENETIC MATERIAL...
...GRAFTED INTO HER HUMAN DNA.

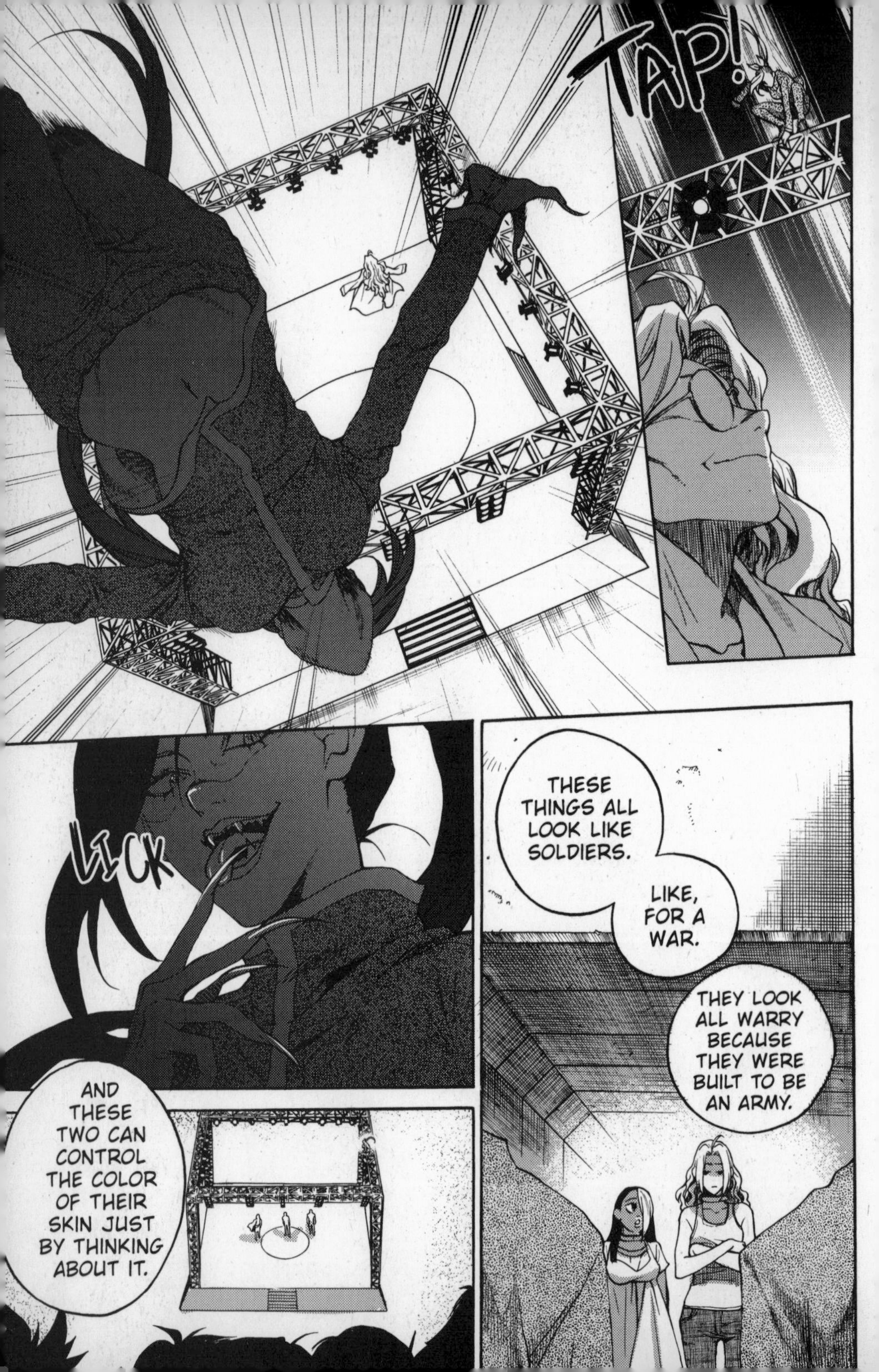
TAP!
LICK
THESE THINGS ALL LOOK LIKE SOLDIERS.
LIKE, FOR A WAR.
THEY LOOK ALL WARRY BECAUSE THEY WERE BUILT TO BE AN ARMY.
AND THESE TWO CAN CONTROL THE COLOR OF THEIR SKIN JUST BY THINKING ABOUT IT.

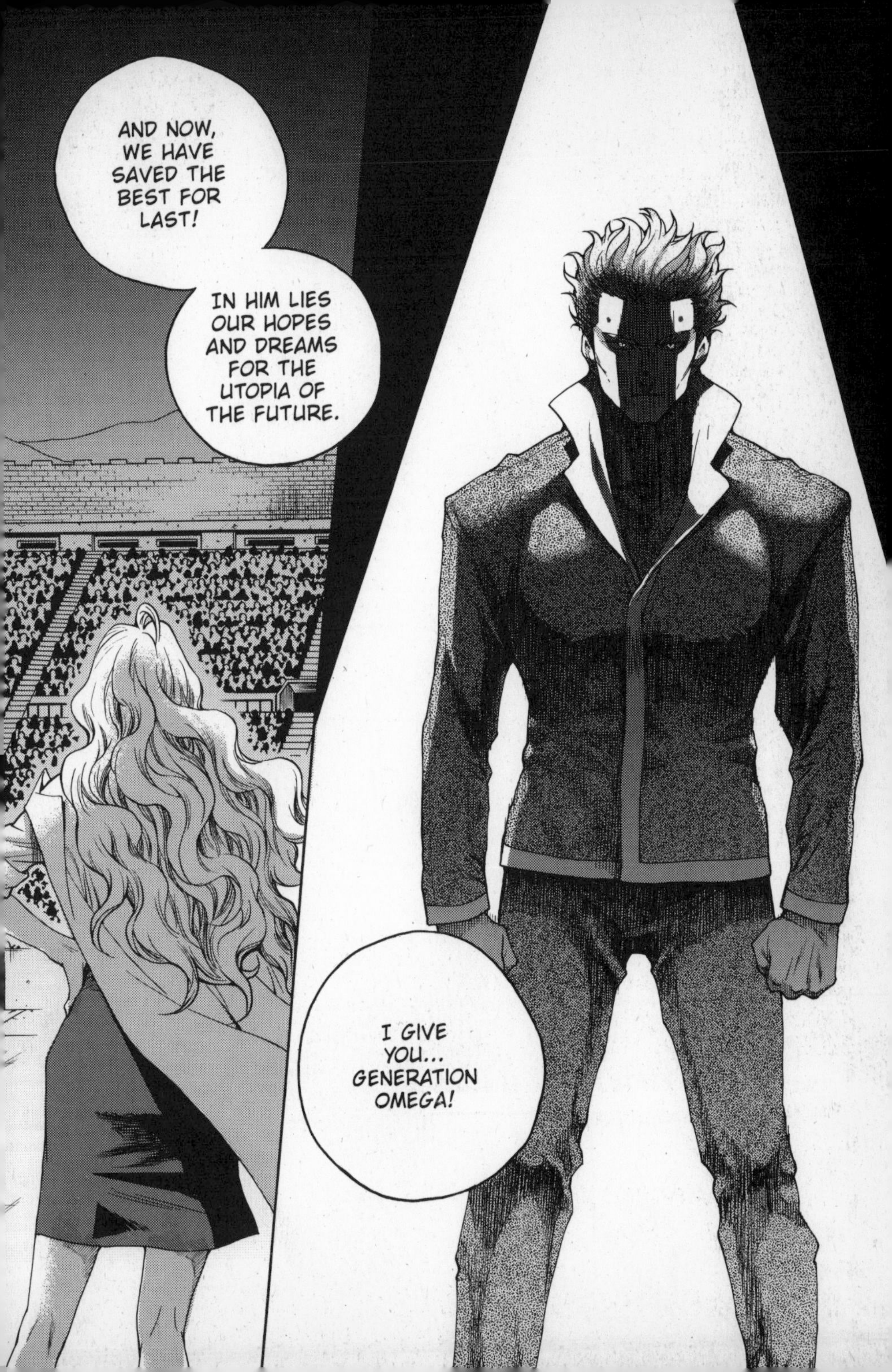
AND NOW, WE HAVE SAVED THE BEST FOR LAST!
IN HIM LIES OUR HOPES AND DREAMS FOR THE UTOPIA OF THE FUTURE.
I GIVE YOU... GENERATION OMEGA!

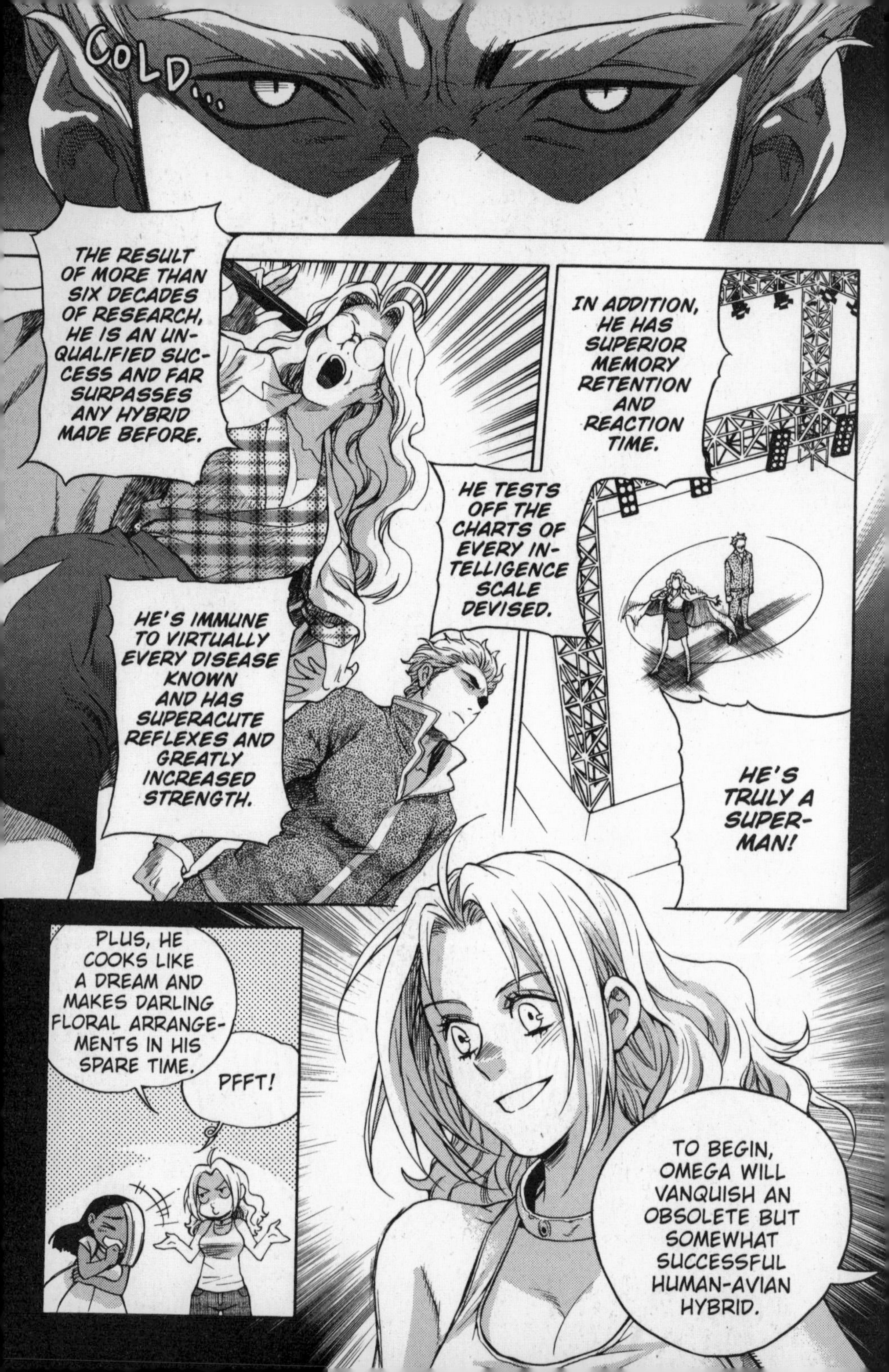
COLD...
THE RESULT OF MORE THAN SIX DECADES OF RESEARCH, HE IS AN UN-QUALIFIED SUC-CESS AND FAR SURPASSES ANY HYBRID MADE BEFORE.
IN ADDITION, HE HAS SUPERIOR MEMORY RETENTION AND REACTION TIME.
HE TESTS OFF THE CHARTS OF EVERY IN-TELLIGENCE SCALE DEVISED.
HE'S IMMUNE TO VIRTUALLY EVERY DISEASE KNOWN AND HAS SUPERACUTE REFLEXES AND GREATLY INCREASED STRENGTH.
HE'S TRULY A SUPER-MAN!
PLUS, HE COOKS LIKE A DREAM AND MAKES DARLING FLORAL ARRANGE-MENTS IN HIS SPARE TIME.
PFFT!
TO BEGIN, OMEGA WILL VANQUISH AN OBSOLETE BUT SOMEWHAT SUCCESSFUL HUMAN-AVIAN HYBRID.

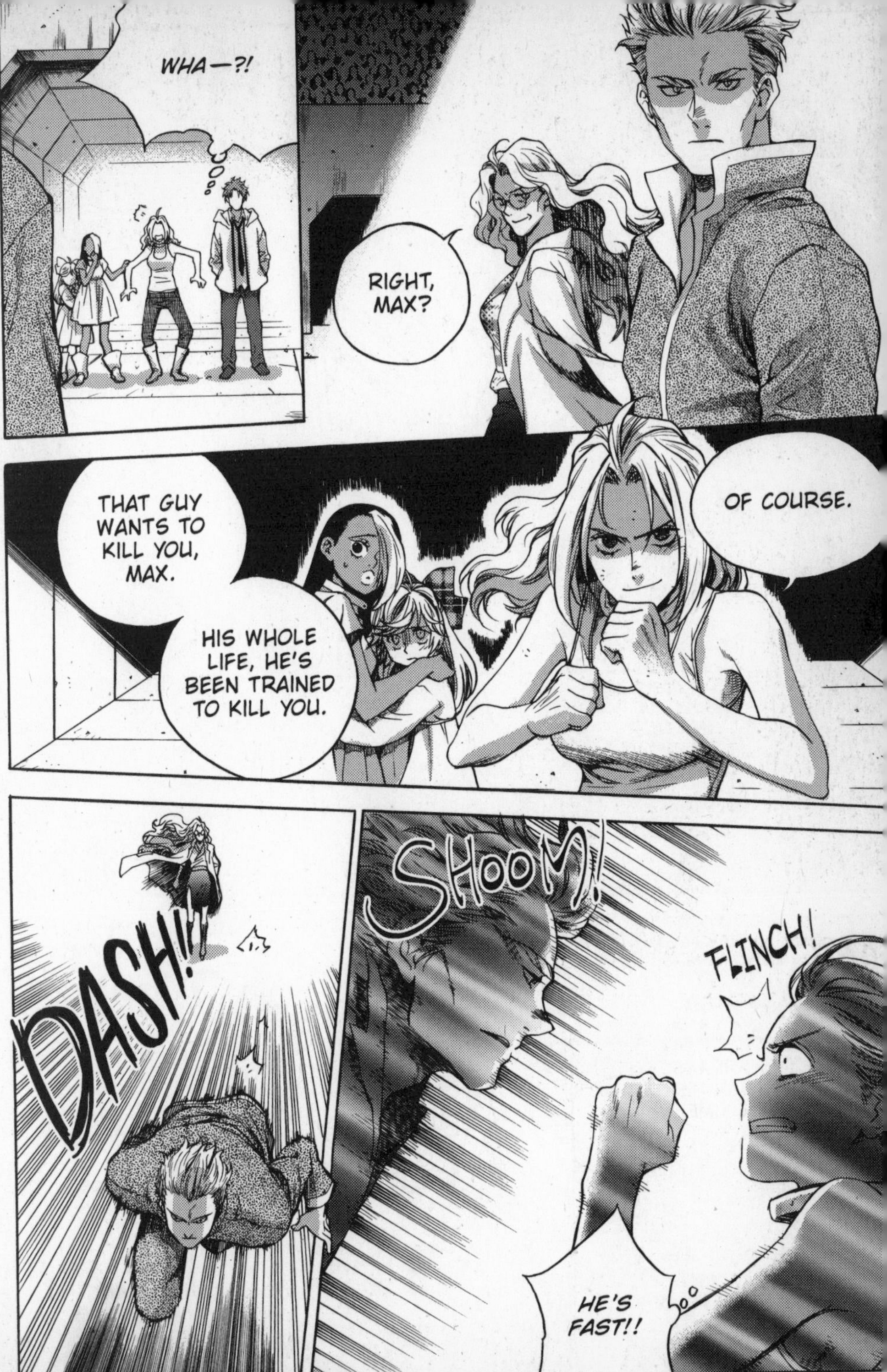
WHA—?!
RIGHT, MAX?
OF COURSE.
THAT GUY WANTS TO KILL YOU, MAX.
HIS WHOLE LIFE, HE'S BEEN TRAINED TO KILL YOU.
DASH!!
SHOOM!
FLINCH!
HE'S FAST!!

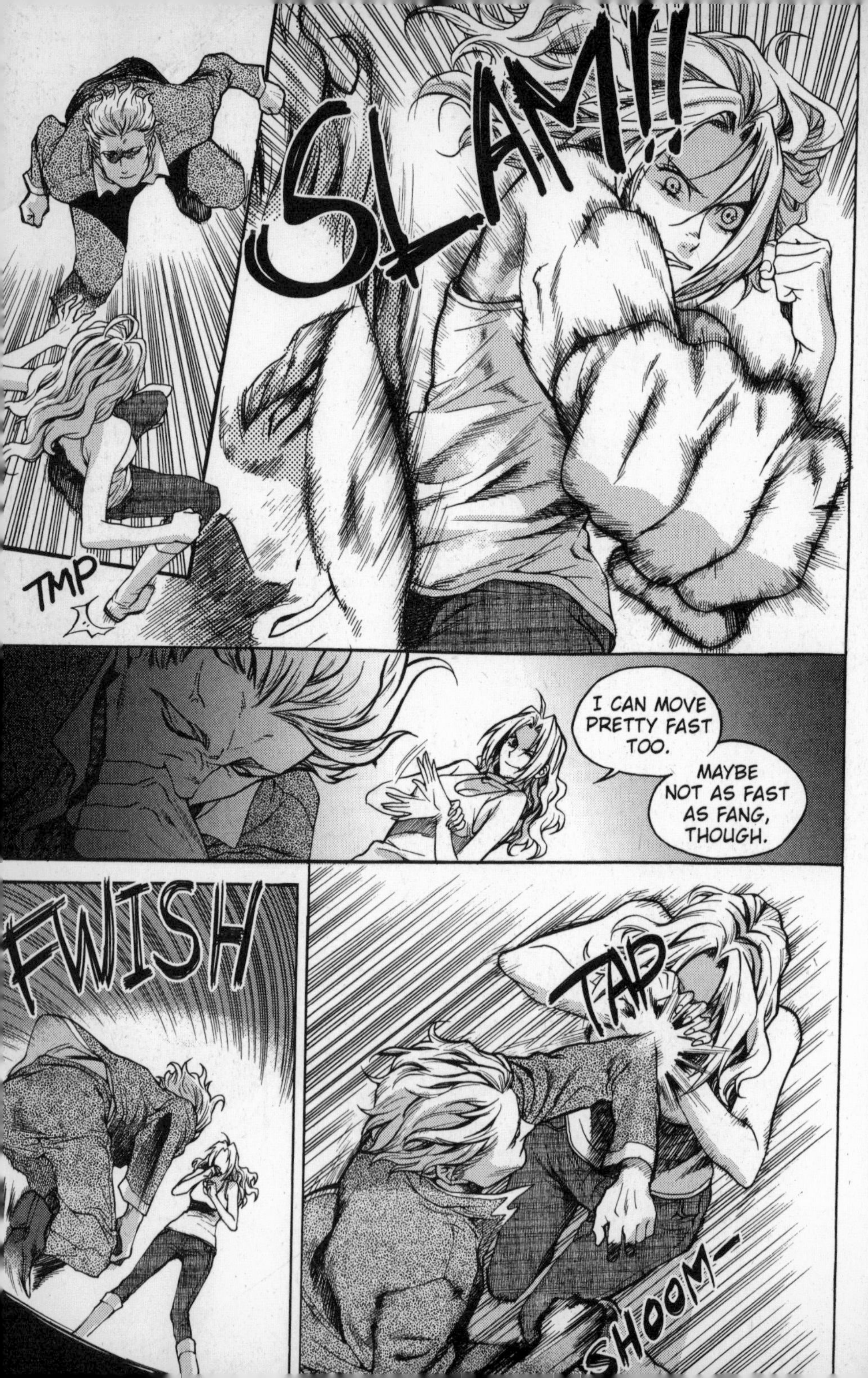
TMP
SLAM!!
I CAN MOVE PRETTY FAST TOO.
MAYBE NOT AS FAST AS FANG, THOUGH.
FWISH
TAP
SHOOM—

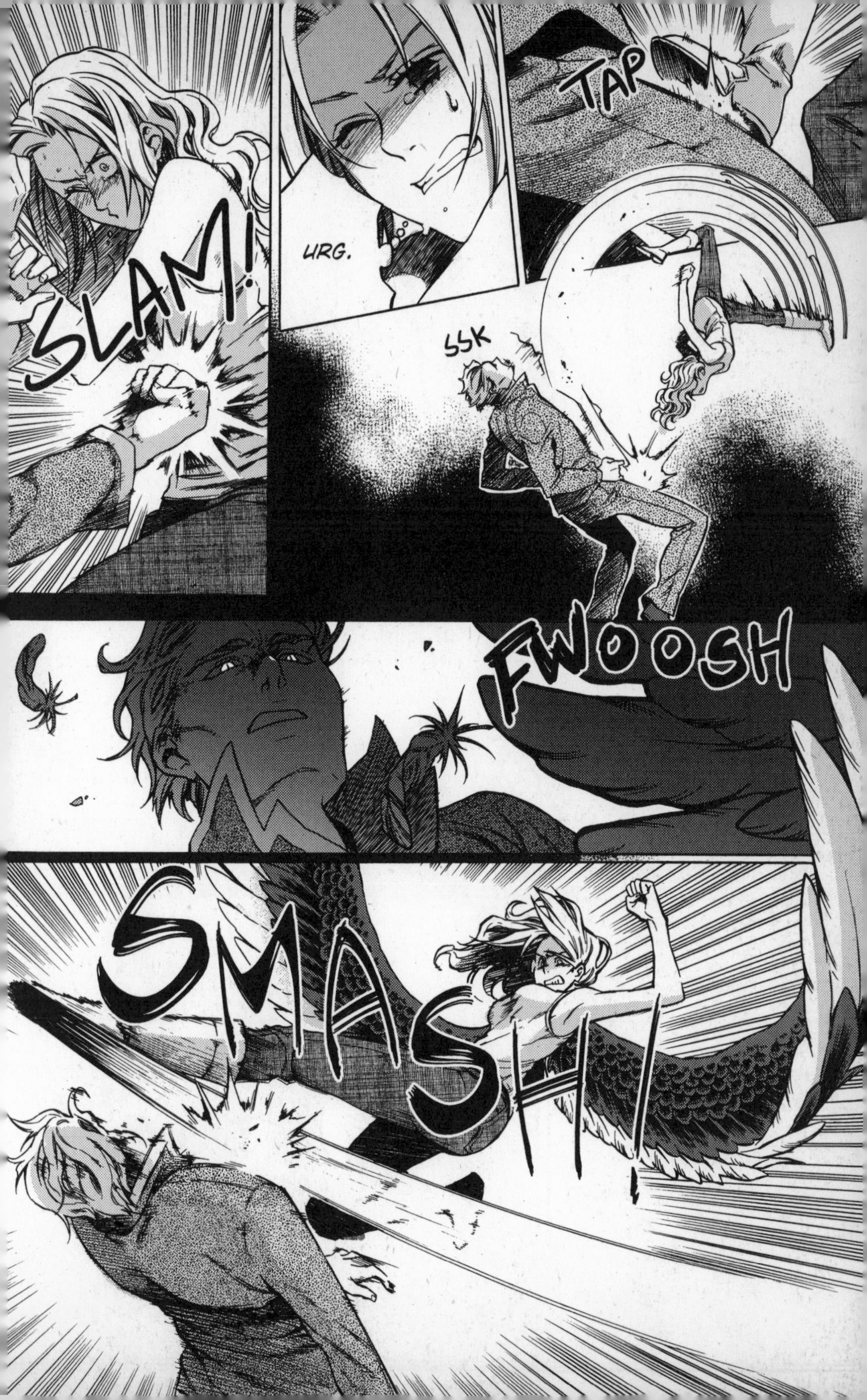
SLAM!
URG.
TAP
SSK
FWOOSH
SMASH!

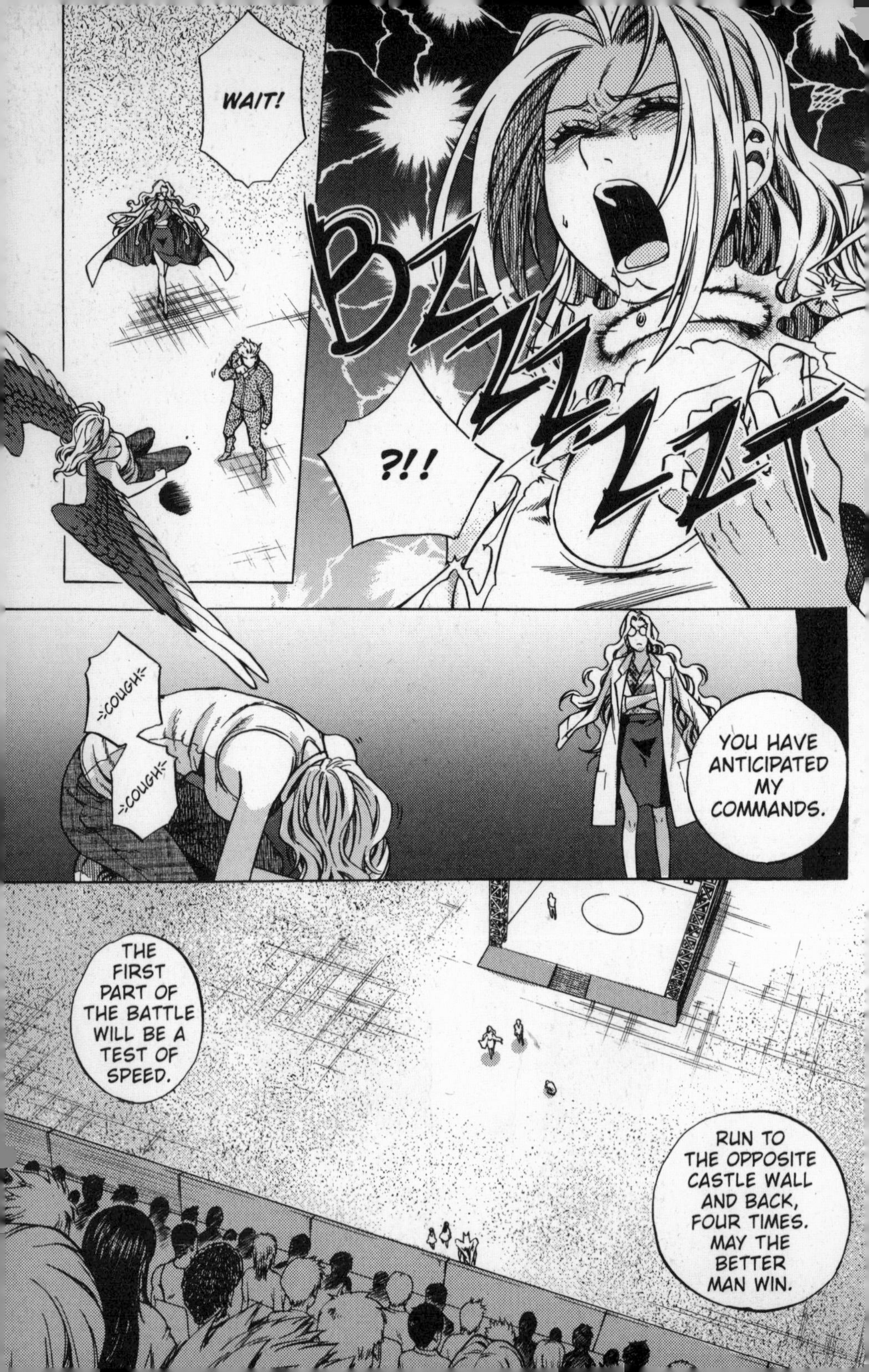
WAIT!
BZZZZZZT
?!!
YOU HAVE ANTICIPATED MY COMMANDS.
COUGH
COUGH
THE FIRST PART OF THE BATTLE WILL BE A TEST OF SPEED.
RUN TO THE OPPOSITE CASTLE WALL AND BACK, FOUR TIMES. MAY THE BETTER MAN WIN.

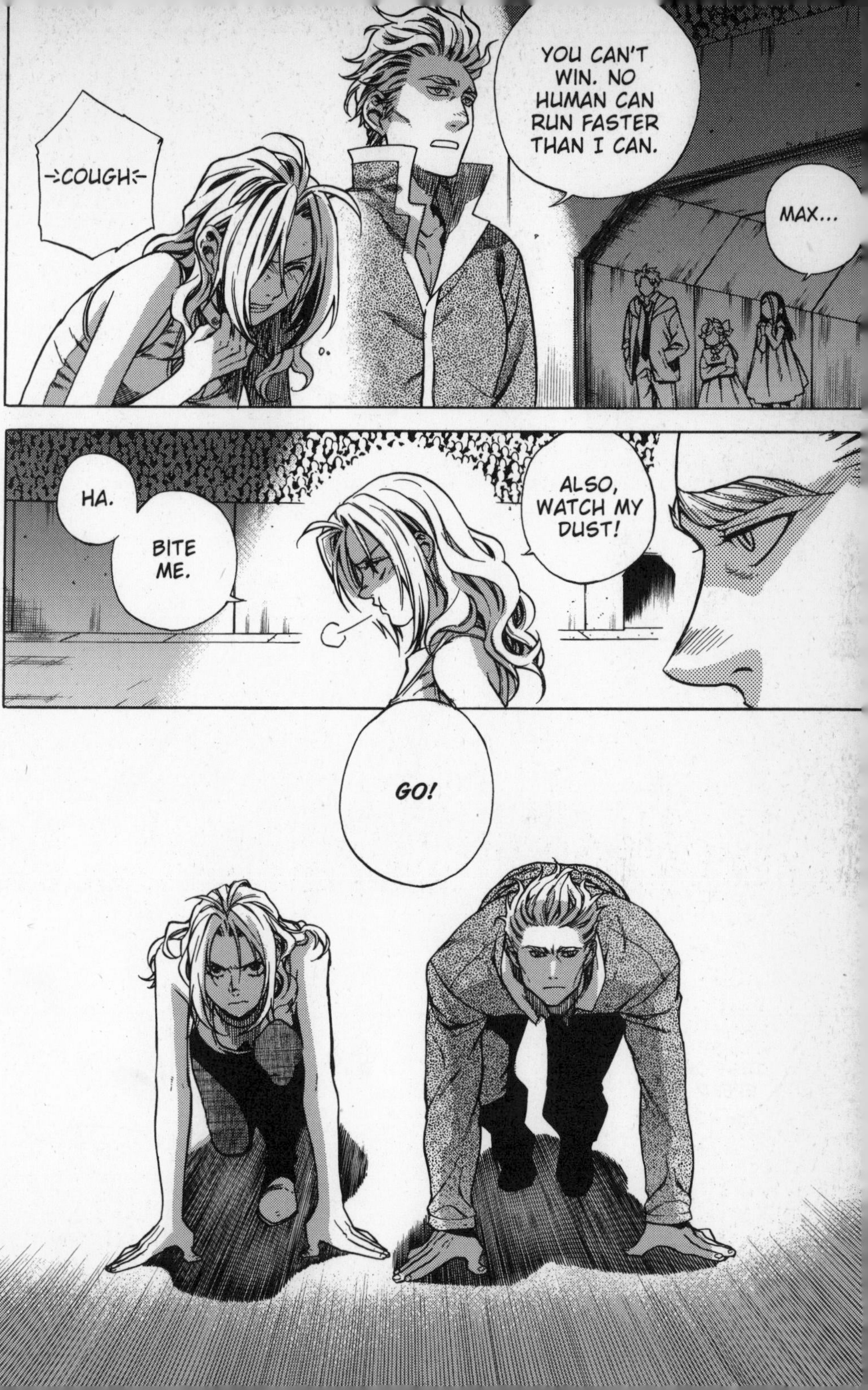
-COUGH-
YOU CAN'T WIN. NO HUMAN CAN RUN FASTER THAN I CAN.
MAX...
HA.
BITE ME.
ALSO, WATCH MY DUST!
GO!

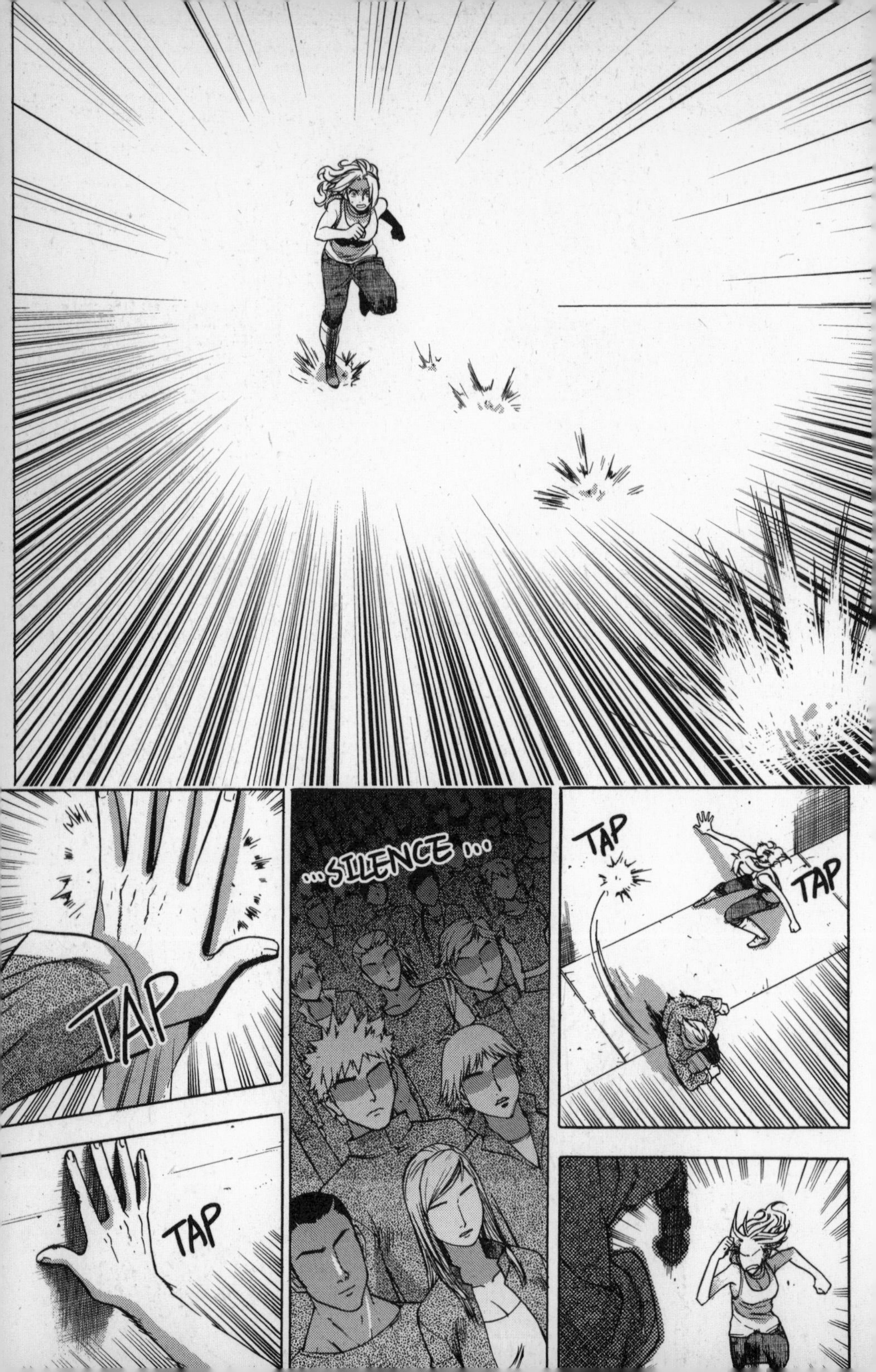

TAP
...SILENCE ...
TAP
TAP
TAP

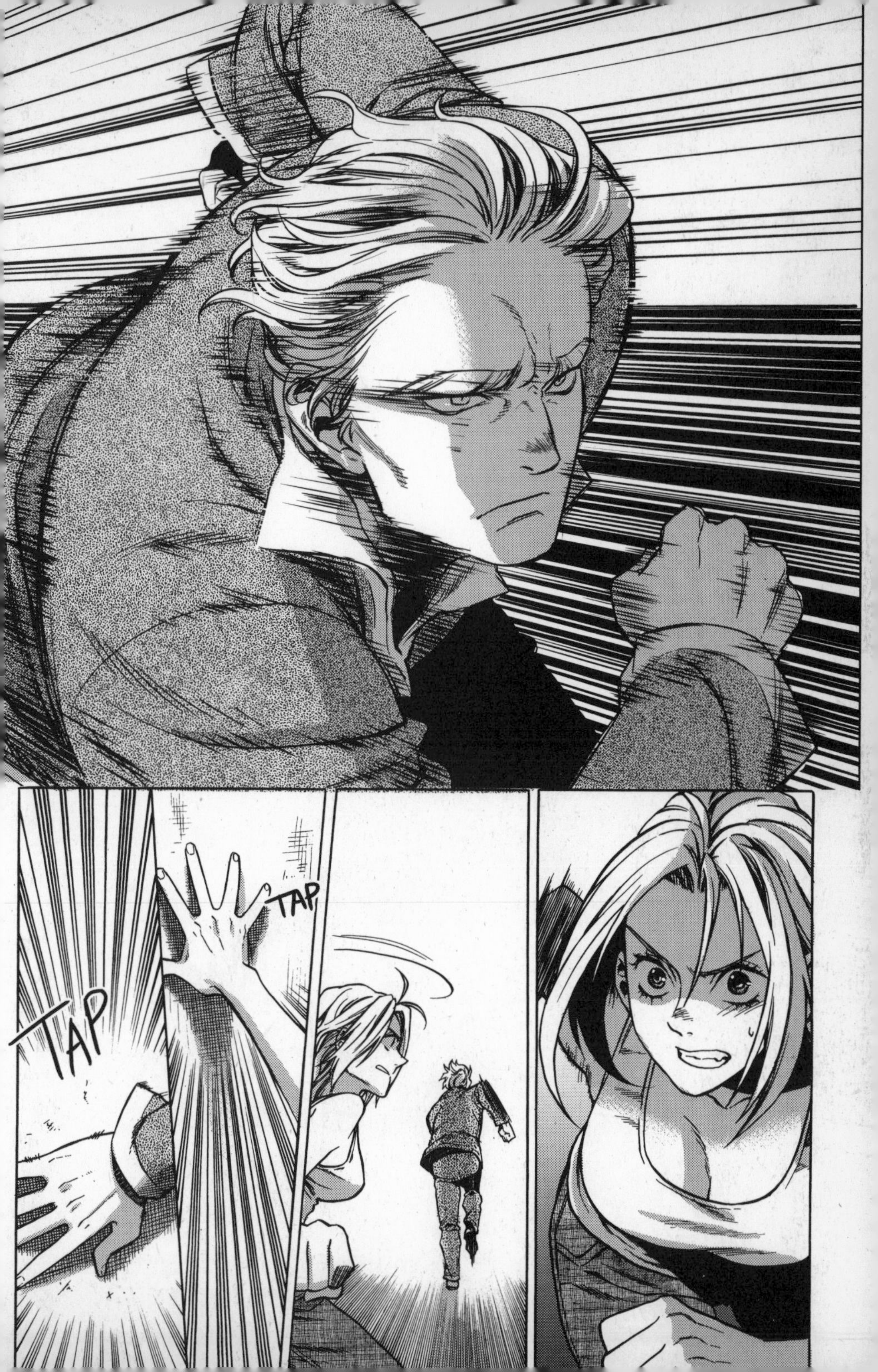
TAP
TAP

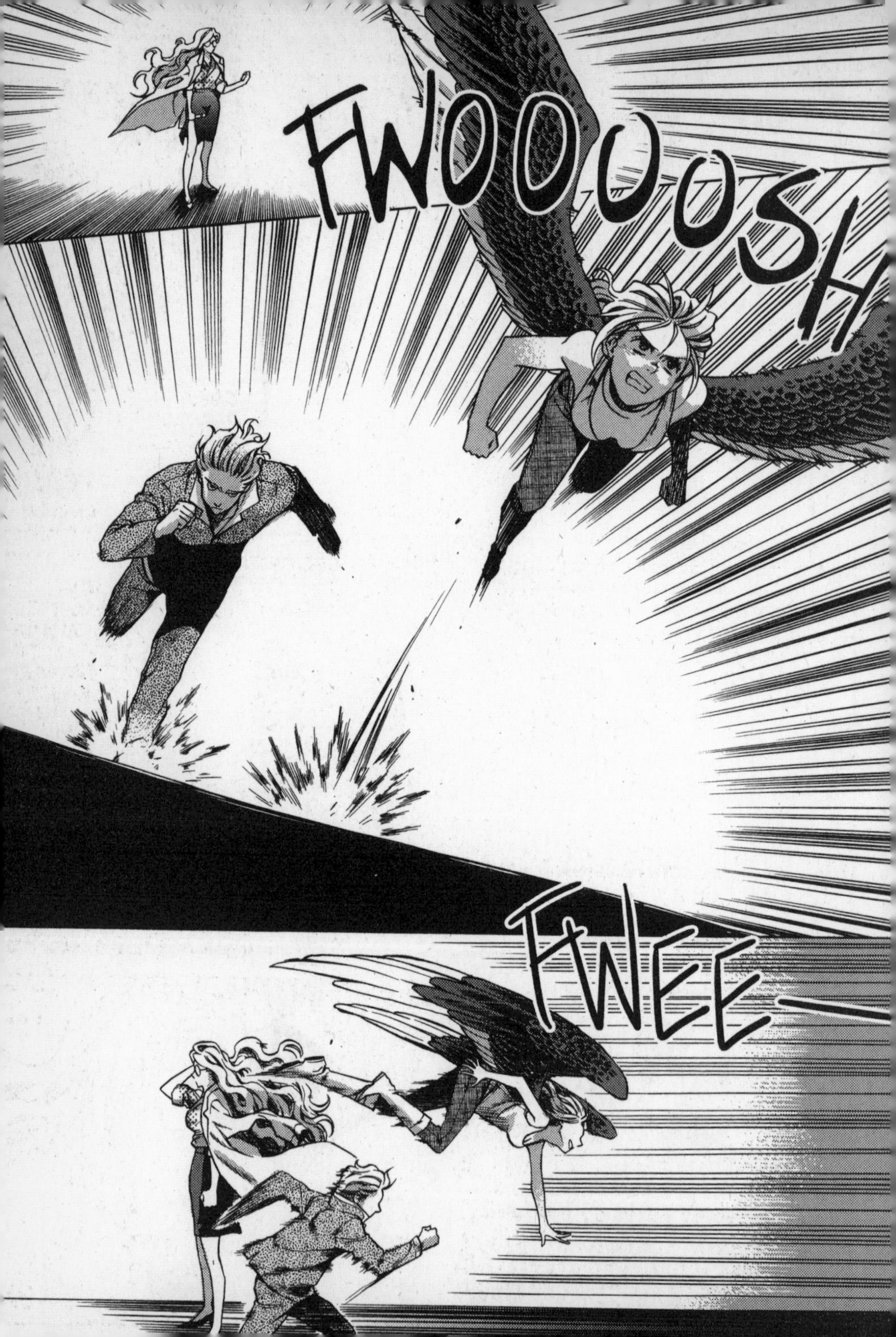
FWOOOOSH
FWEE—

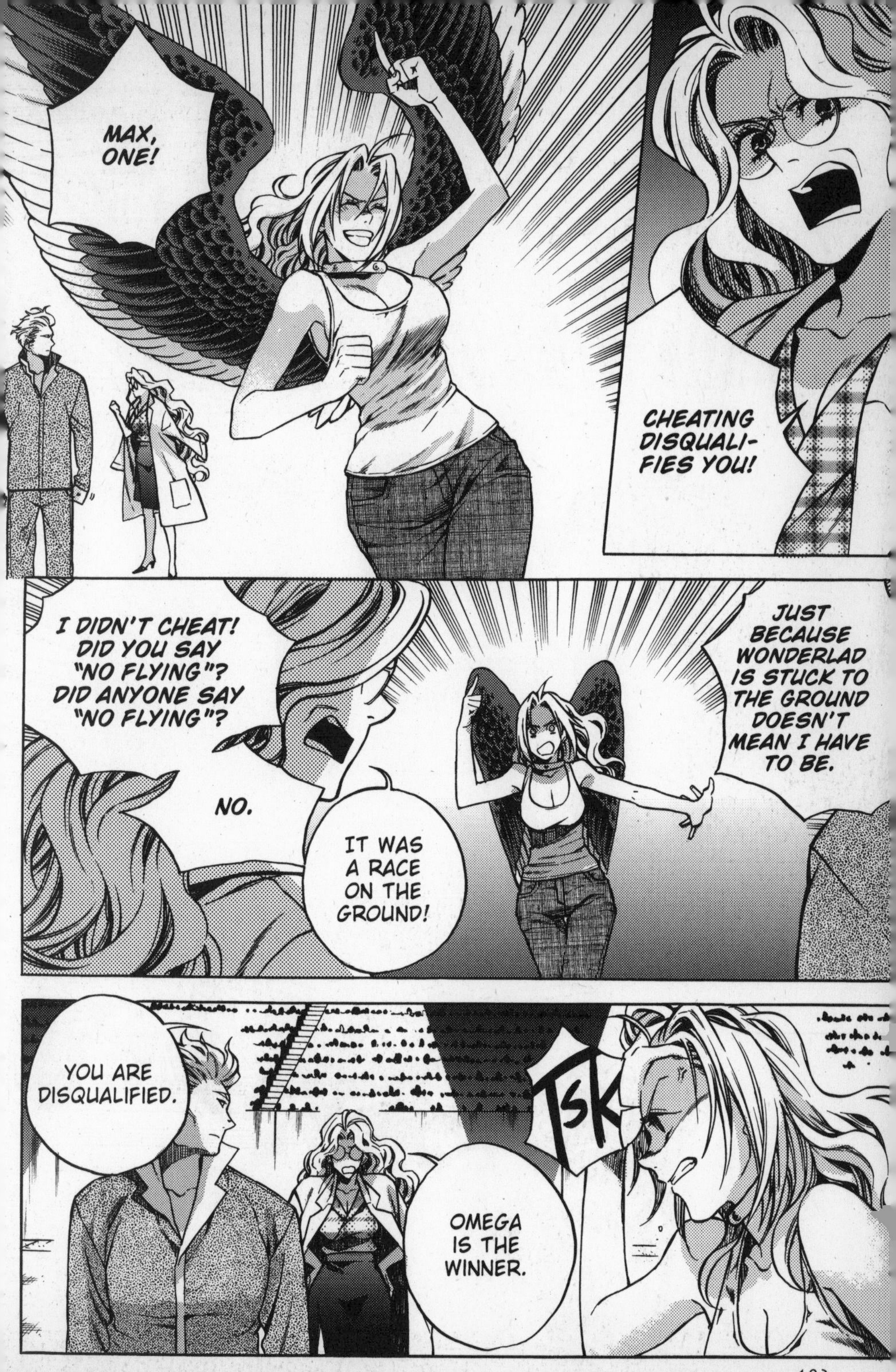
MAX, ONE!
CHEATING DISQUALIFIES YOU!
I DIDN'T CHEAT! DID YOU SAY "NO FLYING"? DID ANYONE SAY "NO FLYING"?
NO.
JUST BECAUSE WONDERLAD IS STUCK TO THE GROUND DOESN'T MEAN I HAVE TO BE.
IT WAS A RACE ON THE GROUND!
YOU ARE DISQUALIFIED.
TSK
OMEGA IS THE WINNER.

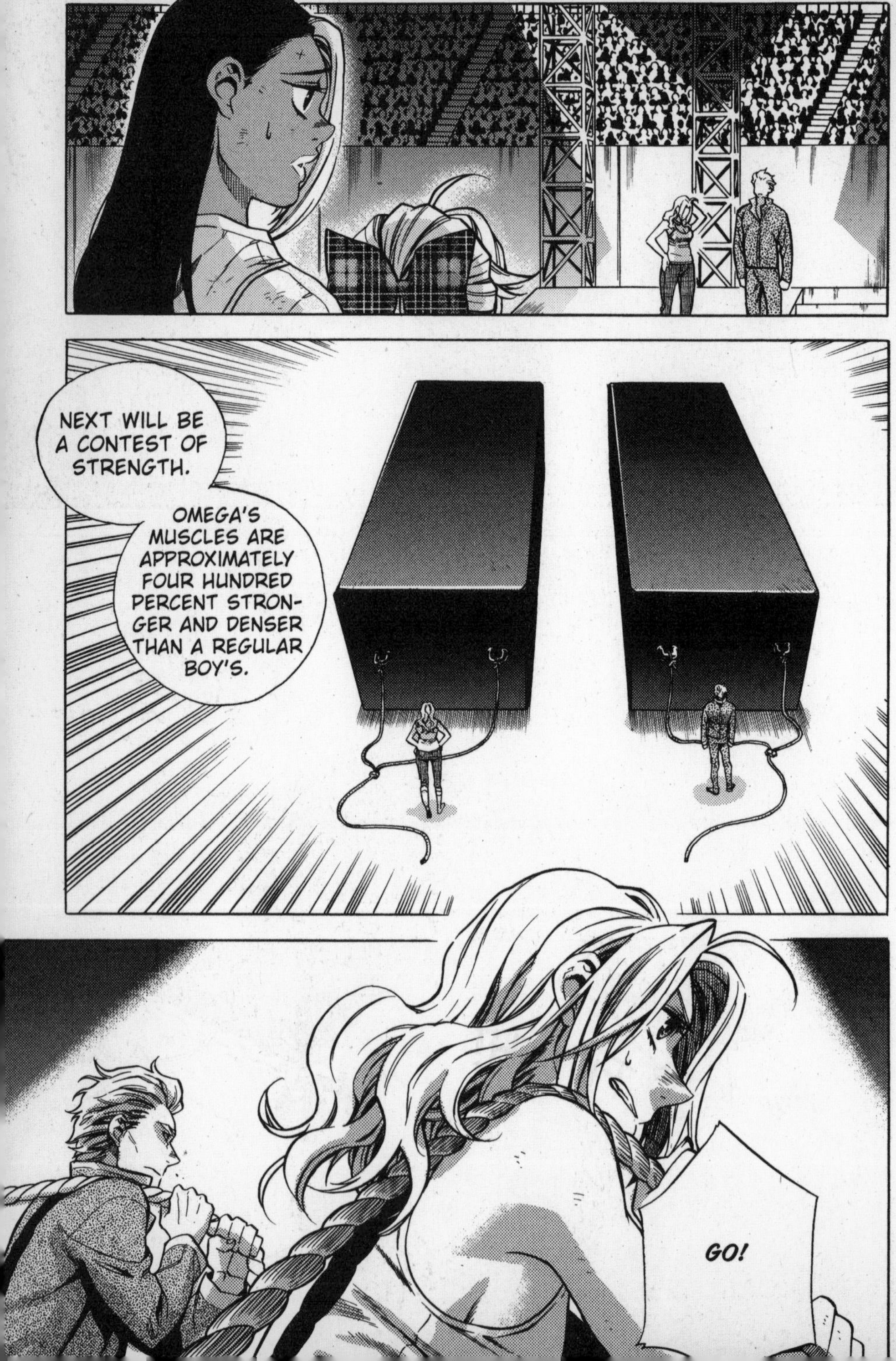
NEXT WILL BE A CONTEST OF STRENGTH.
OMEGA'S MUSCLES ARE APPROXIMATELY FOUR HUNDRED PERCENT STRONGER AND DENSER THAN A REGULAR BOY'S.
GO!

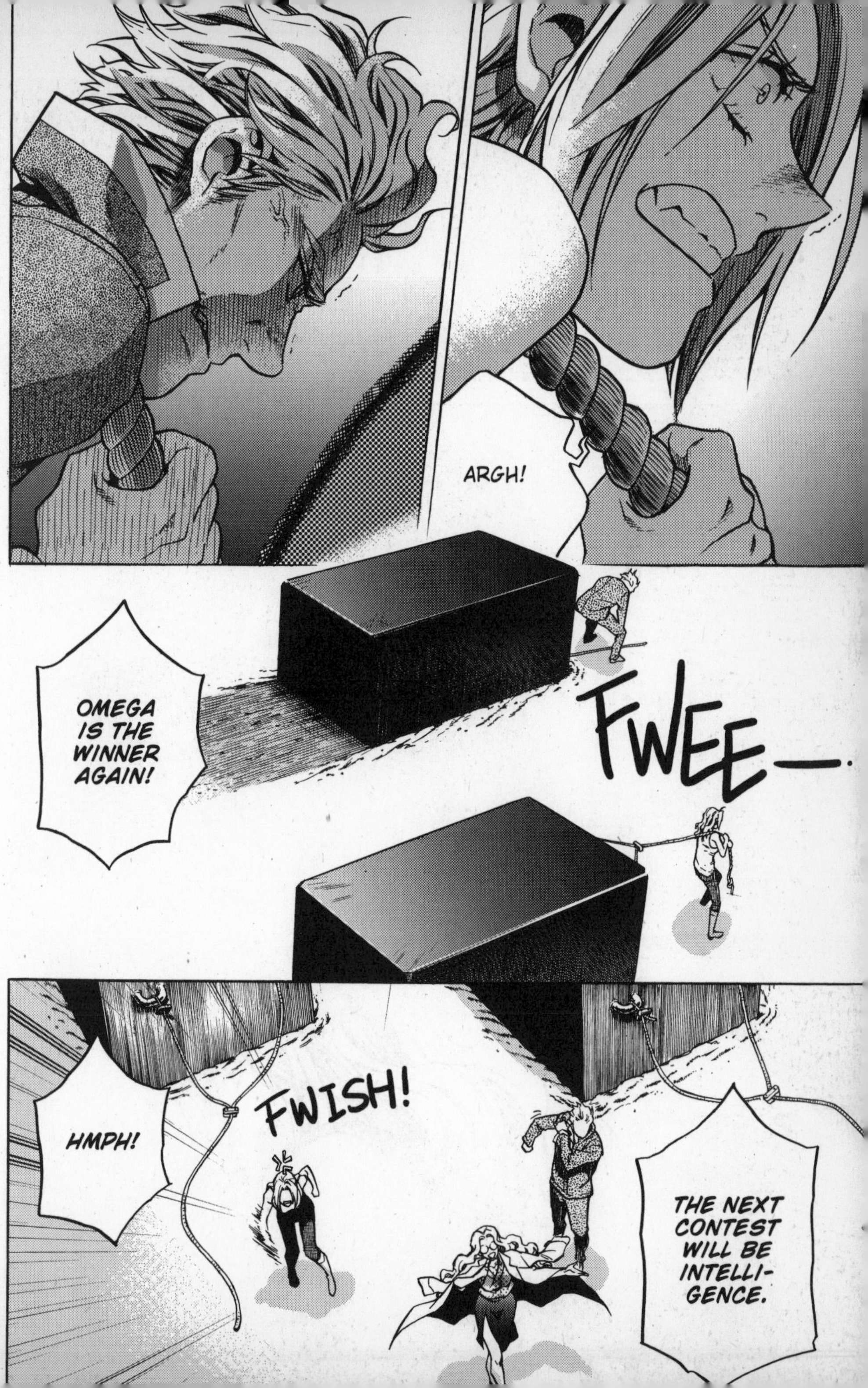
ARGH!
OMEGA IS THE WINNER AGAIN!
FWEE—
FWISH!
HMPH!
THE NEXT CONTEST WILL BE INTELLI-GENCE.

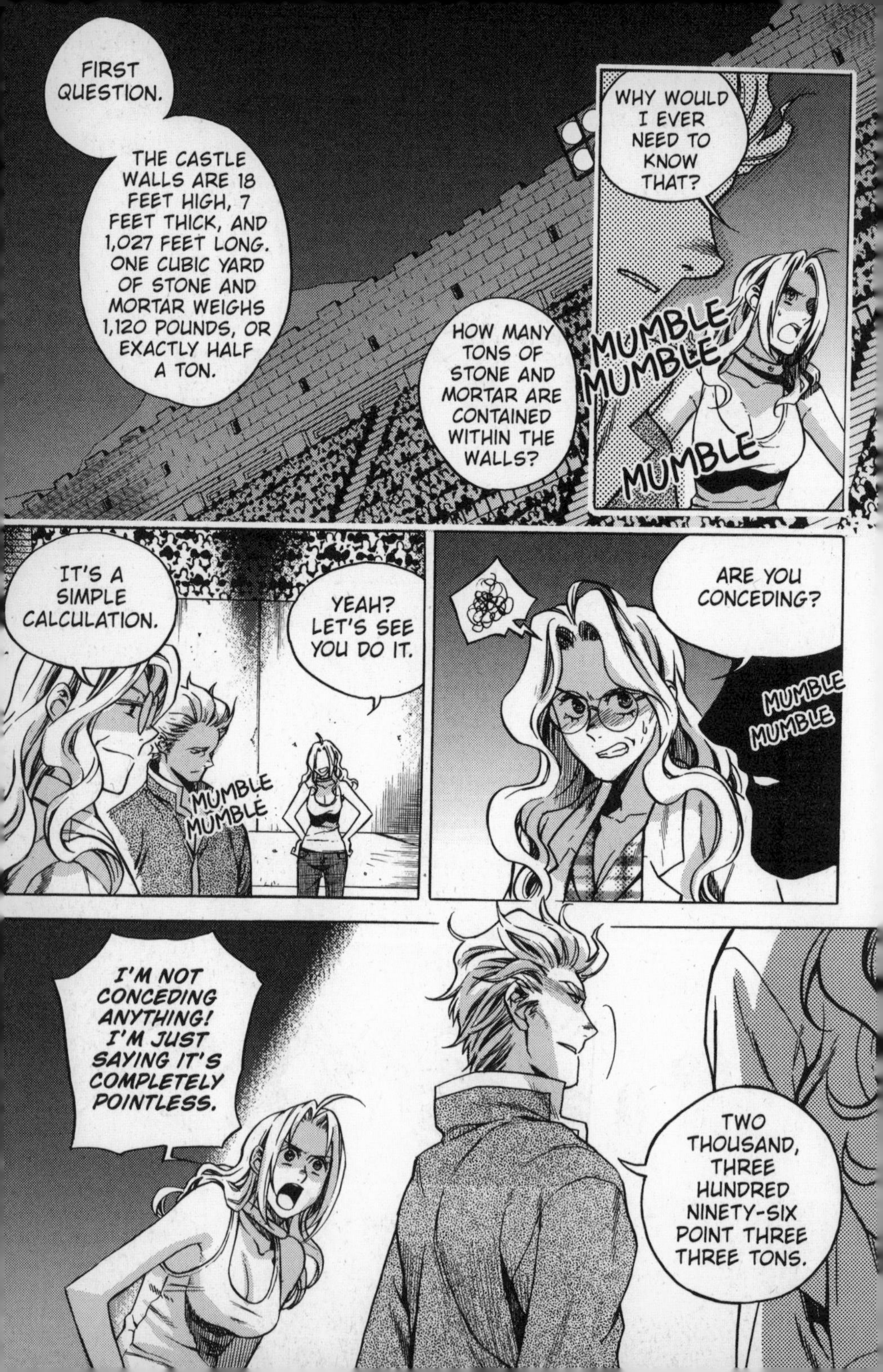
FIRST QUESTION.
THE CASTLE WALLS ARE 18 FEET HIGH, 7 FEET THICK, AND 1,027 FEET LONG. ONE CUBIC YARD OF STONE AND MORTAR WEIGHS 1,120 POUNDS, OR EXACTLY HALF A TON.
HOW MANY TONS OF STONE AND MORTAR ARE CONTAINED WITHIN THE WALLS?
WHY WOULD I EVER NEED TO KNOW THAT?
MUMBLE MUMBLE
MUMBLE
IT'S A SIMPLE CALCULATION.
YEAH? LET'S SEE YOU DO IT.
MUMBLE MUMBLE
ARE YOU CONCEDING?
MUMBLE MUMBLE
I'M NOT CONCEDING ANYTHING! I'M JUST SAYING IT'S COMPLETELY POINTLESS.
TWO THOUSAND, THREE HUNDRED NINETY-SIX POINT THREE THREE TONS.

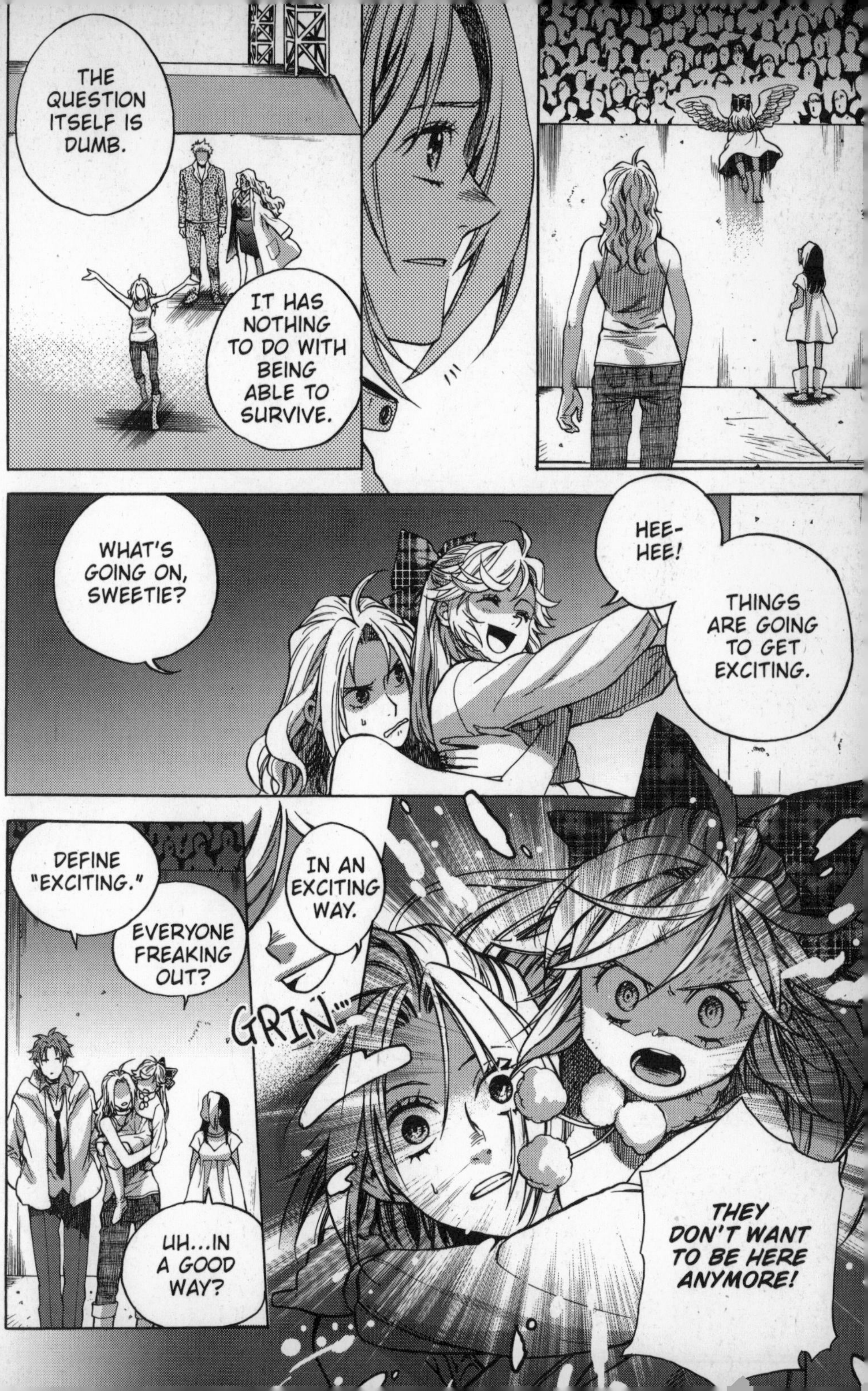
THE QUESTION ITSELF IS DUMB.
IT HAS NOTHING TO DO WITH BEING ABLE TO SURVIVE.
HEE-HEE!
THINGS ARE GOING TO GET EXCITING.
WHAT'S GOING ON, SWEETIE?
THEY DON'T WANT TO BE HERE ANYMORE!
IN AN EXCITING WAY.
GRIN
DEFINE "EXCITING."
EVERYONE FREAKING OUT?
UH...IN A GOOD WAY?

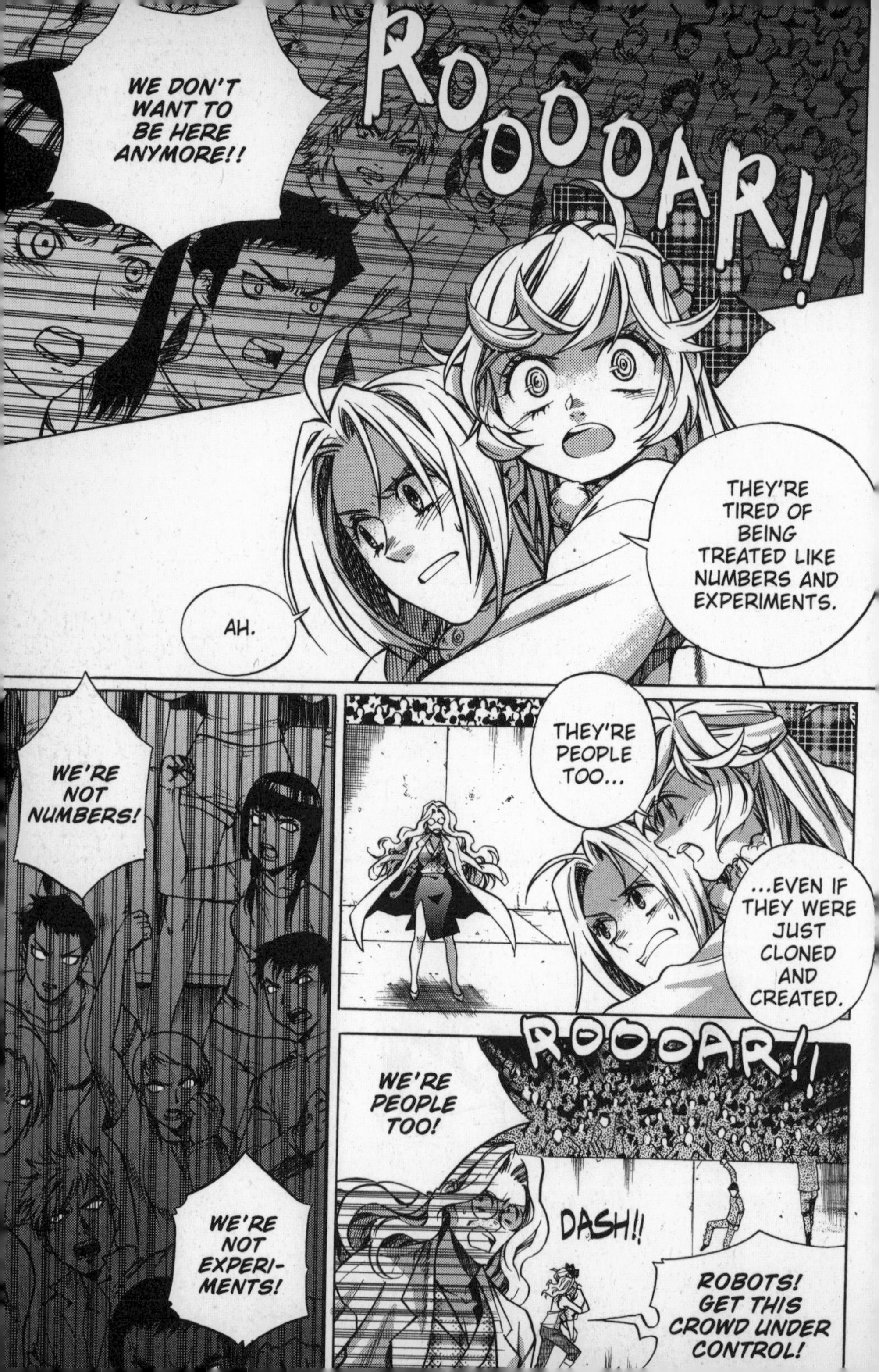
WE DON'T WANT TO BE HERE ANYMORE!!
ROOOOAR!!
THEY'RE TIRED OF BEING TREATED LIKE NUMBERS AND EXPERIMENTS.
AH.
WE'RE NOT NUMBERS!
THEY'RE PEOPLE TOO...
...EVEN IF THEY WERE JUST CLONED AND CREATED.
WE'RE NOT EXPERI-MENTS!
ROOOAR!!
WE'RE PEOPLE TOO!
DASH!!
ROBOTS! GET THIS CROWD UNDER CONTROL!

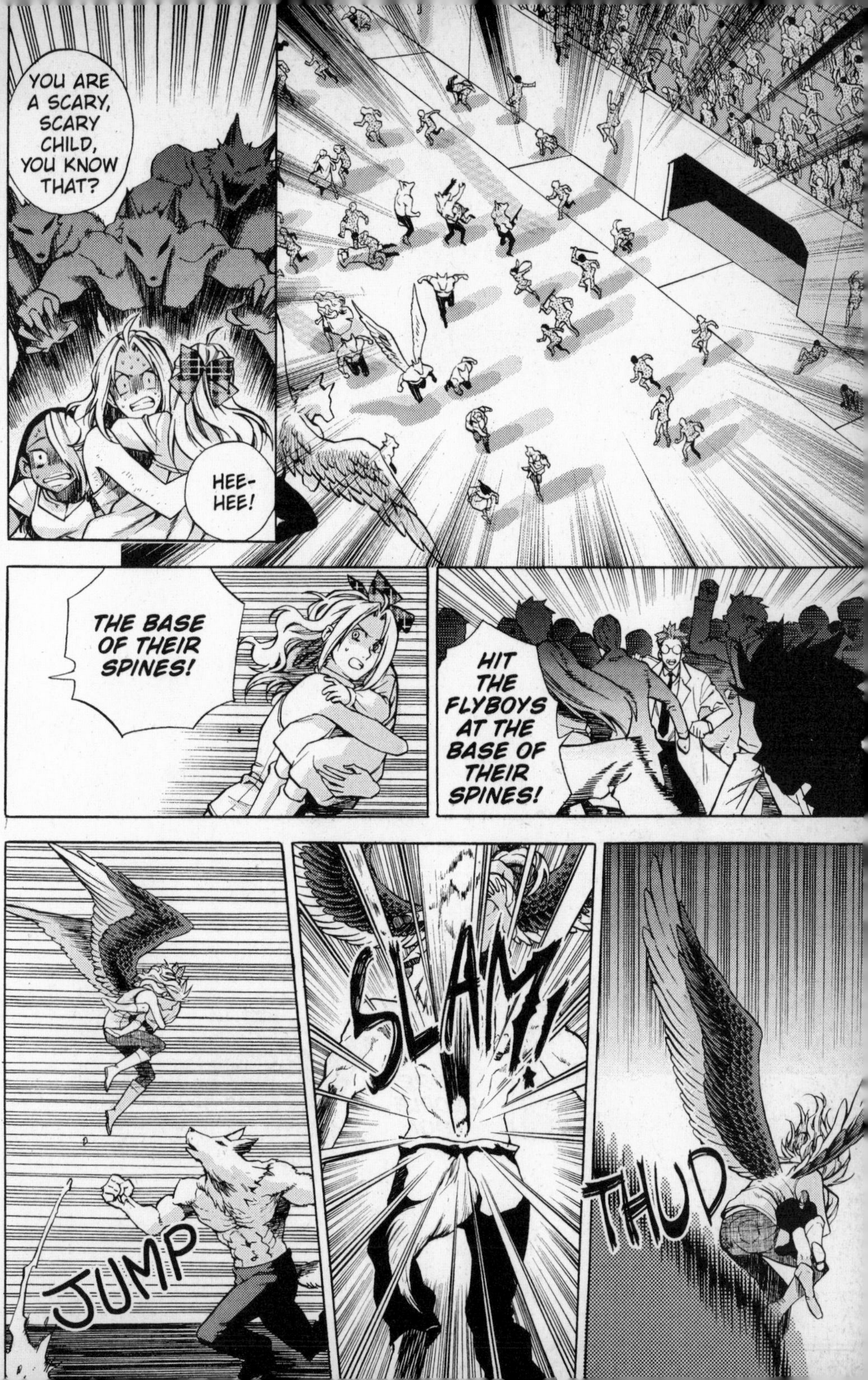
YOU ARE A SCARY, SCARY CHILD, YOU KNOW THAT?
HEE-HEE!
THE BASE OF THEIR SPINES!
HIT THE FLYBOYS AT THE BASE OF THEIR SPINES!
JUMP
SLAM!
THUD

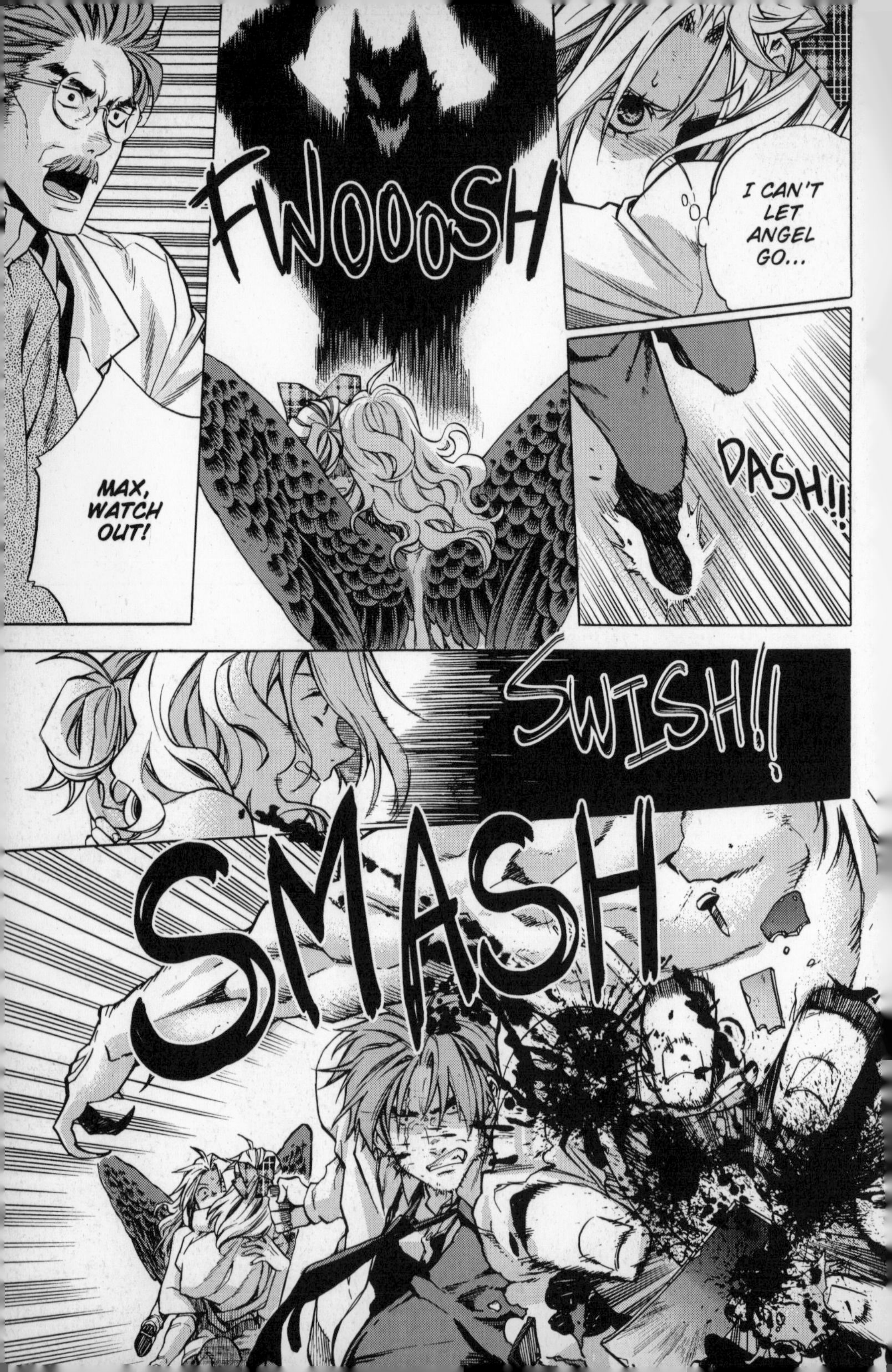
I CAN'T LET ANGEL GO...
FWOOOSH
MAX, WATCH OUT!
DASH!!
SWISH!!
SMASH

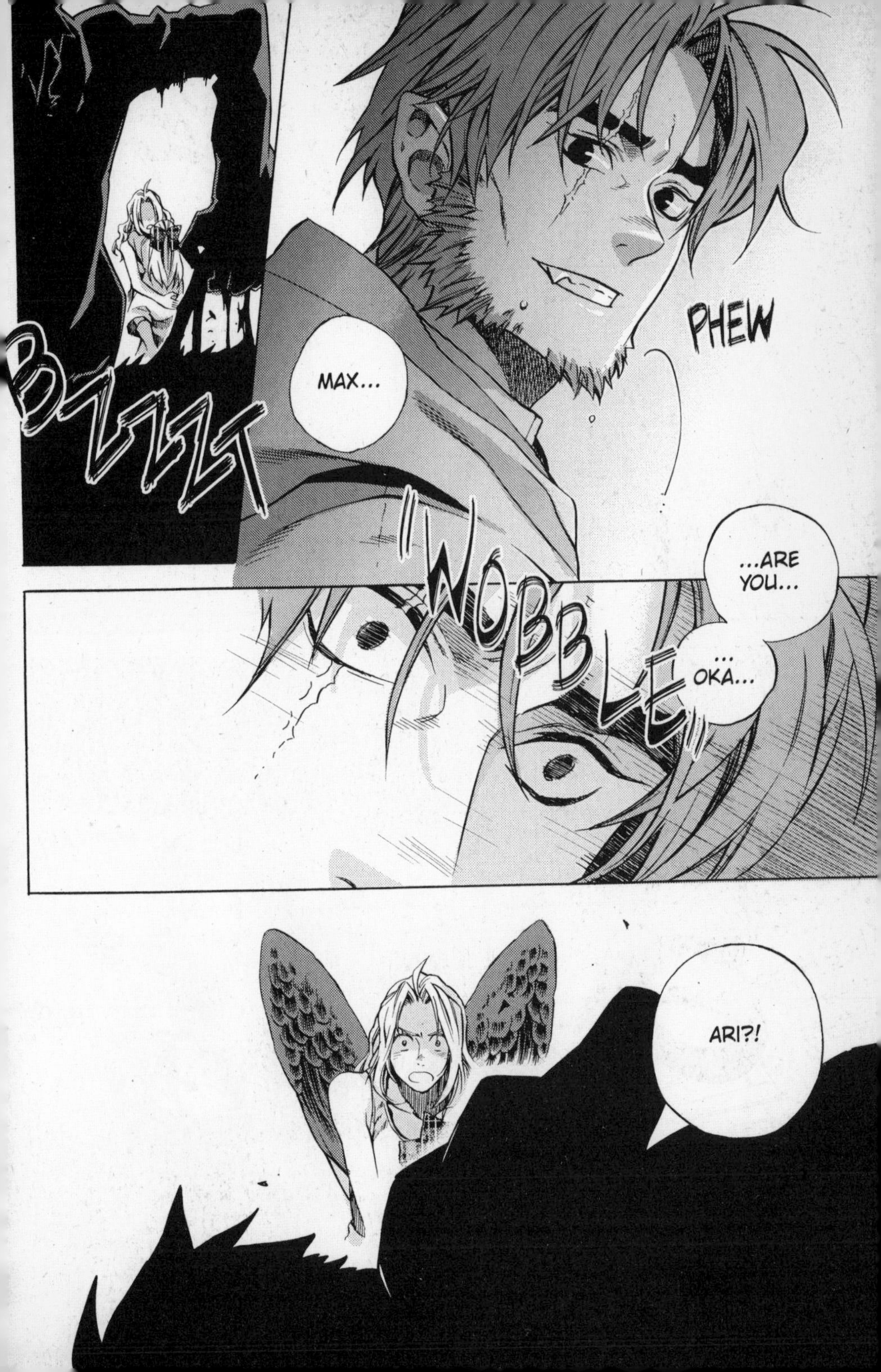
PHEW
MAX...
BZZZT
...ARE YOU...
... OKA...
WOBBLE
ARI?!

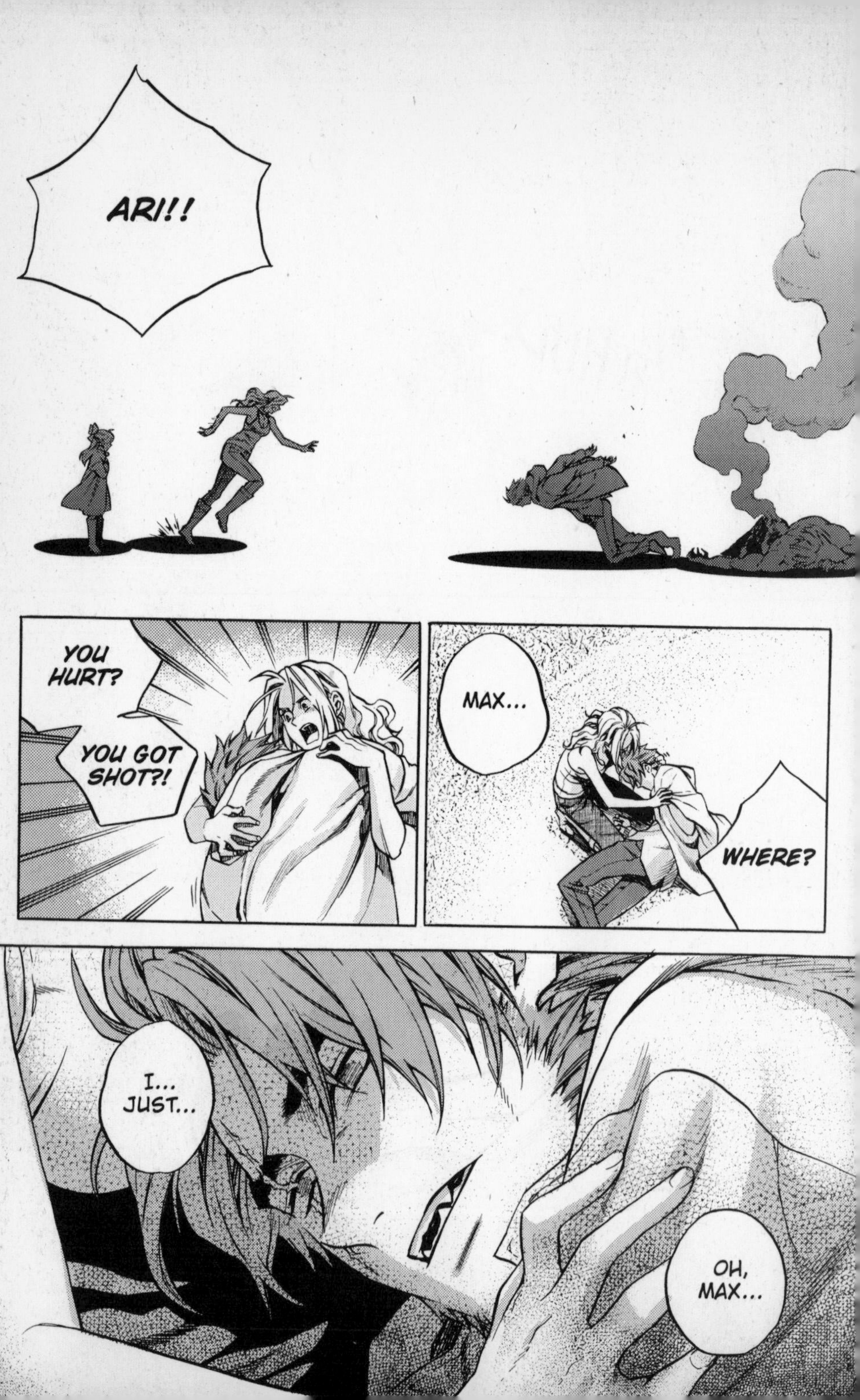
ARI!!
YOU HURT?
YOU GOT SHOT?!
MAX...
WHERE?
I... JUST...
OH, MAX...

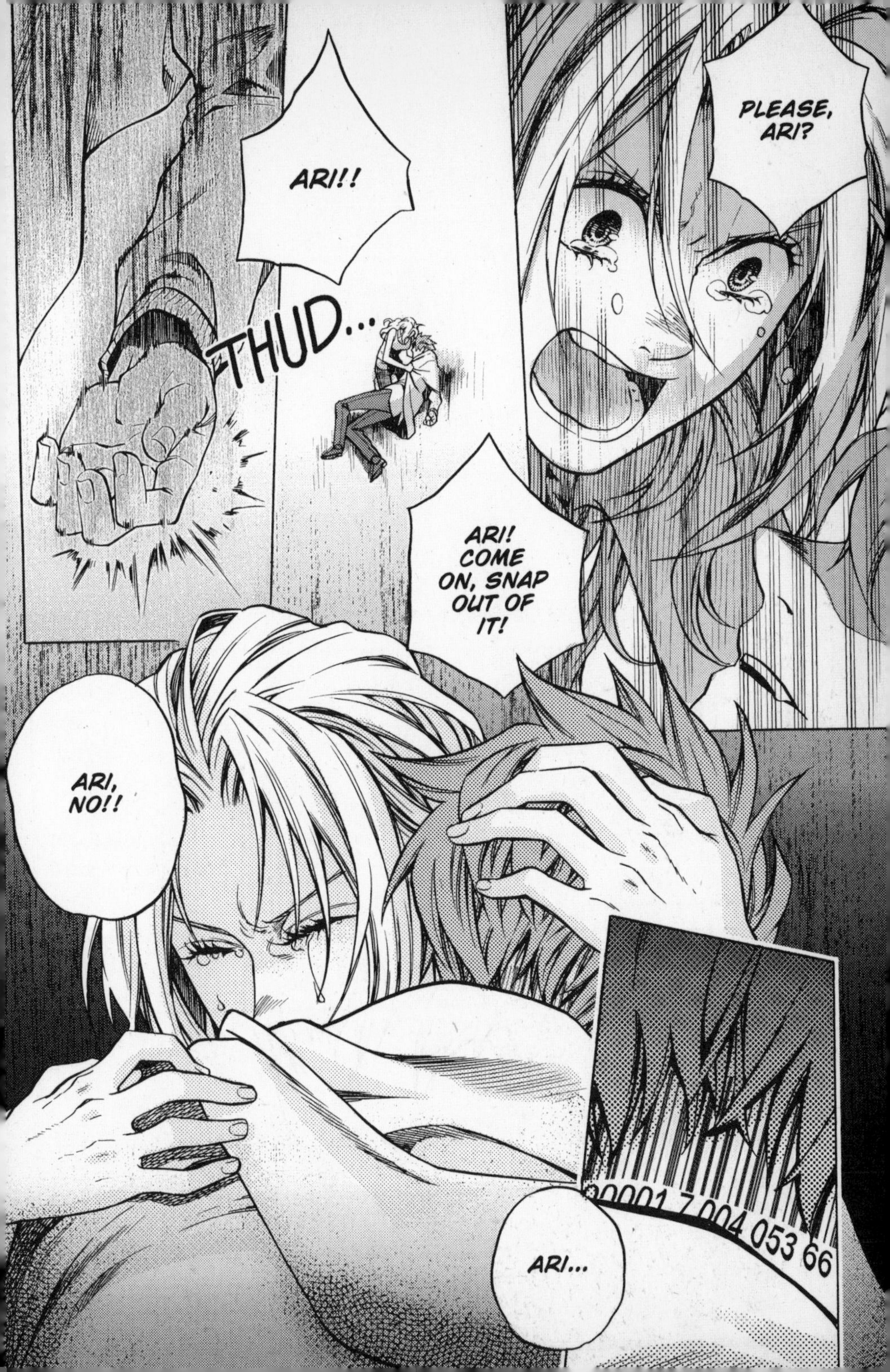

ARI!!
THUD...
PLEASE, ARI?
ARI! COME ON, SNAP OUT OF IT!
ARI, NO!!
ARI...

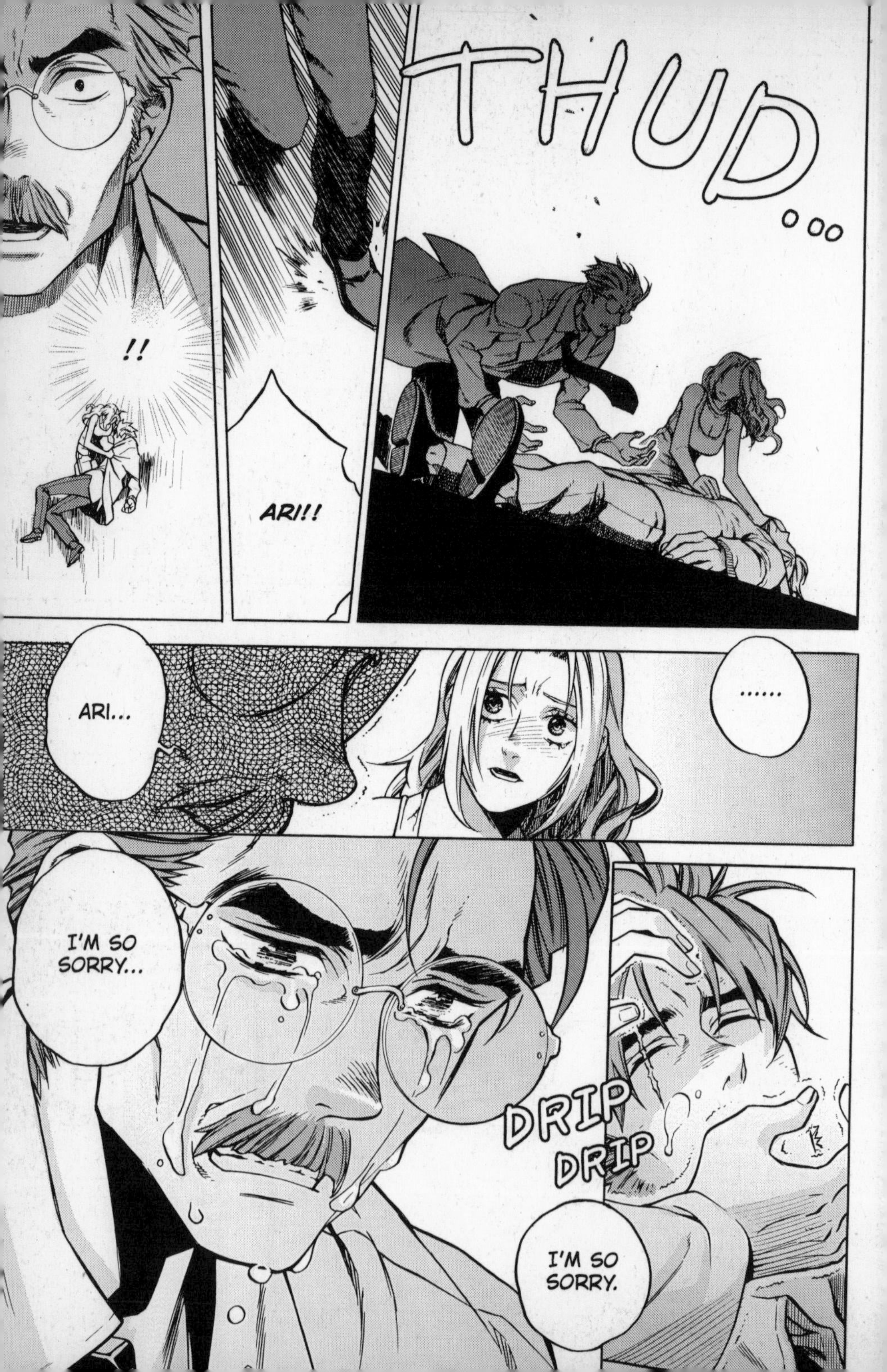
!!
ARI!!
THUD...
ARI...
......
I'M SO SORRY...
DRIP DRIP
I'M SO SORRY.

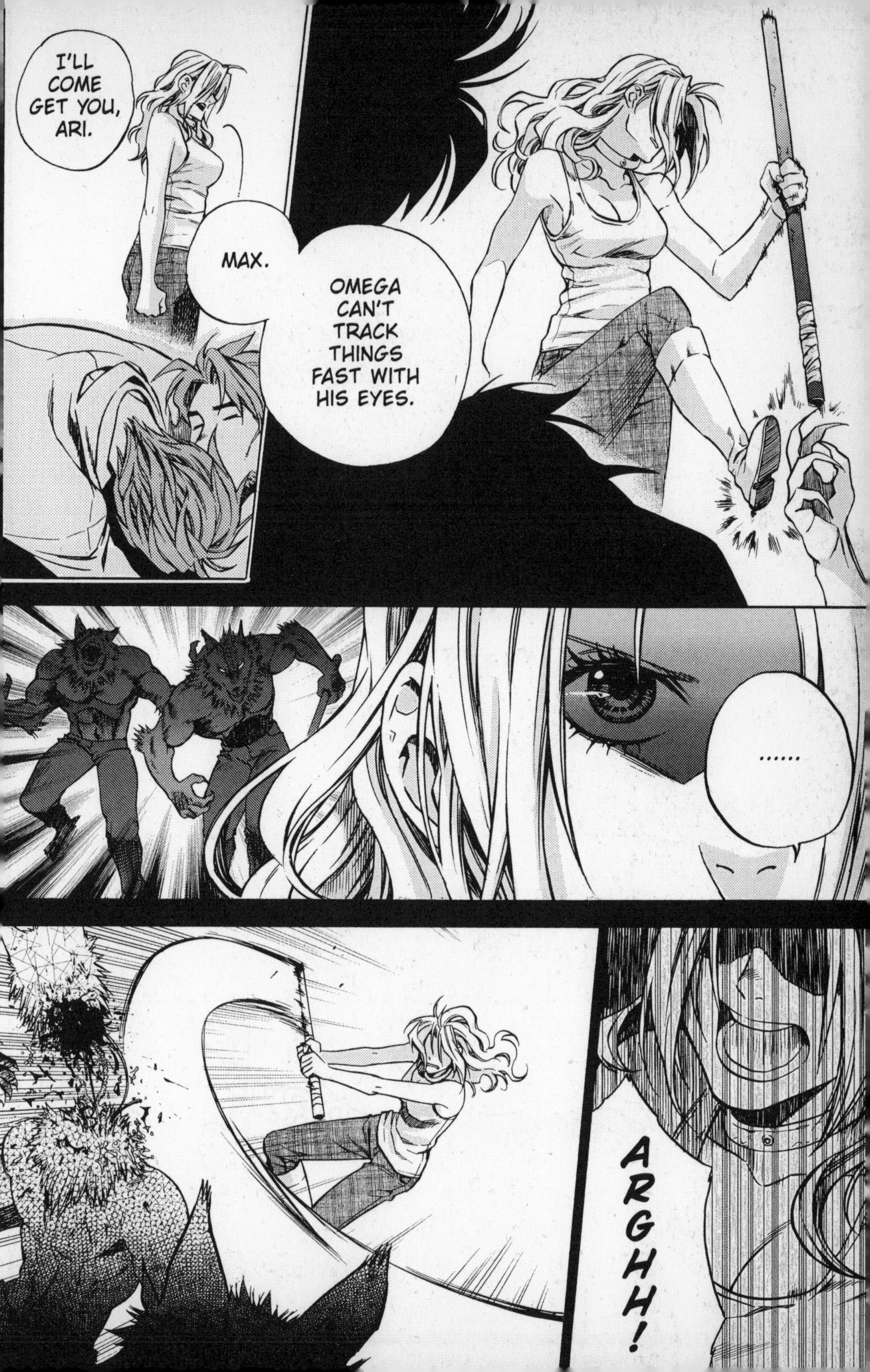
I'LL COME GET YOU, ARI.
MAX.
OMEGA CAN'T TRACK THINGS FAST WITH HIS EYES.
......
ARGHH!

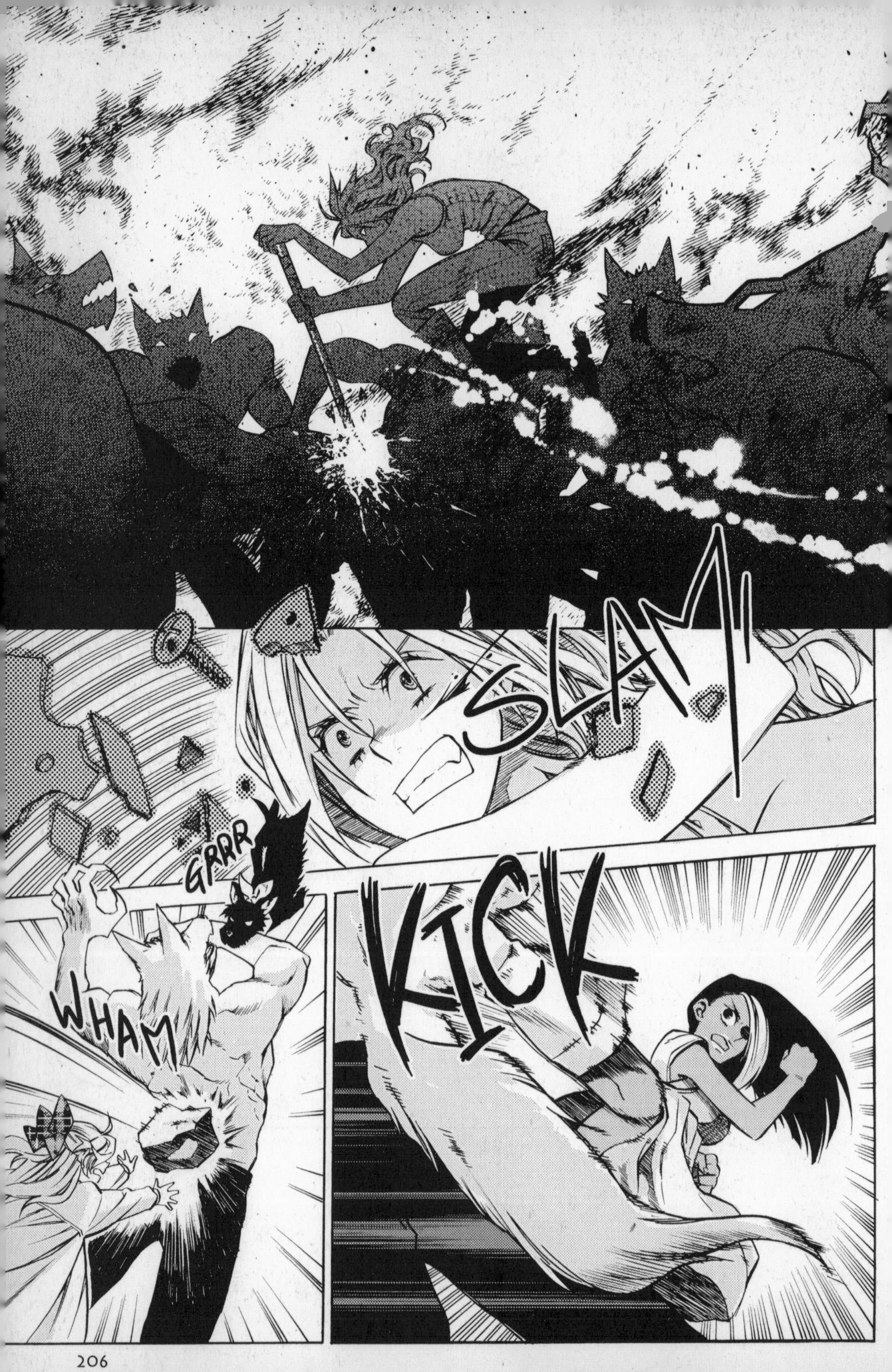
SLAM!
GRRR
WHAM
KICK

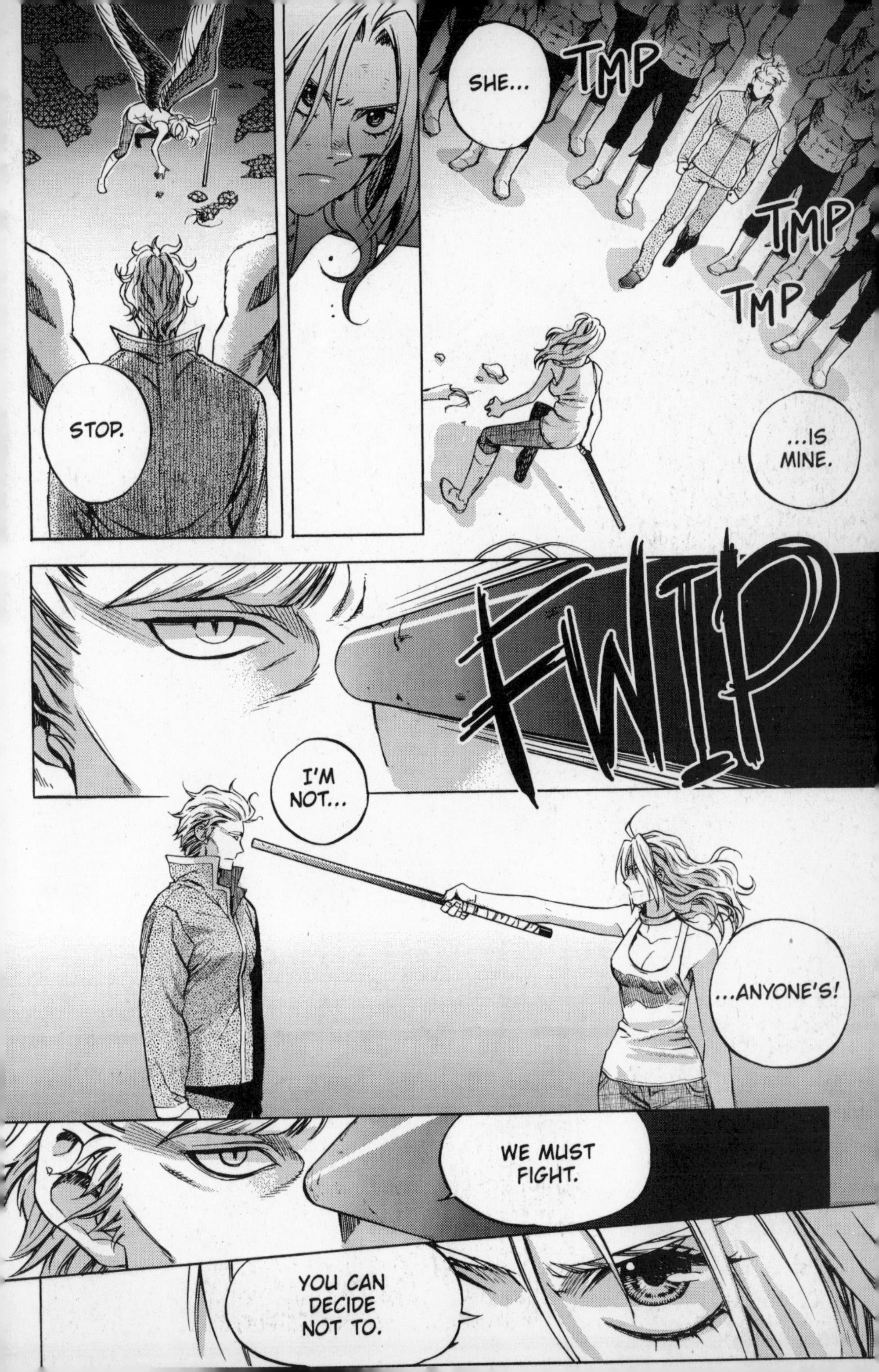
STOP.
SHE...
TMP
TMP
TMP
...IS MINE.
FWIP
I'M NOT...
...ANYONE'S!
WE MUST FIGHT.
YOU CAN DECIDE NOT TO.

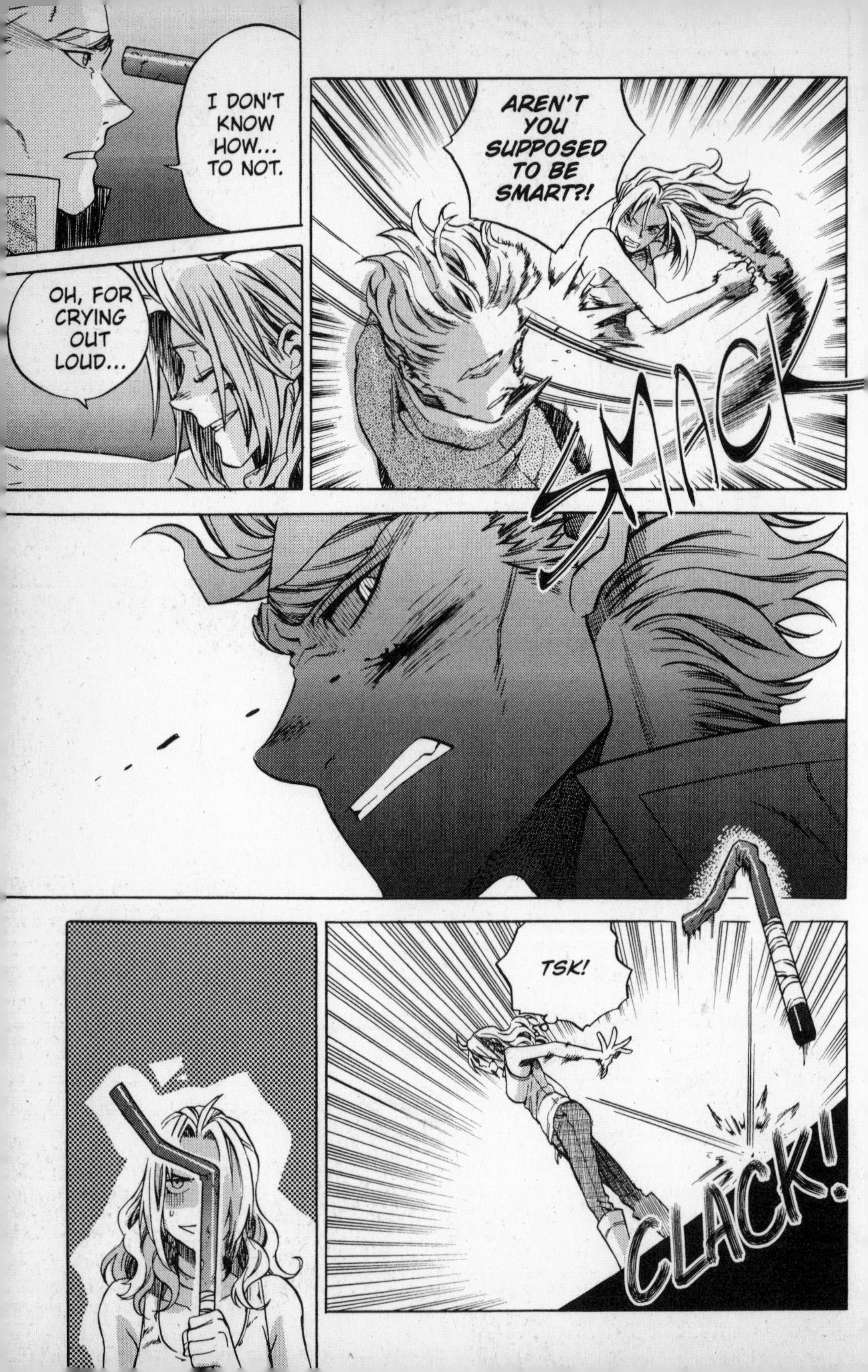
I DON'T KNOW HOW... TO NOT.
ARE'T YOU SUPPOSED TO BE SMART?!
OH, FOR CRYING OUT LOUD...
SMACK
TSK!
CLACK!

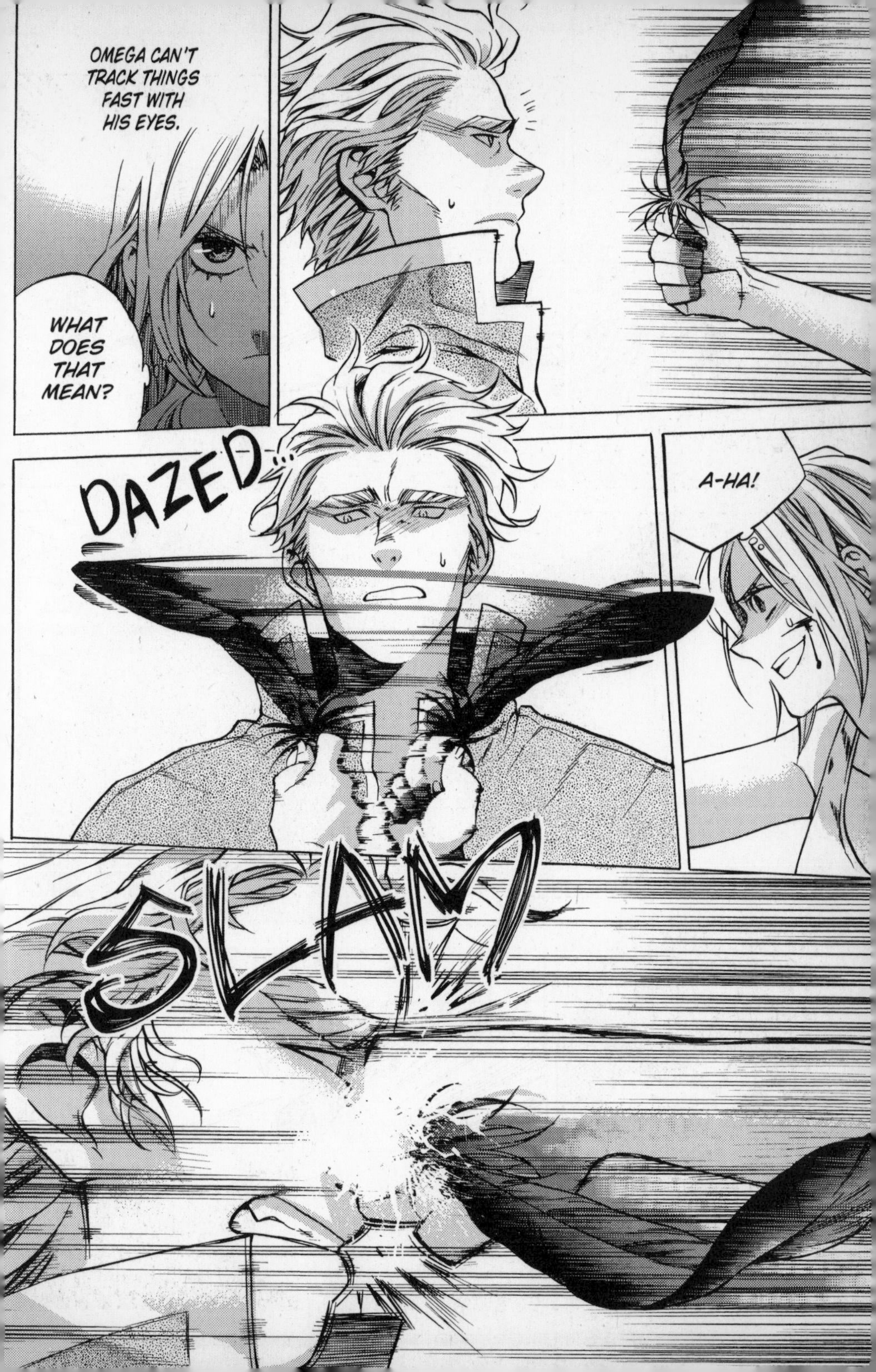
OMEGA CAN'T TRACK THINGS FAST WITH HIS EYES.
WHAT DOES THAT MEAN?
A-HA!
DAZED...
SLAM

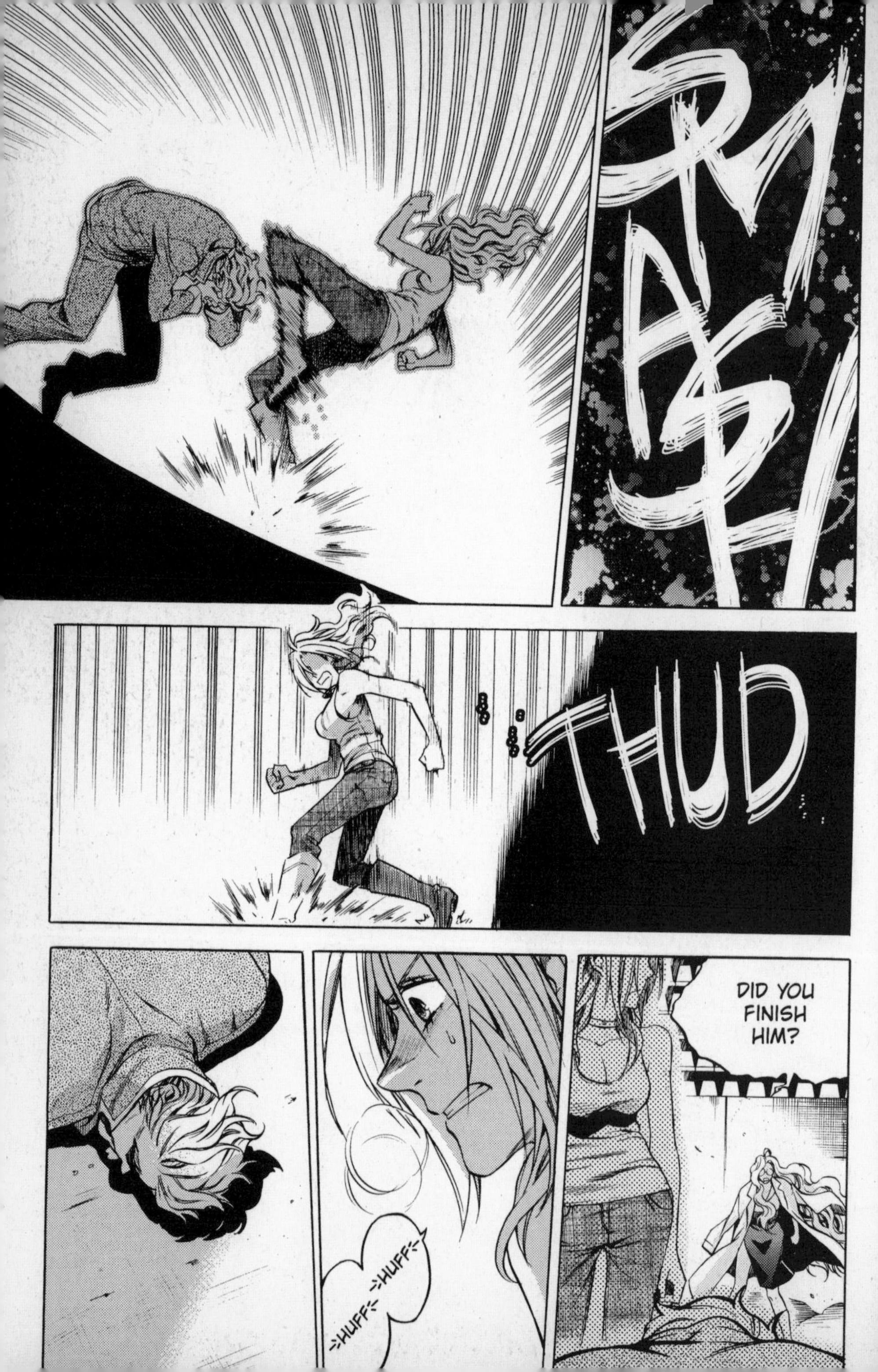

SMASH!
THUD
DID YOU FINISH HIM?
HUFF HUFF
HUFF

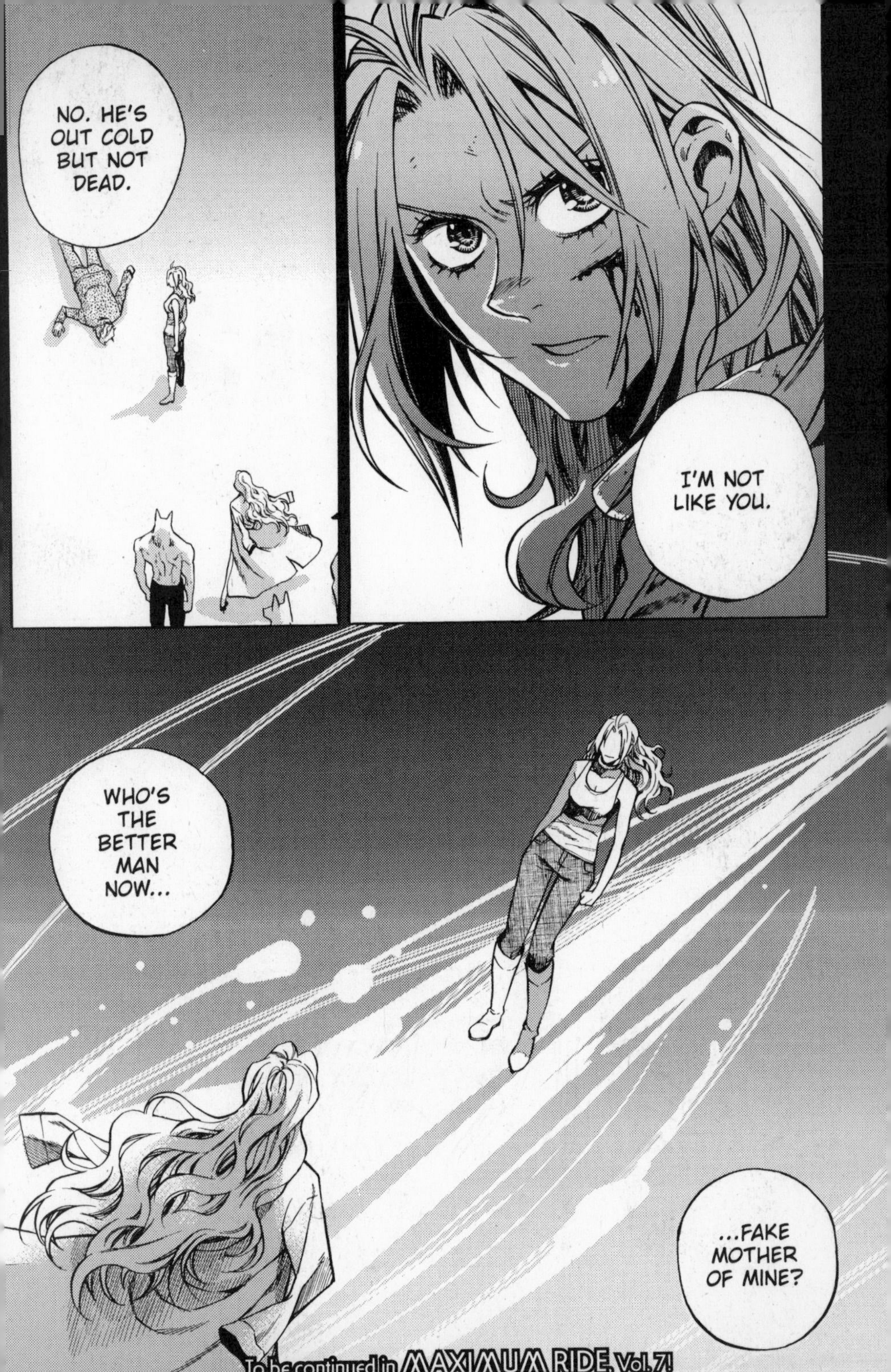
NO. HE'S OUT COLD BUT NOT DEAD.
I'M NOT LIKE YOU.
WHO'S THE BETTER MAN NOW...
...FAKE MOTHER OF MINE?

To be continued in MAXIMUM RIDE, Vol. 7!

MAXIMUM RIDE: THE MANGA

BASED ON THE NOVELS BY
JAMES PATTERSON

ART AND ADAPTATION

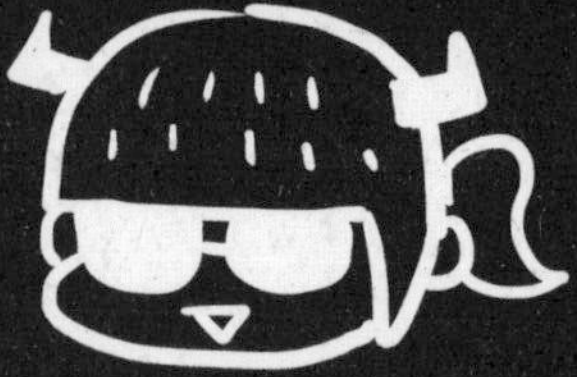

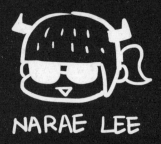

NARAE LEE

BACKGROUND ASSISTANCE

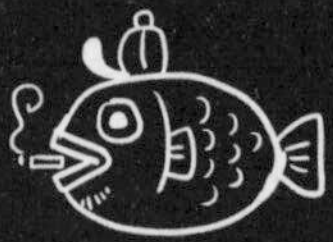

WT. KIM

SPECIAL THANKS

MIMI. Yoon